The Komedie Stamboel

This series of publications on Africa, Latin America, Southeast Asia, and Global and Comparative Studies is designed to present significant research, translation, and opinion to area specialists and to a wide community of persons interested in world affairs. The editor seeks manuscripts of quality on any subject and can usually make a decision regarding publication within three months of receipt of the original work. Production methods generally permit a work to appear within one year of acceptance. The editor works closely with authors to produce a high-quality book. The series appears in a paperback format and is distributed worldwide. For more information, contact the executive editor at Ohio University Press, 19 Circle Drive, The Ridges, Athens, Ohio 45701.

The Ohio University Research in International Studies series is published for the Center for International Studies by Ohio University Press. The views expressed in individual volumes are those of the authors and should not be considered to represent the policies or beliefs of the Center for International Studies, Ohio University Press, or Ohio University.

The Komedie Stamboel

Popular Theater in Colonial Indonesia, 1891–1903

Matthew Isaac Cohen

Ohio University Research in International Studies
Southeast Asia Series No. 112
Ohio University Press
Athens

www.ohio.edu/oupress
Printed in the United States of America

14 13 12 11 10 09 08 07 06 5 4 3 2 1

The books in the Ohio University Research in International Studies Series
are printed on acid-free paper ∞ ™

Cover image: King Darsa Alam senses the presence of a heavenly nymph (in the cutout) in a 1906 stambul performance of *Jula-Juli bintang tiga* (Third star Jula-Juli) in Gombong, Central Java. Photograph from the Rob Nieuwenhuys Collection, Koninklijk Instituut voor de Tropen.

Library of Congress Cataloging-in-Publication Data

Cohen, Matthew Isaac.

Komedie Stamboel : popular theater in colonial Indonesia, 1891–1903 / Matthew Isaac Cohen.

p. cm. — (Ohio University research in international studies. Southeast Asia series ; no. 112)

ISBN 0-89680-246-9 (alk. paper)

1. Komedie Stamboel (Theater company)—History. 2. Komedi stambul—Indonesia—Surabaya. 3. Indonesian drama (Comedy)—History and criticism. 4. Theater and society—Indonesia—History—19th century. I. Title: Popular theater in colonial Indonesia, 1891–1903. II. Title. III. Research in international studies. Southeast Asia series ; no. 112.

PN2904.5.K66C64 2006

792.09598'2—dc22

2005030022

For Aviva sayangku *and* mijn mooie meisje *Hannah*

Contents

Illustrations

Figures

Maps

Notes on Sources and Acknowledgments

I began my research on the Komedie Stamboel as a postdoctoral research fellow at the International Institute for Asian Studies (IIAS) in the Netherlands from 1998 to 2000. At the outset I had no intention of writing a book on the history of Indonesian popular theater. I was at the time working on an ethnohistorical project on traditional shadow puppet theater in the Cirebon area on the north coast of western Java (Indonesia). This research had led me to look at newspapers published in Cirebon in the late nineteenth and early twentieth centuries to glean details about *wayang kulit* and related artistic forms. I still recall my excitement on encountering a series of eight articles in the Dutch newspaper *Tjerimai* describing a run of performances of the Komedie Stamboel "under the direction of the Heer Mahieu" in 1893. As a student of Southeast Asian theater, I was familiar with the name Auguste Mahieu (1865–1903) and the pivotal position this Eurasian actor-manager played in establishing popular Malay-language theater. That much was, and is, common knowledge from the available secondary sources. I had no inkling that primary sources, in the form of newspaper sources, existed—and in such substantial numbers. Curiosity got the better of me. What other materials might be available about Mahieu? Might there be also press reports about the founding of the company in 1891? Might it be possible, in fact, to reconstruct the entirety of Mahieu's career?

The topic fascinated me from the start, for Mahieu's theater was a multiethnic enterprise in which mixed-race performers had a prominent place. Researching an Asian theater, especially one so close to the cultural psyche as wayang kulit, always leaves a non-Asian feeling that he or she is missing something essential by virtue of not having been born into the culture of that theater. I felt no such discomfiture in investigating the hybrid theater of the Komedie Stamboel. In fact, living in Europe with my Javanese wife and Dutch-born daughter, I felt a curious affinity for the between-two-worlds Eurasians of colonial Indonesia. This affinity has only deepened over time as I have learned more about Mahieu and other personalities behind the theater, and the theater world they constructed and inhabited. I am Jewish-American by birth, but having spent most of my adult life in Indonesia, the Netherlands, and Great Britain, I have become (almost by default) of mixed heritage. In terms of language, food, and artistic taste, I imagine the Eurasians of colonial Indonesia to be my close kin.

Tracing the history of the Komedie Stamboel from 1891 until Mahieu's death in 1903 proved to be a hit-and-miss affair. There are no photographs, no complete scripts, few detailed descriptions of performances, no contemporary biographies nor detailed historical overviews of popular theater. Nothing like a route book of the Komedie Stamboel has survived, nor have prior scholars or archivists compiled newspaper clippings. When I decided to expand my account of the first year of the Komedie Stamboel's existence into a book on Mahieu and his theater, much time was necessarily expended combing the pages of periodicals for references to the Komedie Stamboel's itinerary. Newspapers often note that a Malay-language troupe is playing in a particular town but without mentioning proper names, making it difficult to determine which of the dozens of professional troupes active in the 1890s and early 1900s it might be. This is related to colonial protocol. A combination of colonial libel law and decorum meant that people were often dealt with anonymously in newspapers, referred to by initials, or even disguised. Mahieu is often referred to in reviews as M. The most detailed contemporary source on Mahieu's life, a two-part article by the art critic Otto Knaap that originally appeared in a newspaper published in the Netherlands and was subsequently reprinted in 1903 in the *Bondsblad,* refers to Mahieu by the pseudonym Tardieu—and accordingly takes certain liberties in the subject's representation.

Such challenges notwithstanding, I have for the most part been able to reconstruct Mahieu's travels through Java, Madura, Sumatra, and Singapore and have traced the journeys of rival theater troupes to even more distant parts of Southeast Asia. There are stretches of time when Mahieu's whereabouts are unknown and it is possible on one or two occasions that I have ascribed certain activities to Mahieu and his company that should properly be credited to other theater makers. This is not so great a concern for me, for I do not pretend that this book is a proper biography of Mahieu. (Such a biography is not possible, granted the nature of available sources.) Rather, I understand the contours of Mahieu's career, and the careers of fellow theater makers—including Yap Gwan Thay, Lien Gemser, Wim Cramer, Carel Snabilié, and Bai Kasim—as being iconic of the fields of theatrical culture and popular entertainment in colonial Indonesia.

There is clearly much additional research to be done on fin-de-siècle popular culture in Indonesia, a period that saw the introduction of not only the Komedie Stamboel but also the phonograph, cinema, and many other cultural forms associated with modernity. There are undoubtedly documents related to the Komedie Stamboel to be found in the diplomatic pouches, court records, and other nonpublic archival sources of colonial Indonesia. These texts, particularly relevant to the often strained financial circumstances of the theater's Eurasian actors and the numerous legal entanglements of the Komedie Stamboel and other performing groups, will certainly provide rich material for future scholars. This book is largely concerned with the position of popular theater in the public sphere. I anticipate that future work will focus on backstage machinations and politicking, drawing on as yet unexamined archival material available in Jakarta and The Hague.

The Dutch and Malay newspaper sources from the late nineteenth and early twentieth centuries, preserved in libraries in the Netherlands and Indonesia, predate the standardization of vernacular Malay as Indonesian, the national language of Indonesia. At the time they were written, there was no regular system of spelling or official grammar for Malay as written and spoken in the Netherlands Indies. For the most part, Malay orthography follows Dutch conventions. So oe = oo (as in *tool*); ie = ee (as in *peel*); tj = ch (as in *chat*); j = y (as in *yet*); and so on. But the obvious influence of French and English orthographies can also be detected. Thus, for example, Komedie is also occasionally spelled Comedie or Komedi, and Stamboel is sometimes spelled Stambool or Stamboul. A proper Malay or Chinese name, such as Yap Gwan Thay, might likewise be subject to numerous orthographic treatments (e.g., IJap Gwan Taij, Jap Goean Thaij, Yap Goan Thay). The newspaper *Selompret Melajoe,* published in the city of Semarang, is also spelled *Slompret Melayoe.* My initial intention was to use the spelling of the original sources to give the flavor of the hybridized linguistic environment of the popular sphere. A need for legibility has taken precedence. As a rule, I use the standard Indonesian orthography established in 1972, with the exceptions of proper names, titles of published texts, and Dutch words. Dutch orthography circa 1900 also was not absolutely standardized; hence there is some variation in usage (i.e., both *toneel* and *tooneel* can be found). I follow the scholarly convention of not pluralizing Indonesian nouns. For example, I write "Indos lived in urban kampung," not "urban kampungs." Play titles and character names tend to use contemporary Indonesian orthography, except when there are well-known English equivalents (e.g., Aladdin).

The representation of the book's central subject involves an orthographic quirk. Komedie Stamboel (in period spelling) or Komedi Stambul (in contemporary spelling) is both the name of a theater troupe that originated in the eastern Javanese port city of Surabaya in 1891 as well as a designation for a theatrical genre named after the first company. For simplicity's sake, this book will use the capitalized form Komedie Stamboel to refer to the company and the lowercased *komedi stambul* (or simply *stambul*) to refer to the genre. The use of the Dutch spelling for the group both signals the foreignness of the name when it was first used—an alienating effect that was intentional—and anticipates the links to the Dutch revival of the 1950s, discussed in the book's final chapter.

Research was initially carried out in the Netherlands, in the library of the Royal Netherlands Institute of Southeast Asian and Caribbean

Studies (KITLV) at Leiden; the Leiden University Library (UB); and the National Library of the Netherlands (KB) in The Hague. Most of this library research in the Netherlands was conducted in 1999 and 2000, when I was a postdoctoral research fellow at the IIAS. The IIAS provided a utopian environment for the project, and my daily train trips to the KB and regular bicycle rides to the UB and KITLV to peruse microfilm and immaculately bound newspapers remain vivid in memory. Two days were also spent at the British Library Newspaper Reading Room in London.

My library investigations in Indonesia were conducted in the summer of 2002 at the Perpustakaan Nasional (National Library) in Jakarta. That summer was an exercise in historical stereoscopy, as I was reading century-old historical sources describing the physical topography of the city in which I was residing. My body was located in the complex environment of post-Reformation Indonesia. Terrorist bombs were being detonated nightly at discotheques, churches, and shopping malls; Indonesian students were in the streets protesting abuses of power and corruption. My imagination was one hundred years out of focus, though, and I was constantly looking for and finding traces of the past.

All the National Library's books and other materials are stored in a modern, multistory white edifice on Jalan Salemba that sometimes benefits from air conditioning. But adjacent to the main building is a hall used today for receptions, meetings, and other official library functions that in the nineteenth century functioned as the Gymnasium Willem III, opened in 1860. "Regarded for many years as a 'Eurasian' school, the Gymnasium Willem III was an important step towards the emancipation of Eurasians in Batavia and thus helped them to rise further in society."[1] Much the same could be said of the Komedie Stamboel as a company and institution. A weekly reminder of my project's beginning came on a Friday, when the amplified strains of *tarling dangdut* drifted in through the open windows of the microfilm reading room. Tarling dangdut is a popular musical genre from Cirebon, and it played to accompany the morning calisthenics of the library staff.

After closing hours, I typically drifted to the open-air cafes at the Taman Ismail Marzuki arts complex, located at what had been Batavia's zoo, or Botanical and Zoological Gardens (Planten en Dierentuin), established in 1864 with land donated by the celebrated painter Raden Saleh. During the 1890s the zoo was a site for both elite and popular entertainment, including stambul and *bangsawan;* the Komedie Stamboel made an unsuccessful bid to perform there during the Batavia Exposition of 1893.

Evenings were often spent watching theater at the Jakarta Art Building (Gedung Kesenian Jakarta or GKJ), adjacent to the Pasar Baroe (New Market), established in 1821. (The old-style spelling is nostalgically used on the sign over the market's entrance, across the street from the GKJ). Sometimes, before a show, I would stop by for a quick bowl of noodle soup at Restoran Tropic, a Chinese restaurant that occupies the site, and many of the same features, as the famous colonial *toko* (store) of Tio Tek Hong. Among the merchandise for sale at this store in the 1920s were phonographic recordings of stambul songs and sheet music for *kroncong* and stambul songs published by Tio Tek Hong himself. In colonial times the GKJ was known as the *schouwburg,* or European-style theater, opened in 1821. For the most part, the schouwburg housed local European amateur and visiting European professional companies of theater, opera, and ballet. Mahieu repeatedly tried, and failed, to perform in this bastion of European high art at various stages of his career. The schouwburg functioned as a B-movie theater after Indonesian independence. It was reopened as a theater in 1986. Since then the GKJ has mostly catered to Indonesian and foreign "serious art." In 2002, however, the GKJ's regular fare was the sort of Javanese popular theater that had been strongly influenced by stambul over the last century, including *ketoprak humor* (humorous ketoprak, presenting costume dramas in a mix of Indonesian and Javanese for television broadcast), *ludruk,* and *wayang wong.* At one particularly memorable ketoprak humor performance I sat next to a madam of a brothel. During the performance, she regaled me with stories about finding prostitutes for foreigners in Bali and repeatedly shouted at one of the clowns (her personal screen and stage idol) to sing a song. She had requested the song by throwing a note onstage attached to a package of cigarettes and a number of banknotes, a typical village practice. This "cultural decolonization" of the GKJ felt right to me, though I know that there are many Indonesian ballet dancers, pianists, and performance artists who would rather see the building put to other, more "high-minded" uses.

The research environments of contemporary Holland and Indonesia could hardly be more different, but the staffs at all the libraries noted above were helpful in the extreme and for that, much thanks. I also thank IIAS and the University of Glasgow for providing the time and support needed to pursue my research. Research and writing were supported by the John Robertson Jr. Bequest Fund (for summer 2002 research) and the Arts and Humanities Research Board (for research leave in 2004).

Parts of the book have been presented as lectures at the University of Glasgow, SOAS, Leiden University, the Janáček Academy of Music and Performing Arts, and Leeds University. Earlier versions of sections of this book have been published in *Bijdragen tot de taal-, land- en volkenkunde; Indonesia and the Malay World; Seleh Notes;* and *Middle Eastern Literatures.* An essay I have written entitled "A Chinese *Pujangga* from Surabaya? Yap Gwan Thay in an Age of Translation" will be published in a forthcoming volume on the history of translation in Indonesia and Malaysia edited by Henri Chambert-Loir. This essay covers the same historical period from the perspective of the Komedie Stamboel's first owner and can be read as a companion piece to this book. I have also edited and annotated a forthcoming anthology of Indonesian popular drama for the Lontar Foundation that begins in the Mahieu period but extends the history of Malay- and Indonesian-language popular theater up through the New Order.

An illustration from the 1891 edition of *Syair Indra Sebaha* is reproduced courtesy of the British Library Board. Ben Snijder's lyrics for "Indisch ABC" are published courtesy of *Moesson.* Photographs from the Rob Nieuwenhuys collection are published courtesy of Querido Publishers and the Royal Tropical Institute.

People meriting particular thanks include Ben Arps, Marthinus van Bart, A. L. Becker, Gillian Berchowitz, Michael Bodden, Siem Boon, Hanne de Bruin, Henri Chambert-Loir, Joost Coté, Catherine Diamond, Rob Dumas, Lilian Ducelle, J. Joseph Errington, Keith Foulcher, Annabel Teh Gallop, Cobina Gillitt, Kathryn Hansen, Barbara Hatley, Doris Jedamski, A. Kasim Achmad, Werner Kraus, Henk Maier, Jan Mrázek, Laura Noszlopy, James Peacock, Harry Poeze, N. Riantiarno, Jacques Roumimper, Suryadi, Tan Sooi Beng, Melanie Tangkau, Hae-Kyung Um, Reed Wadley, Wartaka, Robert Wessing, Wim van Zanten, and my former colleagues and students at Leiden University and the University of Glasgow. Aviva Kartiningsih Cohen and Hannah Sita Cohen provided the trust and understanding essential to the project's completion. All faults, errors in transcription and translation, and overly free flights of imagination are my own.

Introduction

POPULAR ENTERTAINMENT IN NINETEENTH-CENTURY INDONESIA

Blitar, 20 July 1900

> Recently, I happened to be outside the post office of Blitar and heard lively sounds [*rame-rame*] and was surprised to see that in the yard next to Babah Tjan Tjin Hianak's store, the store employees were practicing how to perform stambul. *Wah,* my friend Babah Oei Sing Bi made a good impression of a komedi stambul clown named Ahmat Sokrok, and when he put on his costume and took off his shirt and put on glasses and stuck out his stomach, everyone laughed for he made such a good clown as he was an inch away, meaning almost the same as, Si Ahmat Sokrok, and I stayed to watch until after ten. Oh, I don't know what happened after that as I went home, amen.
>
> —*C. Aswotoendo (alias B. Tjitoroso),* Bintang Soerabaia

At the turn of the century in the small towns and larger cities of the Netherlands Indies, the island group roughly corresponding to the Southeast Asian archipelagic nation known today as Indonesia, the Malay-language musical theater of komedi stambul was omnipresent.[1] Itinerant professional troupes with casts and crews of fifty or more visited regularly, performing four- or five-hour tent shows for paying spectators. Diverse audiences attended—drunken European men, middle-income Muslim families, Chinese store owners, prostitutes, sailors and soldiers, Eurasian clerks, and nearly everyone else. Those who could not afford the price of a ticket might listen outside the tent or try to sneak in. Men and women fell madly in love with actors and actresses and lavished gifts and attention on them. Songs from this theater, known as *lagu stambul,* were sung on the streets, issued as cylinders for music boxes, and incorporated into diverse musical genres including *kroncong, gambang kromong,* and *gamelan.* Stories based on stambul plays or those destined to be performed on the stambul stage were published regularly in the vernacular press, and professional companies advertised and were reviewed in the Dutch- and Malay-language newspapers. Amateur and semiprofessional groups multiplied, performing scaled-down versions of plays such as *Ali Baba, Snow White,* and *Faust* for their own amusement and on the streets during communal celebrations such as the Chinese New Year. Ethical aspects of the theater, performers, and spectators were debated, and the theater was appropriated for charitable, social, and political causes. Not everyone was interested in watching komedi stambul, but almost everyone had an opinion about it. Stambul was integrated into the rhythms of everyday life; it was an involving site of lively (*rame*) amusement and distraction realized in counterpoint to the city's stores, post offices, and like sites associated by many with the drudgery of urban life.

Stambul theater was a peripatetic cultural formation and a popular movement in the arts and culture of Indonesia. Its beginnings can be traced to the eastern Javanese port city of Surabaya in 1891 and the founding of the musical theater company known as the Komedie Stamboel, with Eurasian actors and Chinese owners. The adaptations of *Arabian Nights* stories which the Komedie Stamboel performed on a proscenium stage with wing-and-drop scenery and offstage musical accompaniment initially took place exclusively in a theater in the city's Chinatown. Within months of its founding, the Komedie Stamboel transformed into a touring company, and it was not long before many imitators, professional and amateur, emerged. The ethnic affinities of the theater were of critical importance during the Komedie Stamboel's early history, but the process of intercity and interisland touring resulted in the theatrical form no longer being associated with a particular city or region: it was a common cultural possession of the Indies.

As the first performing art to emerge in the Indies with currency throughout the archipelago, stambul had a significant role in shaping what Hildred Geertz long ago described as Indonesia's "metropolitan superculture," an "integrating system" connecting cities and towns into a single network.[2] A superculture of this sort is not unique to Indonesia, but its articulation in this archipelagic nation, with more distinct ethnic cultures and languages spoken than perhaps any country in the world, is nonetheless striking. We find today, for example, *sanggar tari* (dance studios) located in all Indonesian cities teaching ethnic dances culled from many ethnic groups, and dance artists such as Didik Nini Thowok creating hybrid choreographies drawing on innumerable indigenous and exogenous traditions. Horror films and *sinetron* (television soap operas) might be set against the background of a particular ethnic culture or urban locale, but draw on a shared body of narrative motifs and a repertoire of gesture recognized and comprehended by all Indonesians. A popular music sensation such as the *dangdut* singer-dancer Inul Daratista can ignite the passions of audiences around Indonesia. All speak to the integration of Indonesians in a shared structure of feeling.

Few memories might remain today of the Komedie Stamboel in Indonesia. Indonesian theater scholars sometimes refer to it in passing as a "transitional" theater, located nebulously between the classical and folk theaters of traditional Indonesia and the modern, Indonesian language theater said to have begun with the nationalist movement in the 1920s. Some actors and aficionados of Indonesian regional theaters, such as *ludruk, lenong, sandiwara,* or *drama gong,* might be aware of the pivotal role that touring Malay-language theater beginning with the Komedie Stamboel played in forming these localized popular traditions performed in regional dialects and languages. The relation between stambul and *ketoprak,* a Javanese-language popular theater form that emerged in Yogyakarta in the mid-1920s, is particularly close. An alternate early designation for ketoprak, in fact, was *stambul Jawa,* or (Javanese [language] stambul), for stambul costumes, music, and stories were at the core of ketoprak's early dramaturgy. Kroncong singers are certain to know stambul as a form of song, and the more experienced singers are likely to know that these songs were once associated with a genre of theater, now long gone. In the Netherlands, Indonesia's former colonizer, older Eurasian repatriates will recognize the Komedie Stamboel as a Eurasian cultural product and are likely to have seen some oft-reprinted stambul images collected by Rob Nieuwenhuys.

At the same time, traces of this popular musical theater, the first theater to be performed on a proscenium stage in a language that could be understood by the majority of Indonesia's urban public, are to be found everywhere in Indonesia today—in language, gesture, and intonation; artistic production and reception; the conceptualization of the public. The horizons of imagination, the possibilities for self-transformation, and the potentials of interethnic solidarity did not emerge as programs propounded by intellectuals or politicians. These were theatrical mechanisms and reflexes that came to inform all aspects of Indonesian society. Tracing the genesis and early development of komedi stambul means mapping the formation of Indonesian public culture.

Komedi stambul's dramaturgy appears at first glance to be derivative of European models, but in fact the theater is an eminent hybrid that, in Homi Bhabha's terms, enunciates cultural difference and "problematizes the binary division of past and present, tradition and modernity, at the level of cultural representation and its authoritative address."[3] Greasepaint, bright lights, wing-and-drop scenery, trapdoors and flies, box seats and stalls, tickets, posters, leaflets, and all the apparatus of theater arrived in colonized Asia and Africa with the growth of European settler populations. Temporary stages and then permanent theaters were constructed; amateur and semiprofessional drama clubs and associations were formed; plays were written and rewritten, performed, and reviewed. Occasionally non-Europeans were recruited as actors in early colonial performances, but it was more likely for Asians or Africans to be present in the audience or work behind the scenes than tread the boards. Starting in the middle of the nineteenth century, however, non-European "colonial mimics" began to put on their own dramas, using European dramaturgical forms and theatrical technology to perform plays in their own languages and idioms. The theater of Europe was appropriated and localized.

Theater, as Raymond Williams has pointed out, is the most social of art forms. The transplantation of this European cultural form into non-European cultural landscapes required not only imitating attitudes and poses and translating dialogue. It also entailed a resituating and redefinition of the "art world" of theater, the organized network of patrons, sponsors, performers, technicians, support personnel, spectators, and critics who produce and consume performances. The remooring of European theater in colonial contexts meant creating, or finding equivalents to, the sites of performance, the networks of patronage and support, the institutions of performer training and methods of personnel recruitment, the mechanisms of publicity and promotion, and the makers and suppliers of theatrical equipment that together allow theater to function. Various local conditions yielded a panoply of theater worlds in Asia and Africa, homologous with the theater worlds of European colonizing countries but not identical. The production of colonial theater was a complex negotiation involving tenacious thespians, erratic local conditions and tools of production, volatile whims and desires of sponsors and audiences, and the restrictions of colonial authorities. The playing out of dramas in the public sphere was simultaneously an enactment of the tensions and conflicts among actors and agents, diverse cultural forms, forces of production, the public, and governance.

Performing arts, at least until the twentieth century, did not flourish in the Netherlands. This was largely due to Dutch Calvinism, with its virulent antitheatricalism and suspicion of ostentatious display. The Dutch in the Netherlands Indies embodied a different cultural ethos than the Dutch in Holland, however. "In contrast to bourgeois Holland," writes W. F. Wertheim in a classic study of cultural creolization, "where the tendency was towards a thrifty frugality and simplicity which concealed a certain prosperity, the mode of living in the 'Indian' towns [towns in the Netherlands Indies] aimed at maintaining colonial prestige in a society predominantly feudal. There was no attempt to create the intimate atmosphere of the cozy Dutch parlor. Instead, Indian social life was a life of balls and receptions. Luxury was not to be found in the confines of interior rooms but in open galleries."[4] Some have viewed this as a European accommodation to the performance economy of the Indies.

The Netherlands Indies had a large variety of indigenous ethnic groups speaking different languages and dialects, as well as substantial populations of Chinese, Arabs, Indians, Europeans and Eurasians, assorted "foreign Asian" and other ethnic groups.[5] Migration and urban growth were stimulated by the passing of the Agrarian Law of 1870, which brought free enterprise to the archipelago. Only about 5 percent of indigenous Indonesians were living in urban areas of Java and other islands in Indonesia at the end of the nineteenth century, but exogenous populations were located predominately in towns and cities. The concomitance of wealth and ethnic diversity in urban centers yielded a cosmopolitan character, or at least aspirations to cosmopolitanism. As an English traveler who visited Batavia (present-day Jakarta) in 1890 snidely declared, "Boston is not the only place in the world which has decided upon insufficient evidence that it is the centre of the universe."[6]

The Netherlands Indies, particularly in the densely populated island of Java, where about three quarters of the populace lived, might be characterized as an open-gallery society, in which social and cultural worth were judged on the basis of display, performance, and public presentation. Open galleries were spaces of coarticulation with porous barriers and minimal restrictions. A musical concert might take place in an ostensibly private space such as a European club, but that open gallery space was permeable to crowds of eavesdropping onlookers. There was even a Dutch colonial word coined to describe the incidental audience members who enjoyed a "passive kind of happiness."[7] They were known as *nontonners,* from the Batavia Malay word *nonton,* "to go to see a sight."[8] Nontonners were omnipresent at cultural performances. They also congregated to witness fistfights; eruptions of amok, mentally ill, and drunken behavior; military drills; and executions and corporal punishment. The hustle and bustle of ambulatory street vendors, marketplace exchanges, the arrival and departure of ships, and the passage of elegantly appointed carriages were entertaining diversions for the lower socioeconomic classes, for whom "the city's streets were both living room and public theater."[9]

Life in late nineteenth-century urban Indonesia was lived at an accelerated pace due to advances in communication and transportation technology. Indonesia was fully a part of what naturalist (and Indonesianist) Alfred Wallace termed "the wonderful century," with its attendant "marvelous character" and sense of "vast possibilities of further development of many of our recent discoveries."[10] Roads with hardened surfaces for the use of wagons were first constructed in 1852. The first telegraph line for public use was laid in 1856. A modern postal service began operation in 1862. The first kilometers of railway were laid down in 1867, and by 1888 there were eight railway lines in operation, connecting the fifteen largest cities of Java. The Suez Canal opened in 1869, shortening the distance between Europe and the Indies by many kilometers. The first automobile was imported to Java in 1890, and a cycling craze swept through cities and towns in Java and other islands around 1895. Lithographs, photographs, phonographs, music boxes, and printing presses delivered sounds, texts, and images to the elite and the masses alike.

Along with this increasing interconnectivity came the inevitable "metropolitan blasé attitude" identified by Georg Simmel as a primary characteristic of urban mental life. But at the same time Indonesians craved all that was novel.[11] The port cities of Indonesia had long been places in which "a multitude of impressions, contrast, institutions, buildings, and types of conduct provided an environment which cultivated awareness" of the particularities and generalities of life in process.[12] This awareness only intensified in the course of the nineteenth century.

Cities brought different sets of performance cultures into contact with each other. Cities were "arenas of conflict."[13] They were also arenas of observation. People from different ethnic groups became aware of how other ethnic groups behaved in daily life. They could also inspect diverse forms of extradaily behavior. Cultural performances that were significant reflexive occasions, in which a group told stories about themselves to themselves, became occasions for intercultural communication. The accomplishment demonstrated in producing and performing art and spectacle acted as a source of group pride and cultural valuation in a multiethnic society.

Indonesia is justly famous for the diversity and vitality of its traditional performing arts. Many of the elaborate art forms practiced by Javanese, Balinese, Madurese, and other ethnic groups of the western archipelago, such as the shadow puppet theater known as *wayang kulit,* have roots in Indonesia that go back a millennium or more. There are numerous forms of trance dance, sometimes associated with shamanism and healing; mask dance and mask theater; communal folk dancing; and storytelling with musical accompaniment. Processions with palanquins, giant effigies, music, and dancing accompany rites of passage in many Indonesian societies. Folk troupes of musicians, dancers, actors, and animals busk in markets and street corners. The royal courts of the western archipelago have been patrons of the performing arts for more than a millennium, packaging their own productions and hiring local and extralocal troupes for royal festivities and bestowing noble titles on performers. In the nineteenth and early twentieth centuries, the courts of central Java produced *wayang wong* dance drama, in which actors took the roles of puppets in wayang kulit plays. These could involve months of rehearsals and casts of hundreds. Gamelan, or gong-chime music, has famously influenced Western composers since Debussy, and is played and heard in numerous social and ritual contexts in Indonesia. Communally sponsored festivals, featuring scores of performing ensembles, commemorate ancestors and propitiate spirits.

Other Asian populations in the Indies were active in the arts as well. Indonesian Chinese were historically important sponsors of both indigenous as well as Chinese performance. Seventeenth-century European travelers describe Chinese opera performed in the trading entrepôts of Java's northern littoral to mark the arrival and departure of junks. Chinese opera was translated into the Malay language, the Indonesian lingua franca spoken as a first language by indigenized (*peranakan*) Chinese, by the eighteenth century.[14] In nineteenth-century Java the majority of Chinese opera troupes were all-female. Performers were often not of Chinese descent. They were usually Southeast Asian women drilled and trained to high degrees of proficiency by teachers imported from China.

The European and other elites who demanded the latest novelties from Paris to furnish their luxurious villas, were keen to consume public performances. A minority of Europeans patronized non-European arts and artists, but most preferred arts of European provenance. In contrast to French and British colonies, the Dutch colonial government was not committed to building and maintaining institutions for the cultural good of the public.[15] In Java, there were schouwburgen, European-style theaters with proscenium stages, in the cities of Batavia, Semarang, and Surabaya. These institutions were often strapped for cash, in the absence of fixed-sum awards from the municipal or colonial state governments, and made regular public appeals for support. Dramatic fare at these theaters and other public spaces of performance was an eclectic mixture of professional touring theater and local amateur efforts.

British troupes "played the empire," performing the latest hits from Covent Garden in a transoceanic circuit encompassing Johannesburg, Bombay, Calcutta, Shanghai, Singapore, Sydney, and other parts of Africa, Asia, and the Pacific with many European settlers.[16] French colonies not only benefited from touring theatrical companies from the Parisian metropole, there were also state-subsidized opera companies in residence in major French colonial cities. The Netherlands, as a rule, did not field international performing troupes in the nineteenth century, and there was little in the way of state subsidy for the performing arts. The public culture of nineteenth-century Indonesia cannot be said to have been genuinely colonized by the Netherlands. Urban Indonesia was a transit zone for itinerant performers, a stopover between mainland Asia and Australia (à la the board game Risk). It had its own independent cultural dynamics and momentum, only indirectly indebted to the culture of the colonizing country.

Commercial entertainment outfits originating in the Indies and those that arrived there from outside shared a circuit of towns and cities connected by steamship and rail. On this circuit, there were large-scale mass entertainments like the circus and Japanese acrobatic troupes. There was operetta, burlesque, and variety companies of various sorts. There

Figs. 0.1 and 0.2. Exterior and auditorium of Surabaya's schouwburg, constructed in 1854. Reprinted from von Faber, *Oud Soerabaia,* 335–36.

were also small-scale entertainments: European, Indian and Chinese stage magicians, balloonists, dog-and-monkey showmen, and marionette artists. Other itinerant showmen displayed magic lanterns, waxworks, and panoramas.

In nineteenth-century Indonesia, public performances of all sorts were referred to as *tontonan*.[17] Commercial entertainments were classified generically as *komedi.* This term has high-culture connotations in European parlance, through association with such venerable institutions as La Comédie Française. It is likely in fact that the term *komedi* was introduced to the Indies through touring French troupes. One of the earliest of these French troupes to come to Batavia was under an actor-manager named Minard. In 1835, Minard and his company graced the schouwburg stage with Eugène Scribe's plays *Michel et Christine* (1820) and *La demoiselle et la dame, ou Avant et après le mariage* (1822), as well as a one-act vaudeville entitled *Angéline, ou La Champenoise* (1819).[18] The komedi designation subsequently went down a cultural escalator in colonial Indonesia, and it was appropriated to refer to a host of traveling entertainments.[19]

Forms of komedi were continually evolving and changing throughout the second half of the nineteenth century and the early twentieth century; entertainments all the rage one year were often obsolete the next. Novelty, or at least the appearance of novelty, was valued for its own sake in fashion and entertainment in late nineteenth-century Indonesia.

Newspapers, those ephemeral bestsellers, both indexed and encouraged novelty by preferentially reporting on whatever was new, striking, innovative. Novelty was particularly important in the field of stage magic. Audiences thrilled to magic shows by European, Indian, and Chinese magicians, featuring astounding and often macabre exhibitions of hypnotism, magnetism, and illusion. Indian magicians swallowed swords; Chinese magicians transformed feathers into doves and made water disappear out of jugs; European magicians mixed stage illusions, technological displays, and discourses on the supernatural. Novel acts in an 1893 show by an Indian magician in the small eastern Javanese town of Situbondo are described at length by a correspondent to Semarang's Malay daily *Selompret Melajoe.* The correspondent dwells on how the magician stabs his eye with a bamboo skewer, makes a marble disappear, cuts flowers from paper, and bakes cake on a child's head. But acts already commonly performed by Javanese or Madurese magicians are not even mentioned "as it will only add to the reader's boredom, and in other cities there is no shortage of this sort of komedi, correct?"[20] Newspaper writers and correspondents clearly and consistently demonstrate an awareness of what was special and original, what was shared, and what was common. This was an act not only of categorization but of valuation; the culture of the new inculcated a respect for and an interest in the novel.

Komedie evoked reactions of astonishment, rather than mystification. In European terms, komedi involved "modern magic" and not "sorcery"; in Malay terms, komedi was a cultural form of the *heran* and not the *aneh*.[21] Heran was an attitude toward the world that encompassed confusion; surprise, astonishment, and amazement; and mystery and wonder.[22] Appreciation of attractions presupposed a degree of sophistication, an ability to recognize and appreciate illusionism and technological prowess, and not confuse the wonders of the komedi stage with the genuine magic of spirit possession in hobbyhorse dancing or displays of invulnerability magic in cultural performances such as western Javanese *dabus*.

The attitude of heran was most prominent and celebrated in the circuses, Wild West shows, and hippodrome attractions known collectively to Malay speakers as the *komedi kuda* (horse show). Circuses attracted the largest audiences of all forms of entertainment; the horse show was the stick by which all other popular entertainments were measured. Circuses were initially irregular affairs. The first small circus known to play the Indies performed in a tent erected in the yard of Batavia's Hôtel de Provence in 1848; another "popped up" in 1856, playing in Batavia's Koningsplein, a major public square.[23] As the century wore on, increasingly larger troupes toured Java and other islands of the archipelago with regularity, playing in big tops for audiences of thousands. Visits from itinerant circus troupes became a normal feature of urban life. A particular favorite in nineteenth-century Surabaya was Wilson's Circus, which first played the city in 1879.[24] So popular were the likes of the Chiarini, Wilson, Harmston, and Woodyear circuses that wage earners would commonly ask for advances and farmers would pawn their valuables to see them.[25]

Ticket prices for horse shows, acrobatic displays, magic shows, and most other forms of komedi were affordable to a large percentage of urban dwellers of all races. But there was a definite class bias; members

Figs. 0.3 and 0.4. Advertisements for performances of the Abell and Olman Circus in Batavia. *Pembrita Betawi,* 21, 22 May 1896.

of Java's *priyayi* class, the traditional aristocratic elite and landed gentry, consistently shied away from such vulgar pleasures, preferentially indulging in more refined cultural pursuits such as turtledoves, horse racing, and gamelan music.[26]

For many urbanites, however, komedi represented a psychological necessity by the late nineteenth century, filling out lives and substituting for the organic and integrated social wholeness of rural life—in effect serving the same function that television and the Internet do today. Urban life was perceived acutely by many as a life of alienation and anomie; this was all the more prevalent before the twentieth-century rise of the mass political organizations that stamped out identities and provided extraindividual purpose for Indonesians. Henk Maier has linked the rise of the Malay-language commercial publishing industry with the feeling of tedium, or *iseng* (a word that did not exist in older Malay), which "had become a ruling obsession in circles of Batavian literati" by the 1890s. Authors report that they wrote, as they did not know what else they might do with the time on their hands and anticipated that their readers would read their work as "a way to fight boredom." "Iseng is dangerous; people who give in to it open their hearts to all sorts of temptation (*penggoda*), to gambling, for instance, to card-playing, and to neglect of the household."[27] The same sort of individual needs are articulated in relation to komedi as to reading for pleasure.

> Thousands of thanks are due that there are a large number of entertainments [*tontonan*] in Batavia because these are greatly appreciated by all residents. It is an improvement on going home after work and staying in and then going to sleep, without any sort of pleasure [*pelesir*]. Is it not true that if there is a place where one can go to soothe one's body, that one's thoughts also might become soothed there? When a person's body is soothed, is not this of benefit in the alleviation of several varieties of erroneous thoughts that congeal in one's heart and result in annoyance or vexation? Such vexation might be acted on, building on one's annoyance and vexation and resulting finally in problems for oneself. Rather, it is better to have a modicum of enjoyment.[28]

The spectators of komedi lived in urban compounds where there was little joy to be had in fraternizing with neighbors. Urban life in the Indies became increasingly atomized during the nineteenth century. Streetcars ran in all the major Indies cities, and horse-driven two-seater carriages known as *sado* (from the French *dos-à-dos,* back-to-back) and two-wheeled wagons known as *delman* (after the carriage's inventor C. Deeleman) rushed through the streets. Nobody walked in the streets, except the very poor; everyone was propelled at high speeds between place of employment and home. When at home, there was scarcely a need to leave. A vast array of peripatetic street vendors hawked their wares in all cities in the Indies. The likes of Madurese satay, seasonal fruits and vegetables, Arabian *martabak* crepes (introduced to Surabaya in 1891), Chinese *bami* noodle soup, and even iced drinks were available on demand. Ambulatory vendors sold toys, barbers gave haircuts and shaves, and locksmiths made keys on the streets.[29] This allowed many to stay at home and purchase all necessities and many luxuries without venturing into marketplace or store. Their leisure activities were oriented to an increasingly rationalized lifestyle. Komedi was entertainment that "opened its doors at preannounced times, charge fees, and was largely divorced from the rhythms of the life cycle or the agricultural seasons."[30]

Komedi was not only a release from the demands of work, it was also a chance for display of status and conspicuous consumption, "a site where Chinese can throw their money away."[31] Other ethnic groups were just as spendthrift. Garments, ornaments, and hairstyles were critical means of discrimination of types of people in colonial Indonesia.[32] Members of the indigenous Javanese aristocratic elite guarded their privilege to wear certain types of batik cloth; Chinese were marked by their pigtails until the twentieth century; devout Muslims identified themselves by adopting Arabic dress. A strictly enforced dress code was used to keep colonial subjects in place and maintain racial and class hierarchical structures. Komedi offered a reprieve from these strictures. It was a place for trying out what it felt like to walk around in the clothes of another type of person. More than that, it helped formulate what it meant to enact a role and fostered a belief that it was possible to transcend the limitations of birth and transform oneself into something else.[33] This experimentalism in relation to the self was not to be found only onstage but also extended to the auditorium; there is more than one account of spectators wearing clothes that are "too classy" (*terlalu kocak*) or inappropriate for their ethnicity or class, thus garnering censure from the press and sometimes fines from the authorities.

Alcohol lubricated this sense of experimentalism. Various alcoholic drinks could be purchased from itinerant vendors who set up their stalls in the vicinity or in buffets run on commission in or immediately adjacent to komedi sheds and tents. Many European and Eurasian spectators

Fig. 0.5. Advertisement for de Bourran wines. "Friend, try this de Bourran Frères and Company Wine." "Don't you think this wine is smooth and delicious?" "You can get de Bourran Frères and Company Wine only at the K. Hinlopen and Company store in Pangung, Surabaya." "The wine was so good that the friend finished the bottle himself." *Primbon Soerabaia,* 26 July 1900.

considered drinking whiskey, brandy and soda, or beer an essential feature of the komedi experience. Non-European men tended to prefer arrack and *towak* rice wine. The carnivalesque atmosphere of komedi, as an interruption of the norms and strictures of everyday, gave license to audience violence among men.[34]

For the numerous towns and small cities of Java and other parts of the Indies, the arrival of a komedi troupe was an event in itself. Posters went up on walls and other public spaces, circulars were distributed, people stopped to watch the touring theater's tent being erected in the town square. Audiences marveled at many a troupe's ethnic "mixture of actors including Chinese, Dutch, Arabs, Javanese and Indians."[35] Such ethnic mixture was rarely to be found in other sorts of enterprises in the Indies. There was likewise a social electricity (and occasionally friction) generated from the mix of people in the auditorium, cutting across normal divides of ethnicity, class, and sex. Tiered ticket prices ranging from three guilders for box seats to as low as ten or twenty-five cents for third-class bleachers meant that audience members was arrayed in the space of the auditorium in a way that mirrored their standing in society.[36] Contumacious male spectators, typically under the influence of alcohol, often snuck into first-class seats, transgressing barriers of both price and class and disrupting the spectacle of social order through displays of belligerent behavior adjacent to higher-class spectators.

Hosting komedi troupes was often represented as a part of what made a town or city *ramai* (lively)—a sign of prosperity and health (*raharja* in Javanese and Javanese Malay) of the civic body. This ramai quality was also highly valued in komedi performances for the signs of activity and life onstage osmosed into everyday life. A stage that is ramai guarantees a society that is ramai as well. "There is no happiness in a city if it lacks an amenity to soothe our thoughts in a ramai atmosphere."[37] When the town of Tegal was not visited by a komedi troupe for most of 1895, there was evident sadness, as this "left the town square appearing hauntingly quiet."[38] The departure of a komedi troupe left a correspondent from Padang Panjang in despair. "All that those of us living in the area of Padang Panjang's market can do at night is sleep and hold hands; there is nothing to lighten hearts of the youths than a Jewish-owned ringtoss game, but many have only lost at it."[39]

There was little resembling coherent cultural policy in the Netherlands Indies in the nineteenth century, and local authorities consequently had much discretionary power. Residents and assistant residents had substantial autonomy to interpret colonial regulations and instigate new administrative practices in the interest of increasing tax revenues and maintaining social order. This had direct results on popular entertainment and its proponents. Some residents and assistant residents issued performance bans on particular genres or troupes due to fighting, carousing, and other violations of public decorum. Others maintained tolerant attitudes to stage activities in the interest of appeasing the local population. Itinerant troupes always were on slippery ground, as they could not precisely predict what the reaction of local authorities would be to transgressive art or excessive audience behavior.

Traffic of komedi and other cultural forms was multidirectional and complex. Many of the foreign troupes came to the Netherlands Indies on world tours that lasted years or even decades. Details of how companies from Britain, Italy, France, the United States, Australia, New Zealand, Japan, China, India, and other parts of the world financed and organized their tours are often sketchy. Take the case of the Harmston Circus, a familiar name in urban Indonesia from the 1890s through the 1930s. This British circus was founded by William Batty Harmston in 1880 and toured the Midlands and East Anglia until it went bankrupt in 1886 and was forced to sell off all but four of the twenty horses the company owned. Harmston recapitalized, but his failure in England apparently convinced him to set off for greener pastures. Harmston's circus reached Asia by 1889 and remained a fixture of popular entertainment in Asia until 1938, playing India, Sri Lanka, China, Singapore, the Philippines, Malaysia, Vietnam, Indonesia, and other parts of the region. Circuses such as Harmston's started off in Australia, Europe, or the United States, but after years of touring "the Orient," they became more and more Asian in their composition. Some of them featured clowns who could speak Malay. Reviews, notices, and a host of artifacts testify to the enduring appeal of Harmston's and other big-top circuses in late-colonial Indonesia. But, as one nonacademic circus historian notes, there are many unanswered questions related to Harmston's touring. "Who asked, organised and paid for them to go out there? How did they get out there (they would know very little about travelling the world)? . . . How did they travel around the Far East? If it was by boat, how did they transport, feed, keep the animals fit and trained during the sea voyages?"[40] Ongoing research into route books, memoirs, and popular press accounts is beginning to answer questions like these about the showmen, entertainers, and artists who traveled the world in the age of empire.

In the Netherlands Indies, a company from China, India, or Malaya composed of "foreign Asians" was generally granted a six-month performance permit on arrival at port. "European" performers could get longer permits, and it was not unusual for peripatetic entertainers and artists to settle permanently in the Indies. French actors arrived with opera troupes and subsequently became language and dancing teachers, hairdressers, and dress and millinery shop owners. These former actors were instrumental in molding the francophile culture of nineteenth-century Indonesia.[41]

There is more. It seems that two of the most famous American sideshow attractions of the nineteenth century perhaps originated in Indonesia. The conjoined monkey and fish that P. T. Barnum hawked as his "Feejee Mermaid" humbug was earlier known as the St. James Mermaid, and was reportedly purchased in Batavia for five thousand dollars by a sea captain and exhibited in England in the 1820s before coming to the United States.[42] Later "mermaids" displayed in London (in fact dugong) likewise originated in the Indonesian archipelago.[43] Krao Farini, who was marketed variously as "the missing link" and as a "gorilla girl" when she performed with big railroad circuses such as Ringling Brothers and Barnum and Bailey, was said variously to be a native of Sumatra or Burma, or captured by a Norwegian explorer in a Laotian forest. Krao's plenteous body hair, coupled with her diminutive stature, allowed her to play the scantily dressed "savage," although she reportedly spoke seven languages and tutored children at a library in Bridgeport, Connecticut, when Barnum and Bailey wintered there.[44]

Polite representations of other cultures from the field of literature and high art tend to be privileged by academics and cultural curators. But it is in circus tents, sideshows, and popular theaters that the first and most lasting impressions of other cultures are formed. Komedi offered windows onto the world. Brightly colored circus posters enticed spectators with the opportunity of seeing "all varieties of animals on the planet."[45] Acrobatic troupes from Japan, which first came to the Indies in 1867, performed astounding feats of plate spinning, bamboo balancing, tightrope walking, human pyramid construction, and parasol juggling. These troupes offered many nineteenth-century spectators, both in Indonesia and throughout the world, their first encounter with and awareness of Japanese culture. The appearance of troupes of "mountebanks, jugglers, clowns, acrobats, equilibrists, and gymnasts"[46] in the commercial entertainment field marked the end of Japan's lengthy isolation from the rest of the world under the Tokugawa shogunate. The dazzling spectacle of efficient, choreographed bodies performing perfectly timed and coordinated feats beyond normal human powers is an image that shaped popular conceptions of "the Japanese" around the world. Komedi bridged cultures and nations and influenced geopolitical relations.

The Komedie Stamboel was distinguished from many other entertainments traveling the komedi circuit by its local genesis, but it shared exogenous komedi's pleasure-seeking public and orientation toward the novel, the heran, and the ramai.

Java and other islands of Indonesia have long traditions of traveling players, "vagabonds and wanderers" who "peddled their specialities on the broader social market."[47] These professional troupes appeared regularly on market days and communal celebrations and irregularly as roadside buskers with masks, hobbyhorses, magic tricks, clowning, drums, gongs, and shawms. Most premodern civilizations—India, China, the Mediterranean world—had their equivalents. The players stood outside the constraints of the social structure and had liberties in behavior and presentation of self. For little communities, the traditional shows of dramatics, comedy, dance, music, and song were portable feasts, performative irruptions into the quotidian agrarian cycle. The nineteenth century saw the beginning of a long decline of this mode of performance. The requirement of travel documents and permits from civil authorities hampered freedom of movement. The traveling players' routines were conservative and increasingly seen as old hat.

Stambul and related forms of komedi were formations with "active social and cultural substance" that plugged into different sorts of social and cultural networks than traditional itinerant genres.[48] Komedi was dependent on a veneer of technical sophistication coming from Europe, equipment and training unavailable in rural areas, modern forms of marketing, and new modes of patronage, spectatorship, and audience construction. Komedi as such presented a new way of "doing" culture in the Indies. Indigenized forms of komedi like the Komedie Stamboel were not dependent on local patronage systems. Placating gestures to tradition were not required. Market demands could be prioritized over the needs of cultural connoisseurs and elite experts. Komedi culture was transregional, brash, and unapologetically oriented to all that was ephemeral and novel. It was the culture of the masses, volatile and sensitive to public taste and opinion.

The Komedie Stamboel was considered naive, sentimental, and populist by cultural elites in its time and after, but stambul was arguably the most important form of commercial culture until the arrival of film and radio. The Komedie Stamboel was the first theater in the Indonesian archipelago to perform on proscenium stages using focused stage lighting and wing-and-drop sets. It was the first theater that did not specialize in a defined dramatic repertoire but mined plays and stories from all over the world. Many other firsts can, and shall, be enumerated. Komedi stambul began as a derivative of imported komedi culture, but as with so many things entering Asia from Europe, it was "locally articulated" as a self-mobilization or cultural movement "and absorbed into the very fabric of local affairs—causing wider ramifications of change."[49]

This book focuses on stambul's earliest, and most formative, phase of existence. The account begins in 1891, with the founding of the first theater company in Surabaya and continues until the death of actor-manager Auguste Mahieu (1865–1903). Mahieu is commonly regarded as the theater's founding figure, and while this is not strictly accurate, it is true that he exerted more influence on the shape and image of stambul than any other artist. An account of Mahieu's theatrical career and his "dwelling-in-traveling"[50] provides answers to some important questions related to the complexities of commercial culture in his times. We observe how a local cultural institution, a residential theater company, transformed into a peripatetic, transregional cultural form. We take stock of the market pressures for the continual hybridization and development of stambul in its first years of existence. We understand how a form of theater engaged popular ideations and obsessions, responding to currents in the public sphere and sparking debates and controversies.

The book does not take a descriptive approach to a theatrical genre but is instead an historical reckoning of the generation of cultural form and value. The book begins with the emergence of the Komedie Stamboel in 1891 as a building-based theater company with Eurasian actors, Chinese owners, and cross-ethnic audiences against the backdrop of Surabaya's heterogeneous entertainment scene. The first year's organizational trials and tribulations, competition with the circus and other komedi, and attunement to the tastes of its urban audience forged a ramai traveling theater with popular appeal. The company was "road tested" when it toured Java in 1891 and 1892. Touring altered the Komedie Stamboel as a company; impacted local cultural scenes in Solo, Yogyakarta, Semarang, and Batavia; and activated cultural connections among cities and towns in the Indies. The Komedie Stamboel achieved a transregional reputation while at the same time engaging in local debates. In 1893 the Komedie Stamboel was at the apex of its popularity. The company was not only reacting to popular culture in this year, it was actively shaping it—defining a demotic language, form, style, and sentiment for mass communication. The legal designation of the Komedie Stamboel as a form of opera rather than *wayang,* and the ways it was defined in contrast to Malay *bangsawan* were instrumental in determining public opinion of this form of theater. Antitheatrical prejudice festered from 1894 through 1898. Public disenchantment with the Komedie Stamboel and its growing reputation as a home wrecker led to the disbanding of the Komedie Stamboel and Mahieu's years as a "jobbing" actor, and the rebranding of *komedie stamboel* as *komedie janboel,* a mess or muddle of a komedi. Much of this shift in sentiment hinges on two infamous crimes—the double shooting of actor-manager Wim Cramer and actress Lien Gemser in 1895 and the murder of racketeer Hubertus Loth during a stambul show in 1898. Mahieu succeeded temporarily in redefining stambul as an "Indische" theater by linking his company to the Indies League, an organization dedicated to the social welfare of Eurasians, in 1900. His luck was not to last. Mahieu and his company were "stranded" in Borneo, resulting in a merger of stambul and bangsawan theater in 1902. A year later Mahieu was dead of malaria. Mahieu's death marks the end of a theatrical era, but he leaves an important legacy in Indonesia and the Netherlands. The Komedie Stamboel has been construed over the century since Mahieu's death as an innovatory cultural form to be imitated, a travesty of European art, a marker of Eurasian cultural accomplishment, and a transethnic Indonesian theater.

The reasoning behind the book's detailed chronological approach is partially pragmatic. Komedi stambul in its earliest years was an itinerant theater that did not have a fixed form. There are few detailed performance descriptions and no photographs nor recordings available; we lack the sources that would allow one to present a precise generic description representative of a particular phase of the theater's evolution. I am also motivated to write processually on phenomenological grounds. Scholars of non-Western theater often take a taxidermic approach to the field, writing descriptive genre studies of theatrical forms as if they were stuffed and mounted specimens. Theater, however, is meaningful only when it is in motion. Any precise description of stambul in this period must be time based and attuned to historical processes.

This study is in many respects a preliminary inquiry into the field of fin de siècle Indonesian popular culture. Much has been written about elite culture attached to the royal courts of central Java, and the Dutch were devoted chroniclers of their own colonial life in the tropics. The diverse preindustrial societies of nineteenth- and early twentieth-century Indonesia were studied by anthropologists and missionaries. The everyday life and culture of non-European urbanites in the nineteenth and early twentieth centuries has been underresearched in comparison. Pre-Indonesian popular Malay literature, long vilified in scholarly circles, has only recently attracted scholarly interest, and very little is still known about its authors, publishers, and readers.[51] The heterogeneous performers who traveled the komedi circuit, and the equally heterogeneous komedi public, are practically unknown, despite the centrality of komedi culture in urban life.

The nineteenth century has long been viewed by historians of Indonesia in terms of how the various islands and regions of Indonesia were consolidated into Holland's colonial empire. This book aims to present a new image of this period through investigating the elements of a subaltern cultural movement. Examining the realm of unofficial culture shows that people in the Indies were busy constructing interregional networks outside direct state control. The komedi enterprise was parasitic of the colonial state, in that it used its modes of transport (railway and steamship). The effects of komedi were to open up new forms of perception and ways of relating that were often antithetical to the *rust-en-orde* (peace-and-order) colonial project of creating good subjects and maximizing production. The historical period described in this book is at the cusp of the great period of "national awakening," the various forms of nationalism that ultimately gave birth to the nation-state of Indonesia. The Komedie Stamboel was a cultural articulation of an aborted form of nationalism, an "*Indische* nationalism" that cut across boundaries of race and creed (see chapter 5). Indische nationalism has been largely overlooked by historians, as it is considered an aberration in the grand narrative of the nation.[52] This is unfortunate, as Indonesians looking for alternatives to divisive politics of ethnicity and religion potentially have much to learn from Indische nationalism, and the forms of culture associated with it. There are valuable lessons to learn from the accomplishments and failings of the generation of stambul as a multiethnic cultural form and its appropriation by intellectuals and activists attached to the Indies League.

The popularity of komedi stambul in "the Mahieu period" in society at large and its thorough coverage in the press allows for the theater to be approached from multiple vantage points.[53] Much of this book is composed of direct translations and paraphrases from period sources.[54] Some of this writing is by professional journalists, but there are many other voices and perspectives to be discerned as well. Reports by correspondents and letters to editors are written from the perspective of ordinary people engaged in ordinary pursuits, including theatergoing and theater making. The newspapers are replete with accounts about fights between actors and spectators, men and women running off with performers, street singers performing stambul songs, amateur stambul club activities, company disputes with tax collectors and local authorities, anticipation of the arrival of an itinerant troupe, accidents and crimes at or adjacent to theaters, public drunkenness and other lewd or impolite behavior at theaters, the pleasures of theatergoing, and organizational problems of theater making. Theater was part and parcel of the texture of life that people lived and dreamed. "Babah H.," according to an 1893 news item about a certain Chinese man from Semarang, "is so enamored of singing stambul songs that from his enthusiasm it often happens that he sings in his sleep; his wife was shocked and thought he was only pretending [to sleep] but his eyes were firmly shut."[55] Many of the reported items fall firmly in the category of *faits-divers,* "exceptional events that happened to ordinary people."[56] Vanessa Schwartz, in her fascinating study of Parisian popular culture, has argued that such faits-divers (like the practice of people watching in Paris's numerous boulevard cafés or public visits to the morgue, wax museums, panoramas, and early cinema) served to frame everyday life as spectacle. There were strong reciprocal relations among these and other sites of public culture. Newspapers provided stories for enactment in sites of public display and in turn interpreted for the masses the proper attitude of spectatorship in fin de siècle Paris. Newspapers in the Netherlands Indies had a more passive role in shaping public culture during the period I am concerned with, because of relatively limited distribution and readership. However, the understanding that the public theater constituted a viable and significant topic for press discourse filtered into the vernacular press by way of Dutch journalistic models. The newspaper sources quoted are not only reflections on the public culture, they are also part of it. The heterogeneous theater scene potentiated a diversity of viewpoints and subject positions related to class, ethnicity, gender, and cultural orientation.

> I liked *Kamaral Zaman* as a play, as it was quite astonishing and funny, with many kings and attractive princesses, and the beautiful leading actress was prominently featured, and elite, beautiful spectators attended, dressed in trashy, flashy, unseemly clothes, wearing what I estimate as two inches of makeup on their faces. Ah! Indeed, these days someone with a knowledge of facial powder, even

> if dark-skinned, can appear as white as marble at night, to the benefit of the cosmetic factories of Europe, which reap the profits from the sale of their wares.[57]

Itinerant performance culture of the nineteenth and early twentieth centuries anticipated the ways that today's global mass culture shapes our understanding of who we are and the world we inhabit. Railroad circuses provided American audiences with "a global sensory blitz—immediate, live images that mirrored the nation's position in the modern world."[58] Medicine shows offered miracle cures and transformed beliefs about possibilities for overcoming bodily afflictions through performance and chicanery. Stage magicians engaged audiences in debates about the limits of the laws of physics and the existence of the supernatural by merging the most sophisticated technology with the most revered ancient wisdom. "Exotic" dancers such as Sadayakko and Mata Hari redefined norms of propriety for women in dress, appearance, and role. Minstrel shows articulated a lore cycle for conceptualizing racial inequality, manifested possibilities for self-transformation and developed class consciousness. Displays of "freaks" and ethnological side shows both expanded senses of human diversity and inured patrons to degradation, brutality, and the exploitation of Others.

The early history of stambul coincided with a great moment of possibility for Indonesian society. Urbanization and advances in transport and communications technology ruptured settled lifeways and opened up new horizons of movement and transformation. Minke, the journalist-narrator of Pramoedya Ananta Toer's bildungsroman *This Earth of Mankind,* emblematizes the wonder of the age and the abrupt transition away from an agrarian feudal society to a market-oriented, urban-centered, modern society. He speaks as a youth growing up in Surabaya in the 1890s:

> One of the products of science at which I never stopped marveling was printing, especially zincography. Imagine, people can reproduce tens of thousands of copies of any photograph in just one day: pictures of landscapes, important people, new machines, American

> skyscrapers. . . . Trains—carriages without horses, without cattle, without buffalo—had been witnessed now for over ten years by my countrymen. And astonishment remains in their hearts even today. The distance from Betawi [Batavia] to Surabaya can be traveled in only three days! . . . Power was no longer the monopoly of the elephant and the rhinoceros. They had been replaced by small man-made things: nuts, screws, and bolts. . . . The forces of nature were beginning to be changed by man and put to his service. Machines will replace all and every kind of work. . . . Modern! How quickly the word had surged forward and multiplied itself.[59]

The Komedie Stamboel was the first Malay-language theater to embrace this sense of the modern. The world of this popular theater was a "stage of modernity" promising an emotionally involving "complete, unmediated, self-present, immediate reality."[60] Stambul's theatrical machinery and stage images multiplied the astonishing world of "the wonderful century" for the contemplation and delight of a multiethnic public.

Chapter 1

SURABAYA'S RESIDENT THEATER, 1891

> Surabaya compares unfavorably with other Dutch East Indian towns, on account of the greater part of the dwelling-houses not being detached, in the midst of beautifully shaded grounds, but built close together, and bordering on the streets. Besides this, the offices, warehouses, stores, shops, and dwelling-houses, European, Arabian, and native, are a great deal too much mingled together; and a separation between the lower or mercantile part and upper or European part of the town, is more difficult to define than in Batavia or Semarang.
>
> Now this may give to Surabaya a livelier and more European character, but it makes it at the same time dirtier, more oppressive, and less desirable to live in. Next to the finest private houses, we find little native tumble-down shops, or Chinese hovels, that are called "*Warongs.*" As there was no room for shady trees in many of the streets, the hot midday sun is left to have full play over the dusty roads and dirty white houses. Once past the Concordia Club, the outward appearance of the town gets a little better. Here we come upon a cross-way, that to the left leads to the station, and to the right past the "Hoogere Burgerschool" (the high school) to the Alun-Alun [central square], on which there is a beautiful mosque. Before us, the road has the appearance of an avenue of cemara-trees, on the right side of which there is a small park, called the STADSTUIN (City Gardens), where military concerts are given twice a week, and at the end, a small square where a beautiful building is situated. This is the GRIMM RESTAURANT, the only real café in the whole of the Dutch-Indies.
>
> —*J. F. van Bemmelen and G. B. Hooyer,*
> Guide to the Dutch East Indies

Such is a description of the eastern Javanese city of Surabaya, the Netherlands Indies' major port city and principal mercantile center, in the only

English-language guidebook available on the Dutch colony before the twentieth century. This same guidebook advises tourists to avoid staying in this overly mingled together city any longer than necessary, despite the attraction of French pastries, fresh coffee, and iced drinks at a "real café."

Surabaya was the largest city in the Netherlands Indies through the early twentieth century; in 1895 it had a total population of approximately 124,000. Most Surabayans were Muslims (including both Javanese and Madurese and other Southeast Asians), but in the public sphere Muslims rubbed shoulders with substantial populations of "Foreign Asians" (including Chinese, Arabs, and Indians), and about seven thousand "Europeans" (mostly Eurasians, in fact).[1] Surabaya was not the seat of government nor was it perceived as a cosmopolitan metropole, as Batavia was. As historian William Frederick describes, "Surabaya still possessed in those days a distinctly frontier flavor, and while European visitors were impressed with its mercantile prominence and even luxury, its obviously unplanned growth and unsophisticated *Indische* culture were often considered odd or laughable."[2] Surabaya was not known as a cultural center, but as a "city of work."[3] Two rail lines had their termini in the city. One line led to the principalities of Yogyakarta and Surakarta and the southern port of Cilacap. The other went east along the coast to the towns of Pasuruan and Probolinggo. Ships and steamers departed daily for destinations such as Semarang, the Lesser Sunda Islands, Borneo, Makassar, Timor, and points further afield. The city was famous for its dockyards, artillery workshops, factories, and inconstant, roughhousing sailors of the sort immortalized in the Brecht-Weill song "Surabaya Johnny."

Surabaya was a city, as Frederick says, "of relative calm and prosperity. Indigenous peoples accounted for about 90 percent of the city's population and were attracted by the availability of employment and higher wages than could be obtained in most rural areas."[4] Muslims lived in densely populated kampung, or urban shantytowns, in houses with thatched roofs and plaited bamboo walls, and worked as hawkers, petty tradesmen, shop employees, factory workers, washerwomen, and in a variety of crafts and home industries. Where there was space, kampung dwellers planted fruit trees and tended small gardens. Many kampung

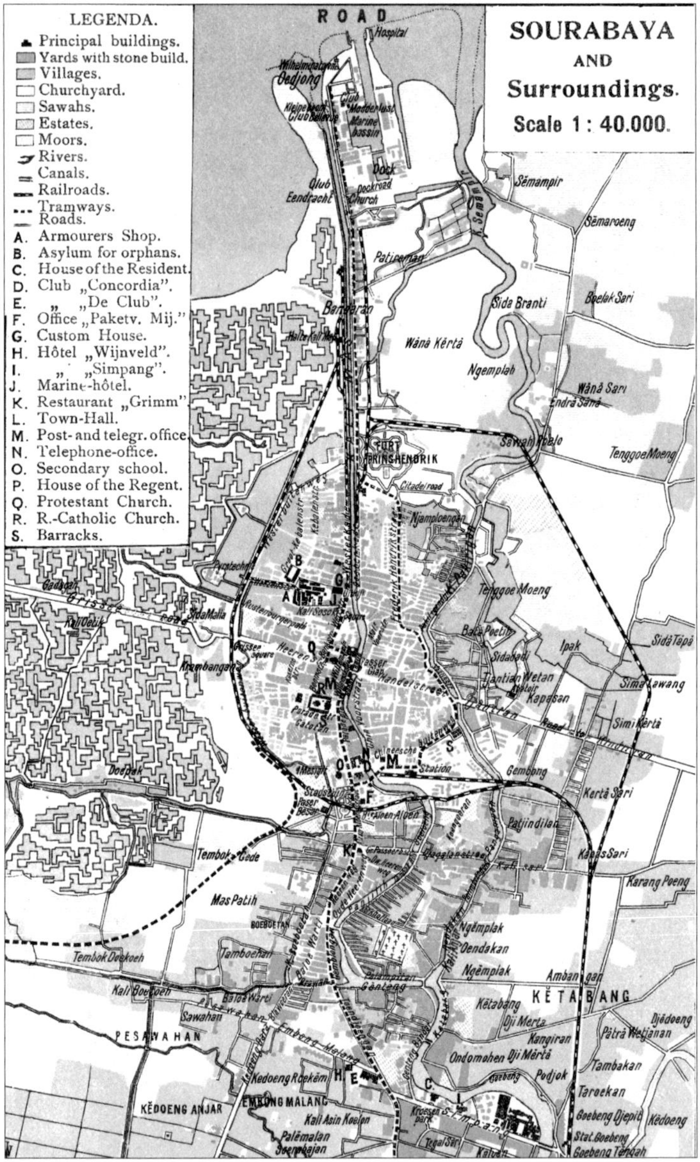

Map 1. Surabaya. Reprinted from J. F. van Bemmelen and G. B. Hooyer, *Guide through Netherlands India, Compiled by Order of the Koninklijke Paketvaart Maatschappij* (London: Thos. Cook and Son, 1903), facing p. 78.

dwellers were recent migrants to the city, and the degree of intimacy among neighbors was not as high as in rural villages.[5] Some of Surabaya's kampung recognized and revered ancestral founding spirits, however, and celebrated local identity in annual rites of thanksgiving such as *sedekah bumi* (offering to the earth) with communal meals, social dancing, and artistic performances.[6]

The Chinese in Surabaya were legally required to live in designated Chinese quarters of the city. Throughout colonial Indonesia, Chinatowns assumed a certain insularity and self-sufficiency. Chinese-run stores, eating establishments, opium dens, and pawnshops were concentrated in Chinatowns, as were Chinese-owned theaters and other places of entertainment. This pattern continued well into the twentieth century. Social anthropologist Leslie H. Palmier wrote apropos of a small Javanese town in the 1950s that "a Chinese never needed to move outside his own community, [and] could, in fact, restrict his life to the confines of the *kampong* and the shops. . . . But a Javanese had, at some time or other, to come into contact with the Chinese and enter their territory. It might be as a worker in a *batik* factory, it might be on a visit to the cinema, he might have to use the pawnshop, and he would have to use the shops at some time or another. And this residential pattern reflected the social: the Chinese rarely had to beg anything of the Javanese, high or low, the Javanese often had to do so of the Chinese."[7] The insularity of Chinatowns was particularly prominent during the late nineteenth century. Chinese in Surabaya were governed by a Dutch-appointed major and his council of officers (*kongko*). These officials had a police force at their disposal and even a lockup to detain prisoners.

As in Chinatowns in other parts of the Indies, Chinese domiciles and places of business in Surabaya lined the main streets in closed rows.[8] Many of these were shop-houses, in which the front part of the house facing the street was used as a store, typically selling "foodstuffs, household notions, wares, and necessities, and some textiles," while the back part and upper story was used as a living area.[9] Some of the Muslim employees of such stores were both domestic servants and shop employees and typically slept on the floor of the shop at night. The wall-shutters of these shop-houses could be removed during trading hours, and baskets

Fig. 1.1. The Songoyudan district of Surabaya's Chinatown. Reprinted from von Faber, *Oud Soerabaia,* 53.

and trays containing an immense variety of brightly colored goods spilled out onto the streets. Store signs were in Chinese characters as well as in the Latin script used for writing Dutch and Malay. The front and roofs of shop-houses and homes lining the main streets were richly decorated. "Nothing could be more delightful than the setting of the red-tiled roofs, with their dragon-decorated ridges and parapets, on the wooden trellis fronts and canvas blinds of the Chinese houses," writes one British traveler.[10] Elite members of the *kongsi* (Chinese business associations) that controlled the opium trade, pawnshops, and gambling houses lived opulently. At the backs of their houses were fantastic gardens, replete with miniature waterfalls, miniature mountains, arched bridges, a luscious array of plants, and song birds.

The other major portion of the "Foreign Asian" population was the Arab community. Some 2,482 Arabs are registered as living in Surabaya in 1892. Many of them lived in the vicinity of the Kapasan market and the neighborhood of Ampel. Most of these Arabs, as well as Bengalis and other nonindigenous Muslims, were closely integrated with the Southeast Asian Muslim populace and worked the real estate and cloth trades.[11]

Europeans were drawn to Surabaya by its many industries and occupied all the important positions in marine and factories, artillery workshops, pyrotechnic workshops, and sugar factories. Surabaya was the seat of a resident and the headquarters of eastern Java's military authorities, which provided numerous civil service and military positions. The city's rail, post, telegraph, and telephone companies also employed European managers and engineers. The wealth generated by these industries allowed many Europeans to live luxuriously in spacious mansions. European elites were attended by scores of servants, ate canned foods from Europe, and wore the latest fashions from Paris. There were two main clubs (*sociëteit,* or *soos*) for Europeans, the Concordia (founded 1843), and the exclusive Simpang Club (1887). These clubs were sites for socializing, gossiping, drinking, and partying. The clubs had their own house bands and amateur theater and music societies. Visiting performance groups were hosted by the clubs as well.[12] Two Dutch-language newspapers, the *Soerabaiasch-Handelsblad* and the *Soerabaija-Courant,* were published in Surabaya in the early 1890s. Much of the news they contained concerned the social activities of the city's most prominent European citizens, but there was also attention to local events involving other ethnic groups.

Poor "Europeans" (mostly Eurasians) lived lives not readily distinguishable from most Muslims. Many lived in kampung at the edges of Muslim society and were deemed an embarrassment to the status of Europeans in the colony.[13] Around 1900 a governmental inquiry into the causes, conditions, and possible solutions of "pauperism" (poverty among whites) in the residency of Surabaya showed that a high percentage of poor European women were sex workers. Some women took in sewing work. Men had military and government jobs and worked as vendors, manual laborers, shopkeepers, and in a variety of trades. Thirty-five percent of poor white men were either unemployed or would not identify their source of employment. One suspects that many among the latter group were criminals.[14]

Surabaya was undergoing major changes in the last two decades of the nineteenth century. Urban populations were being moved, slums demolished, and avenues paved in the name of progress. A telephone office was opened in 1884, and by 1897 it was possible to telephone Batavia. A twenty-kilometer tramline from Ujung to Sepanjang was opened to the public in 1890.

> Surabaya . . . was discernibly altered to meet the needs and tastes of a small minority of Europeans. Dry docks, machine factories, jails, banks, newspaper offices and presses, import-export firms, elegant Victorian pastry shops and stylish clubhouses were built in rapid succession. Beyond the well-established eye of the city and beyond even the famous Simpang area, which fifty years before had been pleasantly rural, suburban thoroughfares were laid out and lined with large Western-style homes and luxuriant gardens. The old alun-alun . . . was turned over to commercial and government buildings and replaced with a new square lacking any traditional significance and designed by a Eurasian in what has been described as Greco-Gothic-Moorish style.[15]

This imposition of European architectural style on an Indonesian urbanscape was mirrored in many other cultural and social realms. Surabaya was distinguished, for example, by the fact that "European" holidays, such as the Saint Nicholas festival, were enjoyed in different ways by one and all as early as 1875.[16] The case was otherwise in other cities of the Indies. It was not until the first decade of the twentieth century, for example, that Muslims appear to have taken an active interest in the queen's birthday celebration in the city of Cirebon.[17] Surabaya was not a model plural society, in which ethnic groups interacted only in the market place.[18] It was a multicultural city, where ethnic groups took pride in their cultural accomplishments, mingled and interacted in public spaces, and could see and be seen in "open galleries" around town.

Surabaya was also a ramai theater city, a center for komedi, amusement, and leisure. There were skating rinks, merry-go-rounds, brass bands, and entertainments in public spaces that appealed to all language and ethnic groups.

Fig. 1.2. The café of Surabaya's schouwburg. Reprinted from von Faber, *Oud Soerabaia,* 336.

Surabaya's schouwburg at Komedieplein (Theater Square) was the third theater by this designation to exist in the city, completed in 1854 at a cost of 55,000 guilders and renovated in 1877 under the supervision of an actor from a touring French operetta company.[19] The schouwburg hosted touring English music hall companies, stage magicians from India and Italy, Italian opera, French troupes performing opéra comique and opéra-bouffe, and Australian burlesque outfits. The arrival of the major Italian and French opera companies, performing operatic workhorses such as *Rigoletto* and *Il trovatore,* was a cause for celebration among the city's European elites. Opera residencies were often supported by subscription, and culture lovers living in adjacent towns and outlying areas of Java's East Hook traveled to Surabaya to be present during an "opera season."

A typical visitor to the schouwburg of Indonesia and other Southeast Asian public theaters during the late nineteenth and early twentieth centuries was "the Pollards," also known as the Lilliputian Opera Company. The Pollards was a family theater started by Tom Pollard, a London piano tuner who migrated to Tasmania in 1854. Pollard was a musician and his wife a dancer, and they educated their seventeen children at home in the three Rs and in music. Pollard's piano tuning income was supplemented by engagements from an orchestra the family formed in 1877, which played local social functions. In 1880, the Pollards produced a juvenile *HMS Pinafore,* with a cast of sixty local children, ages four to fifteen, including his own. This production was a commercial success and was taken to New Zealand the following year. This was the beginning of a thirty-year life on the road. Tom Pollard and his family fielded both child and adult companies that traveled theater circuits to Europe, South Africa, Mauritius, India, Burma, Malaysia, Singapore, Indonesia, China, and elsewhere. The Pollards specialized in British musical comedies but also displayed a kinetoscope, a cinematic device invented by Thomas Edison, during an 1897 tour.[20]

Local amateur European groups, such as Ons Tooneel, Vereeniging Apollo, Vereeniging Constantia, Vereeniging Eendracht Zij Ons Doel, and the military theater of the Onderofficiers-Vereeniging te Soerabaia, frequently performed farces and costume dramas at the schouwburg and other Surabaya stages. Many of these amateur groups were all male, for local European women of standing were reluctant to appear onstage due to modesty. Ticket prices tended to be high, and attendance was limited to Europeans and the thin upper crust of affluent, Dutch-speaking Asians. It was common for these performances to conclude with a ball. The local thespians were mostly enthusiastic "dilettantes" of remedial theatrical ability, but they were sometimes buttressed by seasoned professionals. Play scripts in Dutch, French, and English were available for sale at Surabaya bookstores and could be purchased through the post from Batavia book dealers.

European music was played at many private and public events. Chamber ensembles—known as *strijkje* and typically composed of stringed instruments, harp, and flute—played at balls and other functions at European clubs and private homes. Surabaya's premiere ensemble of this sort in the 1890s was the Italian Quintet. Military brass bands gave *bataljon muziek* concerts of marches, polkas, and mazurkas. European music was not exclusively for or by Europeans. Europeans had long employed indigenous workers who could double as domestic servants

Fig. 1.3. A Surabaya strijkje. Reprinted from von Faber, *Oud Soerabaia,* 373.

and musicians for the entertainment of household and guests.[21] Even when these concerts took place in private, closed-off spaces like the private clubs, it was customary for crowds of nontonners to eavesdrop. An American traveler who visited Java in the 1890s observed that subsidizing opera and providing military bands were ways to "secure all the advantages of civilization and make life tolerable in the far-away tropics."[22]

Surabaya stores stocked a variety of musical instruments, including pianos especially constructed for the tropics. Professional musicians also ordered instruments from Europe. Music teachers regularly placed advertisements in the newspapers, and in the late 1890s Surabaya had an active violin study group, De Violin, with eight members. One of Surabaya's violin teachers, Charles Maij, also was an orchestral composer, and one of the first Europeans to write music for an ensemble combining Western and gamelan musical instruments.[23]

The phonograph was introduced to the Indies in 1892 and only became a common item in elite households in the twentieth century, but a variety of organs and music boxes was available for purchase by elites before this. Some organs were put to commercial use and could be heard on the streets.

There were also, of course, many entertainments specific to Surabaya's various Asian populations. The Muslim population sponsored cultural performances, which were as a rule free and open to a general public, though infrequently announced in newspapers. Performances of *wayang kulit* (shadow puppet theater), *tandakan* (social dance), and *wayang krucil* (theater with flat wooden puppets) were held in conjunction with circumcisions, weddings, and annual communal celebrations. These events seem to have been rowdy affairs, at least judging from newspaper accounts; drunken brawls sporadically broke out. Ensembles of singers and percussionists playing frame drums were often sponsored by more devout Muslims to intone Islamic praise songs in Arabic and Javanese. *Ludruk*, a form of folk drama, was performed in urban kampung as well as the countryside.[24] Itinerant *topeng* troupes from Java and Madura featuring masked actors and gamelan musicians, and performing tales from Javanese legend and history such as Damar Wulan and Panji, played in Chinese-owned public theaters as well as at the private residences of Muslim and Chinese elites. Topeng was in favor in Surabaya in the 1880s but declined in significance beginning in 1891, with the arrival of itinerant wayang wong troupes from central Java. Wayang wong, known as *wayang orang* in Malay, was originally a dance drama associated with Java's royal courts. It was adapted to the commercial stage in the 1880s and became enormously popular in central and western Java, until the assistant resident of Batavia clamped a ban on performances in 1890. That ban was later rescinded, and troupes toured freely throughout Java by the mid-1890s.[25]

Surabaya's Chinese community, in addition to patronizing Javanese entertainments such as wayang kulit and owning theaters where itinerant topeng troupes performed, fostered their own cultural traditions. During private and religious celebrations, houses were "trimmed with flags, lanterns, garlands, and tinsel flowers; orchestras tinkled and thumped, and great feasts were spread."[26] The annual celebrations of the Chinese New Year and Rebutan, or Pu Du, were enjoyed by all elements of Indies society as street festivals in the Chinese wards.[27] The

Cap Go Meh celebrations at Chinese New Year brought hoards of spectators to Chinatown to see the procession of lions and fire-spouting dragons. Muslims thronged to the annual Rebutan celebration, when participants did their best to climb greased poles and snatch prizes of watches and sarongs, and the poor vied (*rebut*) to grab offerings thrown to the crowd.[28] The dragon boat racing of the holiday of Pecun was a public spectacle of note. Chinese opera was performed in public theaters for ticket-purchasing audiences and sponsored in conjunction with temple and private celebrations. Some of the opera troupes that performed in late nineteenth-century Surabaya used a combination of Malay and Chinese language. This was also the case for the *po-te-hi,* or glove puppet theater.

There is less information available about the performance activities of the smaller ethnic minorities of the Indies. Bridal couples of Arab descent would typically be paraded through the streets, to the accompaniment of frame drumming, and sometimes fireworks.[29] In Batavia "the new year for the people of Bombay" was celebrated as a street festival, with food, social dancing, European music, and a parade, but Surabaya's South Asians did not appear to have comparable ardor for their religious holidays.[30]

Some more affluent Dutch-speaking Eurasians participated in amateur European performance activities, and Malay-speaking lower-class Eurasians attended public entertainments that appealed to all. There is no record of a theater or other art form particularly associated with Surabaya's Eurasians, however, before 1891.

One of the great impresarios of Surabaya's entertainment field was Yap Gwan Thay, who was given the honorary title of *pujonggo* (sage, scholar, man of letters, versed in the mystic sciences) by Surabaya's Malay-language press in 1899.[31] Yap maintained diverse business interests and was a public figure of note in Surabaya, wealthy though never spectacularly rich. He built, owned, and ran public theaters in Surabaya's Chinatown and produced traveling Malay and Chinese language Chinese opera troupes, Javanese topeng, magic and variety troupes, magic lantern shows, and a raft of Malay-language popular theater companies. His other business interests included a fireworks company known as Banyu Urip, a pharmaceutical firm that produced both Chinese herbal medicine and illicit European medicine, and a soft drink company (lemonade was a big seller). He was a store owner and restaurateur. Yap was known occasionally to prepare decorations and entertainments for festive occasions—including decorated gates (*gerbang*) and Chinese dragons—and was responsible for producing the painted backdrops for Surabaya's schouwburg. He achieved national media attention in 1907, when he announced a seven-day malaria cure. Another of his numerous talents (perhaps a hobby) was calendrical calculations; he was versed in European, Chinese, Javanese, and Islamic calendars and could compare them with some authority. He was prone to buying novel luxury goods on impulse and was jailed for debts owed to department stores in Semarang and Batavia in 1895. His business connections extended to Singapore, China, and Europe, and his business correspondence was in English, Dutch, Malay and Chinese. These business connections, and his skills in visual reproduction, implicated him in a counterfeit ring, for which he served further jail time in 1896. Yap comes across as a cantankerous and obstinate man, overflowing with ideas, but limited in managerial skills; he is described in one account as "clever indeed in finding a way to make profit, but without genuine wisdom."[32]

Origins are mysterious. Retrospectively, Yap Gwan Thay has been identified as one of the creators of the Komedie Stamboel—if not *the* creator—which was founded in Surabaya in January 1891.[33] The Komedie Stamboel was initially bankrolled by a *kongsi*. There are many indications that Yap Gwan Thay was a member of this group—indeed he might have been the sole member—but it is not until 1892 that he is explicitly identified as the Komedie Stamboel's "owner" (*eigenaar*) in advertisements. Another member of Yap Gwan Thay's kongsi in 1891 might have been Swie Ban Lian, a fellow producer of Malay-language Chinese opera.[34]

Origins are often unknowable. The Komedie Stamboel was often described in reviews, notices, and advertisements as a Malay version of European opera. There is no doubt that the Komedie Stamboel drew di-

Fig. 1.4. An advertisement for Yap Gwan Thay brand medicines. *Bintang-barat,* 12 October 1897.

rectly on the conventions of European musical theater. The proscenium stage, wing-and-drop set, focused stage lighting, emotive character-based acting, musical orchestra accompaniment, division of plays into scenes and acts, makeup and costumes, and many of the plots of plays all resembled the theatrical technology and dramaturgy of late nineteenth-century European theater.

Another influence, just as formative but less visible, was the Parsi theater.[35] The Parsi theater, sometimes called *wayang Parsi* in Indonesia and Malaysia, is seen by some as the beginning of commercial theater in the Malay world.[36] As one observer notes, popular theater in Indonesia

> started with Wayang Parsi, which delivered songs and dance from Persia, Arabia, and Hindustan, using harmonium, fiddle, and drum for its musical instruments. Its stories were *Ghul Bakwali, Syamerdan, Bujangga Bayu, Indra Putra, Langlang Buana.* Lots of kings, with their golden vestments, sitting on their thrones of gold, in their audience halls, attended by viziers, generals, admirals, heralds, and servants, with unsheathed swords in their hands, heads topped with sparkling crowns. Many princesses, queens, princes, concubines, and slaves singing and dancing in palaces, in royal gardens. Many sunset-red spirits, genies, and celestial nymphs, as well, in cloud kingdoms, descending to earth to involve themselves in the affairs of humans. . . . The field of battle where fierce combat is waged; the untamed jungle where kings exile themselves after defeat in battle, where young knights and princesses roam after

> being banished, the object of the wrath of their lord or beloved father. The cave where a sage or priest meditates, who gives his magical aid, resulting in the fateful union and happy marriage of *him* and *her.*[37]

Parsi theater companies from Bombay and other parts of India toured Indonesia starting in 1883, and possibly earlier.[38] These companies were complex hybrids, drawing on Urdu and Hindi literature, north Indian dance and music, and European stage technologies and management structures. The theater's legacy lives on today in the Bollywood film—which has inherited the Parsi theater's masala of melodrama, song and dance, and spectacle. The ownership of the early Parsi theater companies were in the hands of Parsis from Bombay who practiced the pre-Islamic Zoroastrian religion of ancient Persia and functioned as a comprador class for European business interests. Later "Parsi theater" troupes were multiethnic and multidenominational and originated from many parts of the Indian subcontinent.[39] Parsi theater was tremendously popular from its first appearance in Indonesia, and its tunes and plays were imitated in western Java as *lagu Parsi* and a Javanese language version of wayang Parsi, at least until a ban was placed on wayang Parsi performances.[40] The Parsi theater primed Indonesian audiences for a theater using Western stage technology to present non-Western stories in a non-Western language. The ban on wayang Parsi in western Java was a window of opportunity for Surabaya.

A century after the Komedie Stamboel's emergence, it is no longer possible to judge the precise degrees of influence on the origin of the Komedie Stamboel of Yap Gwan Thay and his kongsi, the Eurasian theater makers who formed the company, Parsi theater, or European theater. One can accurately report that the Komedie Stamboel's beginnings were heterogeneous, diverse, hybrid.

The Komedie Stamboel began with modest fanfare: a short letter to the *Soerabaiasch-Handelsblad,* one of the city's Dutch-language newspapers, which appeared on 16 January 1891.

> The theater company in Kampung Doro consists of sixteen people, including four women. At the head is Mr. J. S. Hartens, named director, known as H. S. (not to be confused with the cologne brand H. S.). As far as the four ladies are concerned, they have already lived here for some time, but did not seem [previously] to have a strong inclination for the theater.
>
> Thus perhaps [they are acting] for other reasons!
>
> From a Reader[41]

Innuendo and suspicion of motive of the troupe's actresses are marked in the report. Actresses were not motivated by love of the muses nor to be counted among the city's European artistic "dilettantes." Thus they must have less elevated goals motivating them, above all an unspoken need for money. The condescension displayed to the troupe's nominal leader (referred to as Martens in another newspaper source) in the linkage to a cologne brand is equally clear. Nothing is said of the name of the company, nor the repertoire, nor even a forthcoming performance date. The interest above all is in the actors—their presentation in the public sphere and their motivations.

Who were these twelve men and four women, and what inspired them to form a new theatrical company? Personal details are scarce and hard to come by about them or most of the other actors to follow in their footsteps. It is evident that they were all, without exception, Eurasians (also known as Indos), and were largely unemployed and in need of money. They were, in other words, paupers, in the terminology used at this time. Most of them came from Krambangan, a part of the city with a high Indo population. This was a slum (*achterbuurt* in Dutch), with an old cemetery, a military canteen, blind alleys and crisscrossing lanes. Krambangan young men had delinquent tendencies and a reputation for brawling, rowdiness, and drunken behavior. A core group of the men who made up the original Komedie Stamboel company were likely friends, or at least associates, before striking out on their shared theatrical venture.[42] A number of the actors worked for the city's civil guard and were known as roughnecks, trouble seekers, and pugilists.

Fig. 1.5. King Darsa Alam and three heavenly nymphs in a 1906 stambul performance of *Jula-Juli bintang tiga* in Gombong, Central Java. Photograph from the Koninklijk Instituut voor de Tropen.

Their violent disposition did not disappear after entering the theater; there are regular reports of fights among actors and between actors and spectators for much of the theater's history. Very likely most of the Indo actors possessed only rudimentary formal education and spoke Malay as their first language, with only minimal competence in Dutch or other European languages.[43] For these actors, and for others that followed them, theater was often less a mode of artistic expression than an escape from economic and social repression. As Andjar Asmara points out: "Stambul functioned as a haven or refuge for those who had been excluded from society or for those who preferred the easy life over fatiguing work, because performing stambul was too easy! A person who is a coachman today can tomorrow be a hero onstage."[44]

Kampung Doro, where they performed, was part of Surabaya's Chinatown, east of the city center. It appears that Kampung Doro was not as salubrious as Kampung Kapasan and Kampung Cantian, the other main neighborhoods in Chinatown. In February 1891 the main street of Kampung Doro was reportedly "in a state of extreme neglect," while "an intolerable stench prevails there," evidently emanating from a garbage dump.[45] In August of the same year, houses in Kampung Doro were condemned by the city as part of the ongoing urban renewal of Surabaya. One reporter writes of the theater as being "a bit isolated in its location, though easy to find," suggesting that it was in a part of Surabaya's Chinatown where Europeans rarely ventured.[46] It must have been especially difficult to reach during January, when potholes filled with rain, and mud and muck were everywhere.

The theater where the Komedie Stamboel first performed already existed before the company's formation. It seems to have been used by itinerant Chinese opera and Javanese topeng troupes. "The tent, or better put, the shed in Kampong Doro can seat a few hundred. The box and dress circle seats are well-appointed."[47] The shed was "well-ventilated and spacious,"[48] and lit entirely by gaslights, which provided adequate illumination. The theater was somewhat of a fire trap: only two days before the Komedie Stamboel opened, a leaking reservoir in one of the lights resulted in a fire that almost destroyed the entire structure. A buffet was set up adjacent to the theater. Initially alcohol was served, but by the Komedie Stamboel's third performance this was prohibited by order of the police, due to unruly behavior associated with drunkenness.

In the first two years of its existence, the Komedie Stamboel specialized in the production of plays based on tales from *The Thousand and One Nights,* the medieval Arabic tales generally known to the anglophone

Fig. 1.6. Another scene from the 1906 Gombong performance of *Jula-Juli*. Reprinted from Nieuwenhuys, *Komen en blijven,* 162.

world as *The Arabian Nights* or *The Arabian Nights Entertainment*. More than 90 percent of the performances that the company gave during 1891 and 1892 were based on *Nights* episodes. All productions in these initial years used costumes, painted backdrops and wings, as well as other scenographic elements that audiences associated with the Near East, constructed for playing *Nights* plays. It is not clear whether the choice to present *Nights* stories was made by the European actors or the Chinese management. Possibly the success that the touring Parsi theater companies had with plays of this ilk in the 1880s was a factor.

Few people today know much of the *Nights* beyond bowdlerized versions of the adventures of Aladdin, Ali Baba, and Sinbad. Today the *Nights* are viewed as children's entertainment of a low order. In the past, however, the *Nights* had a different set of associations. The *Nights* were "inexhaustibly opulent" to H. P. Lovecraft and generative of "a strange mixture of obscure dread and intense desire" for Coleridge, marvelous and moralistic, scatological and philosophical. Through the work of J. L. Borges, pantomime productions of the Aladdin tales, Walt Disney, and a host of novelists, poets, playwrights, and experimental theater makers, the *Nights'* fantastic fictions continue to live in the margins of European and American imaginations. The global spectacle of Baghdad today is perhaps more programmed by CNN and the Pentagon than the storytellers, inscribers, and translators of the *Nights*. However, there is decidedly *Nights*-like imagery at work behind the excesses of treasure troves of a national museum that can magically appear and reappear and infinite networks of hidden tunnels that provide escape routes for genielike villains that after long searching emerge—pop!—out of a spider hole.

Much Arabic and Persian literature was translated into the languages of the Malay Peninsula and the Indonesian archipelago following the rise of Melaka as a trading emporium and the emergence of the early Islamic city-states on Java's northern littoral in the fifteenth century. This translated corpus was largely composed of religious and philosophical texts, but there were also romances such as the tales of Amir Hamzah, Muhammad's uncle, a story cycle believed to have been known in Indonesia as early as the fifteenth century.[49] The *Nights,* though, were unknown until they were transmitted to Southeast Asia through Europe. Selections of the *Nights* were translated into Malay and Javanese poetry and prose; published as books in Batavia, Semarang, and Singapore; and serialized in vernacular newspapers, starting in the 1870s or possibly earlier. The Javanese translations, in particular, were motivated by a perceived need by Dutch experts for suitable Javanese reading matter for use in schools and as belletristic exemplars for aspiring Javanese authors.[50] The original source might have been Arabic, but the Malay and Javanese translations that appeared during the colonial period were mediated through European languages—usually Dutch or French. A cognate pattern is apparent elsewhere in Asia, including Thailand, where English-language translations of the *Nights* provided a regular source for royal drama starting in the 1870s.[51]

The association of the *Nights* with European culture was reinforced not only by the source literary texts, but also by the prevalence of *Arabian Nights* plays in the repertoire of Dutch amateur theatrical groups and visiting European companies. More often than not, the *Nights* were played as farce and parody and exploited as an opportunity to dress up

Fig. 1.7. A musical interlude from a stambul performance by Eendracht Maakt Macht (see chapter 6), circa 1910. Standing is the group's director, Marie Oord. Seated, from left to right, are: Snellaers, Theo MacLennon, and Nellie Houtzangers. Photograph from the Rob Nieuwenhuys Collection, Koninklijk Instituut voor de Tropen.

in "Oriental" attire. A typical example was the musical extravaganza presented by Harry Stanley's English Comic and Burlesque Opera Company during their long run in Surabaya's schouwburg in 1891, Blue Beard, or Harlequin Ali Barber and Sinbad, the Wig Ked Coarse-Hair.[52]

The *Nights* tales were not completely dissociated from Indonesian culture, of course. The long presence of Islam in the archipelago meant that much of Indonesia shared a common body of supernatural lore with the fictional world of the *Nights.* Spirits such as genies and afreets were known—and usually feared. The divinatory arts, invulnerability magic, astrological projections, and snake charming that inform the *Nights* had all been practiced in Indonesia for centuries, while the cosmology and notions of fate, causality, and coincidence that underpin the fabulous Arabian tales are all consistent with beliefs found up to the present in the archipelago. It is also possible that the technological and social changes of the late nineteenth century and the new global horizons of possibility available for Indonesian urbanites allowed them to identify with the spirit of adventure and possibility of the translocal, Islamic mercantile community depicted in the urban-centered *Nights.*

The prevalence of the *Nights* on the Komedie Stamboel stage, and the large number of serializations of the tales in newspapers and books that appeared in the 1880s and 1890s, are indicative of the stories' genuine popularity in late nineteenth-century Indonesia. A contemporary review of the thirteenth volume in an illustrated edition of the *Nights* that began publication in 1891 describes these tales as both addictive and accessible.[53] Armijn Pane, perhaps the most incisive Indonesian cultural critic of the mid-twentieth century, opines, "The stories were fitted to the tastes of the majority of the different ethnic groups and classes, in order to obtain a large profit. That is why fantastic tales from *The Thousand and One Nights* were intentionally selected" by the Komedie Stamboel.[54] The taste for the *Nights,* while common to the majority, was not insipid. The *Nights* are replete with outré violence and sex, including passionate affairs between "blackamoor" slaves and seductive princesses. That explicit content of the *Nights* was offensive to a chaste minority, but added considerably to the Komedie Stamboel's popular appeal in colonial Indonesia.

The Komedie Stamboel opened on Saturday, 17 January 1891, with *The Fisherman and the Genie.*[55] The play was based on one of the better-known episodes of the *Nights.* The protagonist is a poor old fisherman who recovers an ancient jar from the sea. In it there is a genie long ago imprisoned by King Solomon. The genie's fearsome magical powers allow the old fisherman to become a king. It is tempting to read the chosen episode allegorically, in relation to the troupe's Indo actors, who hoped to achieve financial success through the magical powers of theater and the age-old *Arabian Nights* tales.

The opening played to a majority Chinese audience and overall "met with great approval."[56] Reports vary on audience numbers: one newspaper states that it was standing room only, while another states that the auditorium was at less than two-thirds capacity. It was reviewed by

Fig. 1.8. Illustration from *The Fisherman and the Genie.* Reprinted from Gijsbert Francis, trans., *Hikajat 1001 malam* (Batavia: Albrecht and Rusche, 1891), 1:82.

Surabaya's newspapers, garnering appreciative if brief notices in the Dutch papers *Soerabaiasch-Handelsblad* and *Soerabaija-Courant* and a more critical and lengthy review in the Malay-language daily *Pembrita-Bahroe.*

Particular praise was directed at the "dazzling" costumes and the set and scenic effects, "such as waves in the sea, mountains, a forest, a large tree, coral reef and so on, which were all made well."[57] Technical problems, arguably inevitable at any premiere, were duly noted. *Pembrita-Bahroe* critiqued the unduly long time the audience was kept waiting for set and costume changes, suggesting that this was due to not having sufficiently mastered the conventions of European theater. A reporter for the *Soerabaiasch-Handelsblad,* looking back nostalgically to this opening performance ten months on, wrote "alas, the curtain did not go up, but was pushed aside by a few houris."[58]

The acting was less polished, and though "the actors and actresses did their best," the play was evidently underrehearsed.[59] Some of the actors showed signs of being unaccustomed to performing onstage. The actor playing the lead of Mahmud, the fisherman, does merit mention for his "professional and capable" performance, however.[60]

Music at this first performance was provided by "a sort of orchestra, consisting of a few guitars, a violin, and a tambourine."[61] These instruments accompanied the actors as they danced and sung end-rhymed quatrains (*pantun*). The reviewer for the Malay daily *Pembrita-Bahroe,* less gracious and more direct in his criticism than the reviewers for the Dutch-language papers, reported that "the singing was sweet indeed and the music fitted the story, but there was not enough variety in the melodies. Only one song was heard again and again throughout the night, though there are in fact a large range of Malay songs available."[62] The nostalgic *Soerabaiasch-Handelsblad* reporter described the music as "sweet but dreadfully monotonous," though without a doubt *eigenaardig* (strange, out of the ordinary, singular). The reporter notes in this same article overhearing a spectator's quip that the singing sounded "like cats in heat!"[63]

What is striking across these reports is the perceived novelty of the enterprise. There had been no prior attempts to translate the conventions of European theater into Malay, and no attempts to describe, report on, or critique such performance. There is evident discomfiture in the attempts of the press to deal with this emergent performance genre that parallels the awkwardness of the initiate performers.

The reviewer for *Pembrita-Bahroe* understood Komedie Stamboel as a thoroughly hybrid form—a theater that was musically and linguistically Malay but dramatically European. He suggested that the company might seek musical advice from established experts in music from Surabaya's Malay community and also pay closer heed to the dramatic conventions of European theater. Writing in Malay limited the reviewer's ability to describe the steps necessary to emulate European theater, though. He could come up with no Malay word for rehearse and instead relied on the compound *gladi (repetisi),* using first a Javanese word for rehearsal (a word more frequently used for military drilling and training in the premodern period) and then parenthetically a variant of the Dutch word for rehearsal, *repetitie.* The concept of rehearsal might be a basic theatrical process in European theater, but it was evidently not part of the critical or aesthetic vocabulary of Malay culture.[64]

Just the name of the company evokes surprise for *Soerabaija-Courant*'s reporter. "Komedie Stamboel!" is the title of his seventy-word article.[65] The idea that one might link *komedie,* up to that time a largely European cultural formation, to *stamboel,* the Dutch and Malay designation for Istanbul, capital of the Ottoman Empire and indexical of all things Near Eastern in the popular imagination, is astonishing.[66] The exclamatory title marks newness and hints at horizons of possibility.

The company itself demonstrated awareness of the interpretive problems confronting the audience from its very first performance. Before the beginning of this first show, "we saw a man with a black beard who recounted—or, better put—rattled out the story, relating the contents for us for the simple reason that we would [otherwise] not understand it."[67] At the next and at following performances, there were programs of sorts that were sold or distributed free of charge to spectators sitting in the more expensive seats. There was also the practice of beginning plays with a song in which all the actors came downstage and individually introduced their characters in a direct audience address through song and dance. This practice, known to later generations of performers as *ladon-diladon,* is shared with Parsi theater and likely is directly borrowed from Parsi theater.[68] Unlike traditional Indonesian expressive forms, which rely actively on shared knowledge of a reservoir of stories and artistic techniques, audiences at Komedie Stamboel required diegetical prompting to understand what was happening onstage.

THE COMPANY's second performance, on the following Wednesday night, 21 January 1891, was, "by popular demand," a reprise of *The Fisherman and the Genie.*[69] (This was a play that was to stay in repertoire for many years.) The reprise was accompanied not by the pickup band of the first performance, but, as advance publicity emphasized, by the renowned Italian Quintet. This woodwind and string ensemble, under the direction of harpist Signor Prati, was considered one of the city's cultural jewels.[70] Its presence in the Komedie Stamboel was a major draw. Reviews of the Komedie Stamboel regularly noted that the quintet "was a delight to hear" and "provided not a little of the evening's pleasure."[71] "The Italians," as they were called, brought with them their highly developed repertoire of marches, romances, waltzes, polkas, and operatic favorites, appropriately adjusted to the dramatic needs of the theater. The quintet was ubiquitous in Surabaya's cultural scene, despite their sizeable fee of eighty-five guilders a night. It regularly accompanied theatricals as well as played Dutch balls and Chinese parties, not only in Surabaya but in many of the small towns of Java's East Hook such as Nganjuk and Tulungagung. By April 1891 the Komedie Stamboel's management had contracted the Italian Quintet to play at all performances, as long as the quintet was not engaged out of town, at the flat rate of fifty guilders per show. The Italians played with the company regularly through November, when the Komedie Stamboel finally established its own orchestra in anticipation of a tour. The quintet also accepted other engagements in Surabaya during the year. They played *bals champêtres* following amateur dramatics by the Vereeniging Constantia on at least five occasions, provided musical accompaniment for a gymnastic display by Vereeniging Hercules at the schouwburg (and played the ball that followed), performed at a Chinese party in Tulungagung, and accompanied the magician J. Calabressini's show in the schouwburg. The Italian Quintet also regularly advertised the availability of its services in the *Soerabaija-Courant* during this year and for most of the rest of the decade.

Despite this musical draw, the house was smaller than at the first performance, due at least in part to a heavy shower in the early evening that tapered off around nine o'clock. (Future performances were often cancelled due to inclement weather.) Reviews of this repeat performance were politely vague. The *Soerabaiasch-Handelsblad* found the play to be "better launched now, although a little more *entrain* [liveliness] in the performance would not hurt" and while the *Soerabaija-Courant* was sympathetic to the fact that "some actors are on the stage boards for their first time so that they are yet not accustomed" to making theater, the paper does point out that "things are not yet proceeding smoothly and most [of the actors] are not fluent in their delivery."[72]

Both Dutch newspapers threw their support behind the theatrical enterprise, however, encouraging audience attendance. The primary reason for this, it appears, is not that the Komedie Stamboel substantially enriched Surabaya's cultural life. Rather, the papers understood the theater as an exemplary self-help mechanism for Eurasian "paupers." Within one week of the company's founding, in fact, a controversy raged about the venture's ethical merits. The debate engaged with dominant cultural stereotypes of the Indo as shiftless, pugnacious, vulgar, and scheming. One side claimed that the company provided work for its Indo actors, "who are in need of a better life," while the other manifested the typical Dutch Calvinist suspicion of the theater as a site of immoral behavior.[73]

> Speaking of the Komedie Stamboel, one hears entirely different opinions about the Indos than normal.
>
> One finds the members courageous, as they, after repeatedly striving in vain to succeed in trade and other enterprises, formed this company and thus no longer live off their families or charity, but are able to earn their own wages. This was the only way open to them to earn a small wage, and though the occupation of acting was foreign to them, they did not hesitate a moment to seize this opportunity. If only for this reason, the company has a valid reason for existing. It is a very sour bread that these people eat, because each provisionally enjoys a monthly salary of fifty guilders, which is doled out twice weekly. But they can at least have a means of subsistence.[74]
>
> Opinions about the Komedie Stamboel or, more accurately, about its Indo actors and actresses run asunder. There is no shortage of disapproval and side reflections that the group promotes immorality and so forth. Fortunately, there are also other thoughts about the matter. The company shows that it is willing to labor under an unbearable weight of oppression and prejudice. They do not seek profit but depend on advance money from a Chinese with

sufficient means. . . . The enterprise deserves as much [public] support as possible.[75]

This ethical issue was not resolved, but became a focal point for much discussion about the Komedie Stamboel in years to come, linked to ongoing debates about "the pauper problem."

THE KOMEDIE Stamboel staged another of the *Nights,* the tale of *Giafar* (or Jafar, to use the spelling of Disney's Aladdin franchise), for its next two performances, on 24 and 27 January. Performances of this lesser known episode drew praise, as "it was more fluent and the acting was more free" than in the prior performances.[76] "Much work was done on the decor and costumes. The ensemble makes a pleasing impression on the audience. . . . This young company is thus much in public favor."[77] The first show was disrupted by a bellicose spectator who "gave offense to the public with his clamorousness" and attempted to force his way backstage "in order to get a glimpse from behind the side wings."[78] He was roughly treated by the actors and forcefully escorted back to his seat, where he was reprimanded by his fellow spectators. The show that followed was also marred by belligerence: a fight among the actors broke out before the start of the performance. The announcement for the next *Nights* episode the company intended to produce, *Muhassan,* guaranteed that there would not be a repeat of such infighting. But this production was never to be realized, due to the eruption of a crisis between the actors and the company's management.

This episode signals a fundamental discrepancy between Indo company members and Chinese financers in their expectations of the rights entailed by the outlay of money. Indeed, there is evidence of a deep divide in the two parties' understandings of the concept of ownership *tout à fait.* Initial reports on the company's finances had it that the company was founded with a loan or advance money provided by one or more anonymous Chinese backers. This money was then used to refurbish the theater, purchase costumes, build sets, and the like. The *Soerabaija-Courant* went so far as to praise these wealthy Chinese backers for their generosity and faith in the fledgling company. "A few distinguished and influential fellow townspeople have given their financial support to the founding of the company, when they were adequately convinced that this merited a piece of bread, on honest wisdom," opined the newspaper.[79] This version of the company's finances appears to have been the one espoused by the company members. An 1894 report states that the Indo founders "were unable to acquire financial capital from Europeans and thus obtained a loan of money for (reportedly) five thousand guilders from a Chinese man."[80] Versions of this story were later reproduced in the widely cited accounts of Otto Knaap and A. Th. Manusama: both sources describe loans taken out by the Indo actors.[81] It is apparent that the actors of the first company expected that the Chinese investors had a strictly financial interest in the company, with no extrafiscal prerogatives.

Conditioned by patronage patterns of Chinese opera, Chinese expectations of theatrical investment differ considerably from European norms. Chinese opera troupes, even those that performed in public theaters for paying spectators, were considered to be trappings of status for the companies' owners. In premodern China, "Actors were luxury goods traded among the elite . . . . Not only individual actors but entire troupes were sold, bestowed upon friends, and bequeathed upon relatives. Their circulation served to create and maintain networks of social exchange, in much the same manner as did gifts of fine ceramic ware, calligraphic scrolls, and ancient bronzes."[82] Actresses working in Chinese opera troupes in Java were for the most part mistresses or sex workers at the disposal of the troupes' owners for their own pleasure, the pleasure of their friends, or for profit.[83] An extreme example of this is the all-female opera troupe owned by Tan Ing Gwan, major of Batavia's Chinese population in the 1850s. This was one of four all-female troupes active in the city at this time.

> But the best of them was that owned by the major, because many of the actresses were physically attractive and polished performers. There was one actress who was most attractive, named Bweehoa. She delivered her actions with great skill, and it could be said that she was the flower of the stage. Despite that, few people would come

> to see the troupe, as wherever it performed, the major often came along to see it. If a young man was bold enough to get too close to the stage during the performance or flirt with the actresses, it would cause a commotion and he would be beaten by the major's followers, who always carried whips. Nearly all the actresses were used by the major as his mistresses, and that accounts for why they were closely guarded by the makeup artists and female help.[84]

There were undoubtedly individual examples of Chinese opera performers whose accomplishments onstage and off brought them fame and social status in Indonesia, but generally speaking, performers were "viewed as lowly and contemptible and there is no Chinese of good background who mixes with them."[85] One Chinese opera troupe that performed in Surabaya in 1891 was lambasted in the pages of the Chinese-edited Malay daily *Bintang Soerabaia* for being dirty and disturbing the peace in the neighborhood where they were staying.[86] Actresses suffered from venereal disease and abuse, and while their employers were obligated to provide medical treatment, opera performers were, not surprisingly, prone to running away.[87]

Contrary to the impression given in early press reports and the later accounts by Knaap and Manusama, the involvement of the so-far anonymous Chinese backers in the company involved much more than providing start-up capital. The Chinese management was responsible for paying the fifty guilder monthly salaries of performers. The kongsi owned the land and building where the company performed and held the requisite performance permit. Judging from the high Chinese turnout at the first four shows, the Chinese management also was responsible for publicity and other administrative aspects of the company. All the newspapers, Dutch and Malay alike, repeatedly protested the high ticket prices for box and dress circle seats. These tickets were priced at two and a half guilders, approximately the same sum paid at the schouwburg to see Gilbert and Sullivan or Offenbach performed by foreign troupes. There was no concession made to these demands. Evidently, the Chinese management initially understood the fledgling enterprise to be less a business and more an opportunity for the display of wealth and self-enjoyment. The theater's still anonymous principal owner-manager is caricatured by the *Soerabaiasch-Handelsblad* as "the Croesus of Tangul Angin," while the *Soerabaija-Courant* notes that "the enterprise under discussion is irregular in its finances, with quarrels and the like, and without a sense of economy."[88] Such dilettantism encouraged proprietary feelings in the kongsi of a sort if not of a degree as that enjoyed by Chinese opera company owners. The same "Tangul Angin clique" who backed the Komedie Stamboel also planned at one point to construct a private club for their own exclusive use.[89] One might regard the Komedie Stamboel, at least in the first months of its operation, as a sort of social club for its Chinese patrons.[90]

The divide in understandings of proprietary rights erupted in crisis at a rehearsal for *Muhassan* on 29 or 30 January. The Chinese backers, as reported in the Dutch press and translated in the Malay press, "thought themselves free to take liberties with the women of the company, those rogues, because of all the advanced money. At a certain day at rehearsal, a pigtailed dandy beast showed up though he had no business being there and carried on in an inappropriate manner. He received a package that he won't forget in a hurry."[91] This inappropriate behavior was almost certainly molestation or even attempted rape of one of the actresses, and it resulted in an immediate violent confrontation between Indo actors and Chinese management. The *Soerabaiasch-Handelsblad* stated that they would not reveal the details of the disclosures that had been made of the "*chronique scandaleuse.*"[92]

Hartens subsequently issued a declaration that he would not work with the Chinese management again and a dispute arose over the ownership of the performance permit. The management, in turn, took action against the resigned director for the return of advances on the first month's wages. The Chinese financiers planned to appoint a new permanent director. A certain Han Oen Djan put in a request for a new permit from the police in early February. But on 25 February it was announced that the Chinese management would not go through with their plans. The Komedie Stamboel was no more.

Or so it seemed. The very day after that the company's dissolution was reported in the *Soerabaiasch-Handelsblad,* the same paper announced that a second company under the name Komedie Stamboel had been formed. This new company, operating under a new performance permit, would begin giving performances in Kampung Doro at the end of February. There would be new actors and actresses (many of the old ones having broken with the Chinese producers along with the resigned director) and a new director, a man who had been an actor in the first company: Auguste Mahieu.

Auguste "Guus" Constantijn Pierre Mahieu, "a sort of legendary figure about whom we possess little exact data," in the words of Rob Nieuwenhuys, is usually given sole credit for the company's founding.[93] This is in part due to the accounts of Knaap and Manusama but also is related to the public image created by Mahieu himself. In fact, as we have seen, Guus Mahieu was one of a coterie of Indo performers and Chinese managers responsible for the company's creation.[94] As a performer in the first company, he "already appeared to be at home on the planks," that is to say an accomplished and talented actor.[95] As Mahieu's career developed subsequently, he became known for his fine tenor voice, his remarkable comic acting skills, his musical abilities (he played both violin and guitar and occasionally functioned as musical director), his playwriting talents, and his compositional abilities. Mahieu is credited with having created the stambul standard melodies ("Stambul I," "Stambul II," "Stambul III," etc.), used again and again in different plays to indicate certain moods, with the words adjusted to the particulars of the play.

Mahieu's stambul melodies have a life beyond the theater itself. The melody of "Stambul I" provided Malaysia with its national anthem.[96] The melody of "Stambul II" remains a standard of musical ensembles all over the Malay world, and its form has been used as a model for hundreds if not thousands of musical compositions. In a 1972 monograph, the composer Kusbini writes that "Stambul II" should be performed in an "adante con dolorosa" style in a way that is "more refined, softer and moving" style than is customary for other popular tunes. The instrumental accompaniment should not be "lively (*lincah*) or joyful (*gembira*)" but should "stress a longing (*rindu*), sad (*sedih*), and moving (*mengungkapkan*) character. Singing style, too, should be refined and

Fig. 1.9. Piano arrangement of "Stambul II," composed by Auguste Mahieu. Reprinted from K. A. van der Poll, arr., *Bintang Soerabaja* (Amsterdam: Metro Muziek, n.d.), 5.

soft (*halus lembut*), *estetis, dinamis, serieus.*"[97] Mahieu's music is a music of the heart, which speaks to many Indonesians to date.

As the company's director, or actor-manager to invoke Victorian terminology, Mahieu was responsible for propelling the company and in fact the entire emergent genre in new directions and Indies-wide fame.

More can be said about Mahieu than any other figure attached to the Komedie Stamboel; his career serves this book as a kind of narrative through-line into the rapidly changing field of Indonesian popular culture. A few biographical details are thus in order.

Mahieu's genealogy and family history have recently been unearthed by Leiden-trained Indologist Rob Dumas.[98] Much has been made of Mahieu's supposed French descent, for the French were considered to be the embodiment of all things cultural, emulated in the "frantic gaiety"[99] of Dutch colonial life, the endless succession of balls, parties, and receptions, the never-ending project to adapt European high fashion to a tropical clime. Mahieu's French blood has been fetishized by both enthusiasts and detractors as the source of his creative energies, the inspiration and cause of his theatrical career. "The drop of French blood in his blood motivated him to bring Western culture to the ignorant," writes Jan Fabricius, while Hein Buitenweg states that Mahieu's "French blood, though not undiluted by other streams, explains his adventurous spirit."[100] But Mahieu's French origin was imagined and projected, not real. Mahieu might sound like a French name, but Mahieu himself was not of French extraction.

Dumas traces Auguste Mahieu's family tree back to Heimonus Isaacsen Mahu (also spelled Maihu) from Geertruidenberg, a town in the Dutch province of North Brabant. Mahu's descendents (with surnames variously spelled Mahu, Mahui, Mahuij, Mahue, and Mahieu) also lived in the Low Countries. Auguste Mahieu's paternal great-grandfather Abraham Mahieu was born in 1769 in Willemstad, a fortified town in the south of Holland named after William of Orange. Abraham Mahieu arrived in the Indies with his wife and children as a lieutenant-colonel in the army in 1804 (when Holland was ruled by Napoleon) and died in Batavia the following year. Abraham Mahieu's family remained in the Indies.

Some members of the Mahieu family enjoyed social and financial success. One of Abraham Mahieu's daughters married a Dutch colonial administrator who enjoyed the prestigious positions of resident and judge. Auguste Mahieu's grandfather, Johan H. B. Mahieu, enjoyed a less privileged life than his elder sister, working at a salt warehouse and as a tax collector. His wife, Adriana de Graaff, was half Javanese.

Auguste Mahieu's father, Johan Mahieu (born in Gresik, 18 January 1830; died in Kediri, 9 December 1902), was the fourth child of J. H. B. Mahieu. Johan Mahieu, like his father, worked a series of low-ranking civil servant jobs, moving house frequently over the course of his career. Johan Mahieu married his own niece Elise Montiara, who was sixteen years younger. In 1865 Johan Mahieu and his wife moved to the town of Bangkalan on the island of Madura, where he worked in the assistant resident's office. Auguste Mahieu was born there on 22 August 1865.[101]

In 1874 or 1875 the Mahieu family moved to Padang. Johan Mahieu worked in Padang as a first-rank clerk in the office of the government of Sumatra's west coast. Padang was a small city (25,000 people in 1874), and a major center of the coffee export trade. There were numerous auction houses, and ships regularly arrived from the Netherlands and the United States. The international traders, soldiers stationed in the town's large military barracks, and the mix of Indonesian, Chinese, and Indian ethnic groups gave the town a cosmopolitan flavor.[102] Possibly the young Guus Mahieu gained his first exposure to Malay language theater while in Padang. It was around the time that the Mahieus were living in Padang that Si Nong, the son of Radja Boerhan Oedin of Batavia, brought a troupe of actors from Riau to Padang. The troupe performed plays based on Malay literature and possibly plays popularized by Parsi theatrical troupes, to great acclaim, drawing eclectically on techniques and forms of Chinese opera, Parsi theater, the emerging Malay-language bangsawan theater of Penang, and European theater. There were many imitators in Padang and the vicinity.[103]

Johan Mahieu was pensioned from his clerical job in Padang on 31 March 1875. The Mahieu family returned to Java in 1878 or 1879, living initially in the Batavia area. The family then moved to Surabaya, perhaps to be closer to Elise's parents.

The move to Surabaya around 1880 allowed Auguste Mahieu the opportunity to study at Surabaya's *hoogere burgerschool* (higher secondary school, hereafter HBS), a highly prestigious five-year course of instruction that had opened in 1875.[104] The semifictional essay on Mahieu (referred to pseudonymously as Antoine Tardieu) written by Knaap describes briefly Mahieu's circumstances at this point.

> Tardieu's parents were paupers, so Antoine, their only child, could only attend a public primary school in his early youth, where one did not have to pay tuition. His vivacious nature and unusual intelligence quickly drew him to the attention of educators. Supported by a few friends, his parents were able to place their son, and after completing lower school, he was able to enjoy the benefits of a middle-school education at one of the three higher secondary schools. At the beginning it appeared that this young man would in due course make a good functionary of the colonial civil service. He followed his classes with success and shined in his end-of-term examinations.[105]

At the time of Mahieu's studies in Surabaya's HBS, there were only two HBS schools in the Indies. (The other was Batavia's Willem III HBS, opened in 1860.) Graduates of these programs could expect immediate employment in mid-level civil service jobs. Before the existence of these two schools, children born in the Indies could acquire only basic schooling and had to travel to the Netherlands to pursue higher studies. The two schools offered education for the European elite. There were only one hundred pupils at Surabaya's HBS in 1880.[106] Emblazoned on the school's flag was the Latin motto *Per aspera ad astra* (through hardship to the stars). Some of the students were coming from backgrounds of hardship, a few did indeed progress to celestial glory, but for all there was a sense of expectation and hope.

> Tardieu's parents hoped ecstatically that Antoine might one day be a candidate-controller, even an assistant resident or perhaps a resident. A position in the colonial civil service is the most fervent desire for many in the Indies. An ideal position: power over thousands of Natives, a part to play in the domination of the colony. Along the way, one could become a man of importance and prestige on the social ladder, or so they imagined.[107]

It is likely that Mahieu obtained his first exposure to European theater during his HBS years. On 1 September 1879 actress, playwright, and women's rights activist Mina Kruseman opened her school for theater and singing at the large house of one of Mahieu's own HBS teachers, W. L. Megenlijk. There is no direct evidence, but I prefer to believe that Kruseman was an influence on the young Mahieu. She certainly made an impression on many of the Eurasians and Europeans who subsequently wrote about Mahieu and the Komedie Stamboel, including Hans van de Wall (Victor Ido) and S. Kalff. Kruseman was one of the most famous cultural and political activists in the Indies from 1877 to 1883, and during her sojourn in Surabaya (1878–83) she devoted herself in large part to educational efforts, as well as writing occasional newspaper articles, plays, and the like. Her politicking and art were inseparable, as they had been for the Netherlands' most famous artist-activist, novelist Multatuli, who had been a personal friend before an acrimonious break. Kruseman infused the lessons she gave in acting, singing, piano playing, and oratory with her own fiery oratory and passion for the emancipation of women. Kruseman was an inspiring role model for many, even if she and her husband (who was thirty years her junior) did live as social "pariahs" (the title of Kruseman's 1900 account of her Surabaya years).[108]

Mahieu would not have actually attended Kruseman's school (which cost 15 guilders a month) nor taken private lessons from her in piano, song, or oratory (25 guilders a month). As a retired civil servant, Mahieu's father would be earning about 62 guilders a month, a substantial decline from the 250 guilders he earned monthly at the end of his career.[109] But Knaap tells us that Mahieu read Corneille, Racine, and Molière while at HBS, and one suspects that he participated in school dramatics of one sort or another. Kruseman actually lodged at Megenlijk's house for much of her time in Surabaya, and it is more than likely that *den heer* Megenlijk, who taught modern languages and geography at Surabaya's HBS from 1875 to 1884, brought to his HBS teaching knowledge culled from direct observation of theatrical instruction and play rehearsals that took place in his own house.[110] Almost certainly theater was very much in the air at the HBS during Mahieu's studies.[111] Granted the precarious financial circumstances of Mahieu and his family, one doubts claims that Mahieu "had seen art in Europe" or "had seen many theatrical performances and operas overseas."[112] But his HBS years perhaps allowed him to experience the vitality of European theatrical culture vicariously, as if he had traveled there himself.

Available sources are contradictory about whether Mahieu completed the five years of HBS and obtained a diploma. A premature cessation of his studies might have been related to his parent's constrained financial circumstances. But an obituary of Mahieu suggests that he left school not out of economic need but out of "wanderlust."[113] After a period of wandering, Mahieu returned to Surabaya and found employment in Surabaya's civil guard. This position provided a small stipend and had irregular hours, allowing him sufficient time to join the Komedie Stamboel as an actor in January 1891. Possibly Mahieu held a job in a government office before joining the Komedie Stamboel, as well.[114]

Mahieu's involvement with the other actors was more than professional. One of the other members of the company in the first year was Auguste Mahieu's sexual partner, described as Nyonya Mahieu (Mrs. Mahieu) in Malay press reports. Nyonya Mahieu was a capable actor in her own right: she is noted (along with her Auguste Mahieu) in one of the 1891 advertisements, and the sudden onset of an illness forces a show to be canceled for lack of an understudy.[115] The *nyonya* might be considered Mahieu's common-law wife, for their marriage is not registered. Cohabitation outside marriage was common among the actors. "The life and social relations of stambul actors was far from decent. In general, the three vices of life, *Wein, Weib, und Spiel,* were to be found in stambul," writes Andjar Asmara.[116] Mahieu particularly was known as a "*chéri des dames,*" with many romantic affiliations, particularly with actresses.[117]

Mahieu made a powerful impression in private as well as public, and there is no doubt that he stood out from the first. He spoke with great passion and conviction, with theatrical mannerisms and in short, direct sentences. Many women apparently found him hard to resist. He was said to be a sharp dresser, though his looks were not conventionally handsome by period standards.[118] "Tardieu does not bask in his Gallic descent—which has no meaning to him—but presents himself always as a unique individual. He is small of stature, has a dark brown complexion, and his features are sharply etched. His black, abundant hair and his heavy eyebrows offset the rather blithe appearance of his brown eyes."[119]

Mahieu's acting talents were recognized early on, but the decision to appoint him as director seems to have been contested, or at least in doubt for a period, for on the same day the *Soerabaiasch-Handelsblad* announced that Mahieu would be the new director, the *Soerabaija-Courant* reported that a certain J. W. W. Seket was to be engaged as the company's director.[120] It seems likely that Seket was considered as a candidate prior to Mahieu's confirmation as director. Possibly, like Mahieu, Seket was an actor in the first company. The matter is moot: no more is heard of Seket for the rest of the company's history.

THE SECOND incarnation of the Komedie Stamboel, under Auguste Mahieu's direction, debuted on 27 February 1891 with *Abu Hasan, the Chief of Thieves,* another *Nights* episode. The eponymous leading role, performed by Mahieu himself, "was unquestionably in good hands."[121] Mahieu was said to have "cut a good figure in several big scenes," and an unnamed actor playing the comic role was also reportedly "a big asset for the company."[122] Many of the members of this second company had also been members of the first. Some of the actors who departed with Hartens were initially hostile to the resurrected company, for they had intended to form their own company with new backing. But compromises were made and reconciliation occurred. Accomplished actors of the first company rejoined in early March and late April; those with less talent were excluded. The standard of acting went up during these months. Some of the newly appointed actors and actresses were initially not word perfect in their renditions, but they improved with practice.

Mahieu was indefatigable as the company's director, producing fourteen plays in three months. The *Nights* provided the core of the dramatic repertoire. In addition to *Abu Hasan,* the company also performed a whole raft of *Nights* plays, including *Ali Baba and the Forty Thieves* and *Aladdin and the Magic Lamp. Ali Baba* was a perennial favorite with the Komedie Stamboel's audience from its first performance. The addition of a sea battle, which was particularly enjoyed by audiences, distinguishes it from the standard *Arabian Nights* version.

The gruesome dismemberment of Kasim, Ali Baba's brother, was a horrifying spectacle reminiscent of Grand Guignol. The following summary was written for publicity purposes in 1894.

> Ali Baba was a poor man who made a living collecting firewood in the forest. When he was there forty thieves (brigands) came and removed a certain stone from in front of a cave. All went inside the cave, carrying their loot. The thieves subsequently emerged and left. Thus did Ali Baba take the thieves' goods and brought them home. Subsequently Kasim discovers how Ali Baba acquired these goods and he also goes to the cave, but [once inside] he is unable to reopen the cave's door and then he is killed by the thieves. Sometime later, the captain of the thieves learns that Ali Baba has taken his goods. He attempts to kill Ali Baba but he escapes to another city by boat. They meet in the middle of the ocean, and fight, but the thief is unable to get close enough to board Ali Baba's ship and thus Ali Baba is able to sail on. Subsequently, the captain of the thieves dresses as a merchant and attempts to kill Ali Baba but is unable to do so because the captain is killed by Ali Baba's servant.[123]

Mahieu also experimented with adapting European literature with *Raelaman bin Rachmat, or The Rinaldo Rinaldi of Arabia,* based on Vulpius's popular novel about an Italian brigand who uses various deceptions to abduct the fiancée of a count.[124] The novelty of seeing a European novel enacted in Malay attracted a large audience, despite stiff competition from Woodyear's Circus.

Mahieu had to contend with the same problems in maintaining the peace faced by the first company, but his own skill as an actor was a major boon. "Tuan M., the director of the Komedie Stamboel, is the leading man and a very accomplished actor who would be up to performing with a major professional theatre company. We believe that as long as he is the head of the troupe the Komedie Stamboel will have a long life, especially if he can manage to keep things quiet and peaceful without disturbances."[125]

The Chinese management demonstrated that they were even more committed to the new company than to the old. They not only hired a new director, they also provided new funds to improving the troupe. New actors were recruited to replace those who departed with Hartens, including "two sweet heads" (read: actresses) from Singapore, and the overall size of the troupe was increased.[126] New costumes and sets were constructed. The "magnificent," "beautiful" decor and costumes consistently garnered enthusiastic comments. The reviewer for *Pembrita-Bahroe* considered the company's decor to surpass even that used in Surabaya's schouwburg.[127] Construction of a new theater for the company's use in the more elite Kapasan district of Surabaya's Chinatown began almost simultaneous with the second company's opening night. Initial plans entailed box seats, an orchestra pit, a cafe, and even a billiard hall in the building.

Occasional technical problems still beset performances. The company's second outing, on 3 March 1891, was a performance of the play *Bedreddin Hassan, a Very Honest Man, Who Is Always Aided by the Lord Allah, and Marries a City Youth with Great Festivities.* The show's start was delayed by problems with the lighting, and at several points during the show, without warning, the gaslights all went out together—evoking hilarity from the audience. The gas company was blamed. One reviewer also complained that the seating did not provide sufficient legroom for spectators.

Not long after the second company's formation, Batavia's Albrecht and Rusche began to publish the first volumes of a multivolume, sumptuously illustrated Malay translation of *The Arabian Nights.* Priced upward of five and a half guilders each, these books were well out of reach of all but the most affluent of Muslims but could be afforded by select Europeans and Chinese readers of Malay. This publication event was heralded in the *Soerabaija-Courant* as an aid to the spectators of the Komedie Stamboel, which under Mahieu's leadership was increasingly attracting Europeans and "Natives" in addition to its Chinese habitués. "Though the artists might deliver their lines clearly and well, for a large part of the public, much that is spoken is lost, an inconvenience that can only be rectified by knowledge of the story."[128]

Indeed, though the amount of brawling between the actors and the spectators decreased with the appointment of Mahieu as director, the theater remained a noisy place. Salvos of applause and multiple encores followed many scenes. The noise and turmoil issuing from the adjacent buffet disturbed the ability to follow the performance. Fights occasionally broke out among spectators. Men yelled and screamed rude comments during shows. The Dutch-language story summaries in the printed "textbooks," or programs, which were available for sale were undoubtedly indispensable for those Europeans in attendance who were not fluent in Malay. They would otherwise have had a hard time following a plot over the din.

The social status of the Komedie Stamboel's actors, much suspect during the first company's run, appears to have improved somewhat under Mahieu. An advertisement for four ladies to train as actresses appeared in *Soerabaija-Courant, Soerabaiasch-Handelsblad,* and *Pembrita Bahroe* on 20 and 21 March met with positive responses, including one from the wife of a civil servant. A reader wrote to the *Soerabaija-Courant,* apropos of this announcement, that "there are still Indos who raise their noses at the Komedie Stamboel. They forbid their children to go see it, for example—what is more, to perform in it. They should first come to take a look at a performance of this troupe. They will then arrive at other conclusions."[129]

Audiences also grew more robust and diversified under Mahieu's leadership, with increasingly more Europeans in attendance. (This was one of the reasons for building the new Kapasan theater: the Doro hall was simply too small.) At one performance, even the Muslim patients of Surabaya's hospital for the mentally ill attended. "'The director does his utmost for his patients and perhaps this diversion had a beneficial influence on the pitiable creatures," wrote the *Soerabaiasch-Handelsblad.*[130]

Once again, it seemed that the troupe was destined for great success, with a growing audience base for its twice-weekly (Tuesday and Friday) shows and enthusiastic press (despite not giving complimentary tickets). Again, a conflict between the actors and the management resulted in the troupe falling apart.

The immediate cause for the company's disbanding was a planned road trip to Pasuruan, in eastern Java, scheduled for early June. Woodyear's Royal Australian Circus, featuring twenty-six performers, including clowns and Japanese acrobats, had been performing in Surabaya since 13 May and was cutting into the sale of the Komedie Stamboel's tickets. Two additional horse shows, Harmston's and Sons and Abell and Klaer's Excelsior Circus Troupe, were expected to arrive in June. On top of this, there was a report that a Parsi theater troupe from India featuring thirty-six actors would soon arrive from Singapore.[131] The management consequently decided that instead of continuing to lose money, it would temporarily shut down the theater and leave for nearby Pasuruan on 7 or 8 June to give a few shows. It would be the first time the company had performed outside Surabaya. A benefit performance for the actors was held on 27 May of the comedy *Abuhassan, the Sleeper Awakened,* with the troupe's best actors in the lead roles and a summary in Dutch distributed for free. This benefit performance was not a success, partially because the play had been performed several times before and partially as the show took place on a Wednesday night, not a usual performance night. Many patrons apparently did not get word of the benefit. Only about seventy guilders was raised at the door, barely enough to pay expenses. The actors still needed cash to tide themselves over during their "vacation" and demanded a month's wages in advance. The management, which claimed to be temporarily short of cash due to large expenditures on costumes and decor, said they could provide only half a month's wages. No compromise could be reached, the Pasuruan trip was canceled, and the actors refused to work, resulting in the disbanding of the Komedie Stamboel at the end of May, for the second time in five months. Mahieu was serving a delayed, week-long jail sentence in the provost prison as punishment for recurring absenteeism from his job as a civil guard, and it is likely he had no hand in the final negotiations.

The Komedie Stamboel had officially disbanded, but such was its popularity that it was clear it would quickly rise from the ashes. The same article in the *Soerabaiasch-Handelsblad* announcing its end also reported that a certain "European had already declared that he had four thousand guilders available to invest if the actors and actresses were willing to again come together as a theatre company."[132] A name change to

Komedie Perzie was considered in June but then decided against. Work meantime continued on the theater in the Kapasan district in June, and it was expected that the company's third avatar would eventually perform there.

The performers and the Chinese management were in the end able to come to an agreement. The majority of the old troupe members were incorporated into the third Chinese-owned troupe, which was placed in the hands of a new actor-manager, tenor J. D. Charles van der Laan, who was "formerly active as an artist with a British-Indian company" (possibly a bangsawan or a Parsi theater troupe) and also acted in the company. An effort was also made to recruit actors in Semarang. The well-known conflicts between the actors and management had cast an unfavorable light on the company as a source of employment, and it had become hard to attract actors from Surabaya's unemployed Indo population. The management took out a loan of 3,900 guilders to purchase and construct "picturesque Arabian costumes," decor, and the like. New regulations were instated by Van der Laan to improve the quality of the performance. New backdrops were created by Lépinat, a painter attached to the troupe. The actors rehearsed. A new performance permit was acquired and the furnishing of the new building in Kapasan, already considerably over budget and behind schedule in its construction, was completed posthaste.

The Komedie Stamboel reopened in the new theater in Kapasan on 14 August 1891, performing the *Nights* play *The Contending Kings Murat Khan and Harun al-Rachmat* to a sell-out audience that was more ethnically diverse than ever, "and when the spectators went home at the end they chatted among each other about how much they enjoyed seeing the show."[133] Kapasan provided a more salubrious environment than Kampung Doro had. Kapasan was where the Chinese major's house was located, and much construction work was going on in the neighborhood in the 1890s, adding to its sense of life.

The opening had been twice delayed due to problems finishing the decor and insuring that the actors had learned their parts. The new theater in Kapasan had good seats and illumination, provided by petroleum lamps. Journalist S. Kalff, writing under the pseudonym Aboe

Hassan, stated in 1893 that the "theatre rivaled the theatre of the Europeans at Komedieplein [Surabaya's schouwburg], with its spacious hall, double roof, fresh decor, good lighting, and ventilation."[134] Measures were taken so that noise from the buffet would not interfere with the viewing pleasure of spectators. Ticket prices remained the same, except for front box seats, which cost three guilders. The semiweekly (Tuesday and Friday nights), schedule was resumed.

Mahieu appears not to have been part of the third company initially, though he rejoined the troupe for its second performance on 18 August. An advertisement that first appeared in the Malay paper *Bintang Soerabaia* on this date (and was reprinted three additional times the same month) stated, "Tuan A. Mahieu and his wife [nyonya] are working again for the Stamboel." Mahieu is the only actor regularly mentioned by name in Komedie Stamboel advertisements, but other actors in the third company also had something of a reputation. A review of *Ali Baba* stated that "the acting of Margiana was outstanding. She is the public's darling, just as she was in the previous troupe."[135]

Plays based on *The Arabian Nights* remained the third company's staple.[136] The Faust tale was adapted to the Komedie Stamboel idiom as *Fathul Achmat, or The Faust of Arabia* (premiered 22 September 1891). This adaptation was later attributed to Mahieu.[137] The production was said to be faithful adaptation of "the German *Faust*" and featured "eighty pantun, some of them never before performed in the world, absolutely remarkable, and truly delightful."[138] The general outline appears to be true to Goethe's play, best known in Indonesia through its operatic adaptation by Charles Gounod (1859):[139]

> Long ago there was an aged physician named Fathul Achmat, who greatly desired to become young again. Thus did a devil come to him and agree to grant his wish, but he had to pledge his soul to the devil if his wish was to be granted. Fathul Achmat accepted the devil's terms and he became young again and married Marhaji, a young girl of great beauty. When the time came for him to surrender his soul to the devil, an angel came to assist Fathul Achmat.[140]

The Komedie Stamboel's *Faust* was well received at its premiere by the audience, which was primarily European. "John Chinaman appears not to desire a performance of the devil's realm," wrote the *Soerabaiasch-Handelsblad.* "The actors and actresses acquitted themselves well of their difficult task, made even more difficult as most of them have never seen 'Faust' enacted."[141] Van der Laan also introduced farces and comedies into the repertoire, premiering a double bill of one-act plays, *The Sluggards* and *He Is Not Jealous,* on 25 September 1891.

Spectacular scenic effects continued to be emphasized in productions under Van der Laan's direction. Six or more painted backdrops were rolled out in shows. One scene was set in an Arabian ship at sea, "with the appearance of real waves." Another scene featured "a fuming volcano in the middle of an agitated sea." These scenic effects were described in newspaper advertisements and clearly were a major audience draw.

Van der Laan's most significant innovation as director, though, was likely the practice of providing addenda to follow the plays performed. Some performances concluded with choral numbers featuring the entire company. More commonly, Van der Laan would create tableaux vivants, fantasias on themes usually unrelated to the night's main attraction.[142] These living pictures, or relatively static images without dialogue, depicted "Europeans, Chinese, Arabs, Dayaks, and Indians of old times, or the spirit world."[143] Some were scenes out of *The Arabian Nights* or closely related tales, such as the story of King Solomon punishing recalcitrant genies. Others, though, were not. One of the most noteworthy of Van der Laan's tableaux vivants depicted the launching of the steamship *Prins Hendrik.*[144]

The practice of concluding a dramatic evening with a tableau vivant was entirely new to the Malay theater, but was characteristic of many European theatrical troupes at the time. The 1890s in fact corresponded to the tableau vivant's "apogee of popularity" in Australia and its "final blaze of glory" on the commercial New York stage.[145] Most accounts trace the origin of the tableau vivant to Emma Hart, the mistress of Sir William Hamilton during his appointment as the British ambassador to the Kingdom of the Two Sicilies in Naples (and later his wife).[146] The tableau vivant entered the public theater in the first decades of the nineteenth century, interspersed between scenes of plays and incorporated into melodrama and Andrew Ducrow's equestrian spectacles. "Venetian Statue" or "Living Statue" acts were introduced into variety companies in Europe and the United States in the 1830s, staged by specialist performers. By the 1840s, not only were there commercial companies devoted exclusively to creating tableaux, but the form had become a bourgeois pastime, enacted in parlors around Europe and the United States. Later in the century, tableaux vivants were also presented on the streets as part of civic parades.

The tableau vivant was from its beginning a subject of controversy, "simultaneously celebrated as a means of promoting virtue and denigrated as a licentious display of semi-nude women in public."[147] Defenders such as Walt Whitman saw it as a mode of "appreciation of the divine beauty evidenced in Nature's cunningest work—the human frame, form and face."[148] Others pointed out the tableau's merits in introducing high art to the masses in an age before mechanical reproduction made high-quality color copies inexpensive. The focus of most tableaux upon revelation of what New York advertisements called "the female form divine" posed motionlessly for the inspection of the male gaze made tableaux vivants suspect as a form of pornography.[149] Scopophilia is inscribed compositionally, with the characteristic appearance of men at the borders of pictorial compositions as a surrogate audience.[150] The titillating "statue girls" of the Barnum & Bailey Circus, clothed only in loincloths and white or bronze greasepaint, afforded the American masses with the closest form of public frontal nudity available at the time—in the name of the reproduction of high art.[151] Commercial companies were regularly banned on the grounds of public indecency.[152]

In a colonial context, the tableau vivant assumes special pertinence as a way "to imitate home institutions" and embody culture. It has been argued that the great popularity of tableaux vivants both as private and public entertainment in nineteenth- and early twentieth-century colonial Australia was due in part to the unavailability of art masterpieces for actual inspection by art students.[153] In Indonesia as well, tableaux vivants were a favored diversion for Dutch colonialists, performed at private clubs and houses and as part of public displays of theatricals, acrobatics, and the like.[154] Many of the nineteenth-century professional troupes that toured Surabaya and other cities of the Indies incorporated one or more tableaux vivants into their performances.

The introduction of the tableau vivant into the Komedie Stamboel corresponded with a vogue in spectacular realism.[155] There was a burgeoning attention to pictorial illusionism in Indonesia. Forgeries of bank bills demonstrated the remarkable skills of local artists in creating convincingly realistic copies.[156] *Trompe l'oeil* displays were common: a representation of crab salad on a bed of lettuce by C. G. van den Steen at the Batavia Exposition of 1893 was so lifelike that visitors reportedly thought it was free food made available by the exposition's director.[157] There were lifelike panoramas depicting world capitals and exotic vistas. Many of these were created by European artists and were exhibited in Europe before they were shipped to Asia, somewhat the worse for use. Such panoramas, on regular display in the cities and towns of Java and other Indonesian islands for paying spectators, allowed for virtual travel. A panorama was billed as a site "at which people can see the conditions of other continents, as if we ourselves went to those places."[158] Itinerant Chinese and Japanese commercial artists toured the major towns and cities, painting and reproducing portraits. The same representational skills and aims that informed the production of panoramas, forgeries, and portraits were artfully displayed before mass audiences in the Komedie Stamboel's tableaux vivants.

The feature of a tableau vivant following the evening-length play (if not the actual title of the tableau) is regularly noted in Komedie Stamboel advertisements. The tableau was, for some at least, the most entertaining part of the evening there. "The particularly fine tableau vivant formed the largest attraction; one must acknowledge that no care or effort was spared upon it," noted one reviewer in 1894.[159] The tableau vivant allowed audiences to be wowed by displays of carefully composed stage technology; realism was lauded as a virtue. One of the most common subjects for the Komedie Stamboel as well as European theatrical troupes was (not surprisingly) the 1883 eruption of Krakatau, the most spectacular natural disaster of the last millennium.[160] One realization of the oft-repeated eruption featured "volcanic ash, flashes of lightning, sea tremors and earthquakes, praying country people; all appeared natural and just right."[161] This spectacle was vividly recalled decades later by an aged spectator:

> The tableau of "The Explosion of Krakatau" showed a good-sized mountain from which emerged flames (likely Bengal fireworks) that stirred long pieces of cloth that gave the appearance of waves when in motion. Men fled and struggled against the waves but were actually immobile in their sculpted poses. An explosion, the eruption of the mountain. Bengal light in red and blue. An appropriate backdrop. Such a tableau was a display we could watch with a sort of suspense, as we never were sure what would come next. It was the element of surprise.[162]

Subjects of Komedie Stamboel tableaux were often fantastical or mythological—angels, devils, genies, faeries, and Greco-Roman gods all feature prominently. But even when depicting a subject as unworldly as "the protecting angel of innocence," an advertisement promised that "this tableau is *imitated* as beautifully and as *naturally* as possible."[163] The tableau needed to appear "spectacularly real" in order to astound and create the desired attitude of heran (astonishment).

Promotional items or reviews do not suggest that Komedie Stamboel tableaux were ever imitations of recognizable paintings. Possibly some of the images were based on printed engravings, but fidelity to already known images is never explicitly mentioned by either the theater's producers or spectators. These images, like the plays, had to be explained. There are no detailed descriptions of how such diegesis was accomplished in 1891, but later accounts allow some insight into the process.[164]

After the conclusion of the final scene of the play, the front curtain is dropped and the orchestra strikes up a piece. This curtain is painted with an image of the frame story of the *Nights,* depicting King Shahriyar reclining on a divan with a pipe in his hand. He is listening to the tales of Scheherazade, who is seated on the ground. Also represented is

Scheherazade's sister Dunyazade, who in the Arabic original provides an internal audience to the storytelling event, prone to comments such as "Sister, what an entertaining story!" On the Komedie Stamboel's front curtain, Dunyazade is shown seated on a Persian carpet with a lute in hand, suggesting that she is providing musical accompaniment to Scheherazade's stories. An actor from the company then steps in front of the footlights and delivers a direct address to the audience (sometimes still in costume and character) in which he announces the title of the play to be performed tomorrow night (giving both the Malay and Dutch versions) and also explains the title and significance of the tableau vivant that follows. The orchestra then starts to play a musical piece selected to provide the proper ambience for the tableau. The front curtain rises on the carefully illuminated and posed scene of actors grouped and styled in symbolically freighted poses.

Typically, tableaux vivants were composed of more than a single still image, featuring two or three *afdeelingen* (parts) or *tafereelen* (pictures), with short pauses in between. The same characters were shown conveying contrasting emotional attitudes and physical poses. A fragmented story could be told through images—from happiness to sadness, from poverty to wealth, from youth to old age.[165] This fragmentary quality did not appeal to all. S. Kalff complains that the cutting up a of piece entitled "In the Kingdom of the Heavenly Beings" into many tafereelen made it unbecomingly long; the flickering lamps nearly drained of their oil supply mirrored the exhausted state of the actors by this time of the evening. Many of the spectators at the performance he witnessed had gone home even before the tableau—exiting the theater promptly after the play's denouement.[166]

A number of the tableaux were codas for the main story. So for example, after Van der Laan's production of *The Faust of Arabia,* there was a "tableau telling of Fathul Achmat's time in the afterlife."[167] There was also the possibility of recycling spectacular images that proved to be hits from prior play productions. Variants of the Arabian shipwreck spectacle from *Ali Baba* were often presented as stand-alone tableaux after other plays. Sometimes tableau images were later developed into full-length plays.

It is striking how the selection of tableaux vivants from the very beginning of the Komedie Stamboel strove to articulate a kind of universality. No images out of the ancient past of the Indonesian islands are ever represented. Religious images are realized ("Adam and Eve Driven from Paradise," "Abel Murdered by Cain," "Jacob's Dream," "The Justice of Solomon"), but all these images are common to the trove of tales shared by Judaism, Christianity, and Islam. The items out of the recent past ("The 1873 Paris Fire," "The Eruption of Krakatau," "The Death of Captain Revière," "The Death of General Van Ham") are of such import as to be recognized by newspaper readers worldwide.

One of the interests of the Komedie Stamboel's spectators in tableaux vivants was without a doubt that they allowed the free range of the gaze on the company's white-skinned actresses. The attractiveness of the Indo actresses was a major selling point of the company from the very beginning. An 1854 law dictated that Chinese were to be considered as "foreign Orientals," sharing private law with Europeans but subject to the same public law (and criminal procedures) as Muslims. A large percentage of Indos actually had lifestyles and standards of living that more closely approximated Native than European norms, and the majority did not speak Dutch in their daily lives. But those Indos recognized as the legal offspring of European parents occupied a higher legal position in Indonesia's hierarchical code of justice than the Chinese.[168] The spectacle of Eurasian women (and to a lesser degree men) performing ridiculous stories in absurd costumes no doubt afforded ticket-purchasing Chinese spectators a degree of subversive pleasure. This pleasure was redoubled with the tableaux vivants. Actresses were frozen in attitudes for viewing pleasure. Stasis allowed spectators to ogle performers and casually converse about the relative attractiveness of the women on display.

The tableau vivant has also always been a good medium for propaganda; it is particularly effective in the way it conveys strong, memorable images. This side of the tableau was only fully exploited by the Komedie Stamboel in a later phase of its development, however. Initially, tableaux acted more to astonish than convince. The pictures were impressions of the faraway and the past, not the here and now.[169]

Under Van der Laan's management, the Komedie Stamboel continued to face stiff competition from other amusements, particularly horse shows like the Fillis Circus. Rambunctious spectators still disrupted performances by their yelling and whistling. The actors clearly experienced their shares of hardship. One almost lost his life when he nearly drank a vial of hydrochloric acid, believing it contained water.[170] The troupe members (including both Mahieu and Van der Laan) who had side jobs as city guards continued to go in and out of jail for their absenteeism. Most spectacularly, one of the actors, a former cannoneer known as Haholij, was arrested at his first performance with the company, at 11:30 P.M. on 23 October 1891, during act seven of *The Three Crippled Princesses.* The cannoneer had been wanted for some twenty-six months before his arrest. Haholij had just given a fine performance in act six, and was sitting in the orchestra pit when the intrepid sheriff Calmer arrested him and handed him over to the military police. Haholij suspected nothing.[171]

There were also signs that the theater's novelty was beginning to fade during these months. A reporter in *Bintang Soerabaia* suggested that spectators were bored of *Arabian Nights* plays and that if stories were based on Islamic romances such as the tales of Sheikh Abdul Mulia or Abdul Muluk ticket sales might increase. (The paper's editor facetiously suggested in a footnote that the writer apply for the position of director of the Komedie Stamboel himself, if he really desired the company's prosperity.)[172] A special charity performance of *Asam and the Spirit Queen* to benefit European and Chinese orphans on 18 October raised 307.50 guilders and merited appreciative letters to the newspapers from representatives of the Protestant and Roman Catholic religious communities. Its publicity value seems to have been minimal however. The *Soerabaiasch-Handelsblad* reported that at the very next performance "the Komedie Stamboel performed . . . for stools and benches, so to speak, so empty was it. Two performances a week is a bit too much, and a browny [*bruintje,* a racist slur] cannot afford the price, especially if he brings his wife and children with him. Tickets are of course fairly highly priced. If the management must give two shows a week, they should set the ticket prices a bit lower."[173]

Low audience turnout contributed to the practice of undertaking out-of-town engagements in eastern Java. The company's first engagement outside Surabaya was at the Harmonie Club in Pasuruan, a small town on the Straits of Madura. Pasuruan was about sixty-five kilometers southeast of Surabaya, connected by a rail line finished in 1878. This town, famously depicted as the sleepy provincial town of "Labuhan" in Louis Couperus's 1900 novel *The Hidden Force,* was the capital of a district by the same name, but in economic and cultural practice functioned as an annex of Surabaya. The town's elite citizens regularly visited Surabaya to shop and socialize, and they subscribed to Surabaya newspapers, which regularly reported on their own town's events. Pasuruan was in many ways a typical residency town, where both the Dutch resident and the Javanese *bupati* (regent) resided.[174] In the compact town center were a Catholic and a Protestant church, a hotel, the houses of the resident and bupati, European and Chinese stores, and the houses of European elites. An inlet from the sea was lined with colorful Madurese fishing boats. The district of Pasuruan was economically thriving due to its fertile soil and industrious populace, but the town of Pasuruan gave the appearance of a ghost town to visitors. The railway line to Surabaya had resulted in a decline in the numbers of Europeans living in town. Many of the "splendid [European] private houses and large merchant-offices along the quays" were either deserted or falling into disrepair under Chinese ownership.[175]

The Harmonie Club was the center of social life for the European community of Pasuruan. It is represented as the "Concordia Club" in

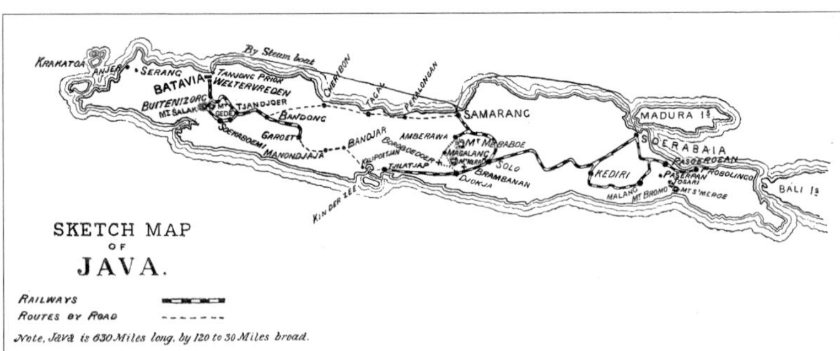

Map 2. Rail map of Java. Reprinted from Worsfold, *Visit to Java,* 84.

Fig. 1.10. Interior of the Harmonie Club in Pasuruan, with the stage arranged for a theatrical performance. Reprinted from Rob Nieuwenhuys, *Baren en oudgasten: Tempo doeloe, Een verzonken wereld, Fotografische documenten uit het Oude Indië, 1870–1920* (Amsterdam: E. M. Querido, 1998), 162.

Couperus's novel, "a handsome villa adorned with slender, fairly correct Ionian pillars of plaster and brilliantly lit with paraffin lamps set in chandeliers." The Harmonie Club was a place of leisure and relaxation for men and women, where Muslim servants dressed in white jackets served colonials sitting at "the great gin-and-bitters table" on "wide cane chairs."[176] As a general rule, club membership was restricted to Europeans. In addition to regular concerts by its in-house band (an inevitable fixture of clubs before the arrival of the phonograph to Indonesia) and amateur theatrics by the local European dramatic society, the Harmonie Club also occasionally hosted small-scale touring arts groups in its multifunctional hall. This is where the Komedie Stamboel played.

From 23 to 25 August 1891, the Komedie Stamboel gave three consecutive performances at the Harmonie Club of *The Fisherman and the*

Genie; Amgiad and Assad, The Two Wronged Princes; and a double bill comprising *Giafar* and the farce *Buekabik*. The Komedie Stamboel's reputation preceded its arrival to Pasuruan through word of mouth and the regular press coverage in Surabaya newspapers. A new catch-phrase was devised in its advertising: Come, see, and judge for yourself! (*komt, ziet en oordeelt* in Dutch). This variant of the Latin *veni, vidi, vici* was used in advertising for years to come.[177] The company used its own painted backdrops, adjusted to the constraints of the hall. Tickets were priced at the flat rate of two guilders (with no concessions available), and "all races could attend."[178] While at least one performance was deemed "very well attended and a great success," overall the company "neither made nor lost money" from the engagement.[179] One commentator suggested that was because "people living in the town of Pasuruan do not easily part with their money for their pleasure, unlike the people of Surabaya."[180] It is also likely that the exclusive status of the Harmonie Club deterred non-European spectators who might have otherwise been drawn to see Malay-language theater. It was an honor to perform in a bastion of European privilege, perhaps, but that did not mean it made financial sense to do so.

The company returned to Surabaya after the three Pasuruan performances, gave a few shows at the Kapasan theater, and then left for another out-of-town engagement. This time the stand was Bangkalan, Mahieu's own hometown in Madura, about ten miles from Surabaya across the narrow Strait of Madura, and only several hours away by steamship. This engagement showed more managerial foresight than the Pasuruan stand. The three performances at the beginning of September were locally contracted, with an agreed fee of 835 guilders for the run, irrespective of box office take. The performances took place in a shed expressly furnished for the company. The location had been scouted by the Komedie Stamboel's newly appointed advance man, who made a special trip from Surabaya to Bangkalan at the end of August. A further offer to perform in Semarang (with a guaranteed income of 250 guilders per night) was tendered and there was talk at this time as well of performing at the Mangkunagaran royal house in Surakarta. The organization was growing.

The management decided by early October that it would soon leave Surabaya for an extended tour of eastern and central Java. A tent that could reportedly seat up to two thousand, similar to those used by itinerant circuses, was built for the tour so that the company could play in towns and cities lacking permanent theaters.[181] Certain modifications were made to the theatrical apparatus: the side wings, for example, could be rolled up for easy storage. The Komedie Stamboel was transforming into an itinerant theater company, modeling itself on traveling troupes, such as the Towers Family from Australia, which toured England, South Africa, and India in the 1880s.

> The Towers' scenery consisted entirely of painted drop cloths and flat canvas wing pieces. For easy transportation the wing pieces were taken apart: the canvas rolled in the same way as the drop cloths; and the wooden frames dismantled. In the big towns there was gaslight, but very often the company worked on stages that were illuminated by kerosene lamps held in "dogs"—iron braces placed against the flat wings out of sight of the audience. Often, too, flat-bottomed oil lamps were strung out across the front of the stage to serve as footlights.[182]

A new musical ensemble was formed to replace the Italian Quintet, which would not be going with the company on its tour. Permission was requested on 7 October to set up the tent at the alun-alun (square) of Surabaya's Pasar Besar, the same space where the circus customarily performed, to give a series of special performances before departing on the tour. The Surabaya police initially denied this request on the grounds that "the Pasar Besar is a European realm and thus a Native theatre company . . . is not in its place" and that "it would disturb the peace of the neighborhood." This reasoning was vigorously condemned as spurious by the *Soerabaiasch-Handelsblad,* on the grounds that the Pasar Besar space had been previously occupied by a Parsi theater troupe from Bombay for weeks at a time and that circuses make at least as much trouble and noise as the Komedie Stamboel.[183] The authorities relented, the permit was eventually granted, and the Komedie Stamboel arranged to give seven consecutive performances during the first week of November of the "best plays" in its repertoire, including *Ali Baba, Aladdin, The Fisherman and the Genie,* and *Siti Senimbar, or Innocence Protected.* Ticket prices ranged from twenty-five cents for second-class benches to two guilders for box seats, and the profits for the last three performances benefited the actors and actresses of the company. During the last nights of the run at the Pasar Besar, Mahieu was instated as the acting director, to temporarily replace Van der Laan.[184]

The transformation of the Komedie Stamboel from a residential to a touring company, a transformation that would eventually allow it to become Indonesia's first translocal cultural form, was greeted with some sadness by Surabaya residents—who even then realized that the gain of other cities and towns was their own loss. At the final performance, the Italian Quintet played a melancholic "Wer weiss ob wir uns wiedersehn!" (Who knows if we'll ever meet again), an 1881 song by Ludolf Waldmann. "*Sic transit gloria mundi,*" memorialized the *Soerabaiasch-Handelsblad*'s reporter over a vision of the "tragic remains" of rubbish left in the Pasar Besar square in the wake of the troupe's decampment.[185]

THE FIRST ten months of the Komedie Stamboel's existence provides many insights into processes of emergence of cultural forms in a modernizing society. Later accounts categorize the company as an initiative of its Eurasian actors, but we see that the Chinese management played a formative role. The company was not simply bankrolled by Chinese businessmen, it was owned and controlled by a kongsi. It is likely that without this patronage and backing, it would not have been able to weather the multiple personnel and financial crises of the first year. The Komedie Stamboel capitalized on Yap Gwan Thay's experience of packaging and touring Chinese opera and topeng troupes, relying on the same mechanisms of publicity and marketing. It was, indeed, at first a theater located in the heart of Surabaya's Chinatown dedicated to the entertainment of Chinese audiences. Only after its first months of operation did it gain a following among non-Chinese Malay speakers. Though manifestly a theater for a multiethnic society, the Komedie Stamboel thus initially relied on clientele and patronage defined in terms of a specific ethnicity. This Chinese leverage over the troupe's European actors was a source of friction and strife. This was graphically instanced by the first breakup around divergent understandings of the concept of ownership.

The Komedie Stamboel was a part of the larger komedi world and was well integrated into the popular culture of its time. The theater where the company premiered was established as a site of entertainment prior to the Komedie Stamboel's founding. The *Nights* in Malay translation provided entertainment for the readership of vernacular newspapers prior to their adaptation for the stage. The Italian Quintet that accompanied most performances was highly regarded among all aficionados of European culture, and was a staple of Surabaya's *soirée variée* and bal champêtre scene. The dramatic form used by the Komedie Stamboel was known to a certain sector of the audience through attendance of operetta and burlesque companies at the schouwburg. Acting was similarly modeled on the conventions of melodrama: actors were encouraged to "project movements" (*buang tingkah*) to their audience and wore white socks on their feet and sequins on their costumes to make their exaggerated postures more visible. From the beginning, the troupe had a translocal orientation. Van der Laan had formerly worked in a "British Indian" troupe and it is likely that the two actresses recruited from Singapore also had theatrical experience abroad. The tent that the company constructed for touring was modeled after circus tents, and it was competition with the circus that drove it to expand its operation to outside Surabaya. Most important for our purposes, perhaps, the Komedie Stamboel advertised and was covered in the newspapers, the same newspapers accustomed to providing regular coverage of other popular entertainments, such as the circus, theater at the schouwburg, and magic shows. Little about the Komedie Stamboel at this phase of its existence could be said to be startlingly new—with the possible exception of its use of Malay and the signature melodies composed by Mahieu. What was exciting was the way the theater combined its heterogeneous elements in a form tailored to suit the "too much mingled together" city of Surabaya.

Chapter 2

AN ITINERANT THEATER, 1891–92

The Komedie Stamboel's first tour outside the Surabaya area covered four cities of eastern and central Java connected by rail and lasted about six weeks during November and December 1891. The tour was a proving ground of sorts. Yap Gwan Thay went with the troupe to collect the gate and oversee the troupe's finances. Overall the campaign was only a partial success; there was infighting and illness among the actors and attrition in the size of both the company and audiences. The *Soerabaiasch-Handelsblad* attributed the company's problems to its diffuse management. For the duration of this tour, Mahieu and Van der Laan functioned collectively as the management (*de directie*), responsible for artistic decisions, while Yap Gwan Thay also took an active role in all decisions. *"Zóó veel hoofden, zóó veel zinnen,"* opined the paper, a Dutch expression roughly meaning that too many cooks spoil the broth.[1] But the Komedie Stamboel demonstrated that it was able to entertain audiences beyond its nurturing Surabaya habitués and earned respectable press notices in Semarang and Surakarta.

The first stop on the 1891 tour was Mojokerto, a small town about thirty kilometers southwest of Surabaya, connected to Surabaya by a rail line opened in 1889. The company performed seven shows between 13 and 19 November 1891 in the town's central square, or alun-alun. Prices ranged from fifty cents for the bleachers to three guilders for box seats, and spectators received programs free of charge. A bad omen marred the troupe's departure from Surabaya to Mojokerto. Johan Frederik Alexander Fortijn, reputedly one of the company's best actors, fell ill on 11 November 1891 and died a few hours later. An actress, likewise reputed to be the best in the company, refused to tour with the troupe. But that did not delay the Mojokerto opening. Audiences turned out in good numbers as the company's reputation preceded it. Another actress left the troupe, however, after her request for a raise was refused.

Madiun, a residency town about 170 kilometers west-southwest of Surabaya, further down the rail line leading to central Java, was the Komedie Stamboel's next stand. The company performed three shows on 23–25 November 1891 in the town's spacious alun-alun. The residency of Madiun had been a center of rural unrest and anticolonial rebellion in the 1880s, and there was still residual paranoia of radical insurgents massacring Europeans. But although there was talk of aggressive "hidden forces," the town was relatively tranquil in the 1890s.[2] Madiun was connected to Kediri and Blitar by a rail line opened in 1884 and benefited from rail links to Surabaya and central Java. Goods and people from the neighboring towns of Maospati and Caruban passed through Madiun in transit to larger markets and shipping centers. This contributed to Madiun's eminence as a prime town for komedi in the 1890s; despite its small size, it was common for troupes traveling around Java to perform here.[3]

The Komedie Stamboel did not fare well in Madiun. A large downpour substantially reduced the audience size at one show. More serious, the actors brawled with each other, becoming a "nightly scandal" that scared away potential spectators—Madiun's urban populace was conditioned to be wary of displays of violence. So serious was this internal fighting, in fact, that a number of the company's members decided not to continue with the tour and returned to Surabaya at the end of November, throwing the entire troupe into disarray. Yap Gwan Thay, however, reported that he was confident the company would have more luck in central Java, and the show went on.

The third stand on the 1891 tour was Surakarta (also known as Solo), a royal court town with two major royal houses, situated at a rail junction. The company succeeded in building a loyal audience in Solo, but not without financial loss. This central Javanese city was more critical to the tour's success than the prior stands. The Komedie Stamboel was an unknown to audiences here, and Surakarta was a far more populous town than Mojokerto or Madiun, with a large Chinatown, locally published newspapers, and correspondents writing for papers in Batavia, Semarang, and Surabaya. More important, priyayi elites throughout Java and elsewhere in the archipelago emulated the tastes of Solo's nobility. The relative lack of enthusiasm of Solo's noble scions to the Komedie Stamboel had important repercussions for future appreciations of the theater.

American traveler E. R. Scidmore, who visited Solo in the 1890s, writes vividly of the city's atmosphere, describing "the stir of camp and court, the state and pomp and pageantry" of the courts of Surakarta and the residency. Scidmore was impressed by Solo's street life, which "could well entertain one for many days." "Bands and marching troops were always to be seen in the street," while the mounted escorts and parasol bearers that accompanied grandees made for a street spectacle of memorable intensity. Solo was a city with a "labyrinthine passer [market] where open sheds and rustic booths have grown upon one another around several court spaces, which are dotted with the huge mushrooms of palm-leaf umbrellas." Shopping for a souvenir, Scidmore found there were "pawnshops galore in this city full of courtiers and hangers-on of greatness, and such array of krisses and curious weapons that there was an embarrassment of choice." The city had an entire street of sarong-shops, "each little shop or open booth glowing with cloths of brilliant colors, and each shop standing in feudal dignity behind a tiny moat, with a mite of a foot-bridge quite its own." Scidmore remarked upon the cleanliness of Solo's Chinatown, where the odor of sesame oil wafts from cookshops. She was struck by the city's rich Chinese peranakan, who "sit rigid and imperturbable . . . smoking long black cheroots" as they drive "past in handsome victories, wearing immaculate duck suits, patent-leather shoes, and silk hose."[4] The intense jockeying for status of this royal court town was played out not only in material trappings but also in entertainment and the arts; Javanese,

Chinese, and Europeans alike were concerned with being seen at prestigious functions and events, where the right guests were in attendance. The *sunan* (king) of Surakarta was not only the defender of traditional culture, he also had "the finest ball-room in Solo—a vast white-marble-floored *pringintan,* or open-sided audience-hall, which is lighted with hundreds of electric lights, and on whose shining surface great cotillions are danced."[5]

An agent for the Komedie Stamboel had visited Solo in October and had attempted (without success) to arrange command performances from the sunan of the Surakarta court and the prince of the Mangkunagaran royal house. He did manage to secure permission to erect the tent in the *alun-alun lor,* the square directly north of Surakarta's royal court, a prime performance venue. Despite the efforts of this agent, there had been little advance publicity for the troupe (which was still effectively unknown in central Java), and Solo audiences initially perceived ticket prices as overly expensive. The Komedie Stamboel consequently played the crowd-pleasers *Siti Senimbar* and *Ali Baba* to small houses during its first two nights in Solo in early December. The local paper reported that if the heirs to the thrones of the Surakarta and Mangkunagaran royal houses "had not been in attendance, it is certain that all the box seats would have been empty."[6] One of the crown princes, the future Pakubuwana X, appears to have taken an extra-aesthetic liking to the Komedie Stamboel. He engaged a talented actress on a permanent basis—she became one of his numerous mistresses. Once again inclement weather for the duration of the run put a damper on audience attendance, as did a government ban on Chinese entering Solo. Audience turnout increased over time, however, and although the company reported a net loss from the Solo engagement, the management attempted (unsuccessfully) to extend the performance permit.

Solonese spectators commended the Komedie Stamboel for its finely executed and lifelike backdrops in which "the picture of the sea appeared like the real sea" and appreciated its "costumes which faithfully imitated the [*Arabian Nights*] chronicles."[7] A group of "Dutch" (mostly likely Indo) devotees were so enthusiastic that they celebrated New

Year's Eve by putting on their own impressions of the songs and dialogues of the Komedie Stamboel's *Ali Baba* and *Aladdin* for their own amusement at the house of a certain Tuan H. The host was so pleased with this performance, said to differ only in costume from the bona fide company, that at the end of the show he spontaneously mounted the stage and did a dance, to the great hilarity of everyone present.

Semarang, a city with a population of about seventy-five thousand, located about 110 kilometers northwest of Surakarta, was the final stand on the 1891 tour. Semarang was connected to Solo by a rail line completed in 1870, and by telephone to Batavia and Surabaya by lines completed in 1882. Hundreds of thousands of tons of goods were annually transported by rail between Semarang and the Principalities (Surakarta and Yogyakarta), and via a north-coast rail line that extended as far as Mayong.[8] Semarang's harbor was not a deep-sea port like Batavia's or Surabaya's, but the twenty-three-meter-wide Kali Baru canal was lined with warehouses and busy with incoming and outgoing steamships and sailing vessels. The city's Europeans had a strong sense of civil pride, and by the early twentieth century Semarang was renowned as a model city of urban planning and development.[9]

The Komedie Stamboel played Semarang under the patronage of officers of Semarang's Chinese community. Semarang's Chinese populace, numbering ten thousand by the early 1890s, had a reputation for forward-thinking entrepreneurship.[10] The most wealthy Semarang Chinese, the so-called *cabang atas* (highest branch), had interests in opium farming, not only in Semarang but throughout Java.[11] Much of the clandestine opium that reached Java's shores in the "opium funnel" of the Juwana-Lasem area was filtered through Semarang, underwriting the fabulous luxuries the cabang atas enjoyed in their fantasy homes and gardens and their munificence for Chinese causes. A number of Chinese community officers had been to Surabaya in September on business related to the city's opium farm. Most likely they were representatives of the Kian Gwan kongsi controlled by Oei Tjie Sien and his dapper son Oei Tiong Ham.[12] The kongsi had expanded into opium farming in central and eastern Java in 1890–91, using capital acquired from buying and selling sugar and other produce.[13] During their visit to Surabaya, the Semarang officers made a pact with Yap Gwan Thay to engage his company for seven performances for a guaranteed 250 guilders per show. They also agreed to arrange for two performances to take place at Semarang's schouwburg.

The Komedie Stamboel attracted good press for its performances in Semarang in late December, but smaller audiences than was customary for komedi in Semarang turned out for the tent shows in the city's central square.[14] Some complained about the uncomfortable seats in the first-class section, and there was little repeat business with Chinese spectators. Mahieu's common-law wife, who played female leads, fell ill without warning during a 20 December 1891 performance, and the final curtain fell before the play was concluded. There was no talk about extending the performance permit in Semarang, and the company returned to Surabaya at the end of December (most likely by steamship). Mahieu stayed on in Semarang for an extra week to scout for actors and actresses to supplement the Surabaya company members. Numerous actors had left the Komedie Stamboel during the tour, and the supply of theatrically inclined Surabaya Eurasians was by now depleted.

The Komedie Stamboel's first tour might not have been a great financial success, but it brought recognition for the troupe outside Surabaya. The Batavia paper *Bintang Betawi* stoked anticipation of a forthcoming visit to the capital "in months to come," reporting that "the Semarang newspapers give high praise to the fine performances of this komedi."[15] The lukewarm response from Solo's noble elites was a disappointment, for the endorsement of Indonesian kings and sultans meant at least as much as performing before the crowned heads of Europe for nineteenth-century itinerant European and American companies. While late nineteenth-century bangsawan troupes were successful in obtaining royal patronage, accolades, and titles in Sumatra and Malaya and elsewhere, the Komedie Stamboel never managed to forge comparable alliances to the potentates of Java or other hereditary nobility of the archipelago. The greatest support in Solo initially appears to have come in fact from the city's Indo population, who recognized the artistic form as their own (even if they could not afford the Komedie Stamboel's elaborate costumes in their imitation shows).

The routine of touring also prompted new practices in publicity and administration. During this tour, play titles for forthcoming performances were posted on a signboard adjacent to the theater's entrance, programs were circulated free of charge, and advance-sale tickets were available for purchase at the theater starting at eight the morning of the performance. Other promotional innovations, to be described below, also likely were initiated by the need to sell the Komedie Stamboel as an unknown commodity during this tour.

THE KOMEDIE Stamboel had left Surabaya in November at the start of the rainy season, and upon its return, at the end of December, the monsoon was in full force, with overcast skies, daily rain, high humidity, mildew, mud, and rainwater overflowing from open sewers. Making theater in Java during the months of December to February is difficult even under the best of circumstances. Many potential spectators will not go out at night during these months. Even spectators who can afford to hire or own vehicles that can provide door-to-door transport tend to be unwilling to risk getting their clothes mucked up in a mad dash between cab and theater entrance in driving rain. The racket of pounding rain can diminish sound quality and audibility even in well-insulated theater buildings. In such conditions it is not easy to transport properties, costumes, and the apparatus of theater to a theater space without getting them wet; and costumes cannot be laundered, dried, and pressed in short order. Later in the 1890s, stambul companies tended to retire during the monsoon months, just as American circuses today winter in warm climes such as Florida. But Yap Gwan Thay had a newly built theater in Kapasan that needed programming if he was to recoup his financial investment, and after the company's protracted absence during its tour, he was perhaps anxious to reinstate the company's reputation in Surabaya.

The actors that Mahieu recruited in Semarang and the original Surabaya company members were divided into two separate troupes under the direction of Mahieu and Van der Laan. The Semarang actors, directed by Mahieu, came largely from the Karang Bidara quarter of Semarang, a lower-class area populated by poor whites and Indos. This area was sociologically similar to Krambangan—the quarter of Surabaya where the majority of the Surabaya stambul actors originated. The monthly wage of Mahieu's theatrical novices was a pittance, only fifteen to thirty guilders, as opposed to the fifty guilders earned by the original company members. The *Soerabaija-Courant,* which tended to be blunter than other Surabaya papers, editorialized that this salary was an insultingly low figure to be tendered by the "munificent" Chinese proprietor, considering that the actors had to study their lines, attend rehearsals, and perform up to four times a week. "A number of the actors appear to be robust young men. Why wouldn't they rather be wearing the soldier's uniform? It's not as if they would not cut just as fine a figure with a gun over their shoulders. . . . And would there not be more honor for them in this occupation than is currently afforded them?"[16] But the young men evidently preferred the life of the actor: there are no accounts of the newcomers quitting over pay disputes. Perhaps they were not in a position to quit, for all actors were indebted to Yap Gwan Thay by his provision of wage advances.[17]

The Komedie Stamboel opened at the Kapasan theater on 6 January 1892. The initial plan was to perform four times weekly (Sunday, Tuesday, Wednesday, and Friday) with the two troupes alternating shows. (Later this demanding schedule was reduced.) The understanding was that Mahieu's troupe, once it had been sufficiently trained and the weather was more favorable, would become the Komedie Stamboel's road company, while Van der Laan's troupe of Surabaya actors would be in permanent residence at the Kapasan theater.

A major impediment to audience attendance was the insalubrious environment of Kapasan during the rainy season. The lane in front of the theater did not have a gutter. When it rained, water spilled into houses and accumulated on the road. The lane became a slippery, foul smelling swamp. This defect was partially rectified in mid-January by a road crew that dredged the lane of mud and pounded gravel to fill potholes. But there were still a number of derelict buildings in the vicinity that gave the environment of the theater a foreboding look, the location was still perceived as being out of the way for non-Chinese, and it could be hard to find a vehicle for hire after performances.

The company used publicity to counteract the environmental deterrents and attract audiences. Spectators purchasing first-and second-class seats were eligible for a prize drawing in a lottery (*tombola*). One "European" (*ollanda*) spectator purchased fourteen tickets for a performance and did not even see the show due to overcrowding.[18]

Yap Gwan Thay engaged the balloonist Lorenzo to perform a free demonstration in the square in front of the theater on 26 January. Lorenzo had tried to fly an unmanned, tethered hot-air balloon on 10 January 1892 at the Kebon Raja gardens, to the accompaniment of a band. While hydrogen balloons were common to the point that Surabaya audiences were no longer willing to purchase tickets to see displays, hot-air balloons were something altogether more thrilling. Lorenzo's spectacular failure in front of a large, multiethnic Sunday crowd was memorialized in the press the next day with a fourteen-verse *Sair balon* (Balloon poem). The twelfth verse reads:

Balon cilaka waktu lah ini.	The balloon came to disaster at this moment.
Salahnya nyang bikin api.	It was the fault of the person feeding the fire.
Tida priksa dengen setiti.	He was not cautious in his supervision.
Balon terbakar sama sekali.	The balloon burned up completely.[19]

Yap Gwan Thay cashed in on this negative publicity for the unfortunate Lorenzo, derided as "the illustrissimo 'Perfester' [mock professor] of aviation," by recruiting him to make his next attempt at flying a hot-air balloon in front of the Kapasan theater.[20] The show took place at the less opportune time of nine on a Tuesday morning and thus attracted a smaller crowd than Lorenzo's first show. But the balloon succeeded this time in mounting to a height of about thirty meters. "This balloon is magically strange," joked *Bintang Soerabaia,* "as when it is observed by many people it does not appear to wish to rise, but yesterday morning when it was observed by [fewer] people it went up without fail. I don't know why this is so. Perhaps it needs to have offerings presented to it, but then one runs the risk of it getting full of itself and overly inflated."[21]

Another form of publicity involved distributing leaflets on the streets. This is a prosaic device today—in Europe and America at least—but was practically unprecedented in Surabaya at this time. Some of these leaflets were distributed by a pair of Javanese and Chinese employees who carried an illustrated signboard around the streets of the Pasar Besar area and handed out leaflets to one and all. One of them reached a newspaper office and was published in full and touted as a "mouthwatering program," "a kind invitation that literally nobody can turn down."

> From the tales of *The Thousand and One Nights*.
>
> Tonight we present the story of *Ali Baba and the Forty Thieves,* armed with Heaven knows how many guns. Ali Baba shoots cannons from his ship and his brother Kasim is cut in half.
>
> If one is terrified of seeing Kasim hacked in two, one need only bend one's head down, to avoid collapsing in a faint.
>
> This piece has previously been performed here, but has been entirely reworked and is much more attractive. It is presented anew due to popular request. The actors and actresses who perform in it have carefully prepared their parts for this show.
>
> What is more, at each performance Dutch and Native police will be present outside as well as in the theatre, so that Ladies and Gentlemen absolutely do not need to fear.
>
> Performances twice a week, Wednesday and Thursday.[22] Even if it rains, the show will go on.
>
> And at the end of each show there is a splendid "Tableau Vivant."
>
> I hope, thus, that Ladies and Gentlemen will come to see this splendid presentation.[23]

A Malay-language variant of this Dutch advertisement explains further that Kasim is "cut in half by a real knife, as in a magic show" and that police had been detailed to insure that "there will be no violent disturbances outside or in the theatre."[24] The invitations might have been mouthwatering, but not everyone paid equal notice to the signboard nor accepted the proffered leaflets. *Bintang Soerabaia* suggested they might have more luck the next time if music was played when the handbills were distributed.[25]

The leaflet's emphasis on special effects reflects an increased attention to scenography, stage magic, and spectacle in 1892. Yap Gwan Thay had made improvements to the Kapasan theater, purchasing sophisticated lighting equipment, constructing new scenic decor, and renewing the stock of properties before the Komedie Stamboel's return from its tour.[26] The new decor included a palette of spectacular effects of the sort regularly encountered in nineteenth-century boulevard theaters in Paris and in the theaters of London's West End but previously unknown in Malay-language theater. Newspaper advertisements from early 1892 describe "angels that appear and disappear into thin air; devils that emerge from the ground"; "an arrow shot by a prince from his bow that hits an Arabian king in his eye" and "the appearance of many robbers, tigers, and elephants in the middle of a forest"; "a prince who is killed by his step-mother and then possessed by a genie and thus comes back to life—all genies dressed in new costumes and shown flying in the sky and emerging from the earth"; "sword play and the sight of hell with people getting tormented, including having their stomachs slashed open"; and "a man burnt alive, angels flying in the open air, and the emergence of devils from the ground."[27]

Surabaya audiences would have been familiar with many of these sorts of illusions from the work of stage magicians working in the tradition of Hermann the Great, Ching Ling Foo, and Harry Kellar. It is likely in fact that some of the Komedie Stamboel's illusions were devised and constructed with the assistance of stage magician J. Calabressini.

"Professor" Calabressini was one of the most enduring itinerant performers on the komedi circuit of nineteenth-century Indonesia. There is an account of his display of "electricity, galvanism, and magnetism" in Surakarta dating from 1870.[28] His magic shows and technological

Fig. 2.1 Advertisement for a performance by stage magician Professor Anderson in Batavia. Magicians like Anderson and Calabressini were the amazement and delight of the Indonesian public; their technologies transferred easily to popular theater. *Hindia-Olanda,* 27 April 1893.

displays played theaters, halls, clubs, and tents for the next four decades.[29] Some of his shows were solo acts, but often he hooked up with other acts, such as the Great Australian Burlesque and Variety Company, under the direction of circus managers S. O. Abell and J. Olman.[30] A typical evening with the Calabressini show was a transformation act called *Exchange of Souls* (*Pengganti jiwa* in Malay or *Metempsychose of zielsverhuizing* in Dutch), which played Surabaya in July 1891. A *Bintang Soerabaia* article (which reads as a promotion placed by the magician) gives the flavor of it.

> It is genuinely and extraordinarily astonishing, as magical effects are called into being before your very eyes.
>
> At the start, a statue head is placed on a table and slowly, before your very eyes, it transforms into a living person's head without being lifted up. What is more, this living person's head transforms into a skull. After this, the skull becomes an empty cage, and then the skull is slowly filled with two finches, and then the cage slowly transforms back into a living person's head. Wah! It is astonishing and there is not a single person who can grasp how it is done. Whoever has seen it once will wish to see it a second time, as one will want to know for certain if one was asleep or really awake when one saw it the first time.
>
> Even more impressive is that the transformed objects are displayed to, and can be touched by, spectators. A ticket price of twenty-five or fifty cents is no waste of money.[31]

Calabressini's association with Yap Gwan Thay was established at least as early as August 1891, when he performed two shows of "conjuring, magnetism, and metempsychosis" at the Kapasan theater. He was back again at Kapasan in March 1892, giving magic lantern shows for children and adults on nights when the Komedie Stamboel was not performing.[32] The timing of Calabressini's reappearance in the Kapasan theater with the Komedie Stamboel's expansion of stage effects certainly does not prove that Calabressini was responsible for the raft of special effects introduced to the Komedie Stamboel in early 1892, but it does suggest it.

The Komedie Stamboel's stage technology was far from perfect—and for some this was part of its charm. Even when effects failed, it still brought pleasure to Kapasan's audience.

> An incident took place at the Komedie-Stamboel that ended well and aroused nothing other than great hilarity at the end. I do not know what the play's title was, but at the conclusion of one of their interesting shows, characteristically full of adultery, blood revenge, and other astonishing revelations, the three main characters were required to sail off to heaven. The mechanism used was naturally not as precise as those employed by Parisian fairies, but a beam and a few ropes generally allow the effect to come off quite nicely. At a certain moment someone working in the wings let one of the ropes slip, and all height gained was lost: everyone quickly toppled from the heavens to the floor, landing on top of one another. Fortunately, they were not yet high enough in heaven to cause serious injury by this fall: the women ended up with a dent here and there and the men came away with bruises on them.
>
> And the public had much more pleasure from this splendid impromptu than from the rest of the gauche and sentimental play.[33]

Surabaya audiences enjoyed the Komedie Stamboel's newly engineered effects and sparkling costumes, along with the increased quality of acting and comedy. (One ad promotes "a new and delightful song sung by a clown.")[34] Opinion was divided about the music. Not only did the company now lack the luster of the Italian Quintet, which had added so much to Surabaya performances in 1891, they were short a number of musicians. Mahieu and possibly other actors played in the band during the overture, playing from eight until nine o'clock, before mounting the stage in costume. This made for an overly sparse musical accompaniment for the duration of the show. One musically minded (but not very literate) critic reported that:

> There was no guitar or harp. I heard nothing other than violin, trumpet, and flute. It would sound better if they used a harp or three

guitars, in my opinion. I had never seen a Javanese person play music like the Italians before. There were two people playing violin, one person on trumpet, and one on flute. So it would be best to try adding a harp, and [then] it would be precisely like the Italian Quintet.

There was one Javanese person who played so well that I was quite astounded. He could play violin like a Dutchman. If they were to add three guitars, I feel that ladies and gentlemen would enjoy the music. All spectators say that the only time you can hear the sound of guitar is when Tuan A. Mahieu steps in to play guitar. When Tuan A. M. appears onstage all I hear are violins, flutes, and trumpet. Why don't they improve things by looking for three able guitar players, Dutch or Javanese, who are acceptable to audience ears, so that audience members can take pleasure in hearing them?

One can compare it to Chinese music without a *sambeyan*. It is not enjoyable. "Dutch" music without a guitar is likewise not enjoyable.[35]

One commentator, however, unequivocally preferred the musical accompaniment in January 1892 over that previously offered by the Italian Quintet, and there were some generally appreciative musical comments as well.[36]

The police presence advertised on the *Ali Baba* leaflet deterred some of the violence inside and in the vicinity of the theater, but the Komedie Stamboel remained a rough place of entertainment, and both actors and spectators were still disposed to violent behavior under the intoxicating influences of Wein, Weib, und Spiel. Once again, police were sent to the theater to arrest one of the actors for unknown offenses. "A pair of Don Juans" fought outside the theater over the affections of one of the actresses. Two Dutch speakers in the auditorium exchanged harsh words, and one slapped another in full public view. The police stood by and did nothing. Sailors and soldiers were known to be particularly rough customers, and though they were offered half-price tickets, they were banned from sitting in the box seats, presumably so as not to offend the more polite classes.[37]

The four-times-a-week performance schedule proved to be unworkable, and the Komedie Stamboel cut back to two to three shows weekly in February, sometimes combining both Mahieu's and Van der Laan's troupes. It was hard to attract spectators on rainy nights, and although the management was reluctant to cancel shows, there were nights when this could not be avoided. Audiences were multiethnic, with Muslims coming in increasing numbers, in addition to the Chinese and Indo habitués. Ticket prices remained high (fifty cents to three guilders), and newspaper contributors were forever offering suggestions about how to improve shows, but all admitted that the Komedie Stamboel was good value for the money. It was predicted that if the Komedie Stamboel were to tour central Java again, large profits would be certain this time.

The success the Komedie Stamboel enjoyed on its return to Surabaya made the following announcement on 16 February 1892 even more surprising:

> *Komedie Stamboel.* I heard from my roving news collector this morning that Tuan Mahieu, the director of the Komedie Stamboel, has requested an honorable discharge and has already received a letter of discharge with great honors. Tuan Mahieu now has a mind to work in the mountains, for it is more pleasing there and perhaps he can climb higher than his current position. Tuan M. is a very able actor and I feel he is the most talented of all.
>
> The Komedie Stamboel has lost Tuan Mahieu, a director and actor who can please the hearts of spectators. If this is permanent, I feel the Komedie Stamboel will soon stop functioning, as Tuan M. is most popular with spectators.[38]

While Mahieu was only one of the two troupe leaders in the company at the time, he was centrally involved in all aspects of the company. A number of ads for the plays carry the tag "written by A. MAHIEU for the Komedie Stamboel"; Mahieu's musical and comic acting talents were known to many.[39] The comment that Mahieu was leaving the company to work in the mountains and thus gain a "higher" position was a jest, but also an indirect way of saying that even the menial work of a mountain farmer was preferable to slaving like an urban coolie for a monthly salary of only seventy-five guilders.

Mahieu's initial plan in fact was to emulate the Italian Quintet and form a musical ensemble composed of two violins, two guitars, and a flute, which would be available for hire for dances and like functions. Mahieu had located a first violinist, someone already accustomed to playing dances and parties, and Mahieu himself was a competent guitarist. He anticipated that the ensemble would cater to European patrons and that the musicians would all wear European formal dress, which required requesting a special permit from the resident, as not all the musicians were classified as European and thus permitted to wear European clothes.

Mahieu's departure left a vacuum in the company. The responsibilities of directing the company had never been evenly proportioned between Van der Laan and Mahieu. While both were actors, Mahieu had played a more active role in writing and directing plays than Van der Laan; some advertisements from February 1892 in fact credit Van der Laan as the company director (*directeur*) while Mahieu is listed as the artistic director (*tooneel-directeur*). C. L. F. Lassing, who had functioned as an acting director for a reprise performance of *Amgiad and Assad* on 19 January 1892, was brought on as the company's stage manager (*regisseur*) in late February. In early March, C. Dinsbach stepped in as producer to look after Yap Gwan Thay's financial interests: advertisements credit Dinsbach as the owner's proxy. A number of actors left with Mahieu as well, and the two troupes were merged into one, with a consequent further reduction of the number of weekly performances. The Italian Quintet was engaged for several performances in March to restore the company's diminished musical capacity.

Despite this shakeup, the touring capacity of the Komedie Stamboel appeared not to be seriously impaired. After a brief delay, the company left town in early April 1892 to give a few shows in the central squares of Pasuruan and Probolinggo, traveling the short distances to these coastal towns in the East Hook area of Java by either train or steamship. Possibly the company visited other towns in the region as well during a period of about two months. There are no reports of Komedie Stamboel performances in May 1892, suggesting that they played small towns in eastern Java that lacked newspapers and artistically minded correspondents. A number of company members, including the actresses Maria and Rika, left the Komedie Stamboel before or during this tour. Semarang's Malay daily, *Selompret Melajoe,* fretting over the Komedie Stamboel's future, noted, "We have received news about this company, whose name is famous throughout Java for its excellent performances and the way it makes young people crazy for its pantun set to music. . . . The gentlemen and ladies who perform with it are in disorder and they are all leaving to look for work on their own."[40]

THE COMPANY weathered the personnel loss before and during the tour of eastern Java and returned to Surabaya to give tent shows in the Pasar Besar square beginning 13 May 1892. The run was initially announced as ten days, but it was extended to a full month. The rainy season was over, but fewer vendors were attracted to set up their stands in the performance area than was customary for komedi attractions playing Pasar Besar.

The end of the opening week was marred by a near fatal accident. At 8:30 P.M. on 19 May 1892, as the band was playing the overture, an elevated gasoline lamp illuminating the tent's entrance fell on a Chinese man, setting a leg of his pants on fire. In his panic, he rushed into the tent, shouting "*ajoh! ajoh!*" (woe! woe!). A pair of quick-thinking actors hurriedly extinguished the flames, preventing the fire from spreading. "The man suffered injuries to his leg only; had it been a lamp closer to the tent, the Stamboel would have gone up like fireworks."[41]

The company showed its concern for the well-being of its "hometown" by offering part of the proceeds of its performances on 29 May to 1 June to the Surabaya orphanage. (The remainder went to benefit the actors.) But the intimacy between company and city had a drawback: performers were prone to be too casual in their relations with audiences. Performers went out into the house during scenes when they were not required onstage, and backstage conversations among actors could be heard in the auditorium. Such slipshod offstage behavior distracted the attention of spectators from the play.

Mahieu went back to work for the Komedie Stamboel in May, agreeing to work for his old salary of seventy-five guilders a month. His plan to form a quintet had evidently not come to fruition, though there is evidence he traveled as far as Semarang and Batavia to scout for musicians. Mahieu was in fact required to serve time in the Surabaya prison in late May, for reasons perhaps related to his shaky finances. Mahieu's return meant that prospects for the Komedie Stamboel now "glowed like the light of the full moon."[42] There was even hope that the actors who had left the company in the preceding months might return with Mahieu's persuasion.

All was now ready for a major tour, which initially was set to cover not only eastern and central Java, but also Batavia and Singapore. Yap Gwan Thay purchased new equipment at the cost of several hundred guilders in preparation. Mahieu again took on an administrative role: advertisements from the tour note Mahieu as tooneel-directeur, responsible for adapting and directing plays. Van der Laan in turn is listed as directeur, responsible for play production and company management. Yap Gwan Thay steps into the limelight for the first time; he too is commonly noted in ads—as the eigenaar (owner).[43]

BANGKALAN WAS the first scheduled stand on the major tour of 1892. The company was already known in this nearby Madurese town from its September 1891 appearance. Its run in Bangkalan's alun-alun, which lasted only a few days at the end of June or the beginning of July, was preceded immediately by a Chinese opera troupe also owned by Yap Gwan Thay. Publicity was shared by the two endeavors: an advertisement for the Chinese opera, which promised pyrotechnics and spectacular martial arts, noted that the Komedie Stamboel would follow it soon.[44]

Yap Gwan Thay's Chinese opera troupe, which played Bangkalan for at least a week, was generally appreciated by Bangkalan audiences for its humor. One commentator severely criticized the Chinese opera's accuracy of realization of the play *Ong ciau kun,* which had been performed on request, saying "not a single thing was correct about it, as if they thought Bangkalan's Chinese did not know" how the story ought to go. The commentator went on to say that if the company was more true to the story, the troupe could play Bangkalan for two months easily.[45] There are no reports about the Komedie Stamboel's Bangkalan performances in late June or early July 1892, however.

THE NEXT reported stand was the royal court city of Surakarta, where the company had last performed in December 1891. The company had an eighteen-day permit, and performances took place on 18 July through 2 August 1892. The tent was pitched in a vacant field behind the Benteng Vastenburg, a Dutch fort constructed in 1750 adjacent to the *kraton* (royal palace). Additional personnel were recruited from Surabaya for this run. A group of Javanese musicians (*muzikan jawa*) from Kampung Kalongan (Surabaya) was brought in by train to Solo to enhance the company's musical capacities. An unnamed actress who had previously decided not to go on tour with the company also reappeared. She had been set up in a furnished house by a love-smitten fan. When her "patron" went out of town on business, she had sold off all the furnishings and left Surabaya to rejoin the company. Her lover believed she was faithful to him until he returned to an empty house.

The Komedie Stamboel attracted large crowds of appreciative spectators every night, making up for its disappointing reception in Solo in 1891. The company wisely opened with the crowd-pleasing *Aladdin*, followed by other prime plays of the repertoire. Apparently not everyone knew exactly what the Komedie Stamboel was at first. In an early notice a correspondent for a Batavia paper writing under the pseudonym Glutak Sengar (Javanese for sharp impact) awkwardly designated the company as a "wayang orang troupe known as the Komedie Stamboel."[46] But the company achieved renown before long. Spectators "who often read from the book of *The Thousand and One Nights* were pleased several times over."[47] When the company decamped on 4 August, they brought two Solonese actresses with them to their next stand in the rival court town of Yogyakarta.

THE SIXTY-FIVE kilometers from Solo to Yogyakarta (also known as Yogya) was traversed via a rail line completed in 1872. Looking out the train window, a traveler could glimpse the ruins of the Prambanan temple complex, endless rows of indigo and cassava plants, "and the frequent roofs and tall chimneys of fabriks [factories] speak[ing] of abundant prosperity for all classes." E. R. Scidmore, who made this rail trip from Solo to Yogya in the 1890s, found Yogya to be "less influenced by Chinese and Europeans" and more "authentically" Javanese than Solo. "The broad streets of the provincial capital are beautifully shaded," reports Scidmore, but Yogya's market, while admittedly "a large and important daily gathering," was deemed to have been "robbed" of its picturesqueness by "corrugated-iron and tiled sheds in formal rows." More impressive for Scidmore was "the residency, a great, low, white building with a classical portico, [which] is set in a luxuriant garden, where Madagascar palms and [other] splendid trees make halos and shadow for the grim stone images, the pensive Buddhas and fine bas-reliefs, brought from neighboring ruins. The government offices adjoin, and on any court [trial] day one may see the crowds of litigants and witnesses sitting around on their heels beneath a shadowing *waringen* [banyan] tree that would be fit bench for Druids' justice." Trials were in fact a form of spectacle in Yogya, and Scidmore herself carried away "a souvenir of one such a court day," a firefly lamp confiscated from a burglar. Scidmore was even more impressed by Yogyakarta's kraton, and its associated Taman Sari pleasure palace, than she was by Solo's royal court. She did, however, find some amusement in the contrast between the heraldry of royal Burmese elephants and a retinue of "gorgeous musicians, singers, dancers, bearers of fan and *payong* [parasol], pipe and betel-boxes" with "a sultan who plays billiards at the club and a sultana who takes a hand at whist."[48]

The Komedie Stamboel speedily erected its tent in one day in a fenced-off area of the alun-alun north of the Yogyakarta kraton. (This square remains to this date a frequent site of theatrical and other performance, overflowing with vendors and show tents during the month-long celebration of the birth of Muhammad.) The company was preceded by good word of mouth and enthusiastic press reports. Yogyakarta's Dutch newspaper, *Mataram,* promoted the company as a charity effort on behalf of the impoverished Indo actors, echoing Surabaya's Dutch press of 1891. *Mataram* referred to the actors euphemistically as "children of the Indies."[49]

The company was enhanced musically by the recruitment of another Surabaya musician, Italian harpist G. de Pierri, whose presence was noted in advertisements. De Pierri had arrived in Surabaya in early 1892, advertising in the newspaper his availability to give harp lessons and play small dance parties and soirées. He was evidently unable to make ends meet as a soloist, and he agreed to join the Komedie Stamboel as harpist and musical director in August. De Pierri was the only European; all the other musicians were Indos or Muslims.

The Komedie Stamboel was a great hit with Yogyakarta audiences, attracting large, multiethnic crowds over the course of its eighteen-day run (4–21 August 1892). The Komedie Stamboel was the talk of the town.

> PETRUK: Hey! Where have you been?
>
> SOROITO: Oh, Truk, I've just seen the Komedie Stamboel.
>
> PETRUK: How much were tickets?
>
> SOROITO: I paid three guilders for a first-class seat.
>
> PETRUK: You have got to be kidding! Well, was the show any good or not?
>
> SOROITO: Oh, it was great, really, with its play about the chronicles of the genie king and the Iblis devil king. And the dialogue and song was excellent, the songs fit with the music and were loud and clear. One could say that there has never before been a komedi like this one in Yogya. It soothed my thoughts.
>
> PETRUK: Was it better than when Tuan Wilson came to Yogya [with his circus]?
>
> SOROITO: Oh, Truk! That was something else altogether. That gentleman presented astonishing sights, but his show did not soothe my heart.[50]

Two poems were published to commemorate the event of the Komedie Stamboel's run in Yogya. Both poems "provide an insight into the way people experienced great events punctuating their everyday life."[51]

An untitled seventeen-verse homage sent to the *Bintang Soerabaia* by "Sendirian Kromo," a Chinese man from Semarang, singles out music and visuals for particular praise.[52] Listeners are said to be immobile "as if tied to a ball and chain," costumes are likened to "pictures in an almanac published by the Van Dorp firm in Semarang illustrating the king of Turkey," and the accordance of scenery with story caused spectators to be astonished (heran).

Tan Tjiook San's "Sair Komedi Stamboel," which appeared in the *Almanak bahasa Melajoe* (Malay Almanac), has a different take on the theatrical experience.[53] The bulk of the syair's 104 quatrains is taken up with a detailed account of *Siti Senimbar,* a play based on an *Arabian Nights* tale and a core item in the Komedie Stamboel repertoire. This story follows the trials and tribulations of the eponymous heroine, the daughter of the raja of Koja from the land of the Tartars. A genie from Mount Kap desires sexual congress with her and transforms himself into a young man to present his suit. Siti Senimbar angrily rejects the genie's offer, but the couple is discovered conversing by the raja, who accuses his daughter of having premarital relations and charges his wazir with taking her to the forest and executing her for her suspected wantonness. (The genie himself conveniently disappears before the raja enters.) Before he is able to fulfill his duty, the wazir is overcome by the power of the genie, who kidnaps the princess. But the genie is defeated by a heaven-sent *bidadari* (heavenly nymph), who descends to earth to defend Siti Senimbar. Two men gathering wood in the forest (conventional comic figures) attempt to rape Siti Senimbar but are prevented from doing so by a bidadari. The sultan of Persia meanwhile has dreamed that he should go to the forest and make the woman he finds there his principal wife (*permeisuri*). He meets Siti Senimbar, she accepts his offer of marriage, and they return to his kingdom. In the end Siti Senimbar is reunited with her father, who has grown sad with regret for his cruel actions and is overjoyed to see his daughter again.

Tan Tjiook San's description of the play is essentially a story summary, rather than a description of a performance. No attempt is made to describe how the various magical effects are executed. There are no descriptions given of costumes or scenery, nor are musical instruments or pieces specifically mentioned. What absorbs Tan Tjiook's attention is the range of emotions manifested by the play's characters, particularly those of Siti Senimbar. Reading the poem, we are drawn into the human side of the stage drama. When, for example, the raja gives his judgment,

Siti Senimbar sangetpun susa,
Hendak di ukum jiwa binasa.
Mata bercucur sahingga basa,
Memuhun ampun senantiasa:

Siti Senimbar is greatly troubled,
For she has been sentenced to death.
Her eyes well up and tears flow,
As she relentlessly begs for mercy:

"Ayahandaku yang amat cinta,
"Anakda muhun kabawah duli
"Hamba bersaksi Tuhan Samista,
"Laku berzina tida sekali."

"My father, whom I love,
I beg your attention.
I vow before God on High
That I have never had intercourse.

"Aduh ayanda jangan kejamken
"Suru membunu jiwaku ini,
"Hamba memuhun ayah ampunken,
"Atas dosaku sekali ini."

"Oh, father, do not be so cruel
To order my death like this,
I beg your forgiveness, father,
"For any sin I have committed, just this once.

"Muhun ayanda punya kasihan,
"Suka ampunin jiwa anakda,
"Jika ayanda tida kasihan,
"Sayang lah hamba sedengnya muda."

"I beg you to have mercy
And grant forgiveness to your daughter.
If you do not grant your mercy,
It would be tragic as I am still young.

"Misi muda terhukum mati,
"Leher terpanggal parang yang tajam,
"Oleh ayanda yang kurang titi,
"Tida kasihan berati kejam."

"Still young, and sentenced to death,
With head cut off with a sharp blade
By a father oblivious to the truth,
Without mercy, that is to say cruel."

Bagenda morka pun tamba bangat,
Hingga badannya basa berkringrat,

The monarch's anger became even greater
Making him sweat and wet all over.

Cinta anaknya pun tida ingat, Wazir di prenta pun sangat-sangat.	He forgets entirely his love for his child, And gives the wazir a most extreme order.
Lekas Wazirku bikin binasa, Ini binatang yang besar dosa, Di dalem rimba kaya biasa, Bangkeinya kasi makan raksasa.	"Go, Wazir, and kill This animal who has sinned so greatly [Do it] in the forest as is the custom And feed her corpse to the *raksasa* [ogres]."[54]

"Sair Komedi Stamboel" is more than just an account of the Komedie Stamboel's first appearance in Yogyakarta. It is an attempt to explore bodily emotion and thereby reproduce some of the excitement surrounding the theater at the time, aptly understood by the poem's author as a *komedi model sekarang,* a contemporary form and model for doing komedi, a theater that "brings happiness."[55]

But while the author of the syair was absorbed by the intensity of the acting, clearly the theater's appeal to Yogyakarta audiences was multiple. Some male spectators were lovestruck by the beauty of the company's ten actresses, others particularly enjoyed the music, the soothing stories, or the exciting visual effects. Spectators reacted viscerally to the performance as individuals. "Sendirian Kromo" was spellbound by the music, and others report rocking in time to the rhythm. The actress playing the eponymous female lead in *Siti Senimbar* was said to be "as pretty as a picture. She made the hearts of spectators pound; they felt compelled to reach out and seize her."[56] Mahieu, who routinely performed the male lead parts, came in for particular praise as an actor: he was said to be graced with "God-given talent."[57]

The Yogyakarta run was not without its hitches. The long intermissions (meant to give time to use the adjacent buffet hall and effect scene changes) resulted in shows that went on until one in the morning—far too late for children, the *Mataram* reviewer noted. An actress disappeared from the company without notice or trace; a reward was posted for information leading to her whereabouts. The company's Chinese cashier, Tan Swi Tjwan, died on 13 August, after suffering from a fever. There was a near tragedy at the 16 August 1892 show, when the gasoline lamps suspended inside the tent were accidentally set into violent motion, generating panic in the audience. "Fire, earthquake, amok!" Gentle ladies shoved each other, mothers shouted for their children, people were trampled underfoot. Even the members of Yogyakarta's royal family seated on stage could not retain their composure. Fortunately, order was soon restored and serious injuries were thus averted.[58]

The Komedie Stamboel also faced steep competition from another show in town: the Abell and Klaer circus. The circus played Yogyakarta from 11 through 15 August in a lot west of the Benteng Vredeburg fort, within earshot of the alun-alun. Circuses were always surefire draws, and tickets were actually cheaper than the Komedie Stamboel. *Mataram* predicted that Yogyakarta was not a large enough town to host two komedi troupes.[59] Indeed, only twenty spectators showed up at the Komedie Stamboel on Abell and Klaer's opening night. The show was cancelled and spectators received their money back. But attendance figures at the Komedie Stamboel bounced back, and the company was able to hold its own against the horse show. Another competing event was a show trial of three thieves who had stolen from the kraton. The trial went on all day and late into the night on 20 August, and the many lights outside the court of law even attracted curious Komedie Stamboel spectators.[60] But even with all these interruptions and impediments, the company succeeded financially as never before, clearing two thousand guilders from the run.

The last night the Komedie Stamboel performed in Yogyakarta was greeted with an unprecedented display of audience solidarity. "The farewell song sung by the ladies and gentlemen of the company delivered the public, particularly those in the fourth ring, into rapture."[61]

Dari Jokja pergi Semarang,	From Yogya we go to Semarang
Kami brangkat lah besuk pagi,	We leave tomorrow morning.
Main di Jokja pun banyak girang,	Playing Yogya has brought much joy.
Lain taun kombali lagi.	We will return another year.[62]

Mataram reported that as they sang this farewell song, "there was such a racket that the artists could not continue and instead of singing burst into roaring laughter. The performance ended abruptly."[63]

The departure of the troupe did not mean an end to stambul activity in Yogya. "The Komedie Stamboel was on people's lips, though the company was no longer to be seen. People recalled it, and decided to imitate its art. People sang stambul songs, they did line dances, they whistled, causing surprise and astonishment. The stambul songs were so sweet. Many enjoyed them. Some decided to use the model and make theater of this sort."[64] Two amateur companies were formed in Yogyakarta in quick succession. The first was composed of young European men and women (burghers), mostly family members of a certain Abraham P. They performed once in Abraham P.'s house for the entertainment of themselves and their friends. The second company was composed of Ambonese soldiers, joined by eight young ladies. Dramatics were a popular activity in the armed forces of the Netherlands Indies, and many garrisons in the Indies produced all-male revues and light comedies, for their own amusement and the entertainment of the general public.[65] The addition of actresses, the glittering costumes, musical accompaniment by a strijkje quintet (minus harp), and the colorful stambul songs made the production of *Orang terbangoen dari tidoernja* (The sleeper awakened) a memorable event. The performance took place in the dance hall of "De Vereeniging," the social club for Yogyakarta's European elite. A dress rehearsal on 26 October was attended by military from the garrison and children of members of the club. The performance occurred on 28 October, in conjunction with an annual celebration in honor of the memory of Jan van Arkelen, a prominent Yogyakarta resident. It was attended mostly (if not entirely) by society members, who paid three guilders each to attend, yielding a tidy profit for the actors.[66]

A slightly more professional effort followed in November. A Chinese man called L. H. G. from Kampung Ketandan established a stambul troupe and gave Saturday night performances at the house of his mistress in Kampung Kerkop. L. H. G. himself played the role of robber chief, and his stature and virility earned him the admiration of the prostitutes and mistresses in attendance. It was L. H. G.'s (apparently unrealized) ambition to make enough money from these shows to finance a touring company. He had good costumes but needed still to construct the scenic backdrops and to purchase other equipment.[67]

The hype surrounding the Komedie Stamboel went up a further notch in Semarang, the next stand on the company's tour. While the Komedie Stamboel had enjoyed only limited success in this central Javanese city in 1891, this time it received rave notices and robust audiences. The company had originally intended to do only thirteen performances here, but it enjoyed such a popular following that in September the performance permit was extended to nearly a full month (24 August–22 September 1892). Semarang's press took an active role in discussing, critiquing, and effecting change on the theater, and the company management, highly sensitive to all criticism, responded with alacrity.[68]

In Semarang the company's advance machine was well oiled and its advertising mechanisms well tuned. An advance man had visited Semarang in early August to arrange the performance permit, scout the performance site, contact the press, and rent a house as a dormitory for the performers and other company members in the Blakang Kebon area of the city.[69] The company arrived in Semarang with a cast of twelve actors and eight actresses on 22 August. A number of these actors and actresses had only been hired that month. It was difficult to keep company members, particularly actresses (who were forever leaving to marry and become mistresses of love-smitten spectators), when the base salary was still only fifty guilders a month, plus travel expenses, accommodation, and a nightly bonus dependent on ticket income.[70] As roustabouts erected the tent in the alun-alun, the actors, including Mahieu, were put to work on the day of arrival distributing leaflets on the street. The handbill stated that the Komedie Stamboel would soon perform in Semarang and that it was "better than before, with new costumes, and would bring pleasure to young men for the songs sung by the actresses please the heart."[71] Exclamation points bristled in advertisements, conveying the sense that the company's visit was a participatory event that could not be missed. "Magnificent! wonderful! nearly impossible! come, see, and judge for yourself!"[72] The company's hyperbolic finances were also on display in notices and advertisements. A single costume reputedly cost a hundred and fifty guilders, and Yap Gwan Thay was said to have invested a hundred thousand guilders in the company to date, of which seventy thousand guilders had been recouped.[73]

Advertisements noted not only the scheduled performances, but also the availability of the Komedie Stamboel Quintet under the direction of de Pierri for engagements before 8 P.M. or after midnight.[74]

The company gave its opening performance at Semarang's schouwburg on 24 August to a small but elite audience. The show finished at 1:15 A.M., prompting *De locomotief* to joke, "[N]obody will therefore complain that he did not see enough for his money."[75] The management did not take this jibe lightly and sought out the reporter to inform him that the late ending was not the company's fault. Rather, it occurred because "the concierge would not give his permission to make use of the scenographic equipment owned by the schouwburg,"[76] implying a European elite prejudice against the company, a social barrier that would have to be overcome collectively by company and audience in performances to follow.

The company opened in its tent in Semarang's alun-alun on 27 August to enthusiastic notices from both the Malay and Dutch press. *Selompret Melajoe* warned readers not to expect the performances to be the same as European opera; the Komedie Stamboel was nevertheless "excellent, attractive, and refined" in its own right.[77] Mahieu came up for particular praise as a director for "boldly bearing the weight of managing [the actors] and rehearsing them."[78]

The troupe played to full houses throughout the alun-alun run, selling out many shows. An itinerant Japanese acrobatic troupe, referred to in Dutch as the Japansche Azoemakomedie and promoted by E. J. Streiff, was in town at the same time, performing in a tent sandwiched between a Montagnes Russes attraction and the newly constructed Kauman mosque (built in 1889–90 by architect G. I. Garnier) in the alun-alun from 10 through 13 September. The Japanese troupe's astounding acts included pole balancing, juggling, rope and ladder tricks; evenings regularly ended with a dramatic pantomime. But the proximity of this spectacular Japanese entertainment did not substantially cut into Komedie Stamboel ticket sales. A chance September rain drenched the ground of the alun-alun and left it a muddy morass, but even as the rain came down, a respectable 213 spectators still turned up for the troupe's show. The alun-alun was reserved to be used as a parade ground on 30 August, necessitating the cancellation of a show. Even then, the Komedie Stamboel's musical ensemble was able to hire itself out to play a ball at the Harmonie Club for the tidy fee of one hundred guilders.

Semarang audiences were rowdy and disorderly, and the management did not always treat spectators with the respect they felt they were owed. The local press, above all Semarang's Malay daily *Selompret Melajoe,* acted to interpret clashes in the theater in terms of social frictions and tensions. It intervened in the interests of propriety and mutual respect. The newspaper understood the theater as being a site of discipline, in which both audience and company were expected to behave in terms of social norms (*adat*). Individuals and groups were "reminded" how to behave properly, though there were no prior instances of such action. In describing inappropriate behavior and insisting on proper decorum, the newspaper was in fact generating a model for how people should act in the public sphere. An unwritten contract was being inscribed.

> Spectators who had purchased second- and third-class seats found these sections already fully occupied. They had not been told of this at the door. They thus snatched up seats in the first-class section, a small infraction of the norms. It is hard to respond to people who do not behave by the norms, but the management is reminded in this regard to insure they institute strictly binding rules.[79]

In another clash over etiquette, the management was faulted.

> We remind the usher at the front entrance that rough behavior is never appropriate. If someone who has received a complimentary ticket comes with his wife, making two in the party, they might not be able to gain entrance as the ticket is only valid for the holder himself. But they should be informed of this before entering. They should not be first let in and then roughly cut off and be prevented [from sitting down]. The babah [Chinese] owner should remember that a newspaper's report can lead to loss [of profit]; therefore one should not behave as one would in a market or a food stall. If one

> wishes to attract morally upright spectators, one must behave according to higher norms.[80]

These accounts suggest that everyone in the field of performance was learning the rules, and their social roles, together. The complimentary ticket holder was more than likely the reporter himself. His assumption that his complimentary ticket was valid for two people marks him as a naive participant in the theatrical field, but the lack of politesse demonstrated by the front-of-house staff makes the management the bigger culprit in the reporter's telling.

Other critiques of audience behavior are marked explicitly in terms of race and gender. The rowdy behavior of *sinyo* (European youths) at a performance reflected badly on all Europeans: "Word has it that last night Sheriff Van der Plas prevented rowdy acts by sinyo and even threatened to eject them. . . . It is true that these sinyo caused embarrassment to their race . . . . We hope they are now more mindful for the sake of racial harmony."[81] When a Chinese spectator came up for criticism for inconsiderate behavior toward female spectators, however, the newspaper made it clear that his faults were individual and should not be ascribed to Chinese more generally.

> The other night, a Chinese man came to see the Komedie Stamboel and idly asked the usher where he should sit. After finding out, he promptly sat down in a seat adjacent to a group of young women [*nyonya nyonya*], despite there being dozens of unoccupied seats nearby. It is true that he paid for a ticket as anyone else and that he was there to enjoy himself, but what he did was not really beneficial to anyone. But there was more. When he was about to sit down he noticed that a shawl belonging to one of the ladies was on the unoccupied seat. He then picked it up and threw it down on another seat. A company member noticed this inappropriate act and approached the babah [Chinese man] to point out a more appropriate seat in the same class.
>
> Because this is the first time that such a gross offense has been so blatantly committed by a Chinese person, it must necessarily be con-

demned, so that the offenses of one or two individuals are not blamed on the entire race. The babah who has behaved so rudely is issued with a reminder. It is not intended that other [Chinese] people become the object of public scorn. The reminder is intended for him alone.[82]

The newspaper's social critique of Komedie Stamboel did not end with what went on below the footlights, but also incorporated the regional orientation and language use of those onstage.

> We hope that the actors and actresses will not take offense if we point out a minor fault.
>
> Every language has its proper intonation, and this cannot but be followed, otherwise people will say "this person is inadequate, that person doesn't stack up." Hearing authentic [*tulen*] Malay language spoken with an eastern Javanese intonation gives us the creeps. It is even more appalling than hearing Dutch spoken very poorly. . . . we [also] suggest that it would be good to try out Malay Javanese proverbs on one or two occasions.[83]

Proper language use—and the differences between various regional forms of Malay—was to become of increasing concern in the years to come.

Even the behavior of actors and spectators offstage was scrutinized in terms of larger social relations, as when a stambul actress left the company to become the mistress of a Chinese man: "Many people here are talking about the son of a rich Chinese who is keeping this woman. The news is that they often go out riding for pleasure in a carriage in the Chinese quarter."[84] Such a tidbit of gossip heightened awareness of class and race: it was not just a man keeping an actress as a mistress, but the son of a wealthy and respected Chinese man. They did not simply ride in a carriage: they rode in the Chinese quarter.

It is apparent from this press coverage that Semarang marks a new phase of the company's history, potentiated by the Komedie Stamboel's increasing presence in the public sphere. It was not only a touring theater but a social barometer. Social issues involving both performers and spectators were on display onstage, and in the auditorium and environs of the theater. These could be inspected discursively in the press and mediated. In this public metatheatrical forum, the press played a crucial role, endowed as it was with moral powers of sanction and prescription. Newspaper articles were no mere mirrors of reality, but tools that shaped reality. The press expected the prerogative of dialogical participation, and the company was responsive to its criticism.

The company tore down the tent on the alun-alun the day after the last show and was on the way to Batavia on 25 September. But its departure, as in other stands along the Komedie Stamboel's route, was hardly the end of stambul for Semarang. A Semarang citizen named F. Simons hatched the idea of forming a resident stambul company in imitation of the Komedie Stamboel. This was conceived as a civil project of the sort so popular in Semarang. It was a way of "injecting life into the ramai quality of the city, to entertain hearts wearied from working," as well as providing work for Semarang's impoverished Indos.[85] The estimated eighty thousand guilders required to found the troupe would be divided into lots that shareholders could purchase. (As *Selompret Melajoe* pointed out, this sum would be sufficient as there would be no need for a resident company to purchase a tent.)

Malay-Language Komedie

In order to form a Malay-language komedi troupe (like the Komedie Stamboel) to provide a source of income for unemployed Europeans who have difficulty providing for their families, it is requested that friends invest in shares at one hundred guilders each, with eighty shares in all.

Each year on 31 January the profits will be divided among the eighty investors. Whoever among the readers is willing to assist please inform the person whose name is noted below how much you would care to invest. At a future date, I will respond to my friends and provide an address for where the money is to be sent.

Very best wishes,
And with fond hopes,
Tuan F. Simons

Simons's letter was published and endorsed in Semarang's newspapers in October 1892, and his project was reported in newspapers published elsewhere in Java.[86] It is not clear how many investors responded, but by February 1893 a stambul company had been established in Semarang. The company was known as the Komedie Perzie (also spelled Persie), the same name as the generic designation given to the Parsi theatrical troupes from the Indian subcontinent that toured Java in the 1880s. The Komedie Perzie, contrary to initial expectations, was formed as an itinerant troupe, the first professional competitor to the Komedie Stamboel. In the year that followed its debut, the Komedie Perzie appeared in Surabaya and small towns in central and west Java including Tegal, Garut, and Tasikmalaya. Its reviews were mediocre (*De Locomotief* said it required more rehearsals at its debut), and it seems to have folded after about a year of operation. But it was the first troupe featuring the notorious actress Lien Gemser.[87]

Batavia was the terminus of the Komedie Stamboel's 1892 tour. While the earliest version of the itinerary included Singapore and other parts of British Malaya, the capital city embraced the Komedie Stamboel with such fervent devotion that the company decided instead to stay in western Java. The Batavia engagement marked the Komedie Stamboel's arrival as a transregional art form, for while Surabaya, Semarang, and the other cities previously visited by the company had their own vibrant cultural scenes in the 1890s, it was cosmopolitan, if-you-can-make-it-here Batavia that set the fashions emulated throughout the Netherlands Indies.

Batavia was a city of approximately 105,000 people in 1892 (including 70,000 Muslims; 24,000 Chinese; and 10,000 Europeans).The headquarters of the most important business concerns in the Indies were centralized here, and while the governor-general in practice ruled from his residence in Buitenzorg (also known as Bogor), officially Batavia was the center of government as well. Batavia was proud of the library and museum collections of the Koninklijk Bataviaasch Genootschap van Kunsten en Wetenschaapen (Royal Batavian Society for Arts and Societies), the oldest scientific society in Asia (founded 1778). Batavia's schouwburg (opened in 1821), adjacent to the Pasar Baru market, was the premiere European stage of the Indies.

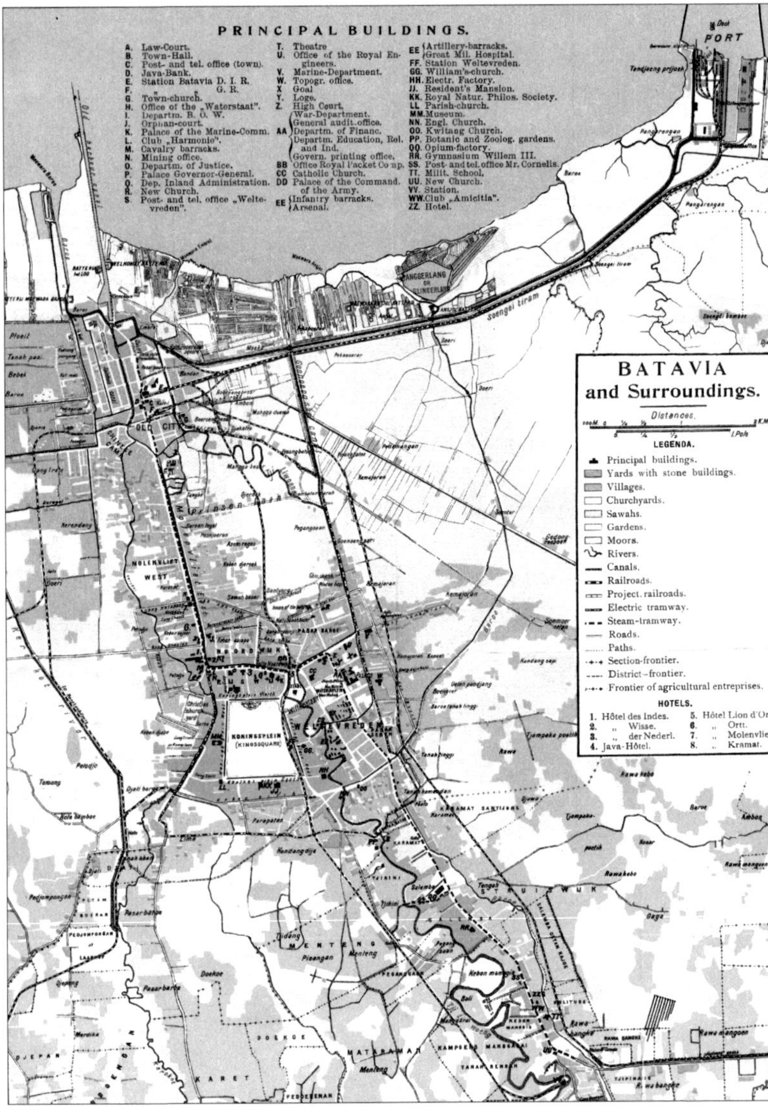

Map 3. Batavia. J. F. van Bemmelen and G. B. Hooyer, *Guide through Netherlands India, Compiled by Order of the Koninklijke Paketvaart Maatschappij* (London: Thos. Cook and Son, 1903), facing p. 16.

While its population was actually smaller than that of Surabaya until the twentieth century, Batavia was a larger, more sprawling town than any other in the Indies, divided into the swelteringly hot, densely built-up northern region (*Betawi ilir,* lit., downstream Batavia) and the more suburban, spacious, and cooler southern upland region (*Betawi udik,* up-stream Batavia). Steam trams (introduced in 1882) provided inexpensive and efficient public transportation; there was also a riot of various sorts of horse-drawn carriages and dogcarts for private hire. Telephones were introduced to Batavia in 1882 and were still somewhat of a novelty. In late nineteenth-century Europe, the telephone was used primarily for business. But in Batavia the telephone was taken as a medium for social interaction. There was some concern among elites that this technology would mean the end of casual visiting and face-to-face socializing.

Many Europeans continued to work in the old town (*kota*) of Batavia in the north of the city, with "its crowded bazaars and streets, [and] bricked canals where small natives splash and swim, women beat the family linen, and men go to and fro in tiny boats, all in strange travesty of the solemn canals of the old country."[88] Few Europeans actually resided in the old town or the ilir region, however, favoring instead the cooler clime and more spacious residences of the southern suburbs. Most preferred the area around the immense Koningsplein (king's square), known in Malay as *tanah lapang Gambir* (Gambir field), where military parades and artillery exercises were regularly carried out. Further to the south was Meester Cornelis (present-day Jatinegara). This army garrison town was only incorporated into the city of Batavia in 1935, but by the late nineteenth century it was already a popular suburban residence for Europeans and Indos. It had a smaller percentage of Chinese than Batavia proper and a majority Sundanese population.

Chinese were largely concentrated in the old "Chinese camp" in present-day Glodok, but some also lived in Chinese wards in Tanah Abang, Pasar Senen, and Pasar Baru. There was an Arab quarter in Pakojan in the old town. Tamil shops were to be found in Pasar Baru and a cluster of Indian domiciles were located in the Koningsplein area. The majority population was, of course, made up of Muslims who lived in urban kampung. There were many Javanese and Sundanese migrants, but most Indonesians were members of the *kaum Betawi,* the locals who spoke a distinctive regional dialect of Malay as their first language, and worked as carriage drivers, barbers, messenger-runners, shop boys, construction workers, and street vendors. "Like London's cockneys, with whom they shared a well-developed sense of humor, they remained basically provincial, and were never in a position to exploit what the town had to offer, and therefore could not play a significant role in the town's economy."[89]

In contrast, Batavia's Indos contributed to the city's cultural life in ways disproportionate to their actual numbers. Indos were active in writing, editing, and publishing newspapers, poetry, and fiction and had also developed kroncong (originally associated with descendents of Portuguese slaves known as Mardijkers) as their own urban folk music. Poor Indos lived in urban kampung such as Kemayoran in the same style as the kaum Betawi. Some Indo men took to criminal activities and became known euphemistically as "crocodiles" (*buaya*), while Indo women from deprived circumstances often became prostitutes.

A troupe performing in the same genre as the Komedie Stamboel was nearly established in Batavia in 1891, bankrolled by "a famous person together with a few wealthy Chinese."[90] The near simultaneity of this announcement with the Komedie Stamboel's first Surabaya performance suggests that the troupes were related in some way. It was expected that performances of "the same Persian tales" performed by the Komedie Stamboel in Surabaya would be staged in a tent in Tanah Abang. Two thousand guilders was committed to purchasing costumes so that "a caliph named Harun al-Rashid will consequently not enter dressed as the cabman in a royal funeral procession, meaning with a tattered coat, and neither will the loquacious Scheherazade appear in the costume of Cinderella."[91] The Batavia troupe never actually performed, likely because it failed to receive the necessary permits. Batavia's authorities were wary of endorsing popular theater in the wake of the 1890 wayang wong ban. News that Surabaya's Komedie Stamboel planned to play Batavia prompted the following comment: "Before arriving, we think that the management of the company should request permission, for as is known, the authorities here do not at all like to give permits for

KOMEDI STAMBOEL.

Tanahlapang Manggabesar.

Soedah termasboer di Hindia Nederland, belon tahoe maen di negri Betawi.

Ini maenan amat bagoesnja, pake bahasa Melaijoe, soepaija pantes didengar orang.

Jang maen semoea toean-toean dan nona-nona pranakan dari Djawa. Ini permaenan sebagi ABDOEL MOELOEK tetapi lebi bagoes, kerna boleh liat Kotta, Straat, Goenoeng, Telaga, Laoet, sekalian Roemah Radja dan Sultan negri Arab.

Tjeritaännja terpoengoet dari boekoe 1001 Malem.

MOELAI MAEN 29 SEPTEMBER 1892.

Ambil tjeritanja

„Toekang ikan sama Djin"

Harga tempat:

LOGE	. . . .	*f*	4.—
KLAS	I	„	3.—
„	II	„	2.—
„	III	„	1.—
„	IV	„	0.50

Tooneel directeur

454 A. MAHIEU.

Fig. 2.2. Advertisement for *The Fisherman and the Genie* emphasizing spectacle. "One can see a city, street, mountain, lake, sea, and also the palaces of kings and sultans of Arabia." *Bintang-Barat,* 29 September 1892.

this and many other sorts of entertainment that can lead to the destruction of Muslim families."[92]

The situation was different in 1892. The Komedie Stamboel arrived in Batavia at the end of September 1892 on the wave of considerable advance publicity and excitement. "Already famous throughout the Netherlands Indies, in its first Batavia appearance," reads the opening of the first Malay-language advertisement.[93] A Dutch advertisement likewise trumpets how the company is "famed for its sumptuous [*prachtige*]" performances.[94]

Mahieu now occupied a dominant position in the company's direction, and while Van der Laan remained an actor in the Komedie Stamboel through 1893, all advertisements with signatures give sole directorial credit to Mahieu (who is noted alternately as directeur or tooneel-directeur). The company's size remained the same as it had been in Semarang (twelve actors and eight actresses) and there were still six musicians in the band, including the musical director, de Pierri (who played harp), as well as two violins, guitar, flute, and trumpet.[95]

Batavia newspaper readers had been following the travels of the troupe for many months now, and numerous notices, advertisements, reviews, story summaries, and the like appeared in all Batavia newspapers. *Bintang-Barat* established a particularly close relationship with the company, covering its activities at length. It appears the paper's editors, J. Kieffer and E. F. Wiggers, regularly received complimentary tickets in exchange. *Bintang-Barat* "catered to readers of all races and religions," featuring "wide-ranging news" that covered local events as well as overseas in unornamented and easy-to-read Malay.[96] The newspaper was also an important vehicle for Malay fiction and poetry in the 1880s and 1890s, serializing numerous translations of what we might now call world literature, as well as original works, including the first publication of Gijsbert Francis's famous novelette *Nyai Dasima*.[97]

Bintang-Barat articles about the Komedie Stamboel were peppered with helpful suggestions.[98] Some of these comments were directly addressed to Mahieu. An offer was made as well to print abbreviated story summaries of the plays to be performed written "in low Malay to increase the pleasure of the public."[99] (This offer was actually taken up in 1893.) The coverage in *Bintang-Barat* was in fact so intense and spiced with superlatives that a rival newspaper accused *Bintang-Barat* of maintaining a "double standard," for it barely referred to other theatrical performances in the first weeks of October, while it "wrote without end about Komedie Stamboel performances and how spectators never get bored as there is a new play every night and how the houses are always at full capacity." The theatrical company was suspected (rightly, no doubt) of benefiting from a nepotistic relation with the newspaper, and indeed *Bintang-Barat* provided detailed coverage of the Komedie Stamboel for the next years—although without such a high degree of enthusiasm.[100]

The Komedie Stamboel opened on 29 September 1892 in the Mangga Besar square in the Glodok area and played there through 13 October.[101] This was the heart of Batavia's old Chinese camp, where "tall, narrow houses, quaintly decorated and crowned with red-tiled roofs, that flame out against the contrasting azure of the sky, stand in close-built rows; the wide street is full of jostling carts and vans, fairly humming with traffic; and the people move with an energy and briskness."[102]

Tickets, at up to four guilders for box seats, were expensive by any standard, and there was some doubt expressed whether Batavia spectators would be willing to pay such prices. And once again, the Komedie Stamboel faced steep competition. The same Japanese acrobatic troupe that had been the Komedie Stamboel's chief competitor in Semarang performed on from 4 to 9 October in Glodok, while Stanley's Comic and Burlesque Opera Company performed operetta and light opera at the nearby schouwburg beginning 9 October.

Audiences were initially drawn by curiosity, tantalized by the company's novelty. Many were keen to see how the Komedie Stamboel compared to other forms of European and Indonesian theater. Before the opening, *Bintang-Barat* made comparisons to French and Italian opera as well as Abdul Muluk theater.[103] The following week the comparison was with bangsawan in Sumatra, as "among the many spectators who came to see the Komedie Stamboel in Mangga Besar there are gentlemen and ladies from Deli, who were frequent viewers of bangsawan in Deli. They report that although bangsawan in Deli is indeed excellent, in their view the Komedie Stamboel is even better."[104] A more sober assessment, almost clinical in tone, was offered by the influential Dutch-language newspaper *Java Bode*. "One should not come in the expectation of seeing an outstanding theatrical troupe, or one will end up let down. But one will not depart disappointed if one is satisfied with observing how a company made up exclusively of Indos possessing not even the lowest standard of direction interpret the art of theater." Even *Java Bode* had to admit, however, that the company exerted an attraction on Chinese, Native, and European alike for the "uniqueness of its mise-en-scène and the acting of its artists."[105]

Some effort was made, as in past engagements, to justify the theater as a form of charity for the actors. *Bintang-Barat* trotted out the familiar rhetoric that "the poverty of these ladies and gentlemen brought them to live the lives of actresses and actors, as a way to work for a living, which is preferable to those in Batavia who live as prostitutes and in the way of 'crocodiles.'"[106] But this same article gives the sense that this was more than a charitable undertaking; the first engagement of the Komedie Stamboel in Batavia was a special occasion, an important event in the cultural life of the city.

> One is sure to think from this name that this komedi is made up of Turkish people. But that is not so. This group is made up of young Indo men and women who have been trained in how to perform komedi in Malay and perform stories adapted from the Arabic chronicle *The Thousand and One Nights*.
>
> When this komedi was still performing in Surabaya we read frequently in the newspapers about how excellent and humorous it was, but we could not report on this as we had not witnessed it with our own eyes. . . . We have just seen two nights of performances and what we observed pleases our heart and is the joy of many.
>
> When one enters and looks around the komedi's tent one is reminded of a circus, as the seating arrangements are of the same sort, with third-, second-, and first-class seats. And if one goes to the border of the first-class seats [between the spectators and the stage] there is a musical band, composed of one harp, two violins,

one guitar, one flute, and one trumpet with a very crude sound. The music is played by Indo men, while an Italian plays the harp.

The music plays before the play begins and during intervals. This is meant to please the hearts of spectators so that they do not wait in silence.

When the play is about to begin a bell sounds and the curtain lifts. Onstage are the actors who act in character according to the roles they play. . . . The actor playing a king is dressed like a king. The actor playing a servant is dressed as a servant. They enact a story adapted from the chronicles of *The Thousand and One Nights* and sing pantun that are appropriate to this chronicle, accompanied by the aforementioned musical instruments. They sing sweet and melodious songs in a European manner, like *Aku ingat pada mu* (I remember you), *Bintang siang* (Morning star), and the like.

Among the actresses there are a number who are attractive and have clear voices, while among the actors are two who are comic actors. Whenever these two appear, they are certain to evoke laughter from the public as they act like clowns. These two men are very funny and capable of gaining the public's sympathy.[107]

It is evident from this effusive description that the Komedie Stamboel introduced a new mode of doing theater in Malay to Batavia. Nobody had seen Malay-speaking actors singing European-style songs accompanied by European musical instruments before. The closeness of fit between performer and character was likewise unprecedented. The company curried favor with other papers as well, including the Dutch-language *Bataviaasch Nieuwsblad,* which praised the quick pace and energy of an eight-act *Ali Baba,* singling out the costumes and dramatic interpretation of character as particularly praiseworthy.[108] The same paper also characterized a tableau vivant entitled "Neptune in His Kingdom" as being "well chosen and pleasing to the eye; it is no wonder that it garnered applause."[109]

Business was brisk from the start, with many notables attending the performances of *The Fisherman and the Genie* and *Siti Senimbar* on the first two nights. After a dip in audience numbers in the first days of

October, house sizes rebounded in the second week of the run "as people in the kampung talk among each other about how good the Komedie Stamboel is, and those who hear these stories wish to attend and when they come back they talk about it with their friends in the kampung in turn."[110] Performances became social events for neighborhoods: men and women arrived in organized groups from the kampung of Poncol Sentiong, Tangki, and Sawah Besar. In a matter of weeks, kroncong ensembles were playing stambul songs in the streets, and people everywhere were whistling the songs they heard in the theater.

The large turnout, and the continual stream of carriages and dog-carts that arrived at the theater tent, had a flip side though: there was an increasing tendency for outbreaks of aggressive and criminal behavior involving both spectators and company members. Some incidents were minor. An infatuated spectator asked the front of house manager how he might procure an introduction to an actress, but received the response, "You'd be better off with an introduction to my bludgeon!" This rough retort earned the company a rebuke from the press—who saw no harm in spectators socializing with performers.[111] All public spectacles in Batavia brought out the criminal elements, who plied their trade as pickpockets and con artists, and the Mangga Besar shows were no exception. One newsworthy item was the theft of a sixty-guilder brooch after a performance by a female spectator's female houseguest.

But some of the incidents were worrisome. A group of actors nearly got into a fistfight with Indos in Glodok on 9 October; further harsh words were exchanged between spectators and performers on 11 October; someone in the theater went amok on 13 October. These fights were likely at least in part over the actresses, for while female spectators came primarily to enjoy the music, male European, Chinese, and Muslim spectators "came night after night as they wished to see the beauty of the Indo women."[112] The actors, some of whom were in relations with the actresses, naturally objected to the forwardness of this type of sexual attention.

The morally upright among the Batavia public saw a connection between the lascivious social atmosphere and the plays performed onstage. The "blue" image of the *Nights* preceded the Komedie Stamboel's presentations of it. People looked askance on the public presentation of

Figs. 2.3 and 2.4. An Arabian harem and an illicit affair between an Arabian princess and a "blackamoor" slave. Reprinted from Gijsbert Francis, *Hikajat 1001 malam* (Batavia: Albrecht and Rusche, 1891), 1:125, 1:14.

tales of sexual dalliance and love slaves. One prudish reader wrote to *Pembrita Betawi* to complain that "the Komedie Stamboel takes its plays exclusively from *The Thousand and One Nights*. Such stories are not fit for girls from good families, because nearly all the stories describe sexual secrets, for example the use of hitting in sex [as foreplay] and matters of this sort that should not be seen by young women. Better for this komedi to look for other [sources] that are appropriate for a general audience to see."[113]

Two weeks after opening night there were calls for the Komedie Stamboel to leave Mangga Besar. After an attempt was made to burn down the tent, even *Bintang-Barat* conceded that "it is best that the komedi quickly move from Mangga Besar. If it does not, one worries that danger and conflict will erupt at some point."[114]

The company in fact gave its last performance in Mangga Besar on 13 October and struck its tent the following day. Company members had been living together "like a family" in a rented house in Mangga Besar. But relations with the adjoining community had apparently become so strained that they moved to a house to the corner of Gang Pasar Baru and Gang Kleijkamp in the Pasar Baru area.[115] The tent was then pitched in the southern part of the city in the Gambir field, where the troupe started giving performances on 16 October, opening with the surefire hit *Siti Senimbar.*[116]

The move to Gambir meant leaving behind some of the more troublesome elements that performances and performers had attracted in Mangga Besar. The move also entailed a need to attract a new audience from the udik part of the city. The Gambir field roughly corresponds with Medan Merdeka (Independence square), where the obelisk of "Sukarno's last erection," the fanciful national monument, is located. Gambir was described by one contemporary observer as "not so much a square as simply a field, vast enough to build a city on," a "brown bare expanse of meadowy ground . . . bordered on the four sides of its irregular quadrangle by a triple row of branching tamarinds."[117] Gambir's public "field" had established its reputation as Batavia's prime site for mass spectacles by the mid-nineteenth century. The first major circus to play Batavia performed there in 1856, while a certain Professor Th. Görs from British India gave a gave a gala display of "sumptuous and costly Vauxhall art-fireworks" in Gambir in 1862.[118] Gambir was also a social space of sorts—a popular nineteenth-century pastime of the elite of Batavia were carriage rides around the square's perimeter in the cool hours of early evening after a refreshing bath. But Muslims in the area of Gambir were less sophisticated in their tastes than their ilir counterparts (*Betawi udik* to date carries connotations of provinciality), and some udik spectators were reportedly concerned that the Komedie Stamboel's plays were overly risqué for their tastes.[119] The same word-of-mouth networks that popularized the company in the ilir part of the city brought the Komedie Stamboel to public attention within a week or so, but *Bintang-Barat* estimated that it would take a full month of performing before the company completely captured the attention of the udik public. And it was not possible to extend the performance permit issued by Batavia's resident beyond 29 October 1892.

Opening night in Gambir was a dud, with fewer than sixty spectators in the house. This was due to the company's still low public profile in the udik area as well as competition from other public events. On the same night Stanley's Comic Opera was doing a double bill of *The Sleeping Beauty* and *Ta-Ra-Ra Boom-De-Ay* at the schouwburg; the amateur military theater of the Onderofficiers Vereeniging "Avendo" was performing a musical send-up of Gounod's *Faust* at the zoo; and there was a big party at the house of Baba Kan Tjeng Si. However, by the 22 October 1892 performance of *Aladdin,* audiences were standing room only, and at performances thereafter second- and third-class tickets routinely sold out. The violence characteristic of the Mangga Besar run did not infringe on the Gambir performances, and in the end the company cleared the goodly sum of six thousand guilders, roughly the amount earned from the Mangga Besar run.

There were, as in Semarang, various violations of public etiquette and decorum committed by members of the public and the company, and *Bintang-Barat* took it upon itself to arbitrate public behavioral norms.

> People who have just returned from seeing the Komedie Stamboel tell that there was a spectator who walked into the auditorium arm

> in arm with his wife, after the manner of Europeans. He was even wearing a gold-lace hat, such as worn by the resident.
>
> People who did not know this spectator thought he had the rank of bupati, but this was not actually the case.
>
> We would like to remind readers that whoever chooses to wear emblems of status that are not his by right can be charged with an offense by law.[120]

Even more offensive than this sartorial infraction was the crudity of loud remarks made by spectators. On one Saturday night performance, a Bantenese fishmonger and a "land crocodile" moved down from the second-class seats after the beginning of the show and disturbed first-class spectators with rude remarks. *Bintang-Barat* admitted that "whoever has money can sit in the auditorium wherever he so chooses, because one person's money is the same as anyone else's." But it was the paper's opinion "that anyone wishing to sit among good people should also behave in a fashion that is beyond reproach and wear appropriate clothing." Spectators sitting in the first-class section should not utter vulgarity, wear hitched-up sarongs, or put their feet up. *Bintang-Barat* warned that allowing such infringements of decorum would lead to loss of business.[121]

On the morning of 31 October 1892, the Komedie Stamboel left Batavia for the western Javanese highlands. The first scheduled stand was Bogor (also known as Buitenzorg), connected to Batavia by an hour-and-a-half rail journey on a line that had opened in 1871. It was planned that if the company made a reasonable profit in Bogor, it would extend its tour to other highland cities.

The town of Bogor "lies cradled in a fold of the undulating country at the base of the Salak [mountain], whose blue top . . . is seen in fine weather from the Koningsplein [in Gambir], rising aerially, fresh and pure above the dusty glare of Batavia."[122] Bogor had a population of about four thousand and was notably the residence of the governor-general of the Indies. Many of Bogor's European residents worked in government; there was also an army barracks not far from the governor-general's palace. Buitenzorg literally means "without a care" in Dutch; its cool climate, pretty rose gardens, and proximity to Batavia made it a popular weekend holiday destination. "It is the pride and show-place of Java, the great center of its social life, leisure interests, and attractions. The higher officials and many Batavian merchants and bankers have homes at Buitenzorg, and residents from other parts of the island make it their place of recreation and goal of holiday trips."[123] The town was famed for its botanic garden, considered one of the finest in the world; the annual horse races in September were a premiere event on the social calendar of the Indies; and "all Java" danced at the ball at the Buitenzorg Club that fell this same month.[124] The area around Bogor had numerous sugar, tea, coffee, and cinchona plantations, and European planters and their staff regularly attended social functions and performances in Bogor. Performing in Bogor thus had social prestige attached to it, and after a grueling five months on the road, Komedie Stamboel company members were likely anticipating Bogor's tranquil pleasures.

The company did not seem to know, however, that the "charming" town of Bogor was also infamous for its torrential late afternoon rains. Guidebooks and travel literature regularly warn that "often between 2–5 p.m. rain falls here accompanied by a severe storm."[125] Most houses in Bogor, in fact, had bamboo walls and thatched roofs in order to minimize damage from such downpours and to withstand the occasional earthquake besetting this mountain town.

On the evening of 9 November 1892, Komedie Stamboel company members were passing out leaflets on the streets when the wind picked up and torrential rain mixed with hail fell. The Komedie Stamboel's tent had not been built to endure such a storm. Tent poles cracked, canvas collapsed, scenery and other equipment was destroyed.

The company immediately telegraphed Batavia in a desperate effort to obtain a Batavia performance permit and rent a tent or shed. There could be no hope of continuing the tour to other highland cities without a properly weatherproofed tent. But the permit was not forthcoming for two weeks, resulting in major losses, and the idea of returning directly to Surabaya was aired. A rumor circulated that the Komedie Stamboel had received a command performance from the governor-general, for a fee of eight hundred guilders. "If this is in fact true, the Komedie Stamboel has certainly received a major honor."[126] Likely the report was false—a flight of desire in a difficult stretch.

Not all news from Bogor was bad, though. A young man named Moll, who had been working as a clerk in the office of the state secretary, quit his job in Bogor to join the company. The idea that someone with a cushy government job might leave it for the Komedie Stamboel made for good press. Moreover, Moll became one of the troupe's stars in 1893, specializing in comic roles as the company's "first comedian."[127] Such was Moll's ability to entertain that he merited bouquets and garlands (along with Mahieu and Mahieu's wife). The comic was an intermediary between the spectators and the play world; he commented on contemporary events and directly addressed the audience in Malay and Dutch, sprinkled for comic effect with a few words in low Javanese.

> Moll, who superbly executed the difficult role of the deaf-mute African, came before the footlights to announce the program for the following evenings. His speech, charmingly delivered in broken Dutch mimicking an African, went more or less as follows: "Ladies and Gentlemen, tomorrow there be good play. *Faust,* that be Dutch, the King of Arab (I cannot speak Dutch), and a tableau of Paris burning. I be born near the Frenchman. And the day after next, there is the violin if you do play him fast, he dances; if you do it slow, he sleeps. And with a tableau. . . . Lho! I does forget. . . . Oh yes, about the burning up of the Krakatau. Now, Ladies and Gentlemen (bowing deeply), bottoms up! If I be free, I come back. If no, forget about it!"[128]

Much of Moll's rough, and mildly racist, humor could not possibly have been represented on the page (let alone translated!); the improvisational talents of this clerk-turned-comedian were greatly valued.

> What role is the most challenging for komedi actors?
>
> A person who asked this question was answered: *performing as a comic is the most challenging.*

> This is my thinking as well, as a comic must perform with earnestness; nothing that a comic does can appear forced, all actions must be funny and pleasing to the public. One cannot exaggerate, everything must be just right. And a comic's words or dialogue cannot be delivered with bravado, like topeng clowns, nor can they be badly *cooked* or *raw,* like circus clowns whom spectators find nauseating.
>
> A comic must be funny by nature, the comedy cannot be artificial. Whatever he says in real life should make people laugh. Only someone like that can properly be called *comical.*
>
> Other roles can be taught, but the role of the comic cannot, it must come from the actor himself. That is why it must be said that the role of the comic is the most challenging among komedi roles.[129]

In time, the company succeeded in renting a tent and obtained the requisite performance permit for playing Batavia. The Komedie Stamboel opened in Mangga Besar in Batavia on 26 November 1892 with the play *Budraim bin Hasap, or Retribution.* Audience turnout was low initially, which *Bintang-Barat* attributed to it being "the tail end of the month, when people's pockets are flat."[130] There was hope that payday, on the first of the month, would yield larger houses, but Yap Gwan Thay was evidently not in a speculative mood, and he sent word that the company should return to Surabaya on 5 December. Affluent Chinese and their families attended the Mangga Besar shows in substantial numbers, but many second- and third-class seats were empty. Performances, as much as spectators' wallets, were likely somewhat flat due to the damage to sets and equipment and the loss of the custom-built tent in Bogor and the fact that Van der Laan was flat on his back with influenza. Mangga Besar audiences remained rowdy during the run. A letter from a reader describes "a number of gentlemen in second-class seats (reputedly good people) who made their own komedi show by looking for fights and shouting. . . . don't those gentlemen have any shame?"[131] The actors were talking about how they wished to be back in Surabaya by the New Year. The performers had done well financially during the tour—one of them had put away a cool five hundred guilders in a savings account—

and did not wish to linger in western Java. The group had overstayed its welcome in Mangga Besar, and when the company departed it "left behind many friends" in Batavia, but it had also successfully "flattened their pockets."[132] It was flat-out time to go home.

When it had departed on its first extended tour in November 1891, the Komedie Stamboel was still essentially a Surabaya theater company. It had constructed a fit-up, installed painted canvas wings, purchased a tent, and hired musicians—but in language, style, and tone it belonged to its city of origin. By the time it had returned to Surabaya in December 1892, the Komedie Stamboel was an itinerant company, with a following across the island of Java. The constant stimulation of travel enriched the company, bringing it performers, techniques, forms, and ideas.[133]

The Komedie Stamboel's tours between November 1891 and December 1892 initiated a new era in Indonesian culture. The company effectively cut a wide swath through Java and established itself not only as a company to watch out for but also as a model for how to do theater. Numerous traditional cultural forms, including batik and *ikat* fabrics and gamelan music, are shared properties of many of the ethnic cultures of Indonesia. But these traditional forms are inflected locally in very particular ways and are expressions of local identity, however much they resemble articulations of similar forms elsewhere in the archipelago. An art form such as wayang kulit is very resistant to being appropriated as a symbol of national or interregional identity, due largely to regional variation in dramatic form, music, and language. Stambul was different from any art that had existed in Indonesia before. It was a phenomenon that united spectators and cultural observers throughout Java and provided a shared discursive topic for newspapers and social intercourse. Not everyone liked the Komedie Stamboel, but everyone had a pretty good idea about what it was, and nearly everyone had an opinion about it.

A visit of the Komedie Stamboel to a city acted as a litmus test for cultural vitality. A city's ability to field stambul actors and mount imitator troupes was an index for artistic strength. "The love of theatre appears to live in our land, for we learn that in each place where the company visits, new actors come forward, and the lovely goddess Thalia has found supporters in our town as well," a Yogyakarta newspaper wrote.[134]

The diverse crowds the theater attracted were expected to behave according to emergent norms and standards, registered and enforced in the pages of newspapers. The theater was both a source of escapist pleasure and a site of discipline.

The alacrity of the diffusion of stambul culture was remarkable. A Chinese correspondent who wrote for the Semarang Malay daily under the name Tjoet Ke Djin found it "astonishing" (*ajaib*) that people in Batavia would be whistling the Komedie Stamboel's catchy songs in the streets less than a month after the company first arrived in that city.[135] Such astonishment diminished over the coming year, as the practice of stambul became increasingly prevalent.

Stambul activity was focused in the theater of the Komedie Stamboel in 1892. There are occasional descriptions of amateur groups in Solo, Yogya, and Batavia, but they were mostly structured opportunities for posturing and tomfoolery. There is also the odd report about stambul songs being sung in other contexts. In May 1892, for example, the sound of a woman singing Komedie Stamboel songs was heard emanating from a suspiciously dark Surabaya house, where Chinese and Europeans gathered to drink and party: it was requested that the police investigate this shady matter. An acrobatics troupe with Javanese and Chinese youths training in the central Javanese town of Klaten incorporated "pantun sung to stambul melodies" along with tightrope walking and tumbling. (Apparently the group still had some way to go in their studies: an aspiring young acrobat named Sie Tjing Wat fell during a tumbling exercise in November 1892 and lost consciousness for a quarter of an hour, to the consternation of his friends.)[136] These are isolated examples, indicative of an incipient phase of cultural diffusion, and not a coherent cultural movement per se.

This picture would change over the course of 1893, as more and more amateur and professional stambul groups were founded throughout Java, playscripts for amateur use were published, music box rolls with Komedie Stamboel songs were produced, stambul songs were sung on the streets and at ritual celebrations, and the music was adapted for various musical ensembles. In 1892 there was great excitement around the Komedie Stamboel as a company, but in the years to come it was stambul as a cultural form that generated popular enthusiasm.

Chapter 3

MAHIEU'S MAGIC, 1893

The Komedie Stamboel returned home from Batavia in mid-December 1892 and remained in Surabaya until mid-April 1893. During these months, the company alternated between performing in the Kapasan theater and a newly manufactured tent pitched on the Pasar Besar square. These four months brought significant changes to the company in terms of repertoire, equipment, and personnel. Many of the improvements can be attributed to "the assiduous director of the Komedie Stamboel, the Heer Mahieu, who . . . is always regaling the public with one or another innovation."[1] Only rarely do the newspapers report fights among actors and spectators marring performances; in general, this was a period of company building and structural reorganization.

Newly recruited actresses from Semarang debuted in early February and their "irreproachable" singing and acting was much appreciated by the public.[2] New songs were composed. A piano was purchased for the band and a pianist engaged to play it. New costumes and sets were constructed. New plays, including Mahieu's adaptation of Vincenzo Bellini's opera *Norma* (originally produced in 1831)—retitled *Normadi,* were added to the repertoire "as people are already bored of seeing plays based on *The Thousand and One Nights.*"[3] *Normadi* filled the Kapasan theater with spectators curious to see how the Komedie Stamboel would interpret this revered *tragedia lirica* about druids and Romans.

Other plays with European sources followed later this year—notably *Sleeping Beauty* and *Bubakam, or Bluebeard.* The Komedie Stamboel's selection of plays was becoming increasingly diverse, and while adaptations from European sources of 1891 and 1892 were remade into the Komedie Stamboel's established idiom, European plays introduced in 1893 and years that followed were frequently (though not always) costumed in European fashion using apposite music. Operatic standards were well known to Surabaya musicians, judging from the Italian Quintet's repertoire and reports of concerts at the European clubs. It would not have been hard for the Komedie Stamboel to adapt the better-known arias, duets, and choral numbers of Bellini's *Norma,* such as the aria "Casta Diva," for their production of *Normadi.* European opera melodies by Verdi and other composers infiltrated other plays in the Komedie Stamboel repertoire as well. A review of *Laeli*—a play about troubles that beset the eponymous Greek heroine on her way to meet her fiancé, the king of Hindustan, first mounted by the Komedie Stamboel in January 1893—notes that "the various airs that are sung, including beautiful melodies extracted from European operas, are well selected."[4]

Musical purists were appalled by such loose treatment of European opera. Justus van Maurik, a cigar dealer who made a business trip to the Indies and subsequently wrote a "chummy and banal" travel book, was voicing a common sentiment when he described a production of François Adrien Boieldieu's *La dame blanche* (retitled *La nyonya blanca*) by the Malay popular theater company Comedie Indra Bangsawan as "abominable vandalism." What seems to have perturbed him most was how "Boieldieu's music was replaced by popular songs such as 'Daisy Bell,' 'Ting-a-Ling Ting-Tay,' 'Champagne Charlie,' and others. They sung 'Die Wacht am Rhein' as a chorus in the first act and 'Wilhelmus van Nassouwe' in the third."[5]

This matching and mixing of old songs and new seems anomalous today, but it was a typical practice for nineteenth-century itinerant troupes. Audiences were accustomed to loose adaptations of operatic standards. American musicologist Katherine Preston writes how in antebellum America "foreign language operas . . . were translated and adapted for the English stage. Recitative, when present, was changed into dialogue, the more difficult ensemble numbers were eliminated, and many of the complex arias were turned into strophic songs. The works essentially became English comic operas. Some 'adapted' operas included a great deal of extra musical material, either newly composed or borrowed from other operas, making them musical pastiches."[6] For example, an 1830 American production of *The Marriage of Figaro* contained not only music by Mozart but also ballads and drum-and-fife songs such as "Bonnets of Blue." Gauche interpolations of this sort were sometimes critiqued in American reviews, but likely had genuine appeal for gallery spectators.[7]

Some of the changes introduced to the Komedie Stamboel in early 1893 were brought about by physical necessity. The troupe's old tent had been damaged beyond repair in Bogor, thus the purchase of a more spacious and better furnished tent. The new tent had good ventilation and was fitted with comfortable seats, but while it was initially advertised as waterproof, it tended to leak when it rained. A tragedy was narrowly averted at a 9 March 1893 performance when the reservoir of a kerosene stage light exploded and a blaze started, nearly setting the highly flammable stage-wings and densely packed stage properties on fire. Yap Gwan Thay had in fact already ordered sixty "safety lamps" of the latest design from Germany for the Kapasan theater and the Komedie Stamboel, but they had not yet arrived. The lights went in later in the month, signaled in March advertisements with the statement that "the sets and lighting are all new, including equipment from Europe."[8] Yap even considered (but apparently did not realize) starting up a printing business to handle the heavy volume of posters, programs, and leaflets the Komedie Stamboel required.

The 1893 Surabaya residence of the Komedie Stamboel is also noteworthy as stimulation for a long descriptive essay by journalist, editor, and literary critic S. Kalff. Kalff's essay is the most precise account of the experience of attending the Komedie Stamboel that is available, and is worth examining in detail. "A Night at the Komedie Stamboel" was published originally on 15 February 1893 in a supplement to *Java Bode,* perhaps the most prestigious newspaper in the Indies. Kalff writes

en
UITREIKING van PRIJZEN der CONCOURS-SPELEN
KOMEDIE STAMBOOL
geeft van af 31 Maart voorstellingen
op de
Aloon-Aloon.
Decoratieven geheel nieuw, waarvan eenige uit EUROPA.
De TENT is waterdicht zoodat bij regenachtig weêr de voorstelling doorgaat
OPVOERING VAN
SITIE SENIEMBAR
Den 14en April
geven wij de eerste voorstelling te
MALANG.
De Directeur
1966 A. MAHIEU.

Fig. 3.1. "The Komedie Stamboel is giving performances on the alun-alun starting 31 March. The sets and lighting are all new, including equipment from Europe. The tent is waterproof so that the show will go on during rainy weather." *Soerabaiasch-Handelsblad,* 30 March 1893.

under his Islamic pseudonym, Aboe Hassan, but there is no trace of imaginative sympathy with his subject. He positions himself instead as a member of the cultural elite, a Eurocentric writer addressing Europeans who share his cultural preoccupations, values, and ideals. Some months before Kalff's essay was published, *Java Bode* had editorialized about the Komedie Stamboel that "one should not come in the expectation of seeing an outstanding theatrical troupe, or one will end up let down."[9] Kalff's stance is consistent with this attitude: he does not purport to take the Komedie Stamboel as art. There are evident joys to be had in seeing the Komedie Stamboel, but these arise out of the observer's ironic detachment. In another era, perhaps, Kalff's reading of the Komedie Stamboel might have been called camp.[10]

Kalff's 1893 essay takes the form of a guided tour, with Kalff himself as our sardonic guide. We enter the performance site arm in arm with the author. Kalff begins by saying that it is curiosity alone that draws European spectators to see the Komedie Stamboel at Kapasan and that few return home enthused. He praises the Kapasan theater's physical amenities, admitting that the fittings rival those of Surabaya's schouwburg. Nonetheless, "the location just outside the Chinese camp appears to be detrimental to visits, and this is possibly why the little troupe brought its business to the heart of the city and pitched a tent in the Pasar Besar area."

Kalff then launches into a representative account of how a European subjectively experiences a Komedie Stamboel performance at Pasar Besar. Spectators arrived with foreknowledge of what was to be performed, as both the Malay- and Dutch-language newspapers printed summaries of upcoming plays and "leaflets in bright red, green, or yellow were distributed, noting the drama the troupe intended to perform. . . . The Native crier standing in front of the tent sounded his brass bell. . . . That drums up business." Kalff goes on to describe the makeup of the audience drawn to this show in "polyglottal Surabaya, the trade emporium of eastern Java." Few upper-class Europeans are visible. "Aside from the throng of Natives in their colorful jackets, one sees low-class Chinese in white *kabaya* blouses and short, wide trousers of polished cotton, Native women in their indigo-blue jackets and batik sarongs and *slendang* shawls, Native soldiers, shipmasters, a few Arabs, and, still less frequently, 'coloreds' [*kleurlingen*] from the slums, the kampung whites," that is to say, poor Eurasians. "In front of the tent there is the customary commotion caused by such a show in any populous town such as Surabaya. The scene is lit with a rosy glow by the smoky oil lamps of street vendors." The sharp odors emitted from portable food stalls mix with the strong smells of pungent fruits, frying coconut oil, and roasting spiced meats.[11]

We then approach the Chinese-manned bamboo ticket booth set up in front of the entrance to the tent, purchase our two-guilder ticket, and enter the theater's auditorium together with Kalff. The first impression is the hall's scale—it is large but there are few spectators in it (as least at the moment). The writer thinks, Perhaps there are few spectators as the novelty of the Komedie Stamboel is wearing off. Kalff then feels the ground beneath his feet and looks down. It is green grass, and Kalff is queerly reminded of a country outing. A dog slips underneath the side of the tent, and roams around inside, barking and "following his canine instinct." Kalff glances presently at the seating. For the first-class seats there are hard-backed Weener chairs; the second- and third-class ticket holders sit on benches. There is an orchestra present, but the writer cannot see where it is situated. An image flashes through Kalff's mind: a Wagner opera performed at the Bayreuth Festspielhaus, with a hundred-piece orchestra hidden from view under the stage. "In this respect at least, the Komedie Stamboel is the equal of Wagner's theatre in Bayreuth," jokes Kalff, though, as the writer later admits, the Komedie Stamboel's orchestra at this show is not to be found under the stage, but backstage.

Kalff finds his seat and sits down. The faint illumination of the house's gaslights allows Kalff to examine the audience. There are a few wealthy Chinese and a handful of Europeans sitting with him in the first-class seats. He turns around and sees that there are more spectators in the second-class seats, including Eurasians, "military men with their mistresses, sailors on shore leave, navy clerks, middle income Natives and Chinese, etc."[12]

The curtain rises on four actors and actresses singing pantun verse in chorus, accompanied by violin, flute, a plucked string instrument, and a brass instrument. Kalff examines the faces of the performers onstage and decides that all four actors and two of the actresses are indisputably "Natives." One or two of the actresses have more Caucasian features and "ruddy blond hair, indicative of a different origin." Kalff's attention is distracted by the noise in the house. Chinese spectators are hollering back and forth, a few *brandal* (troublemakers) are shouting obscenities, Chinese children are running around, "buffet employees hawk cigarettes, Native pastries in lemonade syrup of dubious quality, and candies made in Germany—and there is that stray dog again! . . . In all there are two to three hundred spectators, but the amount of activity befits twice that number."

The introductory song ends and the play proper begins, titled *Het Rokkenei* (The roc's egg) in Dutch and *Telornya burung gorda, atawa rajanja iblis* (The garuda's egg, or The iblis king) in Malay. This was a staple of the repertoire, an *Arabian Nights* episode that the company frequently enacted from 1892 onward. Kalff notes that the garuda bird is entirely fictional, like the elephant-eating roc and the petrifying *bulbul al-syach*—implicitly demonstrating his own knowledge of *Arabian Nights* ornithology. The costumes worn by the actors are fanciful too: Kalff deems them to be more like costumes for children than proper theater attire. "The young ladies wear European skirts and jackets adorned with frills and furbelows, Louis Quinze heels . . . , and turbans and muslin veils. The men are clothed like Arab merchants and Chinese, with long white underclothes, red jackets, and fezzes." Kalff adds that the actors' naturally dark skin means that no stage makeup is necessary.

Two woodcutters enter the stage, with bundles of wood in one hand and small axes in the other. The dialogue is not easy for Kalff to follow, and he warns his readers that "a spectator must be fairly fluent in Malay, including high Malay, to follow the plot." But he gathers that the woodcutters' names are Tasman and Agrib, and that they have been sent by their parents, Barhadam and Rasika, to collect wood in the forest. Tasman and Agrib gripe about their toilsome labor. Exhausted, they lie down under a painted tree and soon go to sleep. A *mulaiḳat* (angel) arrives and tells the sleepers that the tree under which they repose is actually a magic tree with miraculous fruit, for in this tree the garuda makes its nest and in this nest sits the giant roc's egg. The mulaikat commands the woodcutters to break open the egg and free the iblis king who had been imprisoned by a witch inside the egg's indestructible shell for two thousand years. It turns out that the mulaikat is only a dream figment; Tasman and Agrib sleep on.

A beautiful fairy princess named Princess Hamalsadi enters from behind a pasteboard thicket and spies the sleeping woodcutters. Tasman is to her liking. (Her taste in men must not be too high, comments Kalff.) "To my palace!" she commands imperially, and Tasman is spirited off by Hamalsadi and her entourage of fairies.

Agrib awakens and finds himself alone: "Orestes has lost his Pylades." The woodcutter suffers no grief from his brother's disappearance, and maintains a cheerful disposition. He turns his efforts to climbing the magic tree and retrieving the roc's egg, for he recalls his dream of the mulaikat's command perfectly. The egg is perilously perched at the edge of a side scene (*coulisse*). Kalff is initially disappointed that no semblance of the nest referred to in the printed program has been constructed by the Komedie Stamboel's scenic artists, but revising his essay twenty-five years later, he points out that the absence of this scenic element compels spectators to use their "imaginative faculties." Agrib reaches out for the egg but burns his fingers on it and the egg falls to the ground. This affords Kalff a better look at the egg prop. He finds it more closely resembles a squash or watermelon than an egg, "but if the handbill says it is an egg . . ." The egg emits smoke and bright light. Agrib licks his fingers and picks up the egg with both hands. (Kalff likens him to a blacksmith apprentice picking up a nail.) The woodcutter hoists the egg up and throws it to the ground.

"Boom!" goes a sound from behind the wings. The iblis king emerges magically from the egg. Kalff is reminded of Paris's Théâtre du Châtelet and London's Covent Garden, where devils and dragons emerge from the ground and fly in the air and beggars transform into shimmering sorceresses before your very eyes. The Komedie Stamboel's effect is not quite up to this level of stage magic, but that is beside the point: the "terrifying" iblis king has arrived, the two-thousand-year enchantment has been broken, the prophecy fulfilled. What we actually see before us, Kalff describes, is "a long figure with a false beard, skinny unkingly legs, a cheese knife in place of a sword at his side, a shock of hair out of the days of the *rois chevelus,* the sort of kingly garb worn at a costume party, and—in order to demonstrate his quality—a gold paper crown of a Saint Nicholas Day celebrant on his head."[13] The iblis king rages that Agrib has meddled with his affairs—as if he was living the good life in his egg prison, Kalff muses—and he threatens to haul him off to his gloomy dwelling. Once there, the king will do away with him. *Mau di bikin mampus sekalian* (I will kill you dead), Kalff reads in his program.

Kalff finds the scene that follows "vaguely reminiscent of the tale of Theseus and Ariadne," in that both Agrib and Theseus are saved from certain death by the virtuous daughters of murderous kings. The iblis king has a beautiful daughter named Sayalma, who assures Agrib that she wishes to help him and gives him a magic sword from her father's arsenal. They then exchange grandiloquent vows of love in dialogue and song. Kalff catches frequent references to words like *Allah, cinta, dunia, widodaren* (God, love, world, heavenly nymphs). Kalff is less than impressed by the love scene's artistry. The actors' postures evoke images of the stiff joints of Egyptian statuary. The singing is described as *baboedreun* (a Malay-Dutch hybrid coinage meaning "a nanny's lullaby), which is "dutifully accompanied by violin, flute, zither, and saxhorn." Kalff is plainly bored and he looks around and sees that others are restless too. He overhears a European soldier comment that he has never heard such Malay spoken in the barracks and that he prefers listening to military drill songs over this sort of music. The soldier gets up noisily and walks out with his non-European mistress—who was actually enjoying the play and would have preferred not to have been coerced into leaving before the end. Chinese and Native families also begin to leave, in order to take their sleepy children home to bed. Others in the audience also appear bored, but they are determined to get full value for their money and so remain seated until the play's conclusion. "Who knows what will come next!" Kalff exclaims with mock enthusiasm.

The curtain comes up in the next scene on "a domestic interior, which we learn is the house of Princess Hamalsadi." Tasman has exchanged his woodcutter's garb for beaded and laced robes. Kalff says he looks as uncomfortable as an African chief would be upon trying on a general's uniform for the first time. The saucy Hamalsadi takes a quiet pleasure in all this. Agrib shows up with Sayalma. The brothers compliment each other on their new clothes (referred to with the Dutch-Malay term *paķean deftig,* noble garb), magic swords, and newfound girlfriends. The two princesses strike up an amicable conversation. (Kalff is dissatisfied by their apparent nonchalance.) The cannibalistic iblis king has threatened to have Agrib for breakfast and eat his own daughter as well. Agrib does away with the king with his magic sword and also dispatches an evil fairy who has the power to imprison kings in eggs and transform princesses into porcupines.

The couples then return to Agrib and Tasman's humble abode to seek the blessings of Barhadam and Rasika for their marriages. Rasika initially appears displeased that her sons are engaged to get married as she thinks she will have to provide for her daughters-in-law, but her attitude changes when she discovers that her future daughters-in-law are wealthy. The days of hard labor are behind the family. They form a "cooperative society" under a patriarchal head, *sampe pengabisan idup seneng slamanya*—and they live happily ever after.

Many spectators appear to have anticipated this ending and have already made their departure, without waiting to see the final tableau vivant, "In the Kingdom of the Celestials," which Kalff finds "indecently long." The lights, depleted of oil, begin to flicker, and the audience disperses.

Kalff looks at a Malay paper the next day to see what it says about the show. It reports that "the audience went home pleased." Kalff muses that such a statement is on the same level of certainty as an almanac's prediction of good weather. "'Last night,' I told a friend the other day, 'I happened to be in Pasar Besar and saw the Komedie Stamboel's tent. People say that notables occasionally visit there out of pure curiosity.'" Kalff's interlocutor is automatically dismissive. "But you, of course, you walked past?" "No," Kalff replies, "I . . . dropped in!"

In Surabaya in early 1893 the Komedie Stamboel was not the only theater where spectators could "drop in." The company was alternating nights at the Kapasan theater with a popular theater company from British Malaya for much of March and April 1893. This Malaysian company went under the heading Komedie Melajoe (Malay komedi) or Komedie Persi (Parsi komedi), and was owned and managed by Abubakar, who also was the troupe's principal comedian.[14] This may or may not have been the first time that a Malay popular theater group of the sort eventually classified as bangsawan visited Java.[15] But it was the first time that a troupe of this size and polish visited, and it was accorded due attention in the press.

The precise origin of bangsawan is uncertain. Received historiography is derived from a 1960 account of A. H. Edrus.[16] This account appears to be based largely, if not exclusively, on oral historical sources. Edrus describes the popular reception of itinerant Parsi theater troupes in Penang and other cities in Malaya in the 1870s. A man named Tuan Mamat Mashhor (also known as Syed Muhammad bin Abdul Rahman al-Mashhor), of Arabic descent, brought together a group of friends, including descendents of the sultanate of Kedah and Perlis, to form a group to perform Parsi theater stories such as *Indra sabha* in Malay. The musical accompaniment was the same as the Parsi theater was using at

Fig. 3.2. Lithograph from a Malay text published in Singapore with costumes and decor of the sort associated with early bangsawan. Reprinted from Md. Hassan bin Nasaruddin, *Syair Indera Sebaha* (Singapore: Hj Md Siraj, 1891), 32. Original housed at the British Library, shelfmark 14625.d.7. Reproduced courtesy of the British Library Board.

the time—dhol, tabla, and harmonium—and the occasions were those that traditionally instanced theatrical entertainments in Malay society, wedding celebrations, and like rites of passage.

Mamat Mashhor's troupe was all-male, as was the general practice in Parsi theater during the nineteenth century, but after a tour of Sumatra at the invitation of the sultan of Deli, two actresses were added to play female roles. On its return to Penang, Mamat Mashhor's troupe received an injection of capital from a certain Syed Ali (also known as Kapitan Ali). A new troupe founded in 1885 by a wealthy Parsi entrepreneur from Penang named Mamat Pushi subsequently achieved public favor. This troupe was named Indra Bangsawan, after a well-known Malay tale and a central repertoire item. Tradition and extent newspaper documentation has it that Mamat Pushi's company was Penang's preeminent popular theater company of the late 1880s. With a popular following in Singapore as well, it was this troupe that popularized the use of bangsawan to describe the genre, though as late as 1895 the term had not gained complete acceptance in Malaya.[17]

When it played Surabaya in 1893, publicity for Abubakar's company advertised it as being "already famous in British India, having performed for thirteen years already, though this is the first time it has come to Surabaya."[18] If the dating is accurate (promotions tend to exaggerate), then Abubakar's company was one of the first of its sort to be founded. This was a big troupe, "34 men, 5 women, and 2 children strong," with actors from Penang, Singapore, and elsewhere in British Malaya.[19]

Abubakar's komedi took Surabaya by storm, playing to packed houses for two months from March to May 1893. Audiences were bowled over by visions of actors disappearing into pits beneath the stage, flying nymphs picking flowers in a sky garden, and dragons emerging from mouths of actors. The beauty of the actresses portraying the nymphs captivated many, and spectators laughed uproariously at the comic turns. "All enjoyed the performances and took pleasure in them, cheering and clapping and laughing without cease due to the wonderful and astounding performances."[20]

Abubakar's Komedie Melajoe provided an alternative model for doing Malay-language theater. Popular theater in British Malaya still closely resembled the Parsi theater at this time, with Indian musical instruments and songs and the use of a lofty, literary Malay, in contrast to the demotic Malay of the Komedie Stamboel. The extended residency of Abubakar's company in the Kapasan theater allowed Yap Gwan Thay, Charles O. van der Laan, and others involved in the Komedie Stamboel to carefully study their performances. The props and sets of the two companies literally bumped up against each other: the backstage clutter at the Kapasan theater from having to accommodate two alternating companies was one of the reasons why the 9 March 1893 fire was so potentially hazardous.

The Komedie Stamboel had expanded to about sixty members, and it was announced at the end of January 1893 that the company would be bifurcated into two troupes. Mahieu would head up the Komedie Stamboel, with ten actors and five actresses. This troupe would remain under

Yap Gwan Thay's ownership. A new kongsi (including Yap) would be formed to bankroll a second-tier troupe under Charles O. van der Laan's artistic direction, with a half dozen actresses and twice as many actors.

Van der Laan's breakaway troupe was called alternately Komedie Sri Soerabaia Djawi Pranakan Singapoera or Sri Soerabaja Pranakan P. Pinang dan Singapoera. It was also called Sri Soerabaia for short. It was evidently a hybrid of the popular theaters of Malaysia and Indonesia. The core members of the group were Surabaya actors, but Van der Laan himself had performed with a British Malay troupe prior to joining the Komedie Stamboel, and it is possible that actors from British Malaya were recruited to Sri Soerabaia.[21]

Sri Soerabaia did not gain the same accolades as the Komedie Stamboel. It was initially planned that Van der Laan's troupe would tour Singapore, Aceh, Padang, and the west coast of Sumatra, while Mahieu's troupe was slated for the cities and larger towns of Java. But after Sri Soerabaia ended its run in Surabaya it only played small towns in eastern Java: Probolinggo, Besuki, Situbondo, Malang, Bangil. Some of these towns did not yet have a rail link and were never visited by large-scale komedi troupes. Initial performances of Sri Soerabaia at the Kapasan theater in April 1893 were praised for technical polish and sweetness of song. On tour in small towns in eastern Java, it was said that "the select actors, who are all Muslims from Surabaya, speak a good high Malay" and that the "sets are indeed excellent and are certainly not made by Muslims but are manufactured by a Frenchman or someone else from Europe, and they are very costly."[22] Van der Laan introduced new stories to the repertoire, including a play entitled *Malik Mohamad,* based on the Javanese legend of Marmoyo.[23]

Audiences seemed to have trouble placing Van der Laan's troupe. Some classified it as an "imitation komedi troupe . . . with a dramaturgy that is no different from the Komedie Stamboel."[24] Others designated it as Doro Muluk or Indra Bangsawan, apparently equating Sri Soerabaia with the western Javanese theater of Abdul Muluk and the popular theater of British Malaya. One source even referred to Sri Soerabaia by the singular coinage *komedi hartawan* (rich man's komedi)—which seems to be an attempt to translate bangsawan into Javanese Malay.

(*Bangsawan* is an abbreviated form of Indra Bangsawan but also connotes an affluent member of Malay nobility.) This generic confusion surrounding Sri Soerabaia may account for why nothing more is heard of the company after 1893.[25] A different fate awaited Mahieu and his troupe.

In April 1893 the Komedie Stamboel again went on tour. Before departure, Mahieu's troupe gave ten tent shows at Surabaya's central square from 31 March to 9 April 1893. The weather was unaccommodating: planks had to be laid down on the waterlogged square in order for spectators to reach the tent. And the company had to compete with Abubakar's company, still playing at the Kapasan theater, further cutting down audience numbers.

The first stand on the Komedie Stamboel's 1893 tour was Malang, a hill town ninety kilometers south of Surabaya, serviced by a rail line that opened in 1879. Malang was a commercial center and market town for the area's numerous tobacco and coffee plantations and sugar estates. It was a regional distribution center for the surrounding rural area. "Textiles, household goods, petroleum, and ironware arrived from Surabaya, and fruit, maize, and other agrarian products traveled in the opposite direction."[26] At 443 meters above sea level, Malang had a "cool and agreeable climate" and pleasant environs. Its easy access to Surabaya made it attractive to Europeans, and the town was rapidly growing.[27] (It is today the second-largest city in the province of East Java, after Surabaya.) A Malang newspaper correspondent boasted that Malang in 1893 was a "theater city" (*tempat komedi*) behind only Batavia, Surabaya, and Semarang, with two major komedi troupes arriving on average per month, including circuses, Japanese acrobatics troupes, and Malay theatrical troupes. A night fair *(pasar malam)* held in Malang in 1893 in honor of the birthday of the Prophet Muhammad attracted spectators and vendors from as far away as Bangil, Pasuruan, Tulungagung, and Solo.

The Komedie Stamboel performed in Malang's "splendid alun-alun" for about two weeks starting 20 April 1893.[28] A full program with all the plays to be performed in Malang was printed and sold by the company for fifty cents, available before opening in the Jagalan district.[29]

There were high expectations of the much-heralded company as roustabouts erected the tent on 19 and 20 April 1893. In the end, audience numbers were only moderate. A newspaper correspondent who briefly reviewed the company was indifferent to the acting and music but had high praise for the scenic backdrops. Prices could be lower, he added.

Word on the streets of Surakarta in April 1893 had it that the Komedie Stamboel would give a month of shows there in May. But the company actually only performed for eight days (9–16 May 1893) in the same field adjacent to the Benteng Vastenburg, where it had performed in 1892. The Komedie Stamboel's agent was late in acquiring the requisite performance permit, which delayed the opening by a few days. Once again, a program book was for sale.[30] The tent caught fire during the middle of the second night's show, for unknown reasons. The fire was fortunately extinguished posthaste, though the audience was understandably alarmed. Performances drew large and rowdy crowds, and it is possible that the fire was another arson attempt. After the Komedie Stamboel left Surakarta, the local newspaper opined, "It is good that they [the troupe] left in a hurry, as fights were breaking out every night."[31]

Regardless of these disturbances, the Komedie Stamboel was a must-see event in Solo, and many spectators were attracted by these performances, described as "addictive" by one observer who signed his name Ali Baba. This same observer described how "big, little, old, and young in my city at the current time do not stop singing stambul songs. What is more, groups of friends have adapted these songs for *gambang, suling, terbang* and *rebab, ji hian,* and *gong.* These songs are indeed as pleasant as embroidered flowers."[32] The ensemble described uses a combination of gamelan instruments (gambang, suling, rebab, gong) along with terbang (a frame drum usually associated with Islamic chanting) and a Chinese fiddle variously known in Java as *tehyan, gihyan, ji hian,* or *jihyan.*[33] Musical combinations of this sort were used to accompany Chinese dance parties, known as *wayang cokek* in western Java and as *tayuban* in Solo.[34]

Stambul music became increasingly popular among Chinese art lovers throughout Java in 1893. Chinese gathered in Sambongan (an urban ward of Surabaya) every night in March 1893 to "sing pantun in imitation of the Komedie Stamboel," disturbing the peace of nearby residents. (The editor noted that the police would act only if the singing continued after 10 P.M.; otherwise, "one cannot forbid someone pleasure.")[35] The appearance of the Komedie Stamboel in Yogyakarta in 1893 galvanized "Chinese youths to imitate the pantun of this komedi; day and night these pantun can be heard in the streets without cease."[36] In Chinese-owned brothels (*suhian*) in Batavia, wayang cokek musical ensembles and singer-dancers were regularly hired in 1893 on nights of the full moon to perform "very melodious komedie stamboel songs, which are so much loved by residents here (as they are a new form of song)."[37] The 1893 marriage of a grandchild of Semarang's Chinese major was celebrated with stambul music. Many other Chinese in Central Java followed the major's example and incorporated stambul music into public rituals such as the annual dragon boat races and Chinese New Year celebrations, as well as wedding processions and receptions.

This popularity of stambul music among Java's Chinese only increased in 1894. One Semarang writers saw this as a sign of Chinese "cleverness." "The Chinese certainly have clear minds, for whatever they wish to imitate they can do so quickly. Proof of this is that currently Chinese are learning how to play guitar, violin, flute, and *rebana* [frame drum] in the Komedie Stamboel style. A performance last night at Gang Warung was entirely faultless, leading to the pleasure of spectators."[38] Another 1894 report from Semarang further expands on this. "This year in our town there are many Chinese youths who perform komedi stambul songs for pleasure in streets all over the Chinese quarter, playing guitar, violin, flute, and such. There is also someone who sings, mainly Babah L., who has a very melodious voice. People say that these stambul songs are very popular, as they can lighten a melancholy heart. Not only in Semarang, but in other cities as well, there are many who are performing stambul songs."[39] Some found all this stambul singing offensive, and occasionally roving groups of musicians were arrested and fined for disturbing the peace. But in general, there seemed to be great enthusiasm for this new wave of music making activity, in that it added to the ramai, lively quality of life. A letter to *Bintang Soerabaia* from a correspondent in Pasuruan, east Java, reads:

> On Wednesday 31 October 1894 at about nine at night in Kampung Trajeng the sound of violin and percussion could be heard. It was indeed pleasurable to hear. Then three Chinese men [*babah babah*] appeared. One played violin, the other played percussion [*pukul geduk*], while the third sang stambul songs. These three . . . were indeed skilled. . . . I believe they arrived from [Kampung] Tambakan and then walked south, but I am not clear to where. It is not clear whether they were just out having fun. It is a bit of a shame they did not make the rounds in the Chinese quarter. Thanks are due for adding to the life of the city.[40]

It is clear from ordinary accounts like this that stambul music was part of everyday life in urban Java in 1893.

Perhaps the most important Chinese stambul music maker though was the Batavia shop owner and manufacturer Tan Hoe Lo.[41] Tan capitalized on the growing popularity of stambul and was responsible for arranging, manufacturing, and selling many more music boxes and organs with stambul songs between 1893 and 1898, before the phonograph displaced the music box as the music machine of choice. None of Tan's musical creations seem to have survived, but advertisements and other reports demonstrate that he played a central role in mediating stambul music for the elite and the masses. Tan produced both individual rolls and disks as well as a "Continual Stambul Music Box" (*Orgel lagu stambul trus*), which featured "Stambul I" through "Stambul VIII" as well as four additional Malay songs.[42] He also manufactured and sold a hand-cranked music box designed for children with stambul songs including "Stambul Ali Baba," "Siti Marhava," and "Aladdin's March" as well as "various [unnamed] European songs."[43] A rival Batavia manufacturer's music box featuring "Stambul III," "Stambul Bunga Mawar," "Stambul Aladdin," and a variety of Malay songs, seems to have been less popular.[44] These mediated stambul songs could be heard both in people's homes and in public: organ grinders cranked out the tunes in the streets of bigger towns and cities.

The continuing presence of stambul music in the life of the city of Solo made the Komedie Stamboel's departure easier to bear. A three-

Fig. 3.3. "Music Box. Komedi stambul songs and various Malay songs most popular in Batavia. Available for purchase at Tan Hoe Lo, Batavia." *Bintang-Barat,* 12 March 1895.

quatrain poem appeared on the circular distributed on 16 May 1893, the last night the troupe played Solo.

Nyonya nyonya dan tuwan tuwan.	Ladies and Gentlemen,
Komedie Stamboel hendaklah pigi.	The Komedie Stamboel will soon depart.
Melingken tinggal ini mainan,	This show is the final performance,
Melingken tinggal samalem ini.	Tonight is all that is left.
Marilah liat sekali lagi.	Come see it one last time.
Ini mainan masuk di akal.	The performance is lucid.
Hamba main lagi sekali.	We perform once more,
Aken kasi slamet tinggal.	And will wish you farewell.
Jika dapet idinnya ala,	God willing,
Lain taun hamba kembali	We will return another year.
Harep ketemu slamet semua,	We hope to meet again in peace,
Umur panjang murah rezeki.	And wish all a long life and success.[45]

An agent representing the Komedie Stamboel visited Yogyakarta, the next stand of the tour, more than a month before the company opened there on circa 20 May 1893 for a two-week engagement. The company had previously performed in Yogyakarta's alun-alun. This year, the company's agent had arranged to pitch the tent behind the Dutch fort, the Benteng Vredeburg, a space normally reserved for circuses and European entertainments. This was seen as significant, as it placed the company firmly in the middle of the city—symbolically as well as geographically.

News of the company's forthcoming arrival was greeted enthusiastically by the city's Dutch-language newspaper. Rain reduced audience numbers in the first nights of the run, but subsequently the company played to sellout houses. Acting, costumes, lighting, and mise-en-scène were highly praised, but it was Mahieu's name that was highlighted repeatedly in notices and reviews. "The Heer Mahieu is the soul of each piece, and is also a very good actor," the paper avowed.[46] No reviewer or correspondent noticed the loss of Van der Laan and the half of the troupe that went with him to form Sri Soerabaia. The Komedie Stamboel was increasingly being equated with the name of its charismatic actor-manager.

When the Komedie Stamboel rolled into Semarang on 5 June 1893, decked out in attractive Turkish costumes, they made an impression. From the train station, they went to a rented house behind the Paviljoen restaurant in Blakang Kebon, the same area of the city where the company had resided in 1892. The four weeks of shows in the alun-alun were standing room only. Harmston's Circus, a perennial favorite in the Indies, was playing in Semarang at the same, and for the first time the Komedie Stamboel outperformed a major circus, cutting into Harmston's earnings. Not even Harmston's menagerie of lions, tigers, elephants, and bears could contend with the songs and humor of the Komedie Stamboel. "Many are shocked that a horse-and-jungle-animal komedi of this size could fail to compete with the Komedie Stamboel, which is so small and recently formed, but anything can happen and profit is an indisputable indicator of success."[47] Harmston tried to strike a deal with Mahieu for the companies to perform on alternate nights, but Mahieu would have none of it.[48]

Once again, Semarang newspaper writers used the Komedie Stamboel's appearance as an opportunity for social critique involving both performers and audience. One comment was intended to instill a sense that acting was an honorable profession, and that actors should not be looked down on as deviants. A certain Tuan S., an Indo whose father worked for the city government of Semarang, was applauded nightly for his singing and acting in the role of a king. Tuan S. is described as a "good man," in a moral sense. "But sadly his talents do not please his father, for though he might be the mighty king of Baghdad, his father has no wish to see him. Astonishing!"[49]

The Komedie Stamboel also was the target of criticism for a racially discriminatory practice. The Javanese employee distributing leaflets advertising the company allegedly refused to give one to a Chinese person for "these are exclusively for Europeans, as others can't afford the price of seeing this komedi." This comment enraged the correspondent who reported this. He called the employee "a disgrace" (*kurang ajar*) and requested that he be reprimanded by the Komedie Stamboel's director.[50]

The image of the Komedie Stamboel that remained with Semarang spectators is recorded in a seventeen-verse poem that "Djae Wono" (a pen name meaning wild ginger) contributed to the *Bintang Soerabaia.* This poem is worth quoting at length, for it provides insight into how a devotee understood the Komedie Stamboel and what sort of pleasures it yielded.

Babah Yap Gwan Thay amatlah pinter	Babah Yap Gwan Thay is very clever:
Buka komedi dengenlah gambar	He opens the show with a picture.
Sedeng tendanya sampe besar	Also, the tent is big
Tiada kuwatir ujan menyebar.	And one worries not when it rains.
Tuwan A. Mahieu punya buwatan	Tuan A. Mahieu's acting style
Sampe orang jadi ingetan	Is very memorable
Dari cerdiknya suda klihatan	His skill is visible
Lucunya juga jadi sebutan.	And his comic talent renowned.
Komedie Stamboel sampelah garang	The Komedie Stamboel is vivid
Banyak di sukai sekalian orang	And much liked by one and all.
Siapa yang melihat temtunya girang	Whoever watches will surely be pleased
Denger menyanyinya sampelah terang.	To listen to the singing, which is clear.

Komedie Stamboel punya punggawa Nonah dan nyonya ada semuwa Yang suka bikin orang ketawa Nyonya gembuk dari Surabaia.	The Komedie Stamboel's members of The female persuasion are all European. The one who makes you laugh Is a plump young woman from Surabaya.
Tuwan gemuk tersebut bujel Tingkah lucunya sampelah prigel Banyak orang terpingkel pingkel Merasa di perut sampelah pegel.	A fat man called bujel Acts in a very funny way. Many double up with laughter Until their stomachs hurt.
Tuwan Mahieu sampe mengerti Ambil ceritanya ganti berganti Biar penonton panas di hati Tiap malem jangan brenti.	Tuan Mahieu has a real understanding And changes the plays continuously So that spectators fervently desire To come every night without cease.
Pakeannya komedi semuwa patut Sedeng nyanyinya semuwa runtut Dengen biola bisa menurut Banyak orang jadi kepincut.	The costumes worn are all appropriate And the singing follows the melody In tune and time with the violin. Many are enthralled.
Menyanyi Stambul paling pertama Tertiru orang di mana mana Biar di jalan biar di rumah Orang menyanyi tarik rebana.	The song known as "Stambul I" Is imitated by everyone. On the street and in houses People sing and play it on drums.

Djae Wono's opening description shows a complex, multifocal appreciation of the art form. He recognizes the significance of both Mahieu and Yap Gwan Thay in the company, mentioning both by name. To Yap he attributes the physical accommodation of the tent and the opening stage picture, by which he likely means the front curtain with the illustration of the *Nights'* frame story depicting King Shahriyar, Scheherazade, and Dunyazade. Mahieu is given credit for both repertoire and acting. Two more comic actors are noted, but not by their full names. Programs did not contain the names of actors, and even the most devoted spectators rarely could identify actors except in terms of the personae they assumed onstage. The obese young comic actress is nameless entirely, while the fat male clown is called *bujel,* a Javanese word meaning "having a rounded tip."[51] This is a typical stage name used by clowns, and has obvious phallic connotations. The lack of capitalization of this moniker shows an awareness that this is a nom de théâtre assumed by a comic actor, not a proper name per se.

Aside from these individual contributions, the aspect of performance most stressed by Djae Wono is the Komedie Stamboel's music. This is clearly related to the fact that, as Djae Wono says in verse 2, "the songs of stambul are now much imitated by the people of Semarang. / Those singing them are many." This is a poem that was written a full month after the Komedie Stamboel left Semarang, judging from the date of publication. The emphasis is not on momentary impressions but the lasting imprint. In 1893 this imprint was primarily musical.

Djae Wono then highlights very particular aspects of individual plays in performance before wishing his readers and the Komedie Stamboel well in a formulaic conclusion.

Kapan ambil Aladin punya cerita	When *Aladdin* was selected as a play
Orang nonton semuwa rata	All sorts of people watched.
Lihat Aladin berduka cita	One saw Aladdin in his sadness
Pintu di guwa ketutup nyata.	When the cave's door firmly closes.
Cerita Machmud tukang ambil ikan	The story of *Machmud the Fisherman*
Menjala di pinggir lautan	Showed him net-fishing at the seashore.
Dapet guci suda klihatan	He found a jug
Di dalem isinya iblis dan setan.	With devils and demons inside.
Suwatu lakonnya Siti Senimbar	The play entitled *Siti Senimbar* featured
Perkumpulan putri bermain pelan	Noble women displaying gentility
Sedeng bermainlah hendak bubar	Before the show was over
Pableau vevantnya harus di gambar.	A tableau vivant was shown.
Cerita Ali babah dan kepala kampak	The story of *Ali Baba and the Robber Chief*[52]
Orang yang lihat jugalah banyak	Was seen by many people as well.
Mlihat Kasim dapet cilaka	They attended to Kasim's misfortune
Ali belayar menrajang ombak.	And Ali cutting the waves as he sailed.

Apa bila ceritanya Nurmandi	While the story of *Normadi*
Bikin si penonton ngeri di hati	Struck dread in spectators' hearts.
Coba lihat itu prampuwan Padri	Imagine seeing the priestess
Sekalian kepala perang di bakar api.	And the proconsul being burned alive.
Suwatu lakon si bungah mawar	In the play *Sleeping Beauty,*
Perkumpulan pri pista besar	A gathering of fairies at a feast.
Ramenya suwara sebagi pasar	The sounds were lively as a market
Sekalian yang dateng tida kesasar.	And those who came were not confused.

Djae Wono clearly is impressed by special effects, but he was also attentive to the depiction and sympathetic reception of emotional states. The death of Norma and Pollione provided not only spectacle, but an emotionally sympathetic experience of *ngeri*—horror, dread, terror. It is Aladdin's sadness in being trapped in the dark, and not the magic of the genie, that commands Djae Wono's attention. And finally, he is not oblivious to mise-en-scène, alluding to the intricate choreography and overlapping layers of the soundscape of the feast scene of *Sleeping Beauty* in his penultimate verse.

Performing in Batavia brought great strain to the Komedie Stamboel; although sellout houses yielded substantial financial rewards, Mahieu found himself embroiled in legal cases and at the center of more than one controversy when the company played the capital in July 1893. The Komedie Stamboel was recognized by all as Mahieu's company, but that celebrity made him responsible for all the company's deficiencies. The Batavia papers remained very interested in the company and were more attentive to backstage intrigues than ever before. But the press's tone was more critical than celebratory. The Komedie Stamboel was fully engaged with Batavia's public culture—indeed, it was actively shaping it.

Batavia audiences had been avidly awaiting the return of the Komedie Stamboel to their city for months. Imitation performances by a semiprofessional group of Indo actors at the annual Cap Go Meh celebrations in honor of Chinese New Year in March 1893 attracted large audiences, even though the singing was stiff and the plays not well selected. Such amateur or semiprofessional performances had their place and were appreciated for injecting local referents into dramatic action.[53] But they generated only a shadow of the excitement and possessed only a fraction of the glamour associated with the Komedie Stamboel. "The Komedie Stamboel of Surabaya must come here quickly for at this time people in Batavia are crazy for stambul," concluded *Bintang-Barat.*[54]

One Batavia stambul devotee, H. Krafft, even took it upon himself to write two short stambul scenarios in 1893, *The Painter's Story* and *The Story of a Poor Man Who Benefited from Magical Medicine,* collected in a thin volume entitled *Boekoe Komidi Terpaké bagi Komidi Stamboel* (Playscripts for Komedi Stambul). Krafft was likely a Batavia Indo kroncong singer and might even have been a member of the group that performed at Cap Go Meh. In the introduction to this volume (dated 1 February 1893), Krafft writes,

> For some time my friends have asked me to write a book of stories of the sort used in komedi stambul, but I have only now been able to fulfill this request. . . . I have been overwhelmed by work and thus could write only in fits and starts. What is more, I am not a teacher nor an intellectual nor skilled in writing. . . . My only intent was to amuse my friends and myself, and to entertain myself.[55]

The plays Krafft published in 1893, and a longer play entitled *The Boatman's Tale* published a year or two later, all bear the stamp of the amateur, with awkward rhymes and frequent recourse to explanatory footnotes. They can perhaps more effectively be read as acts of homage to Mahieu's company than as autonomous literary works.

The Komedie Stamboel performed from 5 to 31 July 1893 at the Mangga Besar square. Company members stayed in a rented house also in the Mangga Besar area. As in Semarang, the company tried to make an impression by appearing in a costume in public. But Batavia observers were less taken with this Oriental façade than their counterparts in Semarang: "The clothes the Komedie Stamboel actors wear in public are very odd. A white jacket and pants, a red scarf as a waistband, and a red fez with a star on it. The women wear their own clothes: these are

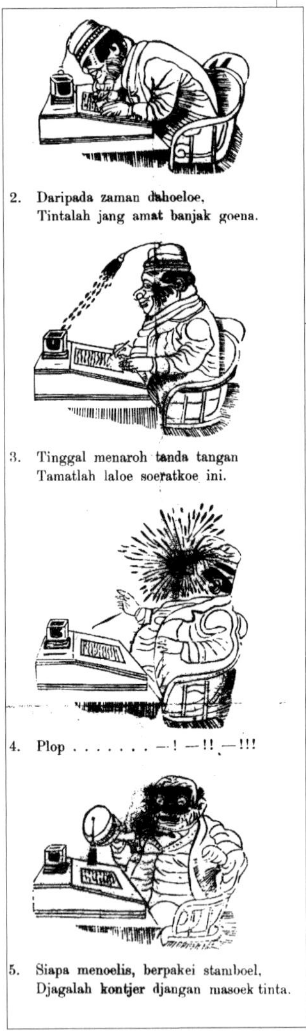

Fig. 3.4. A Malay-language cartoon by Gijsbert Francis entitled "Pleasure Replaced by Regret," burlesquing the fez (stambul). "1. A good pen, white paper. That's what I call pleasurable writing!" 2. "This ink has many more uses than those of the past." 3. "All that's left is to sign the letter and it's finished." 4. "Plop . . . . —!—!!—!!!" 5. "If you write while wearing a fez, be sure the tassel doesn't get in the ink." *Pengadilan,* 22 January 1898.

of good quality, it is true, but a bit odd. I think it would be better for all the employees of the Komedie Stamboel to be given clothes of the sort worn by Turks."[56] Probably the actors were in fact trying to approximate Turkish dress—this is how their outfits are described in Semarang. They just did not do a very good job of appearing Turkish by Batavia's sophisticated standards, and in any case the Turkish fez was an object of ridicule, caricatured as antimodern in an 1898 cartoon by Gijbert Francis.

Other aspects of public front caused problems as well. The company's Muslim distributor of leaflets got into a near fight due to his racial discrimination. This time it was not a Chinese man who was refused a leaflet, but a Muslim fruit vendor in Glodok square.

> Not only was he [the fruit vendor] not given a leaflet, he was abused and insulted by the Muslim who said, "This is not for you Muslims but actually only for Chinese, Dutch, and Arabs." The Muslim then spoke back to the leaflet distributor, who was not ashamed to respond in kind with all sorts of insults. The distributor then walked off to Mangga Besar square, muttering insults as he went. Who knows what would have happened had he not left in a hurry? The matter would have certainly escalated into a brawl.[57]

The leaflet distributor was not the only employee accused of disgraceful behavior. The usher at the theater's front entrance was likewise regarded as not showing a proper amount of respect to spectators.

None of this appeared to discourage spectators from showing up in droves. Any competition faced from other shows in town, including C. Daron's Operetta and Vaudeville Company at the schouwburg, did not appear to affect the size of the Komedie Stamboel's audience. "Many people now are hot for the Komedie Stamboel—that is they are crazy for the chronicles that are sweetly performed and that are appropriate for a mass audience. When it does not rain, the tent is full of spectators."[58] The theater was deemed an apt entertainment for Batavia's consumerist society, for "it is true indeed that the people of Batavia enjoy their leisure and are profligate in throwing a bit of money around as long as their hearts are pleased."[59] The crowd attracted was as diverse as ever. Most of the audience was made up of Chinese and Muslim spectators. There were prostitutes, decorously described as "fragrant night blooms whose odor wafts when the wind blows."[60] There were the usual share of drunks—two of whom picked fight with a hussar during one performance.[61] After a Saturday night show, two young European spectators (likely Indos) hijacked a dos-à-dos from the street and abandoned the horse and carriage on a main road of Kampung Kwitang for the police to pick up the next morning. It was a rowdy crowd but an enthusiastic one.

Many of the plays performed in Batavia appear to be vehicles for Mahieu's comic acting skills. Mahieu was at the top of his form, but attrition in the company meant that some of the principle roles had to be filled by weaker actors, and it was prudent for Mahieu to pick up the slack. Typical of the plays performed was the fast-paced *Ali and the Magic Violin* (most likely written by Mahieu), which was actually introduced to the repertoire in 1892, but had been reworked in March 1893, with new music and costumes.

> A king from the land of Hyderabad has a dream in which a mouse bites through a rope in his palace. The king summons a sage to find out the meaning of his dream. The sage says that the dream means that the king will soon will be beset with major difficulties, but he will subsequently receive the help of a poor person. The king states with great arrogance that he will not allow a poor person to help him, for he is a very mighty and powerful king.
>
> But things come to pass as the sage foresaw. The poor son of a widow assists the king when he is attacked by bandits. This poor man is named Ali and he has a violin with great powers. When he plays it everyone gets tired, and when he plays it softly everyone falls fast asleep. When bandits gain entrance to the king's palace, Ali tricks the bandits and makes them fall fast asleep [with his violin], and after that Ali kills all the bandits.
>
> After that, the king finds out what Ali has done to help the king, and that is why Ali is given the hand of the daughter of the king of the land of Hyderabad in marriage.[62]

This upbeat, rags-to-riches play showed Mahieu at his best. The role of the eponymous hero allowed him to display his musical skills onstage in a role that could be mined to comic effect. "Those that came on Sunday evening to the Komedie Stamboel to see *Ali and the Magic Violin* certainly left with no regrets; from beginning to the end one could hear the public laughing. All were extraordinarily amused," reads one review.[63]

Another review praised the actress playing Ali's mother.[64] While the performer's name is not given, it was almost certainly the actress E. Rensing, who specialized in playing old mothers of the Widow Twankey variety.[65] Rensing's talents are repeatedly praised in reviews in 1892 and 1893—she is said to be "not at all devoid of talent" in the role of a mother; "skilled" in the role of an old and poor mother; and "very funny" in the role of mother of an exiled Tartar prince.[66] Rensing's most extravagant praise comes from an October 1893 performance of *Aladdin,* at which a Muslim spectator wet herself from laughing at the stupidity displayed by Aladdin's mother and the clever wittiness of Aladdin. The spectator's skirt was so wet that she was the last to leave the theater out of embarrassment.

Notices and reviews also are full of praise for the decor. Sets and costumes were recognized as "new and tastefully selected."[67] Not all scenographic equipment functioned perfectly all the time: gas lamps broke at least once, leading to momentary darkness in the theater and fear of a fire breaking out in the tent. Overall, however, the decor was said to rival if not better the Italian opera companies that performed in the schouwburg. The news that the Komedie Stamboel would be performing the story of Adam and Eve raised great curiosity, as "when they were created, there were no other people on earth, aside from these two royals, and they did not yet have clothes to cover their bodies either." Everyone wished to know how Adam and Eve would be costumed before the Fall in the Komedie Stamboel's production, for the company was acquiring a reputation for spectacular realism.[68]

Aside from Mahieu and Rensing, however, the actors in the company were not felt to be strong; while they might be commended for having "done their best,"[69] they were often critiqued by *Bintang-Barat* and other papers. The actress playing the princess in *Ali and the Magic Violin* was disparaged for "speaking words from a book she does not quite understand," while the actress in the title role of *Sleeping Beauty* was "likely performing it for the first time in public because . . . she was afraid to speak."[70] Another actress's weak performance was excused by *Bintang-Barat*'s reviewer because it seemed it was her "time of month." Singing was sometimes out of tune, and at least one of the actors was prone to laughing inappropriately onstage. After a very weak *Sleeping Beauty* (in which Mahieu played the prince), Mahieu was advised to avoid plays of this sort and stick to light comedy.

Ignominy shadowed the actors less for unpolished onstage behavior, however, than for their scandalous conduct offstage. At least two unmarried actor couples had spectacular breakups during this time. It was common for actors and actresses in the Komedie Stamboel and other traveling troupes to live together as unmarried couples (although some were legally married). The loosely communal living arrangements and itinerant lifestyle made such alliances easy and practical: women performed domestic chores such as washing clothes and cooking, while men protected their partners from molestation by love-smitten spectators. This was a very different way of life than that practiced by the bourgeois mainstream, but as actors and other entertainers were not permanent residents of a city it was for the most part hidden from public scrutiny, and Indonesian society was generally more tolerant of a range of sexual relations (prominently concubinage) in the nineteenth century than later.

Precise details and names are vague, but the connubial splits in Batavia hinged on infidelity and affairs. An actor and actress left their partners in the troupe to return to Surabaya together. Another actress, said to be the "fruit of the heart and the object of the gaze of the public," also returned to Surabaya when her partner was unfaithful.[71] The most public breakup, described as a "miniature war," occurred between E. Rensing (referred to as "the woman who customarily performs Aladdin's mother") and her partner, a certain Tuan M., who had worked as a scribe at a Batavia pawnshop before joining the Komedie Stamboel. "Tuan M. received a few smacks from his mistress, and then she struck him with a door bolt so that he ran away swearing with a suitcase filled with his clothes, which he threw into a *kahar* [small carriage], but the horse did not want to go at first. Finally, the horse started to move and he departed, crashing into things left and right on the main street."[72] All this hanky-panky, offstage histrionics, and quarrelling among the actors earned censure from the press. Mahieu was warned that if he "did not make better rules for the relations between his employees, it is certain that the komedi will soon become a real mess."[73]

The actors also behaved disgracefully with members of the public, as illustrated by the following story:

> Two or three days ago three people from the Komedie Stamboel went to a food stall [*warung*] at the bottom of the bridge in Mangga Besar to drink to their hearts' content. After one of them had a few drinks, he appeared half drunk and plumped down his glass so hard that it broke. He then spoke very loudly:
>
> "Who cares if I've broken one glass? I'll replace it with a thousand."
>
> Now it happened that there was a Sino-Malay man [*Cina pranakan*] who reported to the warung's owner what the three men had done and said.
>
> "Hey, *encik* [a term of address for an older Chinese man], he said he doesn't care he's broken one glass because he'll replace it with a thousand."
>
> As soon as the three men heard what the Chinese man had said, the three men got angry and without a further word began to beat him, and the Chinese man was so scared that he ran away and the three men chased him into the kampung. After they had chased the Chinese man, the three men returned to the food stall and vowed as follows:
>
> "Wah, we are not afraid of Chinese or Muslims. If any of you wants a piece of us, come over here. We came to Batavia from Surabaya and we are not afraid of you people from Batavia."
>
> People listened to what they had to say but did not react, as they were half-drunk. So people gave them no mind.[74]

Of course, just because people sitting at a Mangga Besar food stall paid no heed to the drunken performers, does not mean their words were not offensive to the Batavia public. The story was reported without editorial commentary. Indeed, it hardly needed any: the words and deeds of the actors were self-condemning. Slowly, transgression piled on top of transgression. One senses it was only a matter of time before the Komedie Stamboel would be branded a den of vice and its actors viewed as rogues and vagabonds.

Mahieu was conscious of his motley company's indiscretions and weaknesses, onstage as well as off. One attempt to engage the public's sympathy was an announcement that the company would give two benefit performances, with two-thirds of the profits going to Semarang's orphanages and charitable enterprises in Batavia. (It is not clear whether these charity performances ever took place.) Another important sign of Mahieu's recognition of the need to improve his company was that he gave free tickets to the best-known kroncong artists from Kemayoran and recruited three female kroncong singers to join the troupe. This interaction with kroncong artists was recognized by the press both as a mode of advertising as well as a means to "forward" the company.[75]

The relation between stambul and kroncong is complex and worth expanding on. Kroncong was essentially a Batavia art form until 1893, and a low-status art of the streets at that. Many of the accomplished players were Indos who wandered the streets in gangs of three to five, committing petty crimes and wooing women with their romantic songs, accompanied by the kroncong, the ukulele-like instrument that gives the musical form its name.[76] Sometimes guitar, rebana, and other instruments were added. Nobody of status would agree to be serenaded in such a fashion. A few Indo kroncong artists who tried to win the heart of the daughter of a Chinese food stall owner's daughter in 1892 by this means were hit by the girl's father with a door bolt and ran away helter-skelter. Kroncong artists were typically referred to as *buaya kroncong, buaya* (crocodile) being the same term applied to street toughs and petty criminals.

Kroncong performers had been doing stambul songs since October 1892, when the company first played Batavia. The two genres are musically close, and kroncong musicians and singers have always been adept in adapting new melodies to their own hybrid art. Within months, the music of the Komedie Stamboel had become thoroughly part of Batavia's kroncong scene.

> A drum follows the melody: a metaphor for the people of Batavia.
>
> Indeed, the people of Batavia descended from Portuguese known as *serani* have from early times had the pastime of playing the kroncong guitar and singing *pranga, marisku, dangsu cikote* and other songs, but in the short time since the Komedie Stamboel was here, all of Batavia is now performing the songs of Komedie Stamboel, to the point that one is tired of listening.[77]
>
> Whenever Chinese, Muslims, and especially Europeans or Indos wish to sing or whistle, it is a stambul song they do.
>
> Now things have moved on a bit, but the kroncong players have reanimated [the stambul songs].
>
> Every night in the urban wards [*kampung-kampung*] after dusk, especially if the streets are flooded, one can hear kroncong singers' voices, interlocking with the frogs that summon rain.

Ajaib sekali	A great wonder
Adatnya orang Betawi,	Are the ways of Batavia's people.
Ini hari begitu besok begini,	Today like this, tomorrow like that,
Nusanya lagi menukar bini.	The day after tomorrow and there will be a new wife.[78]

Public culture was capricious in Batavia, as described in the above article sent by a reader to *Bintang-Barat.* A love object today was unlikely to be around two days from now. In 1893, Batavia, including its kroncong musicians, was in love with stambul music.

The new stambul songs provided Batavia's kroncong performers with an extended emotional range, plumbing new depths of melancholy and sentimentality. Their affective appeal to kroncong musicians and audiences has to do with their harmonic and modal construction, as described in musicological terms by Bronia Kornhauser.

> From their early days . . . , stambul songs developed a distinctive formal structure within the kroncong music idiom. Stambul songs are allegedly the most melancholy of all kroncong songs. The use of the minor mode for many stambul melodies may have given rise to this notion; such an explanation assumes that the basically Western association of sadness with the minor mode has been transferred into the kroncong medium. Another reason for the idea may be that the subdominant, connected with the melancholy in kroncong, is used extensively in those songs. The vocal part in many cases actually begins in the subdominant, continuing for three or four bars, and then finally progresses to the tonic. Occasionally, vocalists attempt to heighten emotion by singing sustained tones in a relatively slow tremolo fashion.[79]

What Kornhauser does not indicate is that the equation of sadness with melancholy was likely not perceived as purely Western in Batavia or other cities of the Indies by the late nineteenth century. Musicians playing Western instruments such as violin and guitar fully embodied musical aesthetics that came from Europe, but they had set down deep roots in Indonesian soil.

The addition of kroncong singers and their songs to the Komedie Stamboel broadened the musical resources of the company. Just as important, it brought this originally Batavian music to the attention of the entire Indonesian public during the course of the travels of the Komedie Stamboel and rival stambul companies. Instrumentation for kroncong became more standardized, reflecting the musical makeup of Komedie Stamboel's orchestra, and it was not long before musical notation was introduced for the benefit of musicians who were unfamiliar with this Batavia art.[80] The sentiment-tinged kroncong became a significant axis of communication between performers and spectators, as recounted by a spectator of Mahieu's theater in his old age.

> If someone wished for an encore, they would shout out from the hall something like, "Dirk, what about some kroncong?" and Dirk would answer, "Take a gander at this," and the kroncong music would start. Bram and Dirk would launch into tunes with enthusiasm. They had disheveled hair, long lashes, wide-open eyes, with clear voices, and sang kroncong with feeling, and you experienced a tension like one preceding an explosion. When the music, song, and acting ended with the energetic bowing of the violin, emotion broke loose. Flowers and coins were thrown onto the stage. . . . There was direct contact between hall and stage. The musical ensemble in the corner, made up of strings, flute, clarinet, and trumpet, was connected to the company. It went with the group from city to city, country to country.[81]

Kroncong did not begin as an integral part of the Komedie Stamboel, but starting in 1893 the fates of the two popular arts became inextricably linked. Stambul melodies (above all "Stambul I" and "Stambul II") remain standards in the kroncong repertoire and regularly provide forms, or *kerangka,* for composing new songs.[82] Stambul melodies also feature in a variety of other musics of Indonesia and Malaysia, such as gambang kromong. Variants of songs composed by Mahieu and his fellow artists are part of the living heritage of popular performance in Indonesia and other countries, many decades after stambul theater has ceased to exist.

Unwanted attention from the colonial authorities came along with the high public presence enjoyed by the Komedie Stamboel in Batavia in July 1893. The police of Meester Cornelis were perceived as being parodied in one of the plays, and Mahieu was called to the local authorities to answer to a sedition charge. Nothing more is heard of this case, and it can be assumed that charges were subsequently dropped—fortunately for Mahieu and other members of the company, who might have otherwise faced imprisonment or the cane.

A legal case that did not go away so quickly involved the payment of taxes. The residency of Batavia was unique in the Indies for having a tax or permit fee on entertainments designated as wayang.[83] These fees were collected by agents of a revenue farmer, who paid a fee to the local government for the privilege and pocketed the proceeds for himself. The category initially covered as wayang and subject to this special performance tax in Batavia included Chinese opera (known colloquially as *wayang Makao*) and every variety of puppet theater (Javanese and Chinese shadow puppets, Chinese glove puppets, and marionettes). In the 1880s the wayang tax farm was extended to include two new forms of popular theater—wayang wong and Abdul Muluk.[84] The remarkable degree of elaboration of theatrical arts in Indonesian societies forever baffled Dutch colonialists. Many saw the extravagant investment in dramatic performance as a sign of Oriental decadence and took it upon themselves to temper this taste for the theatrical.

The moral danger of entertainment is most clearly illustrated in Michael Theophile Hubert Perelaer's antiopium novel *Baboe Dalima* (1886), in a chapter outlining the corruption of the village of Kaligawe by the plotting opium farmer Lim Yang Bing. The farmer cleverly sponsors a free wayang performance on the green of this prosperous agrarian village, attracting its entire population to see a story "well-calculated to awaken the softest emotions in the breast of the susceptible Javanese."[85] In this emotionally vulnerable state, the villagers fall prey to a familiar ploy and accept free sweets and cigars laced with opium, which get them addicted to the drug. Villagers also gullibly enter into adjacent gambling booths. At first, there are many winners, but as the night grows on the house wins more frequently. Theatrical performance is thus depicted as a trapdoor to turpitude.

The institution of permit fees on wayang was justified paternalistically as a way to mitigate the sort of immoral behavior that Dutch Calvinism associated with sites of entertainment. E. de Waal, in his commentary and apologia for colonial law, provides a justification for the control and taxation of wayang: without monitoring, opera owners might kidnap, enslave, and sexually abuse child actors.[86]

The permit fee for holding a wayang show could be collected from the "owners, managers, or sponsors of a Native or Chinese troupe" according to colonial law.[87] Fees were fixed by an 1862 regulation at the daily rate of eighty guilders for female troupes, sixty guilders for male troupes, fifty guilders for puppet troupes, and twenty guilders for Chinese shadow puppet troupes.[88] Indonesian sponsors of wayang were exempt from this tax for performances taking place in a kampung in connection with a public celebration or a ritual event, but they had to pay twenty guilders otherwise. Failure to pay the requisite fee could result in a jail sentence or a fine. The permit fee was not collected by a government official but rather by the tax farmer who placed the highest bid at a public auction held annually at the residency. The wayang tax farmer (*pachter wayang*), who was inevitably Chinese, then had the exclusive right to collect permit fees and was entitled to pocket the collected moneys. Revenue farms collectively provided the colonial government with one of its most important streams of income, and the access into otherwise off-limits spaces that such farms allowed Chinese farmers was one of the major factors in the rise of Chinese dominance in so many sectors of the economy.[89] The wayang tax farm was considered to be a minor tax farm (*pacht kecil*) and like the farm on permit fees to slaughter pigs (*pacht potong babi*) did not attract big bidders: the wayang farm sold for eighteen thousand guilders for the year 1896, and the highest bid for the year 1899 was only twelve thousand guilders.[90] (This was a pittance compared to the opium farm; opium farm auctions were all-out bidding wars, described by Semarang historian Liem Thian Joe as "the battle of the kings.")[91] It was common that the same person held both the wayang farm and the more lucrative gambling farm, for there were frequently gambling tents set up at wayang performances and the same agents could be used to collect both permit fees. (Indeed, between 1835 and 1848, the gambling farm included the right to collect the wayang permit fees.) As was often the case in revenue farming, the person who acquired the farm tended to engage subfarmers and a host of agents to collect fees.

In practice, the business of running the wayang farm was not easily executed, due to the ephemeral nature of entertainment—one had to know in advance where and when performances were taking place in order to collect fees—and changing and sometimes ambiguous definitions of what constituted wayang. Social dance, for example, might be referred to as wayang cokek in Batavia, but a wayang tax farmer could not collect permit fees on it, though at least one wayang farmer attempted to argue in a court of law that he could.[92] The legal case that involved Mahieu and the Komedie Stamboel entailed just this sort of ambiguity in the application of the wayang revenue farming regulations.

The wayang revenue farmer in Batavia in 1893 was Kan Tjeng Sie, but it was evidently Kan's associate Tan Lan Siong and his company that actually handled the day-to-day business of the farm for him. Tan demanded that Mahieu pay a twenty-guilder daily permit fee for his "wayang" performances, advised by his attorney that there was no substantial difference between the Komedie Stamboel and other forms of popular theater that were required to pay these fees. Mahieu refused on the grounds that the Komedie Stamboel was neither a Native nor a Chinese troupe (although it was Chinese owned and had some Muslim performers), but rather a form of opera akin to European troupes—which were never subject to permit fees. It is in fact at this juncture that Mahieu officially changed the name of the company from Komedie Stamboel to Opera Stamboel. *Bintang-Barat* suspected the name change to be a tax dodge.[93]

Mahieu also mounted a defense that collecting a performance fee was motivated by a personal vendetta. Kan Tjeng Sie had requested that the Komedie Stamboel perform at his child's wedding in 1892, offering a fee of two hundred or two hundred fifty guilders. Mahieu demanded that the company receive a fee of five hundred guilders, plus expenses, and as no accord could be reached Kan Tjeng Sie reportedly was "cross at Mahieu's refusal" and "carried a grudge" against the Komedie Stamboel.[94] Kan Tjeng Sie refuted this charge, saying that he had not acquired the wayang tax farm until 1893 and that in any case it was Tan Lan Siong who ran the farm: he had nothing to do with the decision to collect a permit fee from the Komedie Stamboel himself.

The case was brought in October 1893 before the Raad van Justitie, Batavia's high court. A lawyer named Mr. Fock represented the wayang tax farmer and a lawyer named Mr. Haakmat represented the Komedie Stamboel. It was widely predicted that the Komedie Stamboel would lose the case and be forced to pay the permit fee, but when the decision was finally announced in March 1893, the ruling was in the Komedie Stamboel's favor. The ground for the decision was that if the Komedie Stamboel had to pay a permit fee to the wayang tax farmer, "all sorts of komedi as well as European opera would also be required to pay a fee."[95] Clearly Batavia's wayang legislation had not been designed to discourage Italian opera performances in the schouwburg!

The exemption of the Komedie Stamboel from paying wayang permit fees, and its explicit equation with European opera in the Raad van Justitie decision, served to validate the claim that the Komedie Stamboel had an equivalent aesthetic standing as European high art. The company had used the names Opera Stamboel and Komedie Opera Stamboel (with various spellings) on and off since its founding in January 1891. Supporters recognized the Komedie Stamboel's dramatic form as essentially equivalent to European opera—but with different music and language that was accessible to the Malay-speaking public. One sympathetic newspaper reviewer even suggested that to improve the acting in a stambul troupe a director should "often invite his cast to see French opera. In this spectacle, you can see intentions that are appropriate to imitate, and can change the way actors perform." Significantly, this reviewer urges performers not to act like "wooden dolls" (*boneka kayu*) and to come downstage before the footlights during songs in an acknowledgment of the necessity of direct appeal and emotional linkage to the audience.[96] These aesthetic norms are European through and through; a nineteenth century Javanese actor would hold up the full embodiment of a "doll" (or a puppet) and emotional detachment from the audience as the highest form of acting. Versions of European opera had been part of the Komedie Stamboel's repertoire since the 1891 *Faust* adaptation. But while Europeans often expressed curiosity in seeing how the Komedie Stamboel handled operas such as Gounod's *Faust,* Bellini's *Norma,* Bellini's *La sonnambula* (adapted by Mahieu in 1894), and Verdi's *Aïda* (adapted by Mahieu as *Adiama* in 1900), stambul adaptations were not accepted by Europeans as the genuine articles. "The performance of *Faust* on Wednesday evening was a disappointment for many. There is next to nothing of the plot left in this Malay adaptation of the famous opera, and as a parody it does not hold one's attention for long. The music! . . . but let us be silent about that."[97] These sorts of comments were inevitably European in origin. Non-European spectators came with a different set of expectations and in 1893, at least, were rarely disappointed by the company's appropriations of Western operatic masterpieces. Komedie Stamboel might have performed its operas "on roughly constructed, temporary stages with raised timber floors" rather than at "sturdy, colonial *schouwburg[en].*"[98] But the masses accepted the Komedie Stamboel uncritically and without reserve as *De Oost Indische Opera*—the opera of the East Indies.[99]

Great financial rewards came with the nightly crowds drawn to see the Komedie Stamboel perform in Batavia, and the company was keen on extending its one-month performance permit. It was unable to do so, however, as Batavia's major exposition (*tentoonstelling*) was scheduled to open soon, and the authorities did not wish to grant permits to rival commercial entertainments that might encroach on the exposition's gate.

The 1893 exposition, which took place in Cikini at the zoo and the adjacent grounds of the house of Raden Saleh from 12 August to 19 November 1893, was a watershed cultural event for Batavia and Indonesia as a whole.[100] The exposition was a hybrid celebratory form, drawing eclectically on features of the Dutch country fair, the *garebeg* public celebrations at the kraton, and world fairs. In particular, Batavia's exposition was organized as a response to the Exposition Universelle in Paris in 1889 and the World's Columbian Exposition in Chicago in 1893. Both of these world fairs had generated global excitement for the range of cultures and goods represented, the technological marvels on display, and the quality of amenities available on the fairgrounds. These global events, and Indonesian participation in them, were avidly discussed in the pages of Malay and Dutch newspapers published in the Indies. The 1893 exposition in Batavia was an opportunity for the promotion of local goods and services, the education of the masses in the niceties of consumerism, and the figuring of a culturalist representation of the colony. It was a major financial undertaking, costing 207,672.41 guilders (of which 94 percent was eventually recouped), and attracting many thou-

Fig. 3.5. The Batavia Exposition of 1893. Reprinted from Nieuwenhuys, *Tempo doeloe,* 170.

sands of people daily. There were 110 Dutch, twenty-five French and Belgian, and six British firms participating. The 1893 exposition is notable in many ways for the novelties introduced—the latest styles and fashions from Europe, a teakwood piano designed for the tropics, a new system for teaching music. It introduced a model for organizing similar expositions in residencies throughout the Indies. (Versions of such expositions exist to date under labels such as the Jakarta Fair and *pasar malam*—night fairs.)

The exposition was a site of contrasts and juxtapositions. One report noted "a Catholic priest selling Bibles and such materials; but the priest's stand is adjacent to stalls selling alcohol, where one can drink beer, wine, brandy and soda, whiskey, and such." To which the typesetter added in a footnote: "And other sorts of satanic drinks."[101] Such contrasts and ironies appear to be pervasive but were rarely delineated. This neglect can be attributed to the distraction of the masses in the phantasmagoria of the exposition—a reactionary attitude that, as Walter Benjamin tells us, leads "to that state of subjection which propaganda, industrial as well as political, relies on."[102] Visitors were seeing things with different eyes, on a scale and perspective formerly unknown. This was the first time that outdoor electrification was deployed in the Indies on a wide scale. For years after, exposition visitors associated electricity with the experience of seeing by "electrical light that illuminates the exposition as if it was day."[103]

The exposition was a bringing together of the high and low: crafts, stalls, goods, and people from urban and rural areas throughout the colony. It is appropriate that the exposition's location was divided between the high culture emblematized by the house of Raden Saleh (1811–80), the Javanese "prince" turned European artist, and the low culture of the zoo. Exposition visitors participated in an event that represented the colony as a whole, articulated links between the Indies and other parts of the world, and showed that the world was modernizing.

The bulk of the theatrical performances, appropriately enough, took place in the zoo grounds. This was a realm of the popular and the folk. Companies included C. Daron's operetta and vaudeville company and the internationally famous D'Arcs marionette company.[104] There were also performances of theatrical forms still officially banned in Batavia—Abdul Muluk theater and commercial *wayang wong* dance drama—as well as *topeng dalang* (mask theater), *ronggeng* (social dance with gamelan accompaniment), and *gamelan.* The most popular entertainment at the exposition, however, was a bangsawan group from Penang known variously as the Komedie Bangsawan Permata Johor or Komedie Melajoe Sri Bangsawan or Komedie Bangsawan Johore, under the direction of Abdulrachman—about which more below.

The Komedie Stamboel was in fact offered the chance to perform at Batavia's exposition, but in early July it issued a refusal. The organizers wished to charge the company a seven-hundred-guilder monthly fee to use the grounds, "and whoever wished to see the Komedie would have to pay an entrance fee to the zoo as well as purchase tickets to see the Komedie Stamboel: in effect, paying twice."[105] The troupe's decision not to perform at the exposition proved subsequently to be a mistake.

After its final show at Mangga Besar square on 30 July 1893, the Komedie Stamboel decamped for the Sundanese highlands of western

Java. The company played Bandung, Sukabumi, and possibly other towns, before going once more to Bogor. It timed its arrival there to coincide with the installment of the new governor-general of the Indies.

A newspaper correspondent writing from the sleepy resort and retirement town of Sukabumi, famous principally for the government-subsidized Sela Batu sanitarium, was surprised to see the large and enthusiastic multiethnic audience the Komedie Stamboel attracted during a ten-day run (13–22 September 1893), despite what he perceived as expensive tickets—from fifty cents for third-class to three guilders for box seats. This same correspondent also was surprised by the company's robust finances, saying, "this komedi is not like other komedi troupes that reside permanently in their tent. They are in the tent only when they perform. All troupe members are staying in rented houses. They are renting four houses at the cost of thirty guilders for ten days."[106]

The company enjoyed a month-long run in Bogor, where it played the field in front of the train station from late September to 21 October 1893. The weather was more cooperative than in 1892, although the "old and leaky tent" meant that spectators occasionally got wet during sporadic downpours.[107] Reviews were generally good, and spectators included both civilians and military personnel. (General Ermeling and his wife are noted as being present at the Komedie Stamboel's *Normadi,* the nearly sold-out penultimate show.) Mahieu was praised for his choice of stories, actors were appreciated for their comic skills, and scenic effects were particularly admired. "One can genuinely praise the skill of the leader as he uses stories in which one finds mountains, the sea, and a palace, etc. that are nearly indistinguishable [from reality], as the equipment is so well made . . . spectators simply cannot be bored."[108] Only one critic griped that the music was better last year, before the ensemble added a piano to its band.[109] The Komedie Stamboel attracted such large crowds, in fact, that the Bogor correspondent of *Bintang-Barat* predicted that even the Abell and Klaer circus, which started to pitch its tent at Bogor's horse market on 23 October, would be unable to match its success.[110]

The Komedie Stamboel had vowed that it would remain in Bogor to greet the new governor-general of the Indies (usually addressed in

Malay as *tuan besar,* or big master), Carel H. A. van der Wijck. The company was in its most patriotic mode, evidenced in the performance of the stirring tableau vivant showing the departure of Prince Willem of Orange and his assassination by Balthazar Gerards (performed in Batavia on 23 July 1893 and in Bogor on 15 October 1893). While the Komedie Stamboel's performance permit had expired the day before, the company stayed to be part of the celebrations on 22 October 1893. Van der Wijck's arrival was made a school holiday in Bogor, and people turned out in large numbers to get their first glimpse of their new tuan besar. Van der Wijck arrived at the Bogor station on a specially scheduled "extra train" at 9:30 A.M.

> The train occupied by His Excellency stopped at the station and a military band greeted him with the anthem "Wien Neerlandsch Bloed," as across the street from the station a canon was sounded twenty-one times as a sign of respect. The Komedie Stamboel did not neglect to give His Excellency a welcome and greeted him with music played in front of their stage, as well as singing and cheering. (There was a small and nice tent erected there which had also been used when the former tuan besar left office and returned [to the Netherlands].) But the stambul music could not be heard due to the many gamelan ensembles that were also playing helter-skelter.[111]

The Komedie Stamboel was anxious to obtain governmental recognition and official validation through association with the new governor-general. They just couldn't get themselves heard through the din of competing voices.

Mahieu did not anticipate that Batavia's exposition would be as big an affair as it was. By the end of August 1893 he seems to have realized he made a mistake in not agreeing to perform there, and he desperately tried to obtain permission to play there or anywhere else in Batavia if possible. However, as the Malay saying goes, "Once someone spits, he ought not to try to lick it up again."[112] All efforts in August and September 1893 to get a permit to play Batavia met without success.

The direct benefactor from the Komedie Stamboel's absence from Batavia was Abdulrachman's Komedie Bangsawan Permata Johor company, which played continuously at the zoo from 15 September until the end of November 1893. It was undoubtedly particularly irksome to Mahieu that Permata Johor was privileged to have a direct entrance from the main road of Cikini and that spectators would thus not have to pay for both entrance to the exposition as well as the theater. Abdulrachman's company had all the benefits of being located adjacent to the busy exposition and none of the detractions. Had Mahieu been offered this option, he might not have been so quick to turn down the exposition's offer to perform there.

Permata Johor was a large-scale bangsawan company, with forty actors in the cast and sparkling costumes and elaborate sets. It claimed in press reports issued before it opened to be better than the Komedie Stamboel.[113] The comparison of the two companies opened a debate about the use of language partially that was embedded in ongoing discussions about "high" and "low" Malay language. This debate had important consequences for how the Komedie Stamboel was publicly viewed in subsequent years.

The debate was rigged—in the sense that it was initiated and fueled by Permata Johor itself. A major selling point for Permata Johor was that, despite its use of European-style songs and European stage technology and marketing mechanisms, it was an authentically Malay cultural product, presenting bona fide chronicle plays out of Malay antiquity. Malay in British Malaya was the language of the courts, a literary language for the composition of *syair, hikayat* (prose narratives), and pantun. According to one promotion issued by the company,

> The company's productions are truly the works of Malays, and all the backdrops, curtains, screens, and costumes are made, sketched, cut, and sewn by Malays as well. . . . Performances are distinguished, as all actors speak in authentic Malay language, and the courtesies, ordered interactions, and polite behavior that takes place between the actors does not neglect a single aspect of the courtesies that originally were used by kings of the authentically

Malay people, in accord with the language used in Malay language books and chronicles.[114]

One promotion goes so far as to include a syair, or poetic ode, to the company's authenticity, reputedly by a Batavian writer who had seen theater in both Malaya and Java. In this syair, the company was lauded as being the venerated work of a Malay master from Johor. The language of Johor was said to be the language of the chronicles themselves, a "literary language" (*bahasa yang asal di dalem surat*). This language, and the fine scenic pictures also said to be made by Malays, would be sure to impress on people "the cleverness of the overseas Malays" (*kepandeyan bangsa Melayu sebrang*), that is, the Malays of British Malaya.[115]

The importance of accurately presenting the customs of the court, and particularly the presentation of deference and respect, was inculcated into Malay theater troupes in Malaya through a history of royal patronage. Actors were expected to be well trained in court etiquette by a *guru wayang,* or acting instructor. Those troupes that deviated from expectations were subject to criticism.[116]

Permata Johor's promotional strategy played cleverly on an insecurity related to Malay language and identity in Java. Interisland trade, the need for a single language of communication for indigenous people in the colonial army and civil service corps, and newspapers and "print capitalism" were all determining factors in Malay becoming a lingua franca in nineteenth-century Indonesia.[117] Dutch scholars, evangelists, and administrators represented the Malay language spoken in urban Java as "bazaar Malay" and the language of the popular press as "low Malay." They positioned the linguistic hybridity of Javanese Malay (with its admixture of words and syntax from Dutch, Chinese, Javanese, and other languages) against the imagined purity of a "high Malay" said to be spoken in the area of Riau and the court centers of Malaya and inscribed in the classic hikayat. "Low Malay" was a "language of communication" (*verkeerstaal*) while "high Malay" was a "language of culture" (*cultuurtaal*).[118] An argument of linguistic contagion motivated research into dialects and a variety of reforms into spelling, syntax, and grammar. Malay was slowly being standardized for use as a lingua franca for administration, education, and evangelical activity throughout Indonesia.

The Komedie Stamboel had always prided itself on being able to communicate directly with its audience, with "dialogue and singing in Malay that can be understood by all." It was rare for a Muslim, Chinese, or Indo urban spectator to report difficulty in comprehending the theater's demotic Malay.[119] Dutch critics were split on their views of the dialogue. While some stated that "the Malay is easy to follow," others reported that it was hard to follow the dialogue "unless one is unusually strong in Malay."[120] Jan Fabricius recalled that he "did not understand the elegant Malay spoke onstage, but the jokes of the comics, which normally were spoken in house- or garden-variety Malay, were more than worth" the price of a ticket.[121] Frequent recourse to "garden-variety Malay," repetition, and cross-translation insured that spectators with even minimal Malay competence could grasp the basic plot of a Komedie Stamboel play. Niceties of inflection were not usually noticed by the company's boozy and boisterous audiences.

Some spectators evidently bought into the linguistic claims of Permata Johor and the notion of a pure form of Malay located outside Java. Claims against the hybrid language of the Komedie Stamboel had been mounting for some time. For example, in 1893 a Batavia newspaper strongly critiqued the Komedie Stamboel's flawed politesse.

> The Komedie Stamboel attracts many spectators nightly due to its excellent performances and the fact that it uses the Malay language. But people who know much about the Malay language say they are disappointed that the komedi does not compose dialogue properly. Something that is mentioned once will often be repeated once or twice again. Last Sunday night, Si Jembros Blas said about himself that he is very rich, to the point that kings borrow money from him. He reported this one moment and the next moment he said the same thing again.
>
> A king speaking to Si Jembros Blas referred to himself as *hamba* [a deferential form of the first person pronoun], while Si J. B. referred to himself as *kami* [the royal "we"].

The paper went on to complain that actors mistook the word *suwami* (a courtly word for husband) to refer to "wife," and called people "male" (*jantan*) or "female" (*betina*), although these classifiers can only properly be applied to animals.[122] No reader jumped to the defense of the Komedie Stamboel, although *Hindia-Olanda*'s aspersions on the company's linguistic skill were answered indirectly by a Sumatran correspondent of one Batavia Malay newspaper, who reported that komedi companies who visited his town also were prone to use language that sounded "most improper" to local Malay speakers.[123] The writer seems to be aware that Malay was at this time not a codified universal language but rather a large variety of overlapping dialects. It was only natural that itinerant theaters would differ in their use of Malay from local custom.

When Permata Johor opened at the zoo on 15 September 1893, the Malay press was able to assess directly the validity of the company's preproduction publicity claims of superiority over the Komedie Stamboel, with the different Batavia papers taking sides. The biggest supporter of the Komedie Stamboel was (not surprisingly) *Bintang-Barat.* The newspaper characterized Permata Johor's dialogue as "high Malay of the sort people use in chronicle literature."[124] This was a form of "Malay that people of Batavia can't completely understand."[125]

> Though the bangsawan group's performance and clothes might be excellent, this is of no use to people in Batavia, for a Malay komedi must speak Malay that is good to hear and which even children can understand, like the Komedie Stamboel. Children see the Komedie Stamboel perform one night and the next day they imitate the plays at home, with all the singing. If the Komedie Stamboel were to arrive here today and erect its tent at Mangga Besar field or Glodok, this very night the tent would certainly be full. It is a pity it could not get a permit to stay here long so that people might watch to their hearts' content.[126]

Hindia-Olanda was also mildly critical of the inaccessibility of Permata Johor's language, saying that "the performance and costumes of the komedi are excellent and cannot be deprecated, but sadly most people do not fully understand the language, as the actors speak in Malaccan Malay."[127] Of greater concern to this paper, in fact, was that an urgent need for fire exits in the theater.[128] But Permata Johor found a strong supporter in the *Pembrita Betawi,* which said that it was "a thousand times better" than the Komedie Stamboel, with better costumes, a better repertoire of stories, and, most important, better language. "The bangsawan troupe's language is more refined than that used by the Komedie Stamboel, for the bangsawan group does not use dirty language, like that often used by the Komedie Stamboel."[129]

This debate on the comparative merits of the Komedie Stamboel and Permata Johor arose at a critical moment in the Komedie Stamboel's history. It occurred at the same time the company was making the legal case that it was more like European opera than traditional Asian theater—to avoid paying taxes to the pachter wayang.[130] The Komedie Stamboel had hitched its representational future to being an indigenized form of European theater, a derivative cultural hybrid through and through. The representation of the mythical and legendary past of Southeast Asia was more or less left to other theatrical forms. That orientation, at least in the short term, was the prudent course, if one takes the brute economics of the entertainment world as index. While Permata Johor did relatively well in Batavia, it did not attract large audiences during its subsequent run at the Kapasan theater in Surabaya. And when the company returned to Batavia in 1894, it did so poorly it was forced to sell off its fit-up to a semiprofessional stambul group from Mangga Besar under the direction of sinyo Henri L. One of Permata Johor's actors, a Singaporean named Mohamad Saleh, was forcibly deported for unknown reasons, and the rest of the company returned to Malaya by June 1894. Apparently, audiences in Java interested in seeing authentic Malay customs depicted onstage were in a minority. Most wished instead to see a demotic form of Malay used as a medium of delivery for a wide range of stories and stage pictures outside the scope of Malay heritage. The Malay language was thus uncoupled from Malay traditional narrative literature, and the "low Malay" of the Komedie Stamboel was constructed as the preferential medium for communicating to mass audiences in the Indies. To use the terms of the times, the Komedie

Stamboel's language was reified as a language of communication and defined in opposition to a language of culture.

From the highlands of western Java, the Komedie Stamboel returned to the coast, steaming into the port of Cirebon and then traveling overland to Tegal and Semarang from October to December 1893, playing to great acclaim in all three cities. The Dutch-language papers in both Cirebon and Tegal responded avidly to the first-time visit of the company, lavishing nearly as much attention on the Komedie Stamboel as they customarily devoted to touring European opera companies.[131] Mahieu's name was increasingly prominent in the public eye, and as actor-manager he is often given credit in reviews for scenography, dramaturgy, acting—in fact, he is credited for all aspects of production.

Cirebon, like the principality towns of Surakarta and Yogyakarta, was a city with a number of royal courts, but their cultural significance and economic resources were meager by the late nineteenth century, diminished by centuries of subordination to the central Javanese kingdom Mataram, the Dutch East Indies Company, and the colonial governments of the Netherlands and Britain. Cirebon's royal courts managed to sponsor the occasional dance drama, but these were of minor interest for most people. The coffee and sugar industries and the presence of sizeable minorities of Chinese, Arabs, and other non-Indonesian ethnic groups, with associated small businesses and home industries, had brought the appearance of prosperity to Cirebon in the 1890s.[132] Artistic activity, however, was largely centered in the surrounding villages, not in Cirebon itself. The reception of the Komedie Stamboel served to establish that city as a center for itinerant popular entertainment, which it remains to date.[133]

The Komedie Stamboel arrived in Cirebon on the wave of its good press from Surabaya, Semarang, and other cities, and with a reputation for a big repertoire of both *Arabian Nights* plays and European opera adaptations. The company gave a musical recital on 28 October 1893 at the Sociëteit Phoenix, Cirebon's exclusive European club, as its tent was being erected in the Kebumen square. The audience for this concert was limited to club members, giving the impression that this was a theatrical group with serious musical aspirations. The run in Cirebon (29 October–15 November 1893) brought full houses, thunderous applause, repeated curtain calls, and garlands and bouquets for the principals. It was not long before the Komedie Stamboel's songs were well known to all and sundry—and were even being sung in the sacrosanctly European preserve of the Phoenix club. The company was deemed a "grand spectacle" (in French) and "a great attraction" (in English)—foreign accolades evoking a cosmopolitan aura.[134]

Perhaps the most popular story in the Komedie Stamboel repertoire at this time was *Bubakam, or Bluebeard,* an adaptation of the classic Mother Goose tale.

> There was a man named Bubakam, who was very rich; his huge wealth was the equivalent of one or even three kings. And he had a blue beard: that is why people called him Bubakam or Bluebeard. He courted a merchant's daughter, and as her parents desired him as an in-law they agreed to marry their daughter, Roldia, to Bubakam. One day after they had married, Bubakam went on an ocean voyage and left his wife at home along with his younger sister, named Dinar. He gave keys to all rooms of the house to his wife but told her that while she could unlock all doors of the house and see what was inside them, there was one room she could not unlock, and if she were to violate his order she would be very sorry. After giving his instructions, Bubakam then departed.
>
> After Bubakam departed, Roldia invited her sister-in-law to unlock all the rooms with the keys in hand, and she was able to observe all the riches of Bubakam in these rooms, and they thus performed no work other than opening up these many rooms for days on end. Then came the day that they had looked into all the rooms, except for the one room that Bubakam had instructed them not to unlock. Because she had already seen so many surprising things [inside the various rooms], she also wished to see what was inside the forbidden room. Her sister-in-law told her not to unlock it, but Roldia could not control herself and unlocked the forbidden room.

> When they entered the room, they fainted for they did not see gold, silver, or other ornamental objects, but rather saw large numbers of corpses of women murdered by Bubakam.
>
> After they came to their senses, they quickly locked the door and left this miserable place, but the lock to the room was soiled with a spot of blood. No matter what they washed it with, the blood would not come off. It was less than a few days later when Bubakam returned and met once again with his wife. He then requested that Roldia return the keys he had given her and he inspected the locks one by one and saw the blood on the lock of the secret room. He then became angry and was on the point of killing her but was prevented from doing so by the arrival of Roldia's brother, and in the end he kills Bubakam. . . . The play concludes with a tableau vivant showing Bubakam surrounded by the wives he has murdered.[135]

Audiences in Cirebon and elsewhere thrilled to the "energetically paced" performances of *Bubakam.*[136] At a performance in Cirebon, the depiction of the attempt of Bluebeard's servants, Si Ali and Kadir, to clean the blood-stained lock with brandy was reported to be "charmingly played," and "[t]he public looked on in horror when the chamber of horrors with the corpses of the seven wives was opened and revealed."[137] Audiences in Tegal received the play as a "comical spectacle" when it played there a month later, frequently screaming with laughter.[138] When the play was enacted in Batavia on 16 April 1894, audiences both laughed to the antics of Ali and Kadir and were emotionally touched by the scene in which "Roldia, Bluebeard's wife is about to be killed, and before she is killed she sings a pantun in alternation with her sister-in-law, Dinar, in a voice that is most sad to hear."[139]

Not all the reviews were positive: the offstage chorus in *Sleeping Beauty* was deemed out of tune, and the music in *Faust* considered beneath criticism. But at a time when there were precious few amusements of this sort available to Cirebonese, the Komedie Stamboel succeeded in captivating audiences, creating a lasting impression.

The troupe left Cirebon after midnight on 17 November and went directly to Tegal, where it performed for two weeks (22 November–5 December 1893). Tegal, like Cirebon, was a small town, with a population of about fifteen thousand in 1893. It was rarely visited by komedi troupes. (Its only competition at the time of its performance seems to have been a commercial wayang show performed with cardboard puppets; tickets cost a token one cent.) The town was prosperous nonetheless. Muslims of Tegal were known as carpenters, smiths, stonecutters, and copper workers. The great post road that ran the length of Java bifurcated the town. A Chinese quarter was on the south side of the road and about five hundred Europeans lived on the north, clustered around a four-sided field not far from the coast, where the resident's mansion and a derelict military fort were located.[140] The Komedie Stamboel pitched its tent in the field behind the resident's house, symbolically the European center of the town. The presence of the town's "notables" (*pembesar pembesar*) at the opening performances was enough for a Malay newspaper correspondent to commend the purchase of second-class seats (priced at one guilder). The Komedie Perzie, the stambul troupe that had originated in Semarang in February 1893, had made a poor showing when it had played Tegal, and people were initially skeptical that the Komedie Stamboel would attract audiences. But Tegal audiences turned out to be "crazy" for the Komedie Stamboel; its performances seem to have appealed above all to Chinese women.[141]

A day or two after the Tegal opening, Mahieu departed for Semarang, leaving "the younger Mahieu" (likely his brother Oscar) temporarily in charge. The reason for Mahieu's absence was not clear immediately, but it subsequently emerged that it was related to another of Yap Gwan Thay's komedi stambul troupes, the Komedie Spanjool (or Ispanjool; lit., Spanish Komedie), which was then playing Semarang.

The Komedie Spanjool, which like the Komedie Stamboel was made up primarily of Indo actors, had been founded in Surabaya by Yap Gwan Thay in July 1893, with a female director named Brouwer initially at the artistic helm. (She was replaced several months later by a man named Rossengais.) After playing for several weeks at the Kapasan theater in Surabaya, the troupe left on tour to Malang (where its run coincided with a major night fair) and Probolinggo, and started to perform in Semarang on 30 October 1893. The troupe from the first tried to establish its own distinct repertoire, with plays culled from the *Arabian Nights* along with a raft of Persian and Indian tales newly introduced to Java by touring bangsawan companies. An advertisement for shows at Kapasan gives an impression of spectacular exoticism, with an emphasis on Indian and Persian plays.

Komedie Spanjool

30 July	Playing PARI BANO, see: a cave breaking open and a fairy palace
1 August	Playing AFFATKAR, see: a woman torturing her husband
3 August	Playing BIN DIAP, find out: the secrets of people selling people
6 August	Playing ALBRAHA, see: a boat set on fire that then sinks
9 August	Playing MARHAVA, see: someone turn into stone and a revolving well

Directress
Brouwer[142]

The company also introduced new plays that had yet to be adopted into the *komedi Melayu* repertoire. One of these was the story of Razia and Sadi from the adventure novel *Secrets of the Court of Constantinople.*[143] Another was *Genoveva,* based on the legend of Genoveva of Brabant, well to known every Dutch schoolboy.[144] This last play, which featured a "very attractive Nonah G. [Gemser?]" in the title role, proved to be a hit with audiences, and was subsequently incorporated into the standard repertoire of all stambul groups. "If one thinks about it, this play taken from a Dutch story and adapted into Malay is certainly not easy to perform smoothly, for the troupe is accustomed to performing stories based on the *Arabian Nights* and has only just learned this new play. Many spectators have requested that this play be repeated once more."[145]

The Komedie Spanjool earned high marks for its fresh costumes and lifelike scenery but was criticized for poor acting and a lack of humor. Spectators tended to view the company as a second-rate imitation of the Komedie Stamboel. Inclement weather in Malang, and the destruction of sets and damage to the tent due to gale-force winds in Probolinggo, meant that by the time the company arrived in Semarang it was badly limping. Yap Gwan Thay was evidently concerned about his new troupe's finances and paid a visit to the company when it was in Malang—he was spotted at Malang's train station, setting off speculation that the Komedie Stamboel would soon be visiting. There was talk of the Komedie Spanjool leaving Java for a Singapore tour. Something needed to be done.

It is hard to reconstruct what happened at this juncture, due to the fragmentary nature of available sources. This is what is known. It was announced in December that Mahieu had stepped in as the director of the Komedie Spanjool, starting 24 November 1893, but by 29 November, Mahieu was back in Tegal performing with the Komedie Stamboel. (The company needed him—ticket sales had fallen in his absence.) The Komedie Spanjool, which had been losing money in Semarang, ended its run there by the beginning of December and then "jumped away, nobody knows to where." Nothing more is heard about the Komedie Spanjool again. Mahieu arrived in Semarang from Tegal on nearly the same day that the Komedie Spanjool disappeared, announcing that he was now heading up a new company called Sri Penggoena (The User), or Stambool Ajohaij (Stambool, "Hello There"). It was suspected that Mahieu had a "new model" of komedi to perform.[146] But when Mahieu actually opened in Semarang in December, it was with the Komedie Stamboel, and there was no hint that the repertoire differed substantially from the one the company presented in Cirebon and Tegal.

The "facts" appear contradictory; we are faced with a historical knot. Here is one possible scenario. Mahieu was brought to Semarang by Yap Gwan Thay to head up the Komedie Spanjool on either a temporary or permanent basis. Mahieu acted with the company for a few days and likely did some actor training as well. When it became apparent that the Komedie Stamboel also required Mahieu to make a profit, Mahieu was contacted and returned to Tegal, leaving the Komedie Spanjool get on without him. In early December the idea was hatched that the two companies might merge and perform together under a new name (Sri Penggoena or Stambool Ajohaij). The decision to change the name was later reversed, and the Komedie Spanjool was absorbed into the Komedie Stamboel. (This is borne out by the fact that a number of plays introduced by the Komedie Spanjool in 1893 were performed by the Komedie Stamboel in 1894.)

Whatever the case might be, the Komedie Stamboel enjoyed an acclaimed and profitable run in Semarang in December 1893, with full or nearly full houses every night (except when it rained). This was the company's third appearance in Semarang, and it had a loyal fan base. On 25 December, the company's equipment was loaded into the train that took the company's personnel and apparatus back to Surabaya. Personnel were promised a two-week holiday in Surabaya before starting up again: after all the events of the long tour of 1893, it was certainly well deserved.

During the last months of 1893, as the Komedie Stamboel toured Java's north coast, a rumor circulated in two variants that Mahieu was using a magic spell (*aji*) or talisman (*jimat*) to attract spectators.

> For all plays performed by Tuan Mahieu, one laughs almost continuously, as they are so funny and so very skillfully and smoothly worked out. When he performs *Aladdin,* people are sure to [laugh so much] their stomachs hurt. People say that Tuan Mahieu has a Pengirutan talisman.[147]

> It is certain that Tuan Mahieu uses a Semar Kuning spell, shown by the fact that men and women, Javanese, Dutch, and Chinese come in droves every night to see his company.[148]

This discourse of magic applied to popular entertainment in the Malay press is a discourse that is almost, but not quite, tongue in cheek, conflating stage magic, the "magic" of the theater, and extratheatrical supernatural powers. Reference has already been made to the hapless balloonist Lorenzo, who failed to present the necessary offerings to his balloon (see chapter 2). We read also about a clown (*badut*) in the Sri Soerabaja stambul company who joked at a Bangil performance about raising a big wind and was stunned to see his prediction come true the next day, when a wind knocked over the company's tent. "The clown had learned his lesson and vowed not to summon winds again. We think that it is because he fears that what he says will come to pass once more."[149] The failure of the Komedie Spanjool to make a profit in Semarang "perhaps was because the charms of the *kihai danyang* [the company's tutelary spirit] were not efficacious."[150] A narrative about the Komedie Stamboel's adaptation of Bellini's *La sonnambula* that mixes a splash of supernatural spirits with more than a drop of alcoholic spirits illustrates perfectly the alienated tone of these attributions of magic onstage.

Batavia

> When the Komedie Stamboel performed at the Mangga Besar field there was a very strange [aneh] happening. We would like to report on it to this newspaper. One night the company performed the story of *The Somnambulist,* which is about a sleepwalker. During a five-minute intermission, spectators were busy eating and drinking at the buffet set up in front of the theater. One of the spectators had been treated to so many beers by his companions that he had forgotten about his wife's daughter, a girl with a beautiful face. She had been sitting by herself and then vanished. Nobody knew where she had gone. The poor father asked many people about her, as he looked about to the right and left, but he could not say where the girl had gone.
>
> By chance, the father walked by the back of the theater and saw the lost child coming down the stairs. She was coming from backstage. Her clothes were disheveled and her hair was tousled, like someone who had just woken up.
>
> The father asked her, "Hey, my child, what has happened to you? What evil man has brought you here? Tell me who it is and I will teach him a lesson."
>
> But the child answered, "Ach, father, let's just go back. Nobody brought me here, nobody asked me to come here. I was struck by sleepiness and then walked in my sleep like the Somnambulist."
>
> Do not ask whether the girl had lost anything that she had not already lost before she became a somnambulist.

Heaven only knows! Be careful, be careful all spectators. Do not be inattentive or drink when you bring your daughter or wife to see *The Somnambulist.*

A reader[151]

Such a story reads like it was translated from a European language (and indeed it might be, with only minor changes). It is awkward, filled with innuendo and ellipsis. Real magic was being used on the popular Malay stage at this time. Bangsawan troupes from Malaya customarily employed one or more *pawang,* who inserted pins into actors to make them more attractive, recited spells on opening night, and produced magical water that actors used to wash their faces and make themselves more attractive to spectators.[152] And there are numerous accounts of Javanese and Balinese performers employing the same sort of magic.[153] But the newspaper accounts of supernatural happenings around stambul tell us less about the actualities of ritual practices of theatrical performers and more about the uncomfortably medial belief position of stambul observers. As Tony Day has observed regarding tales of *kaelokan* (mysterious happenings) in rural central Java reported in the pages of the Javanese newspaper *Bromartani* in the mid-nineteenth century, accounts of the supernatural in theater "tell us something about a hunger felt by the multiracial elite . . . for mysteries with which to titillate its own sensation of social strangeness." Day argues that for Surakarta's urban elites, "situated culturally somewhere between the primitive spirit world of Java and the 'modernity' of 19th-century Europe, such manifestations of *kaelokan* . . . , expressed the impotence, the racial unease and bad conscience inherent in the structures of its own unprecedented plurality."[154]

Mahieu and his company of Eurasians had begun working in 1891 as "paupers," living in the Krambangan slum of Surabaya in much the same way that urban Muslims lived. The Komedie Stamboel was moving up a cultural escalator in 1893, as it increasingly associated itself with European opera, through legal, promotional, and aesthetic mechanisms. There are few references of Komedie Stamboel as a relief effort for impoverished actors in the salad days of 1893: this was a commercial theater that functioned to make money for owners, directors, and actors. The Komedie Stamboel was crossing a social barrier, and every transgression brings out anxiety about the validity of the social structure as a whole. The published (half-joking) accusations that Mahieu was using magic to obtain his popularity were expressions of the racial unease in the unprecedentedly plural world of popular entertainment. A group of Eurasians had never occupied a place of cultural prestige before the Komedie Stamboel. Neither Native art nor entirely European, the Komedie Stamboel was an uncanny "un-native" medium of expression.[155] Rendering Mahieu's considerable accomplishments as magic was an act of symbolic deflation. It was an attempt to mystify Mahieu's popularity, expressing the bad conscience of colonial society. The accusations are a warning, much like the one that concludes the innuendo-filled *Somnambulist* story. Be careful, be careful all spectators. You might be seduced by the powerful "magic" of the Komedie Stamboel, and find yourself searching for something you had always taken for granted when it was sitting next to you. And if you do lose that treasured object and are fortunate enough to find it again, there is no guarantee that its virginal purity will be intact. Likely you will be impotent to know whether the object was pure to begin with.

Chapter 4

KOMEDIE JANBOEL, 1894–98

> The Komedie Stamboel, which has been on tour for the last ten months, returned to Surabaya on 29 December 1893. According to our informant, it has been very successful wherever it has performed. The company will stay for a little while in Surabaya and give some shows in the Kapasan theater. We hope that the company will quickly return to Batavia to give shows, because its performances are greatly appreciated by the people of Batavia.
>
> —*Pembrita Betawi*

After nearly a year of accolades on tour, the Komedie Stamboel's three weeks of performances in Surabaya after New Year's earned unreservedly positive reviews. "The actors and actresses now feel more at home on the planks, the costumes are fresh and sumptuous, and the sets are beautiful."[1] In addition to the shows at the Kapasan theater, two special shows were given at Surabaya's schouwburg on 20–21 January 1894. Dutch-language summaries were available at the entrance to the schouwburg for spectators "less conversant in the Malay language."[2] The first of these shows, a performance of *Ali and the Magic Violin* with "The Eruption of Krakatau" as a tableau vivant, drew a particularly large audience. The second show was *Genoveva,* "costumed entirely in old Spanish costumes," with a tableau vivant picturing "The Discovery of America by the Spaniards." After that performance, there was a ball with music provided by the Komedie Stamboel orchestra. The company clearly had "arrived" from the perspective of colonial society, that is to say, it had been validated socially and aesthetically as an art form worthy of consideration and attention from society's elite.

The company did not intend to prolong its stay in Surabaya. The preferential use of the Kapasan theater at this time was as a tryout house for komedi troupes that Yap Gwan Thay could then purchase, revamp, and send on tour. The Komedie Stamboel was too valuable a commodity not to be on the road reaching new audiences. Malay popular theater for Yap was a sort of franchise, and the Komedie Stamboel acted as a groundbreaker for other troupes he owned—stambul companies, bangsawan troupes, acrobatics groups, variety outfits, companies of Chinese opera (sometimes in Malay, sometimes in Chinese, sometimes in a mixture), and topeng shows.

The Komedie Stamboel gave its last show in Surabaya on 25 January and departed for Singapore on 28 January 1894. Yap Gwan Thay had been interested in touring a stambul troupe outside Java for more than a year, but the heavy demand for the Komedie Stamboel in Java had forestalled interisland touring previously. Plans for Sri Soerabaia and Komedie Spanjool to tour Sumatra and Malaya in 1893 had fallen through, and by 1894 both troupes seem to have become defunct. (Many of Yap's troupes had short lives; acts, equipment, and personnel flowed freely among them.) The moment now seemed ideal for the Komedie Stamboel to tour outside Java. Going to Singapore in January would mean avoiding the worst of Java's rainy season. There was evidence that audiences in Singapore and elsewhere in Malaya would be receptive to stambul, just as audiences in Java had appreciated popular theater companies from Malaya: Abubakar's Komedie Melajoe (from Penang), M. Abdullah and Ibrahim's Komedie Melajoe (also from Penang), and Abdulrachman's Komedie Bangsawan Permata Johor (from Johore) had all enjoyed some success in their tours of Java in 1893. Javanese commercial wayang wong troupes had been performing regularly in Malaya since the 1880s. Audiences in Malaya appreciated this Javanese theater. Difficulties in following this theater's Javanese language did not seem to put them off overly much.

Singapore in 1894 was an international emporium, "the great junction where travelers from the East or West change ship . . . ; a commercial cross-roads where all who travel must stop and see what a marvel of a place British energy has raised from the jungle in less than half a century. . . . The Dutch mail-steamers to and from Batavia connect with the English mail-steamers at Singapore; a French line connects with the

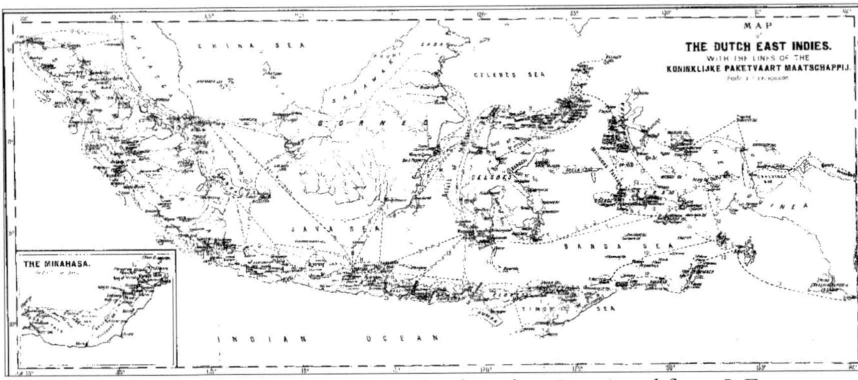

Map 4. Shipping routes in the Netherlands Indies. Reprinted from J. F. van Bemmelen and G. B. Hooyer, *Guide through Netherlands India, Compiled by Order of the Koninklijke Paketvaart Maatschappij* (London: Thos. Cook and Son, 1903), n.p.

Messagerie's ships running between Marseilles and Japan; an Australian line of steamers gives regular communication; and independent steamers . . . leave Singapore almost daily for Batavia."[3] Military steamships from all nations docked regularly in Singapore's deepwater harbor. The man-of-war *Yoshino,* touted as the "fastest cruiser afloat" with a top cruising speed of over twenty-three knots, arrived at Singapore six days after the Komedie Stamboel, causing quite a stir.[4] Singapore was the home port not only for British-owned vessels but also for many Chinese-owned coastal steamers, referred to pejoratively by the Dutch as a mosquito fleet. Singapore was only about sixty hours by steamship from Batavia, and Singapore was the major transshipment center for international freight with destinations or origins in the Netherlands Indies up through the 1890s. The founding of the joint private-public Koninklijke Paketvaart Maatschappij (Royal Steam Packet Company) enterprise in 1888 had gone some way to reduce the centrality of Singapore in the shipping industry of the Netherlands Indies, but Singapore was and remains the most important port in Southeast Asia, with a multiethnic populace and a famously multicultural ethos.

Mahieu and sixty-nine members of the Komedie Stamboel (including fifteen actresses and thirty-five actors) traveled from Surabaya on the steamship *Chiang Hok Kiang.* This ship was a British-registered vessel under the command of a certain Captain Kunath, with a carrying capacity of 956 tons. The company members traveled deck class and likely consumed the customary shipside meals of rice, salted fish, and hot peppers and drank water, coffee, and tea. The company arrived in Singapore on 2 February 1894 and erected its tent (described in Singapore's English-language press as a marquee)[5] on Tank Road, at its juncture with River Valley Road. This stand was adjacent to one of Singapore's biggest Hindu temples—a Tamil temple built in 1859 by Chettiars, a caste of moneylenders and merchant-bankers, known as the Chettiars' Temple or the Sri Thendayuthapani Temple. The opening performance was delayed until 17 February, and the troupe was reportedly able to perform only eight times over the next four weeks. These setbacks were later ascribed to inclement weather. (Singapore's rainy season usually is over by February, but in some years it ends as late as March.)

Due to competition with Chinese New Year festivities, audience figures were initially low, but attendance later picked up. The Komedie Stamboel was experienced as a novelty by Singaporean audiences. In a Malay-language review, the stage is described as being "like that used for theater by White People at Town Hall," Singapore's major theatrical venue used by touring companies. "The painted backdrops are very attractive, like the Town Hall's backdrops, or even more attractive. This theatre company performs in the manner of White People's theatre, not like a circus. The dialogue is in Malay, but is a bit profound [*dalam*]. Costumes are excellent, and in my opinion like those used in Parsi theatre, with lots of beads. The songs are slow and elegant, and there are five or six players in the band. The band also plays slowly."[6]

Singaporeans experienced some trouble with the Malay dialect used onstage. An oral historical account of this first visit of a stambul troupe to Singapore states that the Komedie Stamboel's "accent was not quite suitable with expectations of people" in Singapore.[7] The discrepancies between the Malay spoken in Singapore and the Komedie Stamboel's Javanese Malay is evidenced by the printing of a Malay-language advertisement in the bilingual newspaper *The Straits-Chinese Herald,* or *Surat Khabar Peranakan,* which contains a fair number of spelling and syntactical errors attributable to the typesetter. Some of these errors, including the description of Mahieu as the company's manager rather than director were corrected when the advertisement was printed the second time.[8]

In addition, the Komedie Stamboel's sensationalism might not have been to the taste of the more refined Singaporean audiences. An English-language review of "the old-time story" of *Ali Baba and the Forty Thieves* praised the acting, scenery, and stage effects but reported that the production was "at times of a highly sensational character, and the audience in our opinion might well have been spared the painfully realistic murder of the man found in the robber's cave."[9]

The Komedie Stamboel was billed as a *wayang peranakan Belanda* (Dutch Eurasian theater company) featuring "Dutch Eurasians gentlemen and ladies."[10] Singapore's European elites had low opinions of Eurasians (who were viewed collectively as "a problem"), and this likely contributed to the scant attention the company received in the English-language press. A comparison with the London Lyric Company, which in February 1894 performed mixed bills of variety acts and farces at Town Hall, is illustrative. The London Lyric Company benefited from daily reviews and notices in all the English-language dailies. All shows were recent hits of the London stage, but the London Lyric's productions were of variable quality. A review of *Walker, London* (written by J. M. Barrie in 1892) reported that the production was "a bad mixture of almost forgotten humour, if indeed it be humour at all" and that "the main fault lay in the absence in the play of anything sufficient to warrant laughter."[11] The company nonetheless received the full support of European society. *Jane* (an 1890 farce by W. H. Lestocq and Harry Nicholls) was performed "under the patronage and in the presence of His Excellency Major General Sir Charles Warren," while *Charley's Aunt* (written by Brandon Thomas in 1892) received the same support from the Honorable W. E. Maxwell, the Colonial Secretary.[12] In contrast, the appearance of a solitary Caucasian (*orang puteh*) spectator at the Komedie Stamboel is cause for surprise in a Malay-language review. An explanation for his presence is required: he is said to have been in the audience as "he is Dutch."[13] One English-language paper advised "the management to give a little more publicity to their entertainments," by placing an advertisement in the newspaper.[14] Mahieu did not respond to the paper's offer for cheap publicity, although he did advertise in the Malay press. He knew his target audience in Singapore was not European.

The Komedie Stamboel did not score a financial success in Singapore. The fifteen hundred Singaporean dollars earned from the run did not cover expenses. The theater business in Singapore was a hard nut to crack. This was a lesson that Mahieu learned from both his own experience in Singapore as well as from a certain Babah O. The story of how Babah O. joined the Komedie Stamboel provides an object lesson on the treachery of agents and the collegiality of show folk in the context of international theatrical touring.

Babah O. was a Chinese man from Sukabumi (western Java) who went into partnership with a Singaporean called Hajji A. who visited Java in 1893. Together, they contracted a Sukabumi-based wayang wong troupe to perform in Singapore and paid a local Sukabumi official (*lurah dessa kota Sukabumi*) a two-hundred-ringgit bribe for his permission to let the troupe travel. The troupe then sailed to Singapore, along with the two financial principals. The company was a success in Singapore, drawing thousands of spectators, and earning seventy to eighty ringgit in profit nightly. However, Babah O. only received nine or ten ringgit a night—though his contract with Hajji A. stipulated an equal distribution of profits. Babah O. protested—not only because of his own reduced income but because the performers also saw little of the profits, despite their hard work and popular appeal. The babah put his case to Hajji A., but received a rude response.

"I am not from Sukabumi," replied the hajji. "You know, Babah, that I am a Singaporean. If you want to make a legal case out of this, go ahead. I will not back down. I am used to dealing with the law. What's more, starting now I will not give you any more money, not even half a cent. You want to complain to the authorities, go ahead. You want to get mad, go ahead. Fine and good. But you'll end up with your head split open."

Babah O. had no money at his disposal, but all the same he promptly left the company, only to find out that the hajji had paid a group of forty criminals known as the Ketjo gang to kill him. The babah took refuge in the attic of the house of a *cincau* (gelatin drink) vendor, not daring to go out. For long days, he ate, drank, and even urinated and defecated in the vendor's attic.

Meanwhile, the owner of the wayang wong troupe, a certain D., found himself to be likewise in dire straits. Not only had Babah O. deserted him, not only were his company members being chronically underpaid, he had lost his star performer, an actor-dancer named Si Wen. This performer had won the hearts of thousands of female admirers and the gifts of money, clothes, and jewels that came along with a fan base, but he had also gained the animosity of these fans' husbands and feared for his safety. Wearing soiled and tattered clothing to avoid recognition, Wen boarded a ship to Batavia. With him went another actor and an actress.

D. appealed to the hajji with kind words to sever their affiliation and allow the company to perform in another part of Singapore, at an Indian-owned edifice located about a mile away from the first pitch. Hajji A. appeared initially to consent. However, the hajji subsequently sent out the forty members of the Ketjo gang to raise a ruckus at one of the troupe's first performances. D. turned to the local ward for help, and a battle broke out between the Ketjo gang and some eight hundred residents of the ward. People lost hands and feet, a skull was broken, many fell face down and vomited blood. Babah O., still hiding in the cincau vendor's attic, watched the violent spectacle from the rooftop, invisible in the pale light of the early evening moon. At least fifteen people were seriously injured in the altercation.

D. could gain no assistance from the local authorities. The Indian man who owned the property where the troupe was playing wanted no more trouble from the Ketjo gang and gave the troupe a day to vacate the premises. D. returned to the hajji's employ, conceding full financial control to the hajji and consenting to a fixed nightly pay of only three to five ringgit.

But there was good news for Babah O. The Komedie Stamboel was playing about two kilometers away from his hideout. Babah O. remained unable to show his face in public, but he was able to borrow enough money to hire a rickshaw to take him and the cincau vendor to see the

Komedie Stamboel's director. Mahieu heard Babah O.'s sad story and took pity on him.

"Come, let's eat now, Babah," Mahieu told him. "You can join us and live with the company. We are all 'show folk' [*orang-orang komedi*]. You can work for the company, if you desire, but if you can't work you can also live here without being employed." Babah O. chose to work, and rose to the rank of stage manager, overseeing the complex disassembly process of the troupe's equipment and the loading of the fit-up onto either the steamship *Giang Ann* or the *Kiemtiksing* (accounts vary), which transported the Komedie Stamboel to Batavia at the end of the Singapore engagement.[15] Babah O. also returned to Java on the same ship and was soon home in Sukabumi.[16]

This ideal of "we are all show folk" was as powerful in Southeast Asia as anywhere else in the world in this period. Itinerant entertainers depended on one another for information about travel conditions, the reliability of agents and theater owners, housing arrangements and amenities, local permits and travel passes, the conditions of a theater or tent ground, and a thousand other matters, large and small. Marionette artists, musicians, dancers, actors, acrobats, magicians, sideshow freaks, and a host of other showmen on the road sat down together for drinks, shared meals, and traded gossip, anecdotes, and tales for survival. Life on the road was unpredictable, and while all entertainers hoped for windfall profits, stupendous calamities often lurked in the wings. Often the only "social security" an entertainer traveling abroad possessed was the knowledge that other traveling entertainers were inclined to offer a helping hand in times of need. Assisting a fellow entertainer in need was an investment in one's own future. One never knew when one would need such aid oneself. The Komedie Stamboel was plugged into this international society of performers as much as any troupe. The rescue of Babah O. was not the first time that the Komedie Stamboel had helped show folk in need. In 1893, when the balloonist Ramoth's parachute failed to open fully and he fell forty meters to the Kebumen field in Cirebon, he was brought to a doctor and then recuperated from his injuries at the rented "house of his friends in the Komedie Stamboel," which was playing Cirebon at the same time.[17] Mahieu became "renowned for possessing a good character and readily helping out fellow humans in trouble."[18] This reputation was to stand him in good stead in moments of personal and professional need that lay ahead of him.

FOLLOWING THE completion of the Singapore engagement, the Komedie Stamboel had intended to go to Aceh, Medan, Deli, Padang, and other parts of Sumatra, but an "unbroken stretch of bad weather" resulted in the cancellation of the Sumatra tour.[19] Instead, the company returned to Batavia by steamship, rented a house to serve as the company dormitory in Gang Pinang in the Pesayuran district of Batavia, and, having obtained a two-month performance permit, pitched its tent in Mangga Besar. The Mangga Besar run (30 March–24 May 1894) was financially a great success, reputedly bringing in a clean profit of ten thousand guilders—excluding expenses (about 175 guilders nightly). Inclement weather continued to impinge on the performance schedule, resulting in cancellations due to rain and major damage to the tent during a big windstorm. Even on rainy nights, however, spectators still showed up (typically receiving rain checks for the next night's performance if the show had to be cancelled). And the gallery was so crowded that one night the stands collapsed and the spectators in the third-class seats fell to the ground. (Fortunately, there were no serious injuries.) Dutch- and Malay-language newspapers wrote high praise for performances, with Mahieu's comical acting skills garnering frequent kudos. Much effort was expended on advertising, with ads in all the major newspapers and story summaries appearing regularly in some of the Malay-language papers. An advertisement for *Ali Baba and the Forty Thieves* explicitly compared the Komedie Stamboel's enactment of this "universally famous and beloved piece" with a production at Amsterdam's grandiose Paleis voor Volksvlijt (Palace of Industry), but there is less insistence in general in trying to equate the Komedie Stamboel with European theater than in the past.[20] By 1894, Batavia knew the Komedie Stamboel well—and appreciated it on its own terms.

The company's repertoire had broadened considerably since its last appearance in Batavia, to include a raft of new plays written or adapted by Mahieu, a number of European play adaptations (some, like *Geno-*

veva, costumed in European dress), and many plays derived from the Persian and Indian stories and story motifs mined by Parsi theater and Malaysian bangsawan troupes. One of the more popular of these latter sorts of plays first performed by the Komedie Stamboel in 1894 was *Badarel Dunia, or The World Star,* said to "provide a positive example for those living in this world."[21]

> Asmaru bin Syahda, the king of Jemina, is a very pious and learned man. He wishes to abdicate and appoint his eldest son as king. But his plan is unacceptable to his vizier, who wishes to become king himself. This vizier has gained the support of all the kingdom's warriors and war chiefs. He plots to kill the king, but the king escapes. The queen is terrified that the vizier will try to kill her two sons, Achid and Sasha, and she tells them to run away too. Achid and Sasha meet their father, the king, and the king dies by drowning when he helps his sons ford a wide river.
>
> The vizier becomes king. Presently a mysterious plague strikes the kingdom, spread by Badarel Dunia, also known as World Star, who is the child of a priestess. As the plague becomes increasingly virulent, the people of Jemina become terrified and go to the grave of King Asmaru bin Syadad to ask for his forgiveness and assistance from beyond. For the people recognize their complicity in their king's death and realize that they have done something wrong. Then Badarel Dunia comes to the grave and brings the king back to life. The people wish for Asmaru to become king of Jemina again, but he refuses, and instead appoints his son as king. The evil vizier is then punished.[22]

This simple fable of the value of fealty was appropriately concluded with a tableau vivant depicting Amor, described in Dutch-language publicity as "the god of love" (*god der liefde*) and in Malay-language publicity as either "from love" (*dari ḳacinta-an*) or "that which God causes to come into existence from the pureness of the heart" (*jadinya Tuan Allah dari suci ati*).[23] The Malay subtitles appear to be circumlocutions designed to avoid openly referring to non-Islamic divine beings, as they might

KOMEDIE STAMBOOL,
Mangga-Besar.
HEDEN AVOND
schitterende opvoering van
ALI BABA EN DE VEERTIG ROOVERS,
Dit algemeen bekend en geliefd stukje is eenigszins gewijzigd in den geest zooals 't in AMSTERDAM is opgevoerd geworden in 't PALEIS VAN VOLKSVLIJT.
Het tooneel stelt ALI BABA en DE VEERTIG ROOVERS voor op een groot schip in volle zee. ALI BABA ontvlucht en steekt 't schip in brand.
TABLEAU VIVANT stelt voor
De Jeugd, den Middelbaren leeftijd en den Ouderdom van den mensch.
2868 De Directeur, A. MAHIEU.

KOMEDIE STAMBOOL.
MANGGA BESAR.
HEDEN AVOND!!
BENEFICE VOORSTELLING VOOR DE ACTRICES VAN HET GEZELSCHAP.
GENOVEVA,
waarbij de rollen van GENOVEVA en SIEGFRIED zullen worden vervuld door den heer A. MAHIEU en echtgenoote.
SPAANSCHE COSTUMES!!
TABLEAU VIVANT.
NEPTUNUS OP ZIJN ZEGETOCHT.
Directeur A. MAHIEU.
Vrijkaarten HEDENAVOND niet geldig.
De voorstelling heeft gisteren wegens slecht weder geen voortgang kunnen hebben. 3155

Figs. 4.1 and 4.2. Advertisements for the Komedie Stamboel in Mangga Besar, likening its *Ali Baba* to a production at Amsterdam's Palace of Industry and promoting the "Spanish Costumes!!" of *Genoveva. Bataviaasch Nieuwsblad,* 9 May and 22 May 1894.

offend the sensibilities of Muslim spectators. Such was the degree of sensitivity to the predilections of all spectators in this nonsectarian theater for the masses.

The crowds attracted by the Komedie Stamboel to Mangga Besar remained as rowdy and difficult to control as ever. A Dutch spectator tried to force himself upon the wife of a Chinese man, resulting in a near fight in the audience during the performance of *Sahir zaman,* a new play written by Mahieu.[24] A policeman intervened and escorted the Chinese man out of the theater, called a carriage, and sent him home.[25] A sinyo (young Eurasian) spectator "well known among carriage drivers" started a fight and ended up getting a good beating by other sinyo spectators.[26] Prostitutes and their pimps gathered by the side of the tent.[27] "Drunk and boastful" soldiers tied together dos-à-dos carriages waiting outside the theater as a practical joke, causing great consternation among spectators returning home.[28] All these incidents were artifacts of the theater as a social scene and reflected and represented underlying tensions and antisocial impulses in Batavia society.

More serious was the charge that the Komedie Stamboel itself undermined public morality by attracting female fans who became lovers of actors, resulting in marital and familial crises. This charge had previously been laid against Abdul Muluk theater and had been an instrumental cause of that theater's banning by Batavia's assistant resident in 1882. There was talk now of the Komedie Stamboel being "a second Abdul Muluk."[29] Even if women did not become lovers of their stage idols, their attendance was viewed by some as a drain on domestic economies.

> [W]hen someone without money wishes to go, this can lead to fights between a husband and wife, because the wife is crazy to see it [the Komedi Stamboel], and the husband must stay at home to look after the house. There might not be food at home, and the kids might be screaming from hunger, and the valuables pawned, but the wife just has to go watch, even if it is pouring rain. And what is more, she goes nearly every night! The husband is like a stupid cow and does nothing. . . . We only wish to make the lady, who certainly will read this newspaper, aware of her domestic responsibilities so that she does not neglect her children.[30]

The comment is nominally addressed at one particular married Christian lady (nyonya) but by writing this comment in a newspaper, where it can be read by all observers of Komedie Stamboel and reprinted in other newspapers as well, this woman is made to stand as an icon for all Komedie Stamboel devotees.

Another serious detriment to the company's reputation was the improper behavior that continued from some Komedie Stamboel troupe members and the consequent strained relations with people of various ethnic backgrounds around Batavia. The company's Chinese cashier, Oeij

Tam Lie, was arrested for living in Gang Pinang, a European neighborhood, and not in an officially designated Chinese quarter.[31] An employee of the Komedie Stamboel threw stones at the house of a Muslim named Saman to get the attention of a girl he was enamored with, in the process damaging the roof tiles of both Saman and Saman's Chinese neighbor. The stone thrower was arrested and questioned by the police: it was believed that he was "somewhat mentally disturbed."[32] An exchange of insults and a near fight broke out between Komedie Stamboel company members and Muslims from Kampung Jawa: the actors behaved arrogantly, and in the end the Muslims ran away and a violent conflict was averted. More seriously, a company member abducted and tried to run off with a Muslim girl named Alima living in Pesayuran, not far from the company's rented accommodations. The girl was returned to her parents and the man brought in for questioning by the police.

There is also record of a dispute between the company and people living in Mangga Besar due to the refusal of Tuan L., who ran the buffet in front of the Komedie Stamboel tent, to carry turtledove turnovers (*pastel perkutut*) made by a Mangga Besar woman as a concession. These turnovers, and the squirrel (*bajing*) turnovers she also made, were very popular with people in Mangga Besar, who fancied delicacies of this sort. The woman who made the turnovers and her husband, who had a business selling turtledoves and kept thousands of them, also were much liked by locals. The turnovers had received a bad review in the newspaper, however, and Tuan L. rejected the request to carry them, as he could barely keep up with the demand for alcohol and there was little profit for him in taking in prepared food on concession. This rejection created tension with the locals, and *Bintang Betawi* joked that "new residents in Kampung Mangga Besar should be cautious: if you go out walking in the morning or evening, do not whistle like a turtledove, because their headman lives there."[33]

Mahieu and the other company members appear to have been sensitive to the dangers of bad publicity and responded through various channels. The most important contribution to building a good reputation was a benefit performance for victims of a fire that had recently struck Gang Kancil (in Kampung Pecebokan). The Komedie Stamboel's benefit performance, which took place on 13 April, featured the new play *Muratkhan, or The Horned King* and a Joan of Arc tableau vivant. The announcement of the benefit earned Mahieu support from the press for "his good heart and his sympathy for the [fire's] victims."[34] The benefit cleared three hundred guilders and earned Mahieu and his company a direct vote of thanks from the people of Gang Kancil and surrounding kampung. An announcement that the Komedie Stamboel would soon give a performance at Batavia's schouwburg that would be attended by the governor-general might also have been intended to increase the company's standing. (This report was dismissed by the press as mere rumor, as the announced date conflicted with the governor-general's official schedule.) Finally, early evening displays of kite fighting by Komedie Stamboel company members by a river near the company's dormitory in Pesayuran attracted large crowds of appreciative onlookers, "because in Batavia there has never been kite dueling of the sort the Komedie Stamboel people do."[35]

All these social efforts and the remarkable number of devoted fans and public enthusiasm for the company's performances did not assuage a lurking suspicion that the Komedie Stamboel was somehow betraying its origins. There are no more comments about how the Komedie Stamboel is a noble enterprise formed to benefit its Indo actors, and much concern that this commercial enterprise exerts negative societal influences. The theater had somehow lost its moral rudder, Mahieu's humanitarian spirit notwithstanding. This feeling was most intensely articulated in a letter to the editor of *Hindia-Olanda* that was published a week after the end of the Batavia run. This letter is also an important attempt to look back on the Komedie Stamboel's history, and as such both indexes the variety of stories circulating about the company and provides a strong ethical argument related to the Komedie Stamboel's changing societal value.

> What is the purpose of Komedie Stamboel?
>
> We feel that its producers and owners intend solely to make a big profit and bring joy and pleasure to the hearts of spectators.
>
> Not ten years ago, we saw a form of performance called Abdul Muluk, a theatrical form that had come into being earlier in Borneo

and subsequently arrived and played in Batavia. Abdul Muluk was performed by Muslims and its plays also enacted chronicles of the past. But because many (Muslim) women were attracted to Abdul Muluk, leading to the depredation of good people due to lust for the actors, the police banned this form of performance from being enacted in kampung before the general public.

Now we would like to tell about how the Komedie Stamboel originated in the city of Surabaya: due to the difficulties of gaining employment, a number of unemployed gentlemen without any means of income attempted to form a theatrical company.

A gentleman, probably the same person who now heads the Komedie Stamboel [Mahieu], could not get financed by a European and thus (reputedly) borrowed five thousand guilders—from the Chinese man who is the current owner. This and that occurred, and the komedi did well due to the ability of its director.

At first, these gentlemen hoped that performing stambul would provide enough income to make ends meet, but now that money flows like water, their scruples have changed and they believe that everyone now praises the company.

Word has it that when the Komedie Stamboel performed in the Mangga Besar field in Batavia there were fights every night between company members and outsiders, and while the performance was going on there were fights offstage.

Many women fell under the theater's spell and could not spend a single night at home. All they wished to do was see the Komedie Stamboel. Moreover, there were young women who were coerced into acting with the company.

One gentleman was forced to divorce his wife as she was so crazy for stambul.

If all the stories we have heard are true, we certainly hope that the police will be a bit vigilant.

It is our hope that the authorities investigate this matter proactively and that the matter is treated no different from Abdul Muluk, which has been banned for so long.

K.[36]

This impression of the Komedie Stamboel's public image encapsulates an anxiety of the unbridled power of theater to seduce audiences into a world of fantasy and wantonness. This was an anxiety that was still to crystallize into a concrete form, but there were definite indications that the tide of public sentiment for the Komedie Stamboel was beginning to shift. After the Komedie Stamboel departed Batavia in May, there were, of course, other sources of diversion, including the Indian Circus, under the direction of J. N. Paul and A. L. Ghosal, and a semiprofessional stambul group from Batavia. But the capital was "without doubt very quiet" in the Komedie Stamboel's absence.[37] Some preferred it that way.

The Komedie Stamboel left Batavia and opened in Bogor at the end of May 1894. Batavia's authorities had ruled that only one Malay commercial theater group could play in the city at a time, and Latumeten's semiprofessional stambul company had a prior claim on performing in the Mangga Besar field.[38] With the expiration of the Komedie Stamboel's two-month permit, the troupe needed to leave town, although ticket sales in Mangga Besar were still brisk, and there had been requests for the company to perform in Gambir for the benefit of Batavia's upscale, udik spectators. The troupe clearly did not wish to travel far from its devoted fan base in Batavia and thus arranged for permits in the nearby towns of Bogor (an easy train journey from the capital) and Cirebon (not far away from Batavia by coastal steamship). Other cities of western Java also clamored for the Komedie Stamboel to perform there. A Bandung correspondent for one newspaper suggested that the troupe travel through Bandung on its way to Cirebon, taking the overland "Preanger route," arguing that there was profit to be made in Bandung and that a Bandung stand could "make up for the additional travel expenses."[39]

Ticket sales in Bogor were only mediocre, and on one night a month into the run only thirty people showed up, which was interpreted as a sign that "spectators are starting to get bored and people's pockets are already flat."[40] This low box office was not as substantial a problem as it would have been under other circumstances, as actors were still flush from the profits of the two-month Batavia stand. Mahieu's brother, Oscar, an actor in the Komedie Stamboel at this time, got married in Bogor on 21 June 1894 to F. J. van Lingen, probably using money he had saved from Batavia.[41] There were the usual problems with rowdiness. A Muslim got into a shouting match and was pushed and slapped about by some Europeans during one show, prompting a newspaper correspondent to reflect: "Oh! It is true that wherever there is a performance, men are bound to behave inappropriately."[42] The presence of Governor-General Van der Wijck and his entourage in Bogor meant that the town had unique symbolic cachet. When Van der Wijck's adjutant, Captain Kroll, wrote to Mahieu to reserve seven box seats for a performance of *Ali Baba and the Forty Thieves* on 3 July 1894, it was rumored that the chief of staff would be attending with his wife, Van der Wijck's wife, and the governor-general's children (Van der Wijck himself being otherwise disposed).

The most significant event of the Bogor run, though, was the management buyout of the Komedie Stamboel by Auguste Mahieu. Yap Gwan Thay's finances were often haphazard. He had a talent for latching onto new forms of popular entertainment, but that was offset by his unrestrained desire to speculate in new enterprises of diverse sorts and his profligate spending, on novelty items in particular. In 1894 his finances appeared particularly shaky.[43] Yap's passion for luxury goods from the elite shops of Surabaya, Semarang, and Batavia led to the accumulation of substantial debt, which wound him up in prison for some months in 1895. A particular distraction in the first months of 1894 was a lawsuit against Yap for the unlicensed sale of European medicine, which nearly resulted in three months of forced labor and a one-hundred-guilder fine. The case involved three months of litigation and the temporary shutdown of a profitable pharmaceutical businesses. As previously noted, both of Yap's second-string stambul troupes, Sri Soerabaia and Komedie Spanjool, appear to have closed by the end of 1893 or early 1894 at the latest. All this did not discourage Yap from building a new troupe—the Komedie Laijsing, a magic and variety show headlining magician Laij Sing Pan from Beijing—in May and June 1894. However, it did mean that Yap was unable to devote much attention to the Komedie

Stamboel, and it implies that he was particularly stretched for cash, making him vulnerable to a buyout.

Various estimates of the value of the Komedie Stamboel are to be found in the press. An 1894 letter to *Bintang Soerabaia* that likely originated with Yap Gwan Thay figured the company's assets at "not less than twenty-five thousand guilders."[44] The actual resale value of any theatrical company, however, is much lower than projected assets. For example, when Marie Oord was forced to sell the properties of her quite elaborate stambul troupe in 1917, she was only able to obtain "a meager fifteen hundred guilders."[45] The Komedie Stamboel's most important asset was, in fact, Auguste Mahieu himself.[46] The company was by 1894 so reliant on Mahieu's artistic direction and acting skills that the Komedie Stamboel had little worth without him.

The takeover did not proceed smoothly, which is often the case for management buyouts. It contributed to a lasting animosity between Yap Gwan Thay and Mahieu. A substantial proportion of the sum of eight thousand guilders that Mahieu paid Yap for the company, including all its equipment and its tent, was likely leveraged against an advance payment from an unnamed Chinese backer. Mahieu had arranged to perform for a month in Batavia in July and August 1894 for a fixed fee, with all profits going to this backer. The advance fee was sufficient to cover the bulk of the sum required to purchase the company. The remainder needed to complete the buyout was likely derived from Mahieu's personal savings and the gate of a 24 May 1894 performance of *The Somnambulist,* which was advertised as "a benefit performance for den Heer A. Mahieu."[47] This was the very last show in the company's Mangga Besar run and was guaranteed to bring in a big profit. It is likely that Yap was unaware of Mahieu's intentions to purchase the company at this point. If he had been, he would not have allowed this benefit show to happen. He certainly would not have let Mahieu negotiate independently with a Chinese backer for an advance payment.

The announcement in late June 1894 that Mahieu had purchased the company, including all its equipment and tent, was followed by a report that Yap "had been forced into a corner" by Mahieu, and that he had responded by carting off all the equipment. The report indicated that the performers were now stranded in the highlands of western Java, without money to return home. However, this report's veracity was questioned when it was published, as the reporter "had heard that Tuan Mahieu, the director of the company, had a legally binding written contract with the Komedie Stamboel's [former] owner."[48]

Mahieu's purchase of the company received a warm response from the public. The Dutch press reported that "the director M. has conveyed to us, and it is a pleasure to learn that he need wait no longer to refer to himself as the owner of this komedi, which was started up with the capital of a Chinese."[49] This warmth to Mahieu simultaneously betrays a hostile attitude to Chinese entrepreneurship and rearticulates the Batavia story that Mahieu was indebted to Yap Gwan Thay only for start-up capital costs and that sole control of the company had always been Mahieu's personal prerogative. The final negotiations for the transference of ownership appear not to have been completed until early July. While advertisements for the Komedie Stamboel's shows in Bogor are signed Directie (the management) and an advertisement for the Komedie Opera Stamboel's opening show in Batavia on 9 July 1894 is signed "De Directeur, A. Mahieu," the Komedie Opera Stamboel's 10 July performance of *Snow White* is proudly signed "Directeur-Eigenaar [director-owner], A. Mahieu."[50]

On 6 July the Komedie Stamboel had decamped from Bogor and was on its way to Batavia by train in order to open in the capital on 9 July 1894. It was missed in Bogor. "The city of Bogor has been quiet since the departure of the Komedie Stamboel and on any given night at the site where it had erected its stage there is not a single human being to be seen."[51] The company did not score a success in Batavia on its return, however. The one month (9 July–8 August 1894) in which the company performed in Mangga Besar with a fixed payment from an anonymous Chinese patron marks the beginning of public disenchantment with the Komedie Stamboel. Following the completion of this run, Mahieu vowed publicly not to play Batavia again. The reason, or reasons, for this are difficult to ascertain precisely. Possibly Mahieu's rancor and Batavia's indifference had their roots in the legal troubles and controversies surrounding the Komedie Stamboel's Batavia engagement of July 1893.

The lack of favor shown by Batavia was not for want of innovation. Mahieu continued to introduce new plays into the repertoire, including the perennial bangsawan favorite *Hawai-Majelis, the Sun Princess,* in a version said to be "known from the Hindu tradition and adapted by the director for the stage." A play entitled *Love and Artifice* was reportedly based on an English novel.

Publicity particularly emphasized astonishing special effects. The play *The Three Penitent Sinners, or The Punishments of Hell,* in which three bandits vow to reform after being granted a vision of the afterlife by King Solomon, seems to have been devised to showcase a stupendous vision of the inferno. "You can only see this performance at the Komedie Stamboel, as no other group is capable of depicting the punishments of hell, in which people are burned, have their stomachs cut open and like stuff served up to astonish spectators."[52]

Akhid, or Retribution contains a spectacular resurrection set piece, as well as an astonishing reveal scene, in which layers of gauze and canvas lift slowly in succession to provide a glimpse of a secret figure or realm—a standard feature of European theater of the time. Prince Akhid is killed by his jealous stepmother, Queen Dinar. The queen convinces the king that his son, the heir to the throne, has drowned in a river. Akhid's sisters, Sasha and Fartia, are not deceived by the queen's lies, and they go to a priest and receive a magic item which they are instructed to cast upon a certain cave's entrance. "The boulders split open, and a Genie King emerges and asks the sisters to tell him what they wish. Sasha and Fartia describe all that has occurred and the Genie King instructs them to exhume Akhid from the grave. They place his bones in a fire and he is restored to life and health."[53] The play ends with Akhid waging war against his father, punishing his stepmother for her evil deeds, and replacing his father as king. Publicity emphasized how "people will be astonished when Akhid emerges from the burning flames."[54]

Despite this spectacular repertoire, and the presence of relatively few other commercial entertainments playing Batavia at the same time, the

Komedie Stamboel had trouble attracting spectators by the beginning of August. There simply was not the same excitement and charge to be had from going to see the Komedie Stamboel as before, evidenced in a letter to the editor of *Bintang-Barat.*

> Last night I went out with a friend to Kampung M. [Mangga Besar]. It was my plan to invite my friend to see the Komedi Stamboel with me. But once we got there, . . . my friend said, "Rather than going to see the Komedie Stamboel, better for us to try our luck and buy an exposition lottery ticket for the drawing on 7 August 1894 (this coming Tuesday) at the store of Tan Hoe Lo. . . . What's the use in seeing the Komedie Stamboel? It just tires you, and when you go into work the next morning you might get chewed out by your boss." Oh Tuan Editor, my friend's observation is very true. I ended up going home.[55]

Strong words indeed in a letter addressed to a newspaper that had been, up to this point, one of the Komedie Stamboel's staunchest supporters.

Some spectators were disgruntled by the unprecedented tendency of the company to perform plays that varied from those advertised on the theater's marquee and preannounced in the newspapers. Spectators came expecting one play and were served with another. Unfulfilled expectations resulted in a loss of faith and decreased audience numbers. There is a suggestion of managerial ineptitude caused by the condition of performing for a guaranteed income under their Chinese patron. The company was not dependent on nightly box office receipts and thus was less invested in audience satisfaction. There had never been the same degree of discrepancy between announced and performed plays in the past.

There were also problems with the company's personnel. (Indeed, it might have been because of casting problems that last minute play substitutions were necessitated.) One of the most popular actresses in the company, an older woman known for her acting skills and pleasing voice and known to the general public as *ibu* (mother), resigned from the company early during the Batavia engagement and returned to Surabaya. This actress was most likely E. Rensing, who had been a stalwart company member for the last two years or more. An advertisement signed by Mahieu states that "De Heer Ran has been dismissed from our employ due to his unlawful activities."[56] Ran evidently was causing so much offense to spectators that his dismissal became an urgent matter requiring public notification.

Another, perhaps even more important, detriment to public appreciation of the Komedie Stamboel was the escalating campaign against the Balinese overlords of Lombok. The imperialist ambitions of Governor-General Van der Wijck had opened up a new front in the expansion and consolidation of the archipelagic colony, and the Indies was abuzz with the latest news from Lombok. The theatrical violence and pyrotechnics of the Komedie Stamboel, no matter how astonishing, must have seemed trivial in comparison. The popular theater had in effect been upstaged by a theater of war. Mahieu would soon formulate a response.

Canvasmen from the Komedie Stamboel tore down the tent starting the morning of 9 August 1894 and the troupe left Batavia for Cirebon on the coastal steamer *Giang Ann* the following day. Plans that existed to travel directly from Batavia to Surabaya were scrapped, perhaps due to the animosity between Yap Gwan Thay and Mahieu over the company's buyout.

Originally, the company had planned on opening in Cirebon with a special performance of an adaptation of Verdi's *Aïda* at Cirebon's European club, followed by a ball, on 10 August 1894. But a delay caused by the addition of three extra shows in Batavia resulted in a later arrival than projected, and this prestige show was cancelled. Instead, the company opened immediately in the Kebumen field on 11 August with its ever-popular *Siti Senimbar.*

The three-week stand at the Kebumen field of Cirebon (11 August–4 September 1894) was clouded by none of the discontentment of Batavia. The company had established an excellent rapport with theatergoers of Cirebon during its engagement the previous year, and it was reported that "among the great number of female and male artists there are many old friends of the Cirebonese public."[57] Reviews published in Cirebon's Dutch-language newspaper were, if anything, more positive than those of the prior engagement in this coastal city. "None of the charm of their plays was wasted" on Cirebonese spectators.[58] Plays that had been performed before were described in almost nostalgic terms, actors new to the troupe were pointed out, new plays excited interest. *Ali and the Magic Violin* was said to be "much to the taste of the public, as evidenced by the loud applause, especially from the upper circles of seats."[59] The appearance of a "supple deer" in the "medieval drama" *Genoveva,* also garnered "loud applause" from one and all.[60]

The company was so popular, in fact, that even prior to the company's departure, two Cirebonese of Arabic descent started up an imitation company, the Komedie Opera Konstantinopel, with initial capital costs of five thousand guilders. The company's director was S. S. b. S. Basalama and performers included former members of the Komedie Stamboel as well as Eurasian, Arab, and Muslim actors and actresses. The Komedie Konstantinopel (as it was also known) toured the small towns of western Java in 1894 and 1895, playing Cirebon, Indramayu, Bogor, Cianjur, and Garut, but never attracted first-rate notices or much attention from the public, as it was deemed inferior to both the Komedie Stamboel and the stambul troupes fielded by Yap Gwan Thay. The Komedie Konstantinopel's boorish clowns were reportedly more suited for topeng (masked dance-drama) than komedi, and attempts at using refined language were laughable. Probably its greatest fame to claim was the repeated sale of unlicensed alcohol by buffet manager Tan Tian Pie, which resulted in the confiscation of his stock and a twenty-five-guilder fine after he sold drinks to military personnel in Bogor in 1895.

In contrast, the endearing tone of the Komedie Stamboel's reviews and the company's broad welcome to Cirebon shows that the company was still a much-valued cultural institution in Cirebon. The Komedie Stamboel might no longer have possessed the same level of support it once enjoyed in the capital, but Mahieu had a strong following in the provinces.

WHEN IT played Tegal, the Komedie Stamboel was far from the center of interest of Europeans and the cultured elite. Its tent was pitched in the alun-alun in front of the bupati's mansion, inconveniently far from the European town center, where it had played in 1893. The Komedie Stamboel was also symbolically distant. There was no other commercial entertainment in town for the duration of the company's three-week engagement (10 September–1 October 1894), aside from a carousel erected in the field in front of the *klenteng* (Chinese Confucian temple) in the Banjaran ward of town. European, Javanese, and Chinese children lined up nightly from seven until midnight to pay three to five cents a ride, at least until a child fell off a horse one evening in late September and broke his neck.[61]

The heart of the Tegal public, in any case, was not concerned with light entertainment, but with war. The Lombok campaign was front-page news every day and was a popular obsession. Thousands gathered in Batavia to see the departure of the troops. All over the Indies, local committees to support the Lombok Fund were being formed. Civil-minded communal leaders drummed up a sense of responsibility to provide financial support for the war effort and charitable relief for the war's victims, that is, the war widows and orphans of Dutch colonial army personnel. (The Tegal committee managed to raise a generous 3,376 guilders by the start of October 1894.)

People did come to see the Komedie Stamboel in Tegal. *Ali and the Magic Violin* was said to evoke laughter from start to finish, and *Genoveva* was promoted as a must-see play. "Dutch, Javanese, and Chinese jostled one another and packed the second-class seats, rather than throwing away one guilder," for the first-class seats; the third-class seats were also full to capacity at many shows.[62] The loge seats were sparsely occupied, however, and many Europeans seemed to show little interest. Mahieu was recognized by the local newspaper as the leading director in the field for his creativity, his ability to train actors, and his high-quality performances. "Sundry other troupes have been established and have dissolved while the Komedie Stamboel continues to flourish more and more."[63] Even this degree of recognition and acclaim was not drawing spectators into the first-class and box seats in substantial numbers, however. Mahieu sensed that he would need to break new ground to reengage the interest of the European public. He decided to mount a play based loosely on the events in Lombok as reported daily in the newspapers.

The Dutch forces under Major-General J. A. Vetter and Resident M. C. Dannenbargh had launched their military campaign against Lombok's Balinese overlords under the rule of Ratu Agung-Agung Ngurah of the Karangasem dynasty on 13 June 1894.[64] The Balinese, who had dominated the island of Lombok since the early seventeenth century, were based in western Lombok but ruled the majority Sasak Muslim population of the entire island. The Balinese overlords had been involved in suppressing a Muslim uprising led by a Sasak teacher of Islam in eastern Lombok since 1891. The eastern half of the island had been devastated by this conflict, and the Dutch used humanitarian pretexts for an arms embargo. (The rumored existence of iron, tin, and possibly gold deposits was a strong economic motive for intervention.) There were repeated Balinese attempts to violate this embargo, as it was serving to prolong what would have otherwise been a quickly suppressed local conflict. Exaggerated reports of famine in eastern Lombok and the military's assurance that an expedition to annex Lombok would be swiftly concluded and involve minimal casualties (in contrast to the protracted military campaign in Aceh) prompted the hawkish C. van der Wijck, the newly appointed governor-general of the Netherlands Indies, to send an expeditionary force of 4,400 military personnel to Lombok. Van der Wijck issued an ultimatum demanding acceptance of all commands of the Netherlands Indies government and the abdication of Lombok's Balinese king. The ultimatum furthermore demanded Ratu Agung-Agung Ngurah's replacement by the crown prince, Anak Agung Ketut, who would be a puppet ruler, the extradition of the king's son Anak Agung Made (deemed hostile to Dutch interests), and the payment of the costs of the military expedition. The king sent his sons to negotiate with the Dutch forces. The Balinese royals requested more time to reach a decision. Dannenbargh promptly wired the governor-general that the ultimatum had been rejected. The Dutch forged a pact with the eastern Lombok insurgents against their Balinese rulers and landed their first troops on the beach at Ampenan on 6 July 1894.

The conflict that followed was a tragicomedy of errors. After the Dutch troops landed, they occupied the Balinese strongholds of Mataram and Cakranegara without firing a shot. Anak Agung Jilantik, the ruler of the Karangasem kingdom of Bali who was on Lombok with about twelve hundred of his troops to assist Ratu Agung-Agung Ngurah in his war against the Sasak insurgents, contacted the Dutch and offered his service as a mediator. Jilantik successfully convinced the Balinese king that a war should be avoided at all costs. Ratu Agung-Agung Ngurah ordered his son Anak Agung Made to be executed in the traditional Balinese method—a thrust of a kris to the heart. The death warrant was justified on a charge against Anak Agung Made of classificatory incest with his own niece, Anak Agung Ayu Made Rai. (The corpses of Made and Ayu Made Rai were subsequently examined and identified by the Dutch colonial official, Controller J. H. Liefrinck.) The king also consented to pay the huge indemnity of one million guilders, an annual payment of twenty-five thousand guilders to finance Dutch administration on Lombok, the acceptance of Dutch law, and the other conditions of the original ultimatum. It seemed that the conflict had come to an end. But in the meantime the Dutch had struck a deal with the eastern Lombok Muslim insurgents, effectively guaranteeing them independence from Balinese rule. The new treaty, presented in a Balinese translation at Jilantik's urging on 20 August, was unacceptable to the king. Anak Agung Ketut feigned an illness and negotiations were disrupted—though nearly half of the war indemnity had been paid by this point. The Balinese began to plan attacks on the Dutch encampments in Cakranegara and Mataram. A report of a Sasak village head raised the suspicions of Vetter and Dannenbargh that something was amiss. They consulted Jilantik, who assured them that he knew nothing about any aggressive intentions and promised to inform them if he heard anything. The Balinese launched surprise attacks on the Dutch encampments located in Cakranegara on 25 August (after the Dutch troops had gone to sleep) and Mataram on 26 August 1894. The Dutch troops were caught unprepared and were routed, resulting in heavy casualties. Only the Dutch forces that retreated to Ampenan were not defeated. Jilantik returned with his troops to Bali on the night of 5–6 September—

he knew that waging war against the Dutch was ultimately a hopeless cause.

The Dutch retaliated, increasing the size of their own expeditionary force to 6,700, supplemented by Muslim insurgent forces from eastern Lombok. On 30 August the Dutch began the bombardment of the town of Mataram, resulting in its complete destruction. In the final stage of its siege, women and children joined the fight, and the Balinese warriors rushed the Dutch in a ritualistic suicidal lance attack, or *puputan*. Village after village was ransacked and burnt to the ground. The war ended in late November 1894 with the fall of the house of Karangasem and the capture and exile of its king.

The Lombok War is recognized as one of the most unjust military campaigns waged during the long period of Dutch imperial and colonial domination of the Indonesian archipelago and is a haunting memory in Dutch political consciousness to date. The war's horrific end—looting, burning, mass suicide—stands as one of the most inhumane moments in the history of Dutch colonialism.[65] But in September 1894 the campaign was popularly understood to be an effort to liberate the oppressed Sasak natives from the foreign Balinese despots who ruled the island and a way to surmount the ignominy of the protracted and as yet unresolved conflict in Aceh. News from the front was reported only selectively and with a strong pro-Dutch bias. It was not until well after the campaign's conclusion that all the horrific details would be known.

The play that Mahieu devised to represent the events leading up to the siege of Mataram, *The Fall of Sin Island, or Treason Punished,* was a jingoistic war play, as can be seen immediately from its title. It was programmed to go up as the finale of the Tegal run, on 1 October 1894, as a charity benefit. According to advertisements, a third of the proceeds were earmarked for war widows and orphans of colonial soldiers under the rank of officer. The production's significance for drumming up European support for the Komedie Stamboel was transparent to the press. "The tent will certainly be jam-packed on Monday evening, as the proceeds will benefit the victims of Lombok. Any advertising would thus be practically superfluous."[66]

Concern was immediately registered from Tegal's European community that the play would be in some way disrespectful to the Dutch soldiers injured and killed in the campaign and might serve to undermine the conflict's political objectives. It was in part for this reason, and in part for the sake of publicity, that Mahieu took the unprecedented step of convincing Tegal's Dutch-language newspaper to publish a lengthy summary of his original Malay-language script in Dutch translation. Mahieu, and his supporters at the *Advertentieblad voor Tegal en Omstreken,* wished to allay fears that the play would be a parody or make light of the "profoundly regrettable events that took place on the Lombok field of battle" through comic banter.[67] This detailed summary by Wessels Sr. was published in Tegal's local newspaper four days before the scheduled performance. Prefatory remarks noted that the publication was intended to show how deeply serious the play was about the events in Lombok and how the play was intended to be faithful to the spirit of the dominant view of the conflict, even if it was not documentary in its mode of representation.

The first act of *The Fall of Sin Island* is set in the kingdom of Jambrut (Malay for "Emerald"), also known as Binuwa Bawah Angin (Land below the Wind). The old king announces his imminent abdication, after twenty years of rule. His successor arrives with music. The old king says that the one thing he did not accomplish during his reign was to punish the misdeeds of the vassal king of Pulu Dossah (Sin Island) who has behaved most cruelly to the majority population of his kingdom. The principal miscreant is in fact one of the king's sons, the prince Mohamad Madear (a play on "Made"; *made* is Dutch for maggot). The new king vows to see Prince Madear punished and embarks on an expedition to Pulu Dossah with the principal and vice-vizier. In the following scene, the troops exit with great ceremony.

The second act is set in Pulu Dossah. In the first scene, the troops of Jambrut disembark and set up camp. An ultimatum is sent to the king of Pulu Dossah, demanding the surrender of Prince Madear.

The second scene is set in the throne room of the palace of Pulu Dossah, in the capital city of Matahari ("Sun" in Malay; a play on Mataram).

The king receives the ultimatum. A canon shot is heard, causing fright and dismay. A vassal king of Pulu Dossah, the king of Kebon Manis ("Sweet Garden"; a play on "Karangasem," which in Malay means "Sour Garden") named Gusti Cantik bin Nabdi ("Lord Beauty, son of Servant"; a play on "Jilantik") restores order. He points out that the enemy's weapons are not yet in order. If command is handed over to him, he assures the king that he can favorably resolve the situation. The king gives his consent. Cantik leaves to the enemy's camp to negotiate, accompanied by a few followers.

Scene 3 is set in the encampment of the Jambrut forces. Cantik reports to the Jambrut chieftains that the king of Pulu Dossah has executed his son, Prince Madear, with a kris (submitting to the ultimatum) and that the queen is bereaved. The chieftains say they will go to Mataram to examine the evidence; some of the troops remain encamped.

Scene 4 takes place in the throne room of Pulu Dossah. The Jambrut chieftains arrive. The old king appears to be in a daze, and without comprehension. The viziers of Jambrut, Danu Bagar (a Malayization of "Dannenbargh") and Cincin Ayu ("Beautiful Ring"; an approximate Malay translation of "Liefrinck"), examine and confirm the identities of two corpses: they are indeed the bodies of Prince Madear and his wife. A portion of the war indemnity is paid to the Jambrut emissaries. The commanders of Jambrut's troops leave to inspect the camp where his troops shall stay until the indemnity has been fully paid. Cantik stays behind in the throne room, and boasts (in a soliloquy) of his good fortune. Prince Madear awakens from his feigned death and plots his revenge with Cantik.

Scene 5 is set near the encampment of the Jambrut forces. The camp is visible in the background. Cantik walks arm in arm with one of the Jambrut chieftains. Cantik thanks the chieftain for his trust and claims that he loves him more than his own father. He advises the chieftain to send a portion of his troops to the interior to demonstrate the military capacity of Jambrut to the people. The chieftain accepts the advice and sends another chieftain off with troops; Cantik also exits. A headman from a neighboring land (by implication a Muslim) arrives and warns the Jambrut chieftain of impending danger. The chieftain gives him a flag so that he and his auxiliary troops are recognizable to their allies.

Scene 6: *The catastrophe.* The Jambrut encampment at night. Taps plays and the troops go to sleep. An officer relates his forebodings to his nephew, a private. The officer has been entrusted with his nephew's care and would greatly regret if anything happened to him. His nephew is fearless though, which gives the officer courage. Dead silence. The sound of gongs can be heard at a distance. It is midnight. With the twelfth sounding of the gong, firearms and explosions go off. *Fiasco.* The chieftains order the rank and file to hunch over, so as not to be hit by bullets. The officers themselves stand erect and walk calmly as they give commands.

The seventh scene stirringly depicts the deaths of a chieftain and an officer.

The third act is entitled "Retribution."

The first scene is set in Jambrut's encampment on the beach, where troops are landing. An officer reads a report of the number of wounded and injured soldiers and officers to the commander in chief. The auxiliary troops from the neighboring land arrive. It is resolved to destroy all the buildings in Matahari and take the king captive.

The second scene depicts the bombardment of the royal compound. The old king and his sons are captured and carried off as prisoners to the encampment on the beach, but Cantik is nowhere to be found. A chief reports that Cantik has escaped by a secret passage, but he has an idea about where he is hiding now. The Jambrut forces exit to search for Cantik's hiding place.

Scene 3 is set before one of Pulu Dossah's military posts. There is a statue of the Buddha and a cave. A sentry marches back and forth and then goes to sleep. A headman, scouting for Cantik, arrives and hides himself when he sees Cantik enter with troops. Cantik and his men go inside the cave. The scout states that he recognizes Cantik for who he is. Voices of prisoners singing the "Miserere" from Verdi's *Il trovatore.* A shot is heard and all is quiet. Cantik emerges from the cave and, in a soliloquy, demonstrates delusions of godhood. An unseen voice disillusions him, saying that his gods have forsaken him. A genie emerges from the ground, reproves Cantik for his sins, and disappears. Cantik throws himself to the earth and says, "Yes, I repent. It is true that the king of Jambrut is a mighty king. But it is now too late to turn back. I must now defend myself. I am not afraid. I am a lion, an eagle, a shining star fallen from heaven's pinnacle." He returns to the cave.

In Scene 4, the scout emerges from his hiding place, visibly shaken from hearing the unseen voice from above and seeing a genie. He smashes the Buddha statue (indicating his Islamic faith) and leaves to report to his superiors.

In Scene 5, Prince Madear is captured and bound. The lucky Cantik manages to escape.

Scene 6 depicts the pursuit of Cantik, who manages to evade capture by hiding in caves. He jumps into the sea and eventually washes up on the shore of another island (standing for Bali).

The final scene, or apotheosis, presents a poetic image. In the foreground: the flag-waving guardian angel of Binuwa Bawah Angin encircled by angels. In the background: the princes of Pulu Dossah. The princes have been forced to bend over and a soldier's foot is on each prince's neck.[68]

MAHIEU'S DECISION to devise an imperialist play based on contemporary political events was a radical step. Not only was this the first time that the company had presented a play based on real-life events in the Indies, there were substantial risks involved in representing public figures. Mahieu knew this firsthand from the charges of subversion leveled against him for imitating a police officer onstage in Batavia in 1893. Still in recent memory were the punishments for sedition brought against the Penang-based company Indramawan when it performed *Ali Baba* in Deli in 1888. A scene "where the arch-criminal of the play was judged and punished for his crimes" was deemed "a violation of the laws of Islam," and the actors were jailed for three months, while the manager, Syed Mohamed A'tas, received fifteen strokes of the cane in addition.[69] A wayang wong troupe performing in eastern Java in 1890 got off with a comparatively light punishment when they imitated the functioning of the *landraad* (district council). The punishment for this group's sedition was being banned from ever performing again.[70] Mahieu was undeterred by these precedents. Perhaps Mahieu's security was due to his assurance that the play presented a jingoistic, pro-Dutch stance on the war. Indeed, in the scenario the forces of Pulu Dossah (the Balinese) are referred to explicitly as "the enemy" (*den vijand*), while in the closing scene the forces of Jambrut (the Dutch) are represented as angels. The Balinese sentry in the third scene of act 3 is depicted as sleeping on the job and in the same scene there is the suggestion of the execution of a prisoner—vivid illustrations of the slothful and brutal character of the Balinese. Cantik (Jilantik) is clearly shown to be a cowardly villain and a liar, irrespective of a "yes I repent" soliloquy.

Yet despite the play's strongly pro-Dutch message and the earmarking of proceeds to benefit the families of soldiers fighting on the behalf of the Dutch, the play was banned immediately by the local authorities, "without the slightest explication." Wessels publicly defended Mahieu in the *Advertentieblad* and suggested the ban should be revoked. He argued that the Indies press was filled with accounts that tried to pin the blame of the August 1894 defeat—deemed a fiasco—on the army's chiefs. In contrast, Mahieu's play depicted the ranking officers as perfect gentlemen, standing erect in a hail of bullets, even as they tell their troops to bend down so as to avoid getting shot. Wessels consequently characterized the play as "romantic," as opposed to "realist." The good are rewarded in the play, and the evil are punished—forced into contrition, kneeling under the feet of the military. Wessels's protests were in vain. The ban was enforced, and the Komedie Stamboel substituted an *Arabian Nights* standard, *Siti Safira,* for their final performance in Tegal.

Why was *Sin Island* banned? In the absence of explications from the Tegal authorities, one can only make educated guesses. One strong possibility is that the play was in Malay and had the potential of communicating to an illiterate public, with a fair degree of accuracy, much of what was then supposed to be the facts in the Lombok conflict. It is true that the officers of Jambrut are depicted as behaving honorably under fire in the play, as Wessels pointed out. It is also true, however, that in the play the forces of Pulu Dossah are able to surprise the unprepared

Jambrut troops and that the principal antagonist, Cantik, escapes with his life. Just the idea that one could attack and kill unprepared Dutch troops was a very dangerous one in the colonial context; it was not likely to be an idea that the Dutch authorities wished to see disseminated to a partly illiterate public.

Another possible reason for the ban is that while the final defeat of the Balinese in Lombok looked highly likely by the end of September 1894, the campaign in fact was still ongoing. Mahieu wrote in September out of the position of normative expectation that Mataram would be completely demolished and that Ratu Agung-Agung Ngurah would be captured alive, but these events were only realized in actuality on 11 October and 20 November 1894. This helps account for some of the variation of the play's narrative with ex post facto history. The death of Anak Agung Made was certainly not feigned, and only the most cynical historical observer would characterize it as a ploy. Likewise, there is no strong evidence that Jilantik had foreknowledge of the surprise attack or that his desire to act as a mediator was disingenuous. Jilantik was figured as a treacherous villain in the popular imagination simply because he appeared during the negotiations to be a trusted ally and turned out not to be of great assistance to the Dutch. The discrepancy between *Sin Island* as rounded-out narrative and the Lombok campaign as ongoing event could have potentiated a situation in which a *Sin Island* performance (or its memory) would become unsettling or even subversive. In fact, the outline of the play was mapped out roughly in real-life events to come. But one can envisage all sorts of possible turns that the conflict might have taken—including a betrayal by the allies of the Dutch, the Muslim Sasak forces—which could have made the play as written a problematic text in its interface with reality.

Dutch- and Malay-language novels, histories, and plays on the Lombok campaign were being quickly written and published in newspapers and as books around the time of the conflict. A "Tjakranegara Marsch" was composed by J. W. Portengen, played in public concerts by military bands, and published as sheet music in a solo piano arrangement.[71] A hot item that sold for five cents in roadside stalls and markets in Solo was a handkerchief with a color picture of Ratu Agung-Agung Ngurah captured and bound by the Dutch armed forces. Around the edges was a short poem reading

Ini Bali Lombok	This is Bali and Lombok.
Raja Bali sudah kapok	The Balinese king has given up.
Mangka di pikul mau dodok	That is why he is bent low as he is carried,
Segala orang boleh tengok	As everyone can see.[72]

By early 1897, Yap Gwan Thay even brought out a Gusti Jelantik brand soft drink, with the lord of Karangasem's picture on the bottle. It was said to be charged with extra gas.

These cultural products were largely later efforts, created when the history of Lombok, with its clearly etched cast of heroes and villains, had been firmly inscribed in public memory. (This inscription was later to be challenged by critics of imperialism, including Mahieu.) At the time of the planned 1 October 1894 performance, there was no authoritative version of history available, and any unofficial representation was thus potentially subversive.

A final possible reason for the banning of *Sin Island* in 1894 was the fact that a scenario for the Komedie Stamboel is never a complete text. Wessels's translation summary indicates that a scenario is a scene-by-scene outline of the plot, with notes on music and effects. Some of the scenes are absolutely stock (a genie appeared in a cave in many a Komedie Stamboel play) and do not require elaboration on the page. But the more important dialogue unique to the play (e.g., Cantik's soliloquies) is explicitly notated. The scenario suggests that a significant amount of planning and foresight went into new productions. This planning never encompassed the totality of the performance, however. There was always room for ad-libbed comments and topical referents, particularly via the comical characters, and always the possibility of deviation from the script, intentional and otherwise. A *Sin Island* performance carried the capacity of being somewhat other than complimentary of "Jambrut" and condemnatory of "Pulu Dossah" in its realization of details. The local authorities might well have been aware of this.

It is likely that Mahieu knew *Sin Island* would be controversial; that is likely why he scheduled it as the last show in the Tegal run. He probably did not know it would be banned. (Otherwise, why go to the trouble of writing a full and complex scenario or risk the company's abolition?) The controversy itself might have helped the troupe in the short term. Audience turnout on 1 October 1894, when *Sin Island* was scheduled to premiere, was larger than any other night in the run. Some of the public perhaps did not know of the replacement of the war play with *Siti Safira*. Others, including readers of the local newspaper, did—and came perhaps out of sympathy for the troupe or out of excitement generated by the controversy. Maybe it was ultimately to Mahieu's advantage that the play was not enacted in 1894. When the full scope of the imperial aggression in Lombok subsequently became known, Mahieu reversed his position and depicted it as "an unholy war" in tableaux vivants and as a farcical conflict in revised versions of the *Sin Island* play.[73] After the performance of the first play in the Komedie Stamboel's two-parter *The Expedition to Chili Pepper Island* (a play on Lombok, which means chili pepper in Malay) and *The Death of Jantik* in Surabaya on 27 May 1895, the *Soerabaija-Courant* commented, "Immediately after the conclusion of the Lombok campaign, too much was said for and against the presentation of such transparently topical pieces, full of not-always-kind allusions, to return now to this matter. Where is the boundary between permitted satire and unseemly ridicule of the victor? It is just as well to say no more about this."[74]

The 1894 banning of *Sin Island* is suggestive (at least to me) that something was amiss in the easy fit between popular performance and public taste that characterized the first years of the Komedie Stamboel's existence. The inability to predict a reflex action of the local authorities regarding politically dangerous material could have had far more serious implications than a last-minute schedule change and wasted preparatory hours. The *Soerabaija-Courant* recommends saying no more as the best critical attitude to the Komedie Stamboel's attempt to engage contemporary politics. Silence is not only a form of implicit censorship, it is also a death knell for a popular theater. Mahieu was ready for a new mode of theatrical engagement at the end of 1894, but it took more than five years, and much personal hardship, until colonial society caught up with him.

Bereft of the financial backing and connections of Yap Gwan Thay, the Komedie Stamboel was only one stambul company in an increasingly crowded field of popular performance by the start of 1895. New companies, professional and amateur, sprung into existence, financed largely by Chinese money. Actors moved freely from one company to another, and dramaturgy and repertoire was freely borrowed. Tan Tjeng Bok, a stambul actor in his youth, explained that "stories were all the same for all stambul companies in the past. . . . You could take a thousand stambul troupes, they all had the same stories. The only differences among them were the performers and the technical effects. . . . [That is why] stambul could sprout like mushrooms."[75] Companies such as Yap's Komedie Sri Stamboel and the two stambul companies owned by the Semarang Chinese entrepreneur Tan Kie Bing, Permata Stamboel and Bintang Stamboel, could recruit better performers and afford to produce more spectacular scenic effects than Mahieu's own company.

Other popular theatrical genres, formerly limited in audiences to particular ethnic groups and classes, also began to take on features of the Komedie Stamboel and began to appeal to mass audiences. Yap Gwan Thay had incorporated devices from the Komedie Stamboel into the Chinese opera troupes he owned as early as 1891, using scenic backdrops, concluding plays with tableaux vivants, changing traditional musical accompaniment to fit non-Chinese ears. An advertisement for one of Yap's mixed-sex Chinese opera troupes when it played Kediri evidences a thorough mixture of Chinese spectacle, with the stage magic being developed in the Komedie Stamboel. The ad promises that you can see "someone entering flames, someone doing martial arts with a jug . . . , a presentation of hell with people's punishments, and there is also plate juggling and various martial arts feats."[76] Yap's ownership of the Komedie Stamboel gave him privileged access to the Komedie Stamboel's repertoire of effects, but other Chinese opera followed suit as well. Tan Tjaij Howat's Chinese opera troupe was credited in 1894 as using "scenery and equipment that could be said to be nearly the same as the Komedie Stamboel's. He uses backdrops, and these backdrops are finely drawn." The depiction of the punishments of hell in a production by Tan Tjaij Howat's troupe was said to be "hair-raising in appearance."[77]

A former stambul actor named Remij was appointed director of a mixed-sex Chinese opera company with eighty actors in 1895, bringing his stambul skills with him.

Two Chinese opera troupes stand out for their integration of Komedie Stamboel with Chinese tradition. Both of them were sometimes described in notices and advertisements as *komedi* (or *wayang*) *Cina peranakan* (roughly, indigenized Chinese theater). Their appeal projected well beyond the borders of traditional Chinese opera devotees. One was the Kong Ban Liam (or Lian) komedi troupe, which in 1895 was also directed by a European. Kong Ban Liam used Malay language, tableaux vivants, European-style music and scenography, along with Chinese costumes and staging techniques. The repertoire was dominated by "Chinese blood dramas" until 1900 but by 1902 had expanded to include the staple plays of stambul and bangsawan as well.[78] Tio A Lie's company likewise used Malay and European instrumental accompaniment and was distinguished by its use of European songs as well as the insertion of occasional English-language loan words. Chinese opera devotees could only respond to such innovation by invoking the Malay aphorism "The world is old," meaning that all things are possible.[79]

Wayang wong also increasingly took on stambul characteristics as the 1890s wore on, incorporating scenic backdrops, flying effects, and some of the staging and dramaturgical principles of stambul. This resulted in a revival of wayang wong performance and a recovery of wayang wong's status in the public eye. It was not long that the 1890 performance ban in Batavia, and the lewd female fan behavior that provoked it, were forgotten. Langen Ngesthie Soeka, founded by Solonese Chinese entrepreneur Gan Kam in 1894, was the most famous of wayang wong troupes that integrated stambul techniques. Javanese, Chinese, and European spectators were from the start astounded by Gan Kam's use of realistic backdrops, which integrated features of the contemporary world. The backdrop used in the Siti Hinggil scene set in the outer part of the palace, for example, depicted a line of cannons of the sort one could see at the palaces of Solo and Yogya. Gathotkaca flew with the same technology used by the fairies in bangsawan and stambul. Shows regularly concluded with tableaux vivants. Gan Kam's success encouraged Eurasians, including Charles Houssard (a former soldier in the colonial army) and J. F. Vogel, to establish commercial wayang wong troupes starting circa 1896. Bernard and Raedt van Oldenbarneveldt purchased a full set of wayang wong costumes and other equipment from Gan Kam in 1897 for twelve hundred guilders, for use in a production of *langendriyan* (a dance-drama genre formerly strictly associated with the royal courts) that toured Europe in 1897 and 1898.

The Komedie Stamboel was also competing for audiences with more localized forms of theater that also took on stambulesque features. Ludruk, a form of rural folk theater from eastern Java that originally featured two male clowns (one of them dressed as a woman), gamelan musicians, and a female dancer, integrated komedi with folk drama in 1894 when it started to be performed by urban youths in Surabaya. An informal survey counted eight ludruk groups active in the urban kampung of Surabaya in 1895, all of them mixing features of komedi with traditional ludruk and clowning. These were unofficial groups that performed for free or nearly free. Actors had day jobs. (One Surabaya troupe active in 1899 was made up of restaurant employees from a large restaurant in Pasar Besar, for example.) Most groups lacked permits to perform after midnight. But in 1900 there was at least one ludruk troupe that could afford costumes decorated with gold thread and embroidery, and in the course of the twentieth century ludruk developed into the major popular theater form of eastern Java.[80]

A slightly later development was the emergence in south central Java of a new form of popular theater known as *ande-ande lumut,* named after the well-known Cinderella-like folktale that was the sole item in the theater's repertoire. Ande-ande lumut combined features of both wayang wong and stambul. Some troupes were all male, but others had both actors and actresses. This theater seems to have started in Yogyakarta in 1896; by the end of this year there were reports of local and touring groups in Solo, Kartosuro, Sragen, Pacitan, Ngawi, and Caruban. Ande-ande lumut was in fact so popular in this part of Java that less than three months after the first touring group from Yogya played Solo, a batik pattern was designed in Solo with pictures based on characters from the play. Some ande-ande lumut groups were sponsored for ritual occasions, at a rate of about ten guilders a night; others played in public places and could be hired to perform individual scenes; others erected marquees and sold tickets priced at ten to twenty cents. The lewd behavior of female fans, likened to the behavior of Abdul Muluk fans, resulted in a temporary performance ban being imposed in Solo in October 1896. This ban was soon lifted, however, and ande-ande lumut remained a popular form in urban and rural central and east Java through the first decades of the twentieth century, though today, for urban aesthetic sophisticates of Central and East Java, the form is synonymous with rural quaintness and primitiveness in the arts.

The Komedie Stamboel was only one company in a competitive field of bangsawan, Chinese opera, wayang wong, ludruk, ande-ande lumut, other stambul troupes, and a large variety of other sorts of entertainments during 1895 and 1896. Mahieu remained a lodestone. A company might be described as "no competition for the Komedie Stamboel directed by Tuan Ali Baba, alias Mahieu, who is an able performer and talented in arranging the auditorium in an apt fashion."[81] The good name of the company's owner-director, however, was no guarantee of financial or artistic success for the Komedie Stamboel.

FOLLOWING THE fiasco of *Sin Island* in Tegal, the Komedie Stamboel played the towns and cities of central and east Java. Not all these engagements were reported on in the press, as some of the stands were in towns too small to have either their own newspapers or regular newspaper correspondents. There was in general less attention to the Komedie Stamboel in the popular press after 1894 than there had been previously.

Little of note occurred at an engagement in Semarang from 7 October to 16 November 1894. The company arrived from Tegal by coastal steamer on 4 October, and quickly set up their tent in Semarang's alun-alun. The quality of the acting and music was recognized by *De Locomotief.* "A. J. Mahieu, Augusteijns and Damwijk are exceptionally valued in this genre for their performance and execution. They take on heavy roles every night and have their work cut out for them in getting laughs from the spectators. . . . The owner-director gives his all."[82] This Komedie Stamboel had come of age: it was accepted as an autonomous artistic genre. Yet aesthetic maturity does not necessarily draw spectators. Rain and a lack of brandy at the buffet are blamed for low audience turnout in the middle of the run. But one senses that the problems run deeper. The fickle audiences of urban Java desired something more than repertoire standards such as *Genoveva* and *Aladdin*. They were hungry for novelty. Even J. Calabressini managed to link his stage magic to contemporary events by organizing a benefit show for the Lombokfonds in the Semarang schouwburg that incorporated a demonstration of the phonograph as well as magnetism and conjuring. The Komedie Stamboel was polished, but it was not timely.

The only thing that stands out from the Semarang engagement, in fact, is a change in Mahieu's marital status. Mahieu announced his engagement to twenty-one-year-old Ambarawa-born stambul actress Petronella Wilhelmina "Nellie" Vos, on 18 October 1894. They married on 10 November 1894. No performance was held on their wedding night in honor of their nuptials.[83]

Audiences in Yogyakarta seemed to appreciate the company's *Arabian Nights* standards as much as European folktales such as Snow White and Sleeping Beauty when the Komedie Stamboel performed there from 22 November to 21 December 1894. It was reported that the gate was often as much as five or six hundred guilders a night, but this figure was likely exaggerated. In order to make ends meet, in fact, Mahieu was actually forced to split his company into two troupes for part of this run. The main group played in Yogyakarta, while a splinter group played the nearby town of Klaten.

The Komedie Stamboel retained its loyal following when it performed in Solo in its customary location behind the Vastenburg fort from 23 December 1894 to about 1 February 1895. The company's advance publicity had that it now featured "better performances and equipment. It is certainly true that Tuan Mahieu, now the company's owner, does not cease in his efforts. That is why it is so much better currently, with more songs and attractions."[84] Mahieu also capitalized on the publicity around his hiring a juvenile offender named J. A. Wellen. Wellen was a petty criminal who had recently served a four-day jail sentence for the theft of *soga* wood. Mahieu "took pity on" him, and it was hoped that Wellen would reform now that he was among "the priests and priestesses of art."[85] The gate in Solo was sufficient to encourage Mahieu to extend the run ten days beyond the initially projected one month.

From Solo, the Komedie Stamboel headed to eastern Java, playing Malang and Probolinggo in April 1895. Tickets sales were brisk in Malang, despite competition from a rural-style topeng group that performed in the alun-alun at the same time.

The company then headed for Surabaya, where it played first in the Kapasan theater and then in a tent in Kampung Doro for the month of May and possibly into June 1895. Publicity emphasized that Mahieu's troupe was the genuine article. "Various companies have endeavored to make themselves popular under the name of komedi stambul and have always missed their target and never have acquired the approval of the [original] Komedie Stamboel."[86] Ads proclaimed that the Komedie Stamboel was "famous all over the Netherlands Indies" and Mahieu was heralded as "the proper founder of the first Komedie Stamboel in Java, famous as a sterling actor and an able theatrical director."[87] Surabaya's Dutch newspapers paid the company little heed, other than to report an altercation between actors and a European railway employee.[88]

The Komedie Stamboel played small towns on the north coast of eastern and central Java for the next months, including Gresik, Rembang, and possibly Juwana and Kudus, as well as Mahieu's home town of Bangkalan in Madura. It then headed for Pekalongan, a town on the north coast of central Java well known for its numerous Indo and Chinese batik producers, with a population of 32,327 in 1895.[89] Mahieu's group arrived at almost exactly the same time that Yap Gwan Thay's newest stambul company, Sri Stamboel, was due to arrive—sparking a conflict.

The Komedie Sri Stamboel was established in March 1895 (or possibly slightly earlier) by Yap Gwan Thay. According to a promotional piece sent to Malay newspapers, the core group of actors were "all young Dutch [Indos] with white skin," eleven actresses and twelve actors. There were also two Arabs (said to be *bangsa Said,* or descendants of the Prophet), two Hindus, and two Malays—all of whom took on specialist roles in the company. The Arabs played villains, the Hindus played Hindus, and the Malays played healers. The lead Indo actor, Tuan Laveber, was promoted as having acting skills comparable to Mahieu. All costumes, backdrops, wings, and other equipment were said to be brand new.[90] Musical accompaniment was provided by a quintet composed of flute, guitar, two violins, and piano. Sri Stamboel toured widely in its first months of existence. Not long after opening in Surabaya, it embarked on the steamship *Ban Hin Goan* on a tour of the outer islands of the archipelago, performing in Makassar (Sulawesi) and Buleleng (Bali). It was reported that the raja of Goa had attended a performance of the troupe in Makassar and had commissioned a command performance for five hundred guilders. Sri Stamboel subsequently returned to Java on the steamship *Poo Hin Goan,* played Batavia in July and August 1895, and then left to tour the cities of Java's north coast.

Sri Stamboel seems to have been from its inception fraught with internal conflicts and schisms that often required Yap Gwan Thay's personal attention and intervention. In Makassar, the company's Chinese cashier was accused by one of the actors of stealing five hundred guilders and sending this money to his wife in Java. There were also numerous fights among spectators while performing in Batavia, resulting in the assistant resident for the police banning Sri Stamboel from performing again in Batavia. This news caused local authorities in towns across the north coast to withdraw or reconsider permits offered the company.

Yap Gwan Thay was not about to take this turn of events lying down. After *Pembrita-Bahroe* published an article stating that the authorities of Cirebon had withdrawn a performance permit given to Sri Stamboel in July due to the "very shameful actions of the company's employees," Yap wrote a correction directly to the newspaper.[91]

> When Sri Stamboel was in Batavia in July permission was requested from the resident of Pekalongan to perform there in September 1895. The resident of Pekalongan issued a permit that sanctioned performing in Pekalongan.

> On 9 September 1895, Tuan A. Mahieu's agent requested permission to perform stambul and was permitted to open in his tent on 15 September 1895. The agent for Sri Stamboel, Tuan [A. W.] Bovij (also spelled Bovy), informed the resident that Sri Stamboel had already acquired a permit to pitch its tent in the alun-alun at this time, but the resident refused Tuan Bovij's request and instructed him that the company could perform only after A. Mahieu had left. That means that the resident of Pekalongan allowed the company that had requested a permit last to perform first, while the company that had a permit first had to perform afterward. Do you think the resident of Pekalongan was being fair?
>
> The performers in Sri Stamboel are a select group. None of them behaves in a slanderous fashion. You will find that there has not been a single formal complaint against company members made during all the time it has been in Makassar, Bali, and Batavia. No matters have arisen in the hiring of dogcarts, purchase of alcohol, rental of accommodations, or rental of chairs. Payment has always been prompt and accurate. But you might discover what happened with A. Mahieu when he played Bangkalan and Rembang. Then you will be clear about "his ways" [*dia punya jalan*].

Yap's irate letter not only underlines the personal and professional animosity between A. Mahieu and his former employer after the Komedie Stamboel's buyout. It also indicates the degree of competition between groups in the stambul field in general, as well as the suspicions and doubts accumulating around the public behavior of the Komedie Stamboel, Sri Stamboel, and other groups. Yap was keen to argue that Sri Stamboel was beyond reproach for its business dealings and behavior and that the resident of Pekalongan's decision to allow the Komedie Stamboel access to play Pekalongan prior to Sri Stamboel was unjust. There is a hint that Mahieu in some way influenced the resident's decision. The details of Mahieu's "ways" are not presented, nor does Yap Gwan Thay report what happened when the Komedie Stamboel played Bangkalan and Rembang. This vagueness casts aspersions on stambul in general, for Mahieu's "ways" might be interpreted as open roads that any stambul organization might tread. Cataloguing the possible areas of offense (not providing payment for hiring dogcarts, etc.) did no service to Sri Stamboel nor to itinerant entertainment in general. It only heightened suspicion of the trustworthiness of stambul companies. Yap Gwan Thay publicly aired dirty laundry in his letter. In smearing Mahieu, the writer indirectly befouled himself too.

The latter part of the 1890s was not good for stambul. Java and other parts of the Indies were suffering from a *malaise* (recession) that left the fortunes of the European elite intact but had substantially reduced the disposable income of many non-European peasants, workers, and small businessmen.[92] Spectators still turned up at stambul performances, circuses, and other amusements, but some wondered how they could afford it in this time of malaise.

If this was not bad enough, the Komedie Stamboel was acquiring a reputation as a home wrecker. The theater was viewed as an enticement for women and men to abandon their spouses and families and shack up with performers. It was represented as a seducer of innocents and a cultural site for dissolute behavior. A form of antitheatrical prejudice is barely concealed in a comment made by the resident of Tegal to the Pauper Enquiry, an official government project to unearth the causes and possible solutions to poverty among poor whites.

> "Perhaps," Resident Steinmetz put forward, "a music school in Batavia could issue diplomas for music teachers. What I mean is that there should be training for musicians, and that in connection with this there should be openings in larger cities such as Bandung, Semarang, Surabaya, Padang, Medan, Makassar, and Ambon in the military bands. Do not Spanish sinyos [Europeanized Filipinos] provide the musicians for "Manila bands" in Medan, Singapore, and elsewhere, as well as the horse shows traveling around the East and such? Why should not our Indos, who do not mind working for stambul theater troupes, prefer this sort of work, which is more to their taste than, for example, manual labor?"[93]

There is no trace in Steinmetz's comments of an understanding that stambul provided Indos with a vital form of artistic expression. Stambul is only recognized as a source of itinerant employment—and one that is beneath the dignity of performing in a brass band or circus.

Stambul had found a place in the popular imagination, but it was not a noble one. The fantasy of running away and joining a stambul company was as prevalent in Indonesian public culture as joining the circus in American public culture at the same time. We read reports of "a young woman from Semarang from fairly good parents" who fell in love with an actor when the Komedie Stamboel played Semarang in October-November 1894 and traveled surreptitiously to Yogyakarta in order to be near to her object of desire. "*Aber es hat nicht sollen sein,*" but it was only a dream, and when it ended, the Semarang police enlisted the help of Yogyakarta's resident to bring the girl back to her parents' house."[94] "A much beloved youth" from Malang came under the spell of the Komedie Stamboel's actresses when the company played Malang in April 1895 and dropped everything to tour with the troupe as far as Surabaya. He too was subsequently returned to his parents by the police. Once again, the Dutch press employed a German expression, *die Liebe hat ihn so weit gebracht* (love has brought him so far), to explain the youth's romantic impulse.[95] The Germanic turns might be read as linguistic signs of recognition that such extraordinary events were outside the purview of Dutch language and culture. Yet over and over, "Dutch" (actually Indo, for the most part) children and adults succumbed to the lure of the itinerant theater—to the horror of polite society.

The economic downturn in the Indies had an immediate consequence for both Yap Gwan Thay and Mahieu. At the time of their Pekalongan altercation in September 1895, both Mahieu and Yap were on the verge of serious reversals of fortune. Eleven weeks after he wrote to *Pembrita-Bahroe* to protect his company's good name, Yap was in jail for debt owed to the Semarang department store Brandon and Company. More debtors followed suit, and Yap was forced to declare bankruptcy. All his assets—his theaters in Surabaya, his theatrical troupes including Sri Stamboel, his lemonade and soft drink company—were seized and sold off individually. Members of his social circle in Surabaya came to his rescue and advanced sufficient money for him to leave prison in Semarang, but the express train he took to Surabaya at the end of March 1896 only brought him to another jail cell in Surabaya, where he was imprisoned for some months on suspicion of involvement with a major Chinese-run counterfeiting ring. Yap Gwan Thay was eventually cleared of this charge and released from jail. It took a number of years thereafter for him to rebuild his business concerns, set up new theater troupes, establish a fireworks company, and renew his pharmaceutical interests.[96]

The Komedie Stamboel continued to tour Java under Mahieu's direction through the rainy season, without returning to Surabaya as it had in past years. It seems that it continued to play mostly small towns, for performances are rarely noted in the press. The last report that unambiguously refers to the Komedie Stamboel comes from Purworejo, a town on the southern post road of central Java with a population of about thirteen thousand in 1895. The town was best known for the nearby military base of Gedongkebo.[97] The Komedie Stamboel attracted big audiences in this town during January 1896 but its cash box was stolen, resulting in a net loss for Mahieu. Some months after this, Mahieu seems to have gone bankrupt, and he and his actors were evidently at loose ends by mid-1896.

Mahieu was presented with two job offers at the end of May 1896. The first was to direct a new stambul company being formed by Tan Kie Bing of Semarang. He turned this down in favor of a second offer—to take over as director of the greatly feted but scandal-ridden Komedie Sri Stamboel.

Yap Gwan Thay's bankruptcy had forced him to sell the Komedie Sri Stamboel in December 1895 or January 1896. The company was purchased by a certain Tan Tjing Koen (possibly a relative of Tan Tjing Siang, who purchased Yap's soft-drink business). Tan Tjing Koen resold the theater company to another Chinese businessman named Tan Tjiauw Tjak within a few months. Neither of these two owners seemed to have been particularly involved in running the theatrical company; Sri Stamboel's business matters were routinely handled by a Chinese agent named Oei Tiam Bie who traveled with the company.[98]

Yap Gwan Thay's last months of ownership of Sri Stamboel had been freighted with constant quarrels among the actors, forcing his personal intervention when the company played Semarang in November 1895. It was even rumored (wrongly) that Yap left his jail cell to check up on the company while it was playing Gembong in late December or early January 1896. The infighting among company members only intensified after Yap sold the company.

The company's director, Pieter Wilhelm "Wim" Cramer, a former "famous kroncong singer" from Batavia, did not get along with the Chinese management and had difficulty instilling discipline in his actors.[99] Wim Cramer nonetheless earned the strong endorsement of *De Locomotief,* which reported that "this komedi stambul offers very good entertainment for Semarang people of all ranks and classes. It has been a long time since something of this caliber has come, and it provides good value for money. The shows can indeed be recommended."[100]

Sri Stamboel attracted enormous crowds when it played the alun-alun of Yogyakarta starting 3 January 1896, despite nightly rain and a leaky tent. The bulk of the repertoire was derivative of the Komedie Stamboel, but there were also new plays and innovations. One reads, for example, of "the dancing Afrikaan and his violin" featured in the play *Jenor, or The Revenge of Hassan upon Husin.*[101] Many of the tableaux vivants depicted ongoing or recent military conflicts. The fall of Cakranegara from the Lombok campaign and the battle between China and Japan over Taiwan were particular favorites.

Then, in early February 1896, a story broke of a double shooting. Cramer and the actress Caroline "Lien" Gemser had been shot by Friedrich Wilhelm "Pik" Janitz, Gemser's jilted partner. This spectacular crime occupied much public attention in 1896 and left an indelible mark on the reputation of stambul as a whole.

Lien Gemser was one of the great figures of stambul in the 1890s, an actress originally from Surabaya who performed in and directed many of the key troupes of the time. Gemser was recognized as a "brightly shining star" whose acting and talent as a director "nightly drew full houses."[102] Generations later, Gemser's heavenly body can still be seen in the firmament: Lien Gemser is a distant relation (possibly even a direct ancestor) of Indo actress and model Laura Gemser, star of the soft-porn *Emanuelle* movies. Pik Janitz was a stambul hanger-on, sometimes described as a former actor, sometimes as a *punggawa,* a workman who did manual labor and odd jobs for the company. By January 1896 the couple had been living together "as if they were man and wife" for three years. As was customary for unmarried couples, Gemser was referred to as Janitz's housekeeper (*huishoudster*), though Gemser was in fact supporting Janitz through her earnings as an actress. Gemser and Janitz's relation was on rocky ground by 1895; they had fought in Semarang, and Gemser ended up with a black eye.

Cramer and Gemser developed a mutual attraction for each other while working together onstage.[103] Gemser sent Janitz off to Semarang to sell her velocipede, a type of early bicycle with pedals attached to the front wheel, instructing him to use the income from the sale to redeem eighty guilders worth of her pawned valuables from a Semarang pawnshop. Janitz was a fiercely jealous man, and while he was not prone to displays of anger (indeed, he displayed no anger even on the day he shot Cramer and Gemser), he was suspicious that he was being sent on a fool's errand. He reportedly warned Gemser that if he caught her fooling around with another man he would kill her. But Gemser paid little attention to his threats. With Janitz out of town, she believed that she was now free to hook up with Cramer. Cramer promptly dismissed his own "housekeeper" and had someone escort her back to Batavia.

Gemser then moved out of the rented house near Yogyakarta's alun-alun that she shared with Janitz, Gemser's cook Soetinah, and a number of actresses, including Van der Heijde and Nicola Kent, and moved into the stambul house in the Loji Kecil area that Cramer shared with two actresses named Van Sprew and Van Geerlings.[104] (Cramer occupied one bedroom, while Van Sprew and Van Geerlings shared the other.) Gemser vaguely justified her move to Oei Tiauw Bie, who was responsible for overseeing the accommodations of company members, saying that someone had died of cholera in the alun-alun house and that she could no longer live there, but her fellow actors recognized that moving house meant that Gemser was now Cramer's new "housekeeper." Gemser then wrote a letter to Janitz in Semarang, which began something like: "Dearest Pik! I am going to Surabaya, as I have just received a telegram from mama that she is very sick." Gemser's sole intent was to delay Janitz, so that he did not return directly to Yogyakarta and catch her in the act with Cramer.

Janitz seems to have had his suspicions even before he received Gemser's letter. Janitz was able to sell the velocipede without any difficulty (bicycles were a much-desired novelty in Semarang in 1896), but was unable to redeem Gemser's pawned goods without a claim slip. He thus wrote to Gemser, asking her to send him the slip. Janitz sent copies of his letter to Yogyakarta (in case her departure had been delayed) as well as Surabaya. A week went by without receiving a response, and the suspicious Janitz decided to take the train directly to Yogyakarta, without informing Gemser first. He got out at Yogyakarta's Lempuyangan station a little after midday on 30 January 1896 and hired a carriage. After ascertaining that Gemser had moved out of the house near the alun-alun, he went in search of his missing "housekeeper." Amir, the company's Muslim violinist, who was innocent to the fact that Cramer and Gemser were now living together, informed Janitz that Gemser had moved house to Loji Kecil.

Janitz now was certain that Gemser was up to no good. He went immediately by carriage to the Loji Kecil house, arriving at around 1:30 P.M. He exchanged greetings with company member Jan Nicola, who was lounging on the house's front porch. Van Geerlings, Van Sprew, and Van Sprew's mother were having tea in the front sitting room. Janitz entered the room, and Van Sprew called out to him, "Pik! Pik! I want to speak to you," but Janitz paid her no heed and stormed into the back part of the house, where the two bedrooms were located. Both doors were closed. Janitz barged into Cramer's room. Cramer and Gemser were together on the *bale-bale,* a four-poster platform used in traditional Javanese houses for lounging and sleeping. Cramer was wearing pajama pants while Gemser was wearing a blouse and sarong. At the trial, Janitz testified that they were lying down next to each other, but both Cramer and Gemser said they were in a sitting position. Janitz also testified that he was in a daze, and the precise sequence of events that followed varies according to the teller.

Gemser testified that it was at this point that Janitz pulled a revolver out of his pocket and shot Cramer in the head. Janitz testified that he shot Cramer only after Cramer pulled out a sword (*sabel*) from under the bale-bale, but both Gemser and Cramer disputed that. Cramer admitted that there was indeed a sword in the room (above a cabinet), but from his position on the bed he could not reach it when being held at gunpoint. Gemser ran out of the room in a panic but returned shortly and embraced the bleeding and unconscious Cramer. Janitz then shot Gemser from behind, wounding her above the buttocks. Janitz grasped Gemser's hand and she begged for mercy, "Forgive me!" A police officer was summoned, and Janitz admitted that "an accident" had taken place with the gun he was holding. Gemser and Cramer were both brought to the local hospital, while Janitz was imprisoned (initially in Yogyakarta, and then later in Semarang). Gemser's wound was light. Less than three weeks after being shot, she was again treading the boards on the Sri Stamboel stage. It was thought certain that Cramer would die of his head wound—indeed his death was prematurely announced—but he recovered and was released from the hospital at the end of March 1896. Janitz received a lengthy jail sentence for attempted murder.

The crime and the trial in December 1896 were significant in the way they focused public attention on the private lives of stambul performers. The public became aware for the first time of the discrepancies between the behavioral norms of itinerant performers and those held by the rest of society. The attorneys examining witnesses in the Semarang court manifested extreme detachment from the principals of the case, as if they are interviewing people from an entirely different culture.

> *Question:* Was it customary among actors to enter a bedroom with a door slightly ajar without warning, without for example knocking first?
>
> *Answer:* One would always knock or call out first.[105]

This estrangement from experience was coupled with a concern for details of the lives of theater people that borders on the obsessive.

> The counsel for the defense asked the witness Gemser if it is customary for komedi stambul actors to bear arms wherever they go.
>
> *Answer:* Yes.
>
> The president to the witness Gemser:
>
> *Question:* Was it customary for actors and actresses to live together?
>
> *Answer:* Yes, they lived together and considered themselves as man and wife.
>
> *Question:* Did Cramer ask you to live with him, or did *you* ask him?
>
> *Answer:* Cramer asked *me* naturally, and I accepted [his proposal].[106]

The questions were just as extraordinary as the answers. Both interrogators and witnesses strained to define and defend their points of view and ways of life. *Of course* actors carried weapons—their itinerant way of life and the constant brawling around the theater required them for self-defense. The fact that the counsel for defense and his class were not required to bear swords or guns on a daily basis was a reflex of their sedentary lifestyle; if they were living out of a trunk, they would need such weapons too. *Of course* Cramer propositioned Gemser and not vice versa. Gemser jumped to defend herself as a woman. She knew from her stage experience that a princess would never proposition a prince. Only an ogress in disguise would do that. Gemser did her best to steer clear of the label of vamp.

Some of the questions seem to be so unrelated to the case itself that it is hard to see their relevance. It is as if the questioners, face-to-face with real-life stambul actors for the first time, could not contain their curiosity regarding behind-the-scenes theatrical life.

> *Question:* Are you still performing as an actor now that you have been released from the hospital?

Answer: Yes, I play the lead roles.

Question: When an actor wishes to quit the company, don't they first tender a resignation?

Answer: No, they come and go as they please.

Question: How can you possibly divide up the roles then?

Answer: The division of roles takes place in the theater itself, once all the performers are present.[107]

The entire affair was described as a "notorious drama" in one account; a second article described Janitz as "the main character of the drama," and Cramer and Lien Gemser as "the other characters"; and in a third report Janitz was explicitly represented as an Othello attempting to murder his beloved Desdemona out of jealous rage.[108] This was not a private affair behind closed doors, but a public event that redefined the image of stambul by moving the focal point for spectatorship. Public interest shifted from observing "good value for money" entertainment onstage to fantasizing about a backstage life of sex, violence, and profligacy.

> To make matters worse, this minor incident gave a wag an opportunity to exercise his linguistic ingenuity by rechristening the *Komedie Stamboel* as the *Komedie Janboel.* [*Janboel* means muddle or mess in Dutch, and is also a pun on the name Janitz.] The derisory nickname stuck and caused more harm to Tardieu's [read: Mahieu's] company than the pun lover could have ever suspected. Events are quickly forgotten, but derisory nicknames remain in memory. *Komedie Janboel:* Antoine [i.e., Mahieu] shook with indignation whenever he heard that. Confound it![109]

A FAIR number of actors and actresses promptly left Sri Stamboel in early February following the shooting, apparently unwilling to be attached to the scandal-ridden organization. A new acting director named Oessa was appointed in the first week of February 1896. A number of actors were quickly recruited from Surabaya, including Charles O. van der Laan, the former director of the Komedie Stamboel and Sri

Soerabaia, who temporarily replaced Cramer as the company's leading actor and "first tenor."[110] Gemser was released from the hospital in good time and came before the footlights once more as Sri Stamboel's "prima donna" in a 16 February 1896 performance of *The Lombok War.*[111] Audience attendance remained good, perhaps even augmented by the publicity around the shooting and the return of Gemser. The company left Yogya at the end of February and played a number of small towns and cities in central and western Java, including Purworejo and Bogor, through the end of March, and then traveled to Batavia, opening in Mangga Besar on 8 April 1896 with little advance notice. (Apparently the ban against Sri Stamboel playing Batavia had expired with the change of management and ownership, or had been conveniently forgotten.) Lien Gemser is listed in advertisements as the "acting director" for the opening night, but for the next month directorial credit is split between Gemser (listed as *directrice*) and the "director" A. W. Bovij, who had worked as Yap Gwan Thay's agent in Sri Stamboel in 1895.

Sri Stamboel attracted good notices from Batavia's Malay press during April and May 1896. There were very large audiences for the first month of its run, despite the minimal prepublicity and strong competition from a circus and a French opera company playing Batavia, as well as the horse races in Bogor. The staff writers and other contributors to the Batavia papers display considerable sophistication in their appreciation of the theater and were quick to recognize both strengths and weaknesses of Sri Stamboel. Music received high marks from most critics, and the dramas moved spectators to tears and thunderous applause. Public order remained a problem, both for actors and audience, but one writer pointed out that this was properly the responsibility of the police, who were after all present in order to calm disturbances, not see plays.[112] One of the enduring problems was making sure that the actors kept straight faces while onstage: they were having such a good time themselves that they often burst into laughter to the jests of comedians Long and Short (*si Panjang dan si Pendek*) and at private jokes, much to the distraction of the audience. Lien Gemser herself was prone to exit and enter inexplicably in the middle of scenes.

Gemser's distractions were not only related to directing the company. She had also become involved with a wealthy Chinese fan, and at the beginning of May 1896 she resigned her directorial position and left Sri Stamboel to become her admirer's mistress. The newspapers following the Janitz case had anticipated that Cramer and Gemser would be reunited as soon as Cramer was released from the hospital, but this public drama did not conform to the narrative norms projected upon its actors. Gemser's departure from the company brought about an immediate downturn in audience attendance. Cramer stepped in to replace Gemser and resume his position as director and lead actor of Sri Stamboel on 6 May 1896, and managed to take in a respectable six hundred guilders the following Saturday night. But this seems to have been a fluke. In general, box-office was poor under Cramer's direction. An Indo actor and a young Indo actress and an actress of Indian descent (*perampuan pranakan kling*) left the troupe and traveled to Sumatra to join the Komedie Sri Sumatra, a small Malay-language komedi troupe active on the west coast of Sumatra.[113] Before the month was out, Cramer was replaced by Auguste Mahieu.

It is not my direct interest to trace the careers of Cramer or Gemser.[114] However, two documents appeared in print around the time of the Janitz trial that provide practically unique insight into the inner lives of stambul performers. Both were published anonymously, but internal evidence points to Lien Gemser and Wim Cramer as their authors. These first-person statements provide an intimate window of understanding into the inner life of komedi stambul performers. They are well worth exploring in detail.

The testament attributable to Lien Gemser is a seventy-two-verse poem entitled *Pantoen sindiran* (Pantuns of allusion), written under the name of Si Nona L. . . . , Boenga Hati Negri Betawi (roughly, Little Miss L. . . . , Batavia's Sweetheart).[115] It was published in Batavia as a short booklet in 1896 by the firm of Gijsbert Francis, the journalist and illustrator who translated the *Arabian Nights* into Malay and penned the best-known version of the Nyai Dasima tale. The poem is a long goodbye to the narrator's Chinese lover and is both a justification for a return to the stage and a candid statement about a woman's life in theater.

The poem begins with a personal evaluation. It starts with a sense of worthlessness and lack of agency but quickly moves on to discourse on actorly pride and the empowerment experienced onstage, where the actress wears pants (literally and figuratively) and forces spectators to bend to her will.

Kami seorang memang tontonan, Miskin memang piatu badan, Keluar maen di dalem taman, Seperti bunga bakal ciuman.	I am indeed a spectacle Without worth and without value. I enter and perform in a park Like a flower meant to be smelled.
Miskin memang piatu badan, Jalan di kiri jalan di kanan, Turut perenta kami berjalan, Kami teputer antero alam.	Without worth and without value, I move to the left, move to the right, I obey orders and carry them out And make circuitous travels in this world.
Kami seorang yang bijaksana Keluar maen pake celana, Serta memegang la satu pana, Banyak ati kena kami pana.	I am a tactful person And enter and perform in pants, Carrying with me a single arrow, Many hearts are struck when I release it.
Elok parasku serta rupa Serta bisa berbuang tinka, Siapa liat la tida lupa, Seperti kena ditempel geta.	My face and figure are beautiful And I am a capable actor, Whoever sees me will not forget, As if one has been smeared with resin.

The next twenty-four verses of the poem detail the role types and the variety of plays the narrator has performed, noting briefly the distinguishing features of plays and the characters she has portrayed in them. For example, "when we perform *Aladdin,* a mother is certain to make an appearance, give orders to all the genies, and I become her daughter-in-law." There is again a proud sense of accomplishment marked in this section of the poem in the actress's ability to portray many different characters. In all, twenty play titles are mentioned by name. Most receive only a single verse, but *Snow White* seems to be a particular favorite, and merits three quatrains.

Sneeuwwitje itu carita Olanda,
Satu ma tiri yang joedas ati,
Makan buwa appel dari Olanda,
Lantaran ini la ampir mati.

Snow White is a European tale,
Concerning an evil stepmother,
She eats an apple from Europe
And because of this almost dies.

Tempo Sneeuwwitje suda mati,
Suda ditaro di dalem peti,
Rada hendak membuat istri,
Tida lama idup kombali.

When Snow White is about to die,
And already has been placed in a coffin
A king wishes to marry her,
And shortly thereafter she comes back to life.

Sneeuwwitje itu kami yang jadi,
Serta belonjor di dalam peti,
Siapa yang liat mendadi sedi,
Rasanya ancur di dalem hati.

I am the one who plays Snow White,
And stretches out in a coffin.
Whoever watches will be sad,
And will feel his heart breaking.

Gemser's mimetic abilities were known to stambul devotees, and there was even a rumor that her talents onstage originated from a *siluman* [evil spirit] twin who looked precisely like the actress—the veritable spirit of character impersonation.

The poem's next twelve verses tell the story about how the narrator was lured into becoming the mistress of a lieutenant of Batavia's Chinese community—whom she addresses as Babah. The author depicts herself as being vulnerable to the seductions of wealth by her own low self-esteem offstage. She conflated the love of the Chinese elite, described as *yang besar* (big or important people), with the love of the Batavia public. She allowed herself to be cast into a servile position, enduring drinking, displays of immodest behavior, and the imposition of living in a *suhian,* or upscale brothel, in order to receive attention, praise, and gifts. She had been blinded by the flash of wealth. And all she was able to say in response is thank you.

The next seventeen verses are full of allusions and are difficult to interpret. (It is probably this section that provides the title for the poem.) Some of the quatrains take the traditional pantun form, in which the first two lines are imagistic and relate only obliquely to the third and fourth lines, where a discursive point is made. The mood of these verses is introspective, and there are a number of references to ships and departures. Despair permeates these verses, and both the author and her Chinese lover are depicted as suffering. There are hints that the Chinese lieutenant is not only unhappy in love, he has also suffered some financial reversals that are consuming his attention.

The poem ends with a public declaration of closure. The affair between Gemser and her Chinese lover was carried out with full media exposure—and sparked public debate. Gemser's decision to leave the company and resign her directorial position to become a Chinese man's mistress was described as an "evil act" in one article, discussed in the same breath as Batavia's Indo prostitutes who sit in their dos-à-dos carriages at night waiting to be approached by clients.[116] The poem's ending affirms Gemser's tribulations as a public affair and also marks (a hope for) the end of public attention to her private life.

Selamat tinggal la jantung ati,	Farewell my sweetheart.
Kami mau berangkat pegi,	I am going to depart.
Cari laen pengibur ati,	Look for someone else to amuse you,
Supaya jangan terlalu sedi.	So that you are not too sad.

It is possible that *Pantoen sindiran* was penned by an author taking on the personage of Lien Gemser. However, I find this unlikely. What reason would a ghostwriter have for publishing a poem that alludes to Gemser and her situation but never explicitly names her? I believe Gemser wrote the poem herself and that it can be accurately dated. It was composed in early June 1896, in the confines of Gemser's suhian, immediately before her departure from Batavia. The newspapers reported the severance of her relation to the Chinese lieutenant and her departure for Semarang on the steamship *Tambora,* where she joined the Bintang Stamboel.[117] Gemser maintained her drawing power. "This young woman can rightly be called the komedi stambul's prima donna, and wherever she performs she attracts the public's heart. It is a shame that she is prone to immoral behavior, and that she uses the secret powers of a siluman with a face that is identical to her own."[118]

The story that Gemser writes is a tale of temptation and redemption. She finds the strength within herself to break away from her bondage to the Chinese lieutenant and resume her theatrical career. Her self-portrait is psychologically complex. She represents herself as being easily swayed and coaxed off-stage, but capable and in control when she treads the boards. The return to the theater is thus not only a career move, it is a way to assert agency and maintain identity as a professional woman. It offers a particularly good defense for becoming a stambul actress in an age of limited opportunities for women.

An account entitled "The Path of a Komedi Stambul Director," which appeared in print in late November 1896, offers a strong contrast to Nona L.'s poem.[119] This text, too, is written (mostly) from a first-person perspective and is as strongly gendered as *Pantoen sindiran*. It also was published in 1896, and I would like to think that Cramer issued it as a reaction to Gemser's account.

The stambul director in "The Path" figures himself as a weak man who has been tempted into the theatrical life, primarily through his sexual desire for women. The account has a strong misogynistic streak, for the difficulties involved in controlling women (actresses) also proves to be the director's main obstacle in performing his directorial duties. It is a short text and worth translating in its entirety.

> A gentleman who is a director for a komedi stambul troupe has told the following concerning his path in life.
>
> I hate, said the gentleman, and have contempt for myself. I live a life of deception: I have deceived my parents about what I am. That has been my downfall. I no longer have the strength to free myself from the hands of the demons of temptation.
>
> It started when I was in secondary school and went to see komedi stambul for the first time. I became crazy for it, forgot about school, forgot about my parents, and forgot propriety.
>
> I did not wish to go to school from that time on, and I went off with the komedi stambul troupe, traveling all over with them.

After some time, I became the company's director. What is more, I was greatly enamored of the young ladies who acted in komedi stambul.

My secondary school classmates have become controllers, assistant residents, doctors, officers, and the like. But I became a scoundrel, despised by many, no longer able to associate with people of good standing. But even so, there is no one to blame but myself. I no longer talk about doing other sorts of work because the spirit of stambul has thoroughly permeated me. I must surrender myself to my fate. It is like rice used to make porridge. The rice cannot be turned back to rice again.

This is how things stand now. This has been my path, which is beyond changing. All I can do is close my eyes [to the past].

My greatest difficulty is to find young ladies with attractive faces who are willing to perform komedi stambul.

With money and sweet words, I can find them, but only with patience and time, for many people of European descent, though they might be very poor, are unwilling to allow their children to become komedi stambul performers.

Some among these women are extremely dull witted and very hard to coach. They are able to exploit only their good looks. They are good at making themselves attractive to people through all sorts of ways, but they are of no use at all onstage. That is why I have to come down hard on them when I coach them in their roles in a play.

Once they have become good actors, they can earn a salary of up to seventy-five guilders a month, and once they have become old and stop working as komedi stambul actors, they can get other work that is more enjoyable.

But what do I have to look forward to once I become old? I have no other job skills, I have no money, I have no pension coming to me. How am I going to support myself in my old age?

When I reflect on it, I realize my life will be very hard in the future. I am a child of well-off parents who received a good education, and I have no hope for the future.

> Thus, I would like to provide some advice to my friends in this piece. Do not follow my unfortunate example, because if you succumb even once to the temptations of the demons of stambul, it will certainly be your undoing.[120]

This "composition" (*karangan*) is difficult to place generically and its authorship is conjectural. While it is told mostly in the first person, it opens in a quotational mode. There is good reason to think the piece is based on an interview. One suspects that while the words were spoken by a stambul director, they were written down by a journalist. One can neatly insert the unwritten questions in between paragraphs. ("What is your greatest difficulty . . . ?" "My greatest difficulty is . . .") If the director's statement is mediated through a journalist, the writer seems to share completely the director's bourgeois points of view on women, the importance of education, job skills, and planning for retirement.

It is a useful fiction to consider this statement as a confession by Cramer written after reading Gemser's own book of pantun. One can imagine the komedi director contemplating, perhaps for the first time, what was ahead—after three or four years on the road, moving from stambul house to stambul house, pitch to pitch, surrounded constantly by enchantingly beautiful young women, living with a sword stashed next to his bed, having survived a shooting by a jealous ex-boyfriend of his lover. Gemser derives her strength from the theater, but her involvement as an actress is always conditional and not absolute, as she can anticipate what the director (Cramer) in this piece calls "other work that is more enjoyable"—becoming a rich man's mistress, marrying, raising children. Years devoted to theater can make a woman more desirable to the opposite sex by supplementing and honing the ways she makes herself attractive. The case is different for men of the theater. The options open to the director (Cramer) are more limited. Cramer was known as an "artist *pur sang*."[121] He could not become a kept man nor marry an admirer nor easily settle down to domestic life. The norms of bourgeois society made it incumbent on him to be the provider and to accumulate a nest egg for retirement. None of this was possible given the performer's itinerant life. The newspaper article buys sympathy for the director. We see how he has been ensnared by stambul demons, and we feel sorry for him. But the piece does not leverage a future for either the director (Cramer) or for komedi stambul.

THIS, THEN, was the reality that Mahieu encountered with the loss of his own company. Years of working as a hired actor and director for the benefit of others lay before him, and prospects for the future looked bleak. The Komedie Stamboel was rechristened and mocked as Komedie Janboel, and however much Mahieu trembled at this play of words, he could not eradicate the associations of sex, violence, drunkenness, and public disrepute embedded in the pun.

Mahieu's appointment as director of Sri Stamboel in 1896 was announced as a merger in which "the Komedie Stamboel playing at Mangga Besar and formerly headed by Lien Gemser has now been brought together with the company of Tuan Mahieu, who is very well known as a stage actor."[122] Perhaps more accurately, Sri Stamboel absorbed Mahieu's troupe; there is no indication that Mahieu had a direct financial stake in the company, and he is never noted as its owner.

Mahieu took over Sri Stamboel's artistic direction on 29 May 1896 and acted and directed the company for the next year. There was no immediately discernable effect on the sorts of plays being performed by Sri Stamboel, but ticket sales immediately rebounded. It had been nearly two years since Batavia audiences had seen Mahieu onstage, and he still had his admirers. The Batavia run concluded with a special two-night presentation of Mahieu's two-parter about the Lombok campaign, *The Lombok War* and *The Cakranegara Battle* on 4–5 June 1896. The second play concluded with a tableau vivant showing the death of General Van Ham. These plays attracted very large numbers of European spectators, both men and women. The acting of the male leads was praised highly in one review: "The actor playing Gusti Jelantik was beyond reproach and played the role with power and strength, and he spoke with great force; and the actors playing Generals Vetter and Van Ham deserve praise; and the funniest was the actor playing the captain, Tuan M. [Mahieu], who caused the most laughter from his actions. Indeed, this gentleman is already well known by the public and is a very capable performer."[123] The costumes in *The Lombok War* were critiqued for lack of consistency by this reviewer, while the actors playing Lombok and Sasak characters were dressed appropriately; the Dutch characters were not wearing proper military uniforms, creating an unintentionally humorous visual impact overall.

This seems to have been a chronic problem for Sri Stamboel, predating Mahieu's arrival on the scene. A Sri Stamboel performance on 1 May 1896 of *Rinaldo,* an adaptation of Vulpius's ever-popular adventure novel *Rinaldo Rinaldini, the Robber Chief* (1797), was critiqued along similar lines. While the Komedie Stamboel's 1891 *Rinaldo* adaptation, entitled *Raelaman bin Rachmat, or The Rinaldo Rinaldi of Arabia,* had been a transposition of the Rinaldo story to the fantastic *Arabian Nights* world, Sri Stamboel's version was set more concretely in premodern Poland. Rinaldo himself was dressed appropriately, but his robber underlings were costumed as Turks, while Rinaldo's nemesis "Count Rasouwaki" was dressed in "an Arab vest, with a belt around his waist and a *pet* [cap with a visor] on his head." Even worse, his soldiers wore "cut-off gloves such as worn by Chinese opera soldiers" and were under the command of two officers dressed in "Arabic clown outfits." The reviewer of Sri Stamboel's *Rinaldo* castigated the company for these inconsistencies: plays set in the European past should be costumed appropriately.[124] Mahieu did his best with the material he had to work from and was commended for the very lively atmosphere and excellent performances he produced in Batavia.

Sri Stamboel toured the Preangan highlands of west Java from early June until early August 1896, playing Cianjur, Bogor, and most likely Sukabumi. Cianjur audiences turned up in droves at Sri Stamboel's pitch on the alun-alun to see performances for the entire three-week run (8–28 June 1896). Some complained that they were "sick" (*telah jemu*) of stambul by the end of the engagement, but when the company decamped, "what did these same people say? 'Ach! What a shame that the troupe has vanished, for our city is now so quiet and deserted.'"[125]

Things did not run so smoothly in Bogor. The city's assistant resident instated a new regulation coinciding with Sri Stamboel's arrival.

Sri Stamboel was required to pay a three-hundred-guilder guarantee in order to get a permit. This sum would be used to pay bills incurred by performers from carriage drivers, vendors, and the like. Once the guarantee was spent, the company would be required to fork out an additional three hundred guilders to be used for the same purpose or their performance permit would be instantly cancelled. This news generated protest, as "the action makes no sense, and the assistant resident has no power to do something of this sort."[126] It seems like Mahieu complied with the demand, however: conditions were becoming increasingly hostile to stambul, and it was true that itinerant performers tended to accumulate bad debts. Assistant residents, moreover, did have substantial discretionary powers over local cultural affairs. (Recall that Batavia's assistant resident for the police was responsible for the banning of Abdul Muluk in 1882.) The investment turned out to be a wise one, for Sri Stamboel turned a profit in Bogor. The troupe attracted "men and women, old and young" to performances at its pitch near the rail station, and Mahieu was warmly appreciated for his comic talents.[127]

Sri Stamboel returned to Batavia in August 1896 to perform once again in Mangga Besar. But it was not an opportune moment for the company's return because of a bad precedent set by a rival company. The Empress Victoria Jawi Pranakan Theatrical Company of Penang, owned by Abubakar Siddij and under the direction of B. B. Wanteh, had played Mangga Besar for the last two months, performing in the same tent that Sri Stamboel had used in May and June. Abubakar's troupe, also known as Indra Bangsawan, was a well-established and large company (thirty actors, twelve actresses), said to have been around for more than twenty years. The Penang troupe's costumes, richly embroidered with gold thread, amply impressed spectators. The flying "heavenly nymph" (bidadari) effects were first-rate, without visible strings. Music and comedy were also praised, although stories and story summaries were sometimes hard to follow due to differences between the Malay spoken in Indonesia and Malaysia. The company attracted large but very rowdy crowds. Spectators were prone to shouting out vulgarities during performances. Many in Batavia found the loutish behavior of

Abubakar's company members to be appalling. Ushers routinely insulted spectators; one ill-tempered usher wearing dirty clothes was said to be "fit to live in a jungle, where he can associate with wild animals, because his actions are beastly."[128] A company member was sentenced to six days in the lockup for hitting the company's violinist, a second also received six days for beating his wife, and a third was fined five guilders for striking a fellow company member with a broom.

Even more shocking was the abduction of a girl from the auditorium immediately following a performance of *Zulumi Azioam* by Abubakar's company on 19 June 1896. A man newly arrived from Semarang lusted after a fourteen-year-old Muslim girl watching the show. He paid two policemen two and a half guilders each to accuse the girl of being a prostitute after the show was over. The girl protested her innocence but was roughly escorted by the police, who said they were bringing her to the sheriff (*schout*) and bustled her into a waiting carriage (*kahar*). At a prearranged point on Jalan Sawah Besar, the man from Semarang intercepted the carriage. The Semarang man's interchange with the police went something like this:

SEMARANG MAN: What's going on here?

POLICEMAN: This girl is a criminal, sir, and I am bringing her in to the sheriff's office.

SEMARANG MAN: You most certainly cannot do that. This woman is a good girl. I know her well.

The girl has never met the man before, but she is overjoyed by his unsolicited assistance and pretends that she knows him, out of fear.

POLICEMAN: Very well, if you will take full responsibility for this matter, I will hand over the girl to you, sir.

SEMARANG MAN: Excellent. I will take responsibility for this matter from now on.

The next day the man sails to Semarang with the girl.[129]

The policemen's corruption was quickly found out and they were fired from the force, while the Semarang man was put on a wanted list. This plot—seemingly right out a potboiler melodrama—outraged and horrified Batavia and cemented public association of Malay popular theater with depravity.

Sri Stamboel experienced similar tribulations during its Batavia engagement that began on 10 August 1896 in the same tent occupied as Abubakar's company. Some hostility was expressed even before Sri Stamboel arrived; it was classed by one detractor as a money waster, along with opera, a carnival at the zoo, cockfighting, kite dueling, Chinese card games, and dice.[130] Arguments, fistfights, and drunken brawls regularly broke out among spectators during Sri Stamboel's performances in August and September, frequently disrupting plays. Mahieu's mind was also likely preoccupied with matters of family. His wife, Nellie Vos, was pregnant and had gone home to be with her family for the delivery. She gave birth to Adolphe Joseph Mahieu in Semarang on 24 August 1896. The child died the same day.[131]

Some in Batavia still recognized stambul as a source of pleasure "for those with some [money] in their pockets," but judging from the press reports much of the public in 1896 possessed a hostile and suspicious attitude to Malay popular theater.[132]

> Every night the komedi stambul performs until one in the morning, and every night there is shooting. What is more, near the komedi stambul tent there is a house with young women. After the stambul show finishes, people head to this house for pleasure of a different sort. They yell and cheer until late at night, disturbing the peace and sleep of the people of the neighborhood. It is hoped that the civil authorities will heed the objections of the residents of Mangga Besar and let justice be done, so that these people can have some peace at night. They will hopefully put a stop to komedi stambul shows. What is more, people here no longer appreciate komedi stambul shows. It was different in the past, when komedi stambul performances brought joy to all people of all races.[133]

This request, and others like it, were indeed heeded. It was announced on 26 September 1896 that "on order of the assistant resident in charge of Batavia's police the Komedie Sri Stamboel will not be allowed to perform here any longer, so that there will be no disturbances caused by people fighting." There were some protests, as stambul still had many devotees, and the suspension of Sri Stamboel's permit meant depriving actors of their income. The fights and unruly spectatorial behavior was not the fault of Sri Stamboel per se, but "when one person commits a fault, many must pay the price."[134]

THE TRAVELS of Mahieu and Sri Stamboel over the next year through the towns and cities of Malaya, Sumatra, and Java cannot be reconstructed in detail, but what is known suggests that this was a difficult stretch for the company.

Sri Stamboel toured southern Sumatra in from October to December 1896, playing Palembang (population ca. 54,000) and smaller towns such as Muntok (on the tin-rich offshore island of Bangka, population ca. 4,500).[135] Lien Gemser left Bintang Stamboel and rejoined Sri Stamboel for the Sumatra tour. A correspondent for *Bintang-Barat* who happened to be visiting Muntok caught one of Sri Stamboel's shows and was disturbed to see that actors were laughing inappropriately onstage. He suggested that Mahieu would need to exert more discipline on his actors for this company to come up to the level of accomplishment of his past companies.[136]

Sri Stamboel then toured western Java, including Sukabumi, Ban dung, and Cianjur, in the first months of 1897. Possibly the company also toured central Java. In the resort town of Sukabumi, the company rented a large house on Jalan Cipelang Leutik, at the edge of the city among the fruit trees. Marie "Marietje" Oord, who was ten years old at the time, visited the rented house frequently, mostly to pick fruit. Oord's father was in the colonial army, and she spent much of her time as a child wandering the streets of Sukabumi with her friends. Oord was spotted and recruited as an actress by Mahieu; she became the company's prima donna in later years and was one of the most

Fig. 4.3. Actor-manager Marie Oord, as an adult also known as Laïla or La Gracieuse. Reprinted from Nieuwenhuys, *Komen en Blijven,* 165.

prominent stambul actor-managers of the first two decades of the twentieth century.[137]

Sri Stamboel left Java in March or April 1897 for an ambitious, but ultimately disastrous, tour of British Malaya and Sumatra. The troupe toured under the name Komedie Stamboel rather than Sri Stamboel, apparently in order to maximize name recognition. Mahieu is listed in advertisements as the troupe's director, but there is still no indication of a financial investment in the company.

Once again, reception in Malaya proved poor for Mahieu. The troupe took a Chinese steamship from Penang to Belawan, the principle port on the east coast of Sumatra, but on arrival the troupe was unable to pay the full price of the passage. Fortunately "a good Chinese person took pity on them and paid the cost of the journey," in exchange for the receipts for a predetermined number of shows in the nearby city of Medan, located a few hours from "the damp, warm, and always very unhealthy harbour" of Belawan by train.[138]

Medan was the center of Sumatra's tobacco trade, and its populace was a multiethnic mix of Javanese, Acehnese, Chinese, Malays, Europeans, Indians from the coast of Malabar, Bengalis, Batak, and Indonesians from Bawean, Banjar, and many other parts of the archipelago. Its history as a *plantersstad* (planters' city) dated back only to the establishment of the head office of the Deli Maatschappij te Medan in 1870. Medan rapidly developed in the decades that followed. Chinese shops, hotels, banks, a European club, and a variety of governmental and mercantile offices were established in quick order.[139] Audiences in Medan were cosmopolitan, accustomed to the sounds of the local bands the Manila Muziekcorps and the Cecilia Band, and culturally conditioned to English variety theater and operetta. A large percentage of the European elite were in fact not Dutch, but English; Straits dollars were preferred over guilders at many stores; and British holidays such as Queen Victoria's Diamond Jubilee were public celebrations. Malay speakers were likewise more inclined to share the tastes of Malaysians than Indonesians in Malay popular theater.

Despite this civilized veneer, Medan also was a frontier town, with rowdy crowds and high crime rates.[140] Mahieu's troupe attracted a rough crowd to its shows on Medan's esplanade in May and June 1897. There were fights every night among civilians and military personnel, and an armed robbery took place on 20 May 1897 at a Chinese house across the esplanade from the stambul tent. Lien Gemser, who was still acting with Mahieu's company, had many admirers, but the stambul actors were blamed for being home wreckers. One peranakan Chinese man left his *nyai* (informal Native wife) and child to marry an Indo actress. Receipts were not good in Medan and, it seems, neither were living conditions—the company's Chinese cashier died of dysentery on 24 June 1897. The burial costs and arrangements were taken care of by the Chinese owner of "Betawi store" (*toko Betawi*) Seng Hap and Company, for the company itself had no cash reserves.

The day after the cashier's death, the civil authorities closed down Mahieu's theater. The company was deemed responsible for so much disorder that "the head of the local government forbade them to give any more performances in the residency."[141] That decision was executed with a very heavy hand. At about 5 P.M. on 25 June 1897, the controller, inspector, and a number of police and employees of the public works department arrived at the esplanade. The controller gave the order to tear down the tent, which was duly executed by his underlings. He then instructed his men to place the stage, canvas, and equipment under guard—"for what legal reason only God knows."[142] A good guess is that Mahieu and his company had run up bills with local merchants and vendors, and the local government wished to insure that the company did not skip town before settling their debts.

The company seems to have disbanded in short order. Three former company members who hailed from Bogor, Palembang, and Java joined a local gang and were arrested on 18 August 1897 for the theft of goods from Medan's market. At around the same time, Mahieu sold off Sri Stamboel's equipment to the director of Sri Serdang, a theatrical company of unknown provenance, for two hundred fifty guilders—barely enough to pay for the onward journey of the company members still with Mahieu.

No clear indications exist of Mahieu's whereabouts between September 1897 and January 1898. Somehow, he (and presumably other company members) managed to return to Java, for on 24 February 1898 Mahieu was witness in Batavia to another red-letter day in stambul history: the murder of Hubertus Loth. Mahieu was at the time working as an actor in Permata Stamboel, a troupe directed by actor-manager Carel Jan Willem Snabilié.

Snabilié was an entertainer of diverse experience and a ubiquitous figure in the komedi scene. His first exposure to Malay theater seems to have been as the director of an itinerant bangsawan group from Penang that toured eastern Java from March to June 1894. The outfit was originally owned by a Penang man named Entjik Ibrahim, but it went bankrupt when it played Semarang in early 1894. (Semarang audiences did not appreciate the plays and complained about a lack of humor.) All the fittings were seized by the Semarang court to repay outstanding debts and were sold to the highest bidder. Snabilié also seems to have had difficulty turning a profit with bangsawan. After four months of playing small towns in central and east Java, including Probolinggo, Pekalongan, and Lumajang, Snabilié left the bangsawan company for a new job as the director of the Komedie Laijsing, an outfit owned by Yap Gwan Thay, starting in June or July 1894.

The Komedie Laijsing, as has already been noted, was a variety company starring magician Laij Sing Pan from Peking. It featured magic acts and acrobatics for the most part. Snabilié recruited new performers to the show. Performers from the Indian Circus joined the ranks in July 1894.[143] When the Komedie Laijsing appeared in the Kapasan theater that month, it was described as consisting of "one Chinese from Peking, two authentic English people, [and] three people from Bombay."[144] Snabilié left the company a number of months after the Kapasan engagement, although Komedie Laijsing continued to profit in his absence.[145]

Snabilié then went into stambul, becoming director of the Komedi Stambool Betawi.[146] This company, made up of nineteen "intelligent and well-trained" Batavia youths, was established by Snabilié in November 1895 with the backing of J. Kieffer, editor of the Malay-language newspaper *Pembrita Betawi*.[147] Kieffer's paper provided heavy coverage of early performances in Batavia and even published a casting call.[148] The actors' inexperience was apparent but Snabilié comes up for heavy praise for "possessing a true understanding of how to please the hearts of spectators."[149] The company had less support when it toured southern Sumatra. Two Muslim company members named Salim and Oekoep left Snabilié's company when it played Palembang and returned to Batavia without sea travel passes, for which they were arrested and fined twenty-five guilders each. The company folded not long after.

Snabilié then landed another job as a stambul actor-manager, this time with Permata Stamboel.[150] Permata Stamboel seems to have been from the start an adventurous company. It gained early recognition for a production of *Teuku Umar's Traitorous Work,* a piece dealing with the war in Aceh, performed in Semarang on 19 May 1896. In it the guerilla leader Teuku Umar is described as the "big hero (general) of the Acehnese government." The tableau vivant that followed depicted Acehnese resistance forces ambushed by the colonial army at "Post Lamsut." After the well-attended and enthusiastically received show, Permata Stamboel was forbidden to perform the play again, most likely because the local government recognized the play's subversive potential in relation to the ongoing military campaign in Aceh.[151]

The high quality of Permata Stamboel's backdrops inspired Bandung's Braga Club to ask Snabilié to restore its own scenographic fittings, when Permata Stamboel played the Flower City in October 1896, and led to a series of stambul shows at this European club for members and their children. Permata Stamboel also had a successful tour of Sumatra in 1897, with invitations (and likely financial support) of "important [Chinese] people," playing Padang and the highlands of western Sumatra, as well as possibly Medan and Palembang, at around the same time that Sri Stamboel was in Medan.[152] The company was appreciated for its costumes, sets, and music, but neither the Malay language nor the Dutch occasionally employed in plays like *Faust* (performed in Padang on 28 June 1897) went down well.

Permata Stamboel returned to Java and on 6 November 1897 opened at Tanah Lapang Glodok (Glodok field) in Batavia. It was here where the company made its first acquaintance with Hubertus Loth, a tough from Kemayoran (*jago Kemayoran*) who was well known to Batavia's police.[153] Snabilié's application to play Glodok was initially turned down by the assistant resident for the police out of fear that Loth would create a disturbance. Permata Stamboel was able to obtain a permit only after Snabilié had struck a deal with Loth. Snabilié agreed to hand over 10 percent of profits to the racketeer to guarantee Loth's quiescence. Loth was not content with his agreed-upon cut, however, and demanded more for the company's "protection." He also came to performances regularly, causing commotions. The conflict reached a head at a performance one night.

> On that night, Loth was sitting in the Chinese captain's box, and he was drunk. By chance, Tuan Snabilié himself was scheduled to sing, but the music dragged behind him because Loth had given arrack to the musicians and they were all drunk. Snabilié thus strongly reproached the musicians, but Loth then shouted out that Snabilié had no power over young men [*sinyo-sinyo*] from Kemayoran.
>
> Then Loth mounted the stage and with great anger threw all the equipment he could get his hands on at the center of the auditorium. Spectators quickly dispersed and Snabilié decided that it would be best for him to inform the police that he would not continue to perform in Glodok.[154]

There was nothing the police could do help Snabilié, as the predetermined condition for the permit was that Snabilié himself would arrange to keep Loth under control.

Permata Stamboel decamped to Meester Cornelis, a military garrison town that had developed into a suburb of Batavia, connected to the town center by train and tram. Meester Cornelis was sufficiently outside of Loth's territory to keep him at bay, and he appeared there only sporadically to demand money. Permata Stamboel did well enough in Meester Cornelis to attract two of the great figures of stambul to perform with the company: Mahieu and the celebrated violinist and orchestra director Frans Paulus, for whom "no arrangement was too difficult."[155]

The troupe then pitched their tent at Tanah Abang, in the Weltevreden district of Batavia south of the Koningsplein (Gambir). Loth had business in Besuki, in eastern Java, and stopped by Permata Stamboel's tent the night before his scheduled departure. Snabilié "met with Loth and wished him a pleasant journey to Besuki and drank a glass of medicinal arrack" together with him.[156] More than likely, Loth used the opportunity to extort money from Snabilié. Loth was not alone that night but had come with a female companion named Nona Jet Govert. Loth and Govert got into a terrific row at around 10 P.M. while watching the play, with much shouting. Loth threatened to smash in Govert's head with a chair, but in the end he stormed out of the theater, causing much commotion.

What went on during the next ninety minutes was the source of much contention at the Loth murder trial. A total of eighty-nine witnesses testified at the trial, and few of them agreed on the details. It seems that Loth had an altercation with a group of Chinese at a gambling tent near the theater. Possibly Loth also tried to grab a bag containing Permata Stamboel's box office receipts. Several witnesses reported seeing a group of three men, one of whom might have been Snabilié, roughing up Loth behind the theater tent. Everyone present at Tanah Abang that night agreed that on 24 February 1898 around 11:30 P.M. the hollow percussive tones of the *tong-tong amuk,* a wooden slit gong used to sound the alarm of violence, reverberated. When the confusion of people fleeing this way and that was over, Loth was found dead of multiple stab wounds. Blood was found on a sword belonging to Permata Stamboel and there were also red stains that appeared to be blood on one of the backdrops. (Mahieu claimed in his testimony at the trial that the latter were betel stains.) Seven Chinese men, one of whom had quarreled with Loth on a previous occasion according to Snabilié's testimony, were arrested for murder and held in custody for fourteen months before the trial.[157]

The counsel for the defense, Mr. Van Dijk, attempted in his long closing statement to demonstrate that it was absurd to think that Loth might have been killed by a group of Chinese men who were practical strangers to him in a part of the city where he was unknown. Van Dijk was critical of the police investigation. He highlighted the inconsistency of testimony and pointed to the lack of any physical evidence that might implicate his clients. (The defendants had reputedly killed Loth with sharpened bamboo poles, but these were not found, and the gambling tent was never searched by the police.) Much of Van Dijk's statement was in fact devoted to presenting the counterargument that it was most likely Snabilié who was directly or indirectly responsible for Loth's death. The history of extortion and past altercations gave Snabilié a motive and the stains on the stambul sword and backdrop were physical evidence linking him to the crime. There were witnesses who testified to seeing a group of European-looking men beating Loth that night behind the stambul tent. What is more, before Mahieu and Snabilié returned to Permata Stamboel's rented house, they were spotted by a Chinese friend of the seven defendants talking to each other at Pasar Tanah Abang, the marketplace near the theater. Snabilié reportedly said to Mahieu, "Well, the mongrel is dead. He's been no end of trouble to us."[158] Van Dijk more or less stated that the only thing he was interested in was seeing his clients released. Loth was a criminal, and if Snabilié killed him, he got what he deserved. Nobody else seemed to be interested in trying Snabilié, despite the accumulation of evidence that implicated him. Snabilié did go on trial in 1899, though, for vandalizing musical instruments belonging to the town band of Cilacap.

The death of Loth shocked Batavia to the core. The constant fighting at stambul performances was infamous. There were many stories of stambul "destroying families" and "women who were obsessed with actors."[159] And now there had been a murder. There could be only one response from the civil authorities. A total ban was placed on stambul performances in Batavia, Bogor, and the surrounding area.

Stambul theater had long been a domain of passion and violence, but an actual murder was something new. Not only did it receive an official response from the local government, it forced stambul admirers to reconceive their attitudes to this popular entertainment.

The death of Loth also had an impact on Hans van de Wall, who wrote essays, fiction, and plays under the nom de plume of Victor Ido. Ido recounts in his unpublished memoirs that he was inspired to write the first sketch for his play *De paria van Glodok* (The pariah of Glodok), immediately after a supernatural encounter with the ghost of Loth.[160]

The play tells the story of an Indo man named Leo who is brought up by the kindly Mother Asia (Moeder Asia), a warung (small store) owner, after the death of his own mother. Leo does not know who his father is, though Mother Asia has a ring that was given to Leo's mother by his father. Mother Asia's property is owned by a Chinese man named The Boen Seng, who is seriously ill. The landlord's business affairs have been taken over by his son, The Kwan Liong. Mother Asia's profits are low and she cannot afford to pay the rent. In the first act, set in Mother Asia's warung, The Kwan Liong offers Mother Asia a choice. Either he will have his way with Mother Asia's daughter, Rooslien, or Mother Asia will be evicted. He tells Mother Asia and Rooslien to come that night to a Chinese opera party (*wajangpartij*) being held in honor of the recovery of The Boen Seng from his sickness to give their response. After The Kwan Liong's departure, Leo enters. He has managed to raise the rent money for Mother Asia. Leo notices a still smoldering cigarette left behind by The Kwan Liong, and finds out about The Kwan Liong's designs on Rooselien. He exits, vowing revenge. In the next act, Leo attacks and kills The Kwan Liong against the carnivalesque backdrop of the Chinese opera party. The third act deals with the legal case against Leo. Leo's attorney, Mr. Valkenburg, determines from the ring, a business card, and selected information gleaned from Mother Asia that Leo's father is none other than the president of the high court, the Raad van Justitie. But a death sentence has already been passed upon Leo, and Valkenburg knows that the evidence and testimony of Mother Asia would not be able to prove Leo's parentage in a court of law, in any case. The play ends with Mother Asia praying to Allah for his mercy on Leo.[161]

There is little evident relation between the particulars of the actual Loth case and the drama of *De paria van Glodok,* other than the central event of a murder at a theatrical performance involving a Eurasian. What is significant is that Ido goes to great lengths to build a sympathetic case to show how an underprivileged Eurasian youth might be driven to criminality and murder. The play is a polemical, issue-driven problem drama.

More significant, for our purposes, is the Dutch-language radio address entitled "Goena-goena" (The supernatural) that Van de Wall de-

Fig. 4.4. "J. M. H. Ohl in the role of Leo." Publicity still from the 1916 production of *De paria van Glodok*. Reprinted from Ido, *De paria van Glodok*, facing p. 16.

livered on NIROM under his Victor Ido pseudonym.[162] The details of the case seem to have been purposefully changed. The date of the murder is altered (although the location of Tanah Abang remains the same.) Loth's name is inverted as Tol. As in the stage play, "Tol" was said to have murdered a Chinese man, rather than the other way around. Victor Ido was not speaking history but was rather evoking the cultural mood of an era, speaking the past in an immediate voice at a time of massive political change.

Ido describes how in or around 1893 a young, rich Chinese man was murdered by a twenty-two-year-old man named Tol late one evening at a stambul tent in Tanah Abang. The murderer was said to be "a well-known type in stambul circles. . . . The case as a moral tableau made a deep impression on me. I had never experienced something like this in such proximity. Especially [significant] to me was the revelation through the legal proceedings that the juvenile delinquent must have been the victim of a completely deprived education with insufficient teaching. My sympathy for Tol was boundless and his sad lot was forever impressed on my thoughts."[163]

Ido then recounts a ghost story that took place a few days after Tol's execution. Ido finds and purchases a suling, or bamboo flute, as a present to a friend in Holland and places it in a drawer in his desk, only to forget about it. One day, when a houseguest is visiting, he hears the sound of a flute. Nobody can identify where its unworldly tones originate. The search leads them to the desk: the suling appears somehow to be playing by itself. The mystery still unsolved, Ido and his friend return to the houseguest, who sits in the dimness of twilight, her eyes closed, apparently asleep.

> Her mouth opened slowly and we distinctly heard her say in a strange voice:
>
> "Don't be afraid. I am Tol, sir. You know who I am, the one who was hanged. I did not mean to kill the Chinese, but when wrestling, my knife stabbed him right in the heart. This woman, through whom I speak, is a great trance medium, sir. Through her immense power, I have been called forth. Then I saw the flute. Earlier in my life I could play this instrument beautifully, sir. Now, sir, perhaps I will return later if I so choose. It is so strange that I am not dead . . ."
>
> The impression that this manifestation left was, in a word, disconcerting. (123)

The next day Ido celebrates a birthday at his house with his circle of friends. The company sits in semidarkness as the houseboy is off sick and the gaslights are unlit. Talk naturally gravitates to the incident with the flute, with unbelievers and believers among the company. "The first group explained everything to hallucinations; the latter group spoke of unknown laws of nature, hidden forces, and of ghosts" (123).

> My guest joined the gathering, listened to the lively discussion, and then said, a bit impatiently:
>
> "Ach, you and your ghosts. If a ghost is here, why doesn't he light the lamps, as we're minus a houseboy . . ."
>
> Her mouth was still open with her last word when pop! The whole house was magically, instantly lit up; all the gaslights burned.
>
> Everyone was dumbfounded. (123)

There is a topper to this. The scoffers among the company still attribute the instant illumination, like the magic flute, to the imagination. Their argument is deemed persuasive. Everyone then gathers at the dinner table. Eggs sitting on a plate move by themselves. "A deep silence descended on the table. The unbelievers went as white as sheets" (124).

The hybrid, mestizo social world associated with stambul produced few ghosts.[164] Ghosts and other spirits in Javanese belief are fixed to certain locales, and the itinerant condition of actors and spectators and the ephemeral nature of theater do not yield the solidity of the weird boulder, the gnarled tree, the lonely crossroads, the jutting outcrop of land, or the ruined temple favored by indigenous spirits. Loth was not a Javanese ghost. He did not manifest as a ball of fire, shape-shifter, or hopping corpse. Loth was in form essentially a European ghost, one who had to be summoned into being through a neoséance. Even in death, the spirit of stambul necessarily spoke through the medium of the Other.

Loth literally and figuratively haunted Ido (and likely others of his circle), who figured the "sad lot" of Tol as representative of the general conditions of deprivation faced by Indo "paupers." The word *tol* means toll in Dutch. The depraved behavior of Tol and his mandated death was seen as the toll to be paid for the educational and social neglect of the lowest stratum of Eurasian society. Tol tells Ido that he is not dead. Ido is disconcerted by the spirit's confinement to limbo because, perhaps, he understands that the condition of "Tol" in the afterworld does not differ fundamentally from the betwixt-and-between state that Loth occupied in his living days. Ido is not harmed by Tol in the story, nor is he unduly disturbed by an irruption of the supernatural in daily life. It is implied that his mestizo status and upbringing inures him to the deleterious effects of the otherworldly. He is not about to crack under strain from exposure to "the hidden forces" like Resident Van Oudijck in Couperus's novel *The Hidden Force.*[165] He is able to naturalize disembodied sounds, Tol's apparition, spontaneous combustion, and telekinesis as *guna-guna* (goena-goena), a Dutch-Malay conception of sorcery and the supernatural that Indos and Europeans growing up in the Indies learned from their nannies. An understanding and belief in guna-guna would come to serve as one of the primary identity markers that distinguished those Europeans and Eurasians who identified the Indies as their home (*blijvers*) from those Europeans who were represented as temporary sojourners in the colonies (*trekkers*).[166] Ido's troping of the spirit of Tol as guna-guna thus effectively situates this "well-known type in stambul circles" as an icon of an emergent identity formation. The visage deeply impressed on Ido the necessity of doing something on behalf of people like Tol, who were in no position to do anything themselves. The spirit importuned him from beyond the grave to commit to social action. The spirit was prescient of the rise of group consciousness and the identity politicking to come. As we shall see, stambul, as reinterpreted by Auguste Mahieu and activists like Ido around him, would have a role to play in this political movement.

Chapter 5

AN INDISCHE THEATER, 1898–1903

Auguste Mahieu's days working as a jobbing actor were over in October 1898. He had a new position as actor-manager of Komedie Stamboel Boenga Mawar. This was a newly formed, though ultimately short-lived, company owned by a Semarang entrepreneur named G. A. Vaillant.[1] The name Boenga Mawar (Rose) alluded to the Malay designation for *Sleeping Beauty,* the classic fairy tale first inscribed by Charles Perrault in his collection *Histoires, ou Contes du temps passé* (1697). (In Dutch the tale is known as *Doornroosje*—lit., little rose thorn.) The play based on the tale had been a hit with stambul audiences since Mahieu introduced it to the Komedie Stamboel repertoire in 1893. Both fairy tale and play were associated in the popular imagination with glamour, feminine beauty, magic, and mystery.

Boenga Mawar was a small-scale company. At its formation, it had a total cast and crew of thirty-two, including nine Indo actors and seven Indo actresses. Music direction was in the capable hands of Semarang-based violinist P. van den Broek, described in a Yogyakarta review as a "well-known concern violinist" who is "always the gifted student of the conservatoire."[2] His presence in the band was said to be "a strength in its own right."[3] Boenga Mawar's scenic equipment originally belonged to Tjahja Stamboel, purchased by an anonymous Chinese investor who rented it out to Vaillant. Tjahja Stamboel was a stambul company owned by Semarang businessman Tan Tjin Hian that toured Java to mixed reviews from October 1897 to July 1898.[4] Tan's start-up costs for purchasing sets, costumes, and other equipment was reportedly six thousand guilders, but when he sold off his outfit, Tan recouped only half his initial investment. Tan's company was perhaps more trouble than it was worth to him; there are accounts of legal troubles involving unpaid bills and a sword-and-pistol duel between company members. He was probably happy to get out of the stambul business with three thousand guilders for his used equipment.

Boenga Mawar operation was restricted to the towns and cities of central and eastern Java during the year under Mahieu's direction. A tour to Makassar was announced, but this seems not to have happened. The ban on stambul in Batavia, Bogor, and surroundings contributed to heavy competition in the entertainment field in eastern Java. Semarang had as many as three stambul groups playing simultaneously during October 1899, while even a small town like the "dilapidated" coastal town of Gresik was rarely without some form of commercial entertainment in its alun-alun.[5] Additionally, some eastern Javanese towns appeared to be imitating the Batavia precedent of banning stambul. Banyuwangi's *penghulu* (chief Islamic official) was responsible for the refusal of a stambul troupe's permit in February 1900, several days after the company had pitched its tent in the town's alun-alun.[6]

Komedie Stamboel Boenga Mawar opened in the alun-alun of Semarang on 21 October 1898 in a rented shed with a Mahieu standard, *Ali and the Magic Violin.* Audience sizes were moderate from the beginning of the run, despite praise for the troupe's acting and decor and approval of the great variety of plays presented, including reliable stambul standards such as *Ali Baba, The Fisherman and the Genie, Faust,* and *Genoveva.* Also performed were plays clearly derived from or inspired by the bangsawan and Parsi theater repertoire, such as *Hawai Majelis; Laili and Majenun, or The Power of Love; The Garden of Bakasari, or Queen of the Dark;* and *Indrajaya, or A Princess' Savior, Who was the Prey of a Dangerous Sea Serpent.*[7] In November, attendance dipped to such low levels that Boenga Mawar was forced to lower ticket prices and even cancel performances. When Boenga Mawar departed on 5 December 1898, they left behind many unpaid debts, including outstanding charges for furniture rental.

Possibly Mahieu was distracted by domestic affairs: he is registered as having divorced his actress wife, Nellie Vos, on 17 November 1898. They had no surviving children.[8]

Mahieu temporarily lost a capable company member when Derk van Sprew, an "all-around artist, who was equally capable as actor, stage manager, and technician," was recruited by Semarang businessman Babah Mowa to direct a newly created puppet theater, the Komedie Boneka Stamboel (Stamboel Puppet Theater).[9] This theater used figures in the style of *wayang potehi* (Chinese glove puppets), costumed after characters from the stambul theater, and performed the same stories and music as stambul. For all its ingenuity, the venture was not a success; audience numbers at the tent shows in the Kentangan district of Semarang were small, and the Komedie Boneka Stamboel folded in March 1899. Derk van Sprew later returned to work under Mahieu.

The Semarang run is noteworthy as being the first occasion when a new sort of play was performed, a social drama with a contemporary Indies setting entitled *Secrets of Semarang by Day and Night,* performed as a benefit for the actors on 2 December 1898. This play was the theatrical equivalent of an *Indische roman,* an emergent literary genre in Dutch and Malay writing telling tales set against the backdrop of the Indies and intended largely for an Indies readership.[10] The prototypical text in this genre is arguably M. T. H. Perelaer's antiopium novel, *Baboe Dalima,* a polemical page-turner that pits a young generation of Dutchmen against the evil alliance of a corrupt colonial resident and a Chinese opium farmer. Its initial publication in the Netherlands in two volumes in 1886 was followed in short order by a single-volume English translation from the Dutch and a number of Malay-language newspaper serializations.[11] *Baboe Dalima* sparked a host of like melodramas by Indo and Sino-Malay authors. Some of these were translations of Dutch works, but many were original works. Some were fictional, but the bulk claim to be "true crime stories" based on celebrated crimes of the past or crimes of the present, as reported in newspapers. Virgin abductions, opium smugglers, last-minute rescues, treacherous concubines, desolate hideouts, stalwart heroes, inscrutable mandarins, robber barons, pirate chiefs, lascivious landlords, unscrupulous spies, and dark and stormy nights all figure heavily in the melodramatic Malay genre.[12] An Indische roman was neither strictly naturalist nor realist. Magic and the supernatural spiced up the quotidian. The literary works, and their stage equivalents, did trade on recognizable social types, however, from downtrodden Javanese peasant to haughty Dutch colonial administrator.

Publicity for the theatrical translations of the literary genre refers to such plays explicitly as Indische romans, but to those in the trade they were known as *rusia* (secret) plays, likely after the Malay title of *Secrets of Semarang* and later plays that followed in this line, such as *Secrets of Batavia by Day and Night.* "If you were to ask a company member, 'What story are you doing tonight,' his answer would be 'a rusia story.' This indicated that they were not performing an adaptation of a European opera nor a story from *The Thousand and One Nights,* but a tale set in Indonesia. . . . The term implied that it was not a fantasy story, and included staged Indonesian stories presenting actual occurrences that were not, or not yet, public knowledge."[13] Among the Indische roman plays later performed by Mahieu were *Secrets of Batavia; Nyai Dasima; Rosina* (also spelled *Rossina*); *Si Conat, the Bandit Chief of Tangerang; Siti Rohaya: A Tale from Batavia;* and *Revenge, or Oeij Kim Nio and Lie Koen Njan.*[14] Possibly there were many more. Summaries are often lacking and it is difficult to judge genre from titles alone. Publicity for Indische roman plays sometimes cited the reference for the story's original appearance. *Revenge,* for example, was described in publicity as "a true story that happened in Pasar Minggu, Batavia . . . adapted from the newspaper serial that appeared in *Bintang Betawi* from 17 April through 8 May 1899."[15]

In both construction and reception, Indische roman plays bear much resemblance to Victorian "sensation drama"; possibly a genetic relation exists. A play in both genres has as its "goal . . . neither to make a political point nor to goad its audience to action, inside or outside the theater. Instead, it aims to produce an 'as if' feeling of anxiety, a sense of peril

Fig. 5.1. An Indische roman on the stambul stage. Illustration by Menno van Meeteren Brouwer. Reprinted from Fabricius, *Tempo doeloe,* 79.

that relies on a carefully conceived and executed literalism."[16] The spine-tingling thrills and chills of sensation drama and Indische romans were experienced individually in the company of others. Take, for example, Lien Gemser's harrowing performance as the eponymous heroine of *Ong Tjiauw Koen* in a Komedie Stamboel Zoetelief production. "When Ong Tjiauw Koen was imprisoned, many spectators felt their hearts crushed, to the point where there were even those who shed tears for pity at seeing her [fate]; it was as if Ong Tjiauw Koen was again alive and living in this world."[17] Spectators actively requested this play and came specifically to see Gemser perform.

Mahieu seems to have placed less stress on "secret" plays, in fact, than other stambul troupes, perhaps as the darkly realistic plots tended not to provide suitable vehicles for his own comic acting. Indische roman plays also did not rely on the same spectacular backdrops and costumes in which he was invested.

Boenga Mawar intended to travel next to Surabaya but reconsidered when Mahieu found out that the "adventurous and ambitious" Khurshed Baliwala's Victoria Parsi Theatrical Company was in town, giving performances at the Kapasan theater as well as at Surabaya's schouwburg.[18] It had been a decade since the last major Parsi theater troupe came from India to the Indies. Baliwala's company was one of the most celebrated and widely traveled theatrical troupes in Asia at the time. It was also one of the best equipped, requiring ten freight cars to transport its equipment during its tour of Java. (In contrast, a large-scale stambul company might use one car for its equipment and one car for personnel.)[19] Among Baliwala's attractions in Surabaya were English-language songs, ballet dancers, magical scenic effects, and the cinematograph, an early form of the motion picture. Actors regularly were wreathed with garlands at the end of much-applauded shows. There was no hope that Mahieu and his newly founded company could compete for Victoria Parsi's audience, and any comparison was bound to be unfavorable.

Boenga Mawar instead traveled to Yogyakarta, where it played to good-size houses for a full three months (ca. 10 December 1898–15 March 1899). The troupe opened in the alun-alun, but at the end of January it was compelled to move its marquee to the field behind the Benteng Vredeburg, Yogyakarta's Dutch fort, as its initial location was reserved for *maleman* celebrations.[20] The tent used was substandard, and might have been a rental not designed specifically for komedi use. Nontonners in the vicinity could see into the marquee and watch the show for free, leading to a reduction of tickets sold. Inclement weather hampered attendance in February, but audience numbers picked up in March. Yogya spectators particularly enjoyed the more comical plays.

Polite society in Yogya was again shocked when a number of local youths joined the company. A fourteen-year-old girl from "good parents" was returned to her parents' house after performing onstage for three nights, but it seemed that two young men from Bintaran Kidul stayed on. Some attributed the desire of Yogya youths to act to a "fascination" with the theater, but others said it was economic necessity that drove the young men to be actors. There was some concern that the girl had been permanently altered by her three-day sojourn among the itinerant performers.[21]

After the last tent show, P. van der Broek, the company's violinist and conductor, gave a greatly appreciated *soirée musicale* for the Cecilia music club. There was a humor-filled speech by Mahieu, and the orchestra played dance music after the concert. The music of the Komedie Stamboel Boenga Mawar deserved Yogyakarta's respect, but residents of Loji Kecil, the area of Yogyakarta where the company members were staying, were relieved when the company decamped for Solo on 13 March 1899. No longer did their nerves have to suffer from the late-night brawls and fights. Some Loji Kecil residents enjoyed the "free musical concerts," that is the music that spilled out from the theater and could be heard in the streets until 1 A.M. But even with music there can be something called *des Guten zu viel*—too much of a good thing.[22]

MAHIEU'S COMPANY officially changed its name to Komedie Opera Peranakan India when it opened in Solo on 19 March 1899. No definite reason is given for the change. Mahieu was clearly attached to the opera designation, and it is possible that he had a hand in its inclusion in the company's new name. Peranakan India denotes people of mixed Indian and Indonesian parenthood or culture, and it is likely that the company wanted to re-present its artistic orientation toward the subcontinent.[23] One Solonese commentator described Peranakan India's repertoire: "Formerly komedi stambul would perform plays based on Arabic stories, and occasionally European theater plays, but now most plays are based on legends and stories of India, probably because these are greatly enjoyed by all spectators."[24] The recent tour of Baliwala's Victoria Parsi Theatrical Company might also have renewed interest in Indian theater and served as a reminder of the Parsi theatrical impulse behind stambul's generation.

It is possible the company changed its name to distinguish itself from a rival stambul troupe known as Komedie si Boenga Mawar. The definite article *si* interpolated in the rival group's name is significant; it expressed a sense of cultural intimacy.[25] This was a theater that was recognized as ridiculous and disreputable, a form of fun that served to create a sense of solidarity between and among us.[26] Komedie si Boenga Mawar played small Javanese towns without benefit of a tent. At one performance in the eastern Javanese town of Sidoarjo (population ten thousand), eight drunken European spectators put on "theatrical costumes and then went onstage. All the spectators laughed at how funny their costumes looked. The men played along until the show was nearly open and came onstage again for the tableau."[27] We can all laugh at the onstage appearance of costumed European spectators (who were most likely, but not certainly, Indos), and they can laugh at themselves, without apprehension and with brio. This culturally intimate aspect of stambul was important to later commentators and cultural actors, as we shall observe. It was at odds, however, with Mahieu's aspiration for respectability.

Komedie Opera Peranakan India received a fourteen-day permit from Solo's authorities, though it had applied for a permit to perform for a month in the alun-alun north of the royal palace. The authorities allowed the permit to be extended an additional two weeks, however, perhaps because of the theater's great popularity and the relatively well-behaved crowds it attracted. No violent incidents are recorded during the duration of the run (19 March–15 April 1899). Equipment in use was still substandard. The third-class stalls collapsed on opening night (fortunately, without causing any serious injuries), and tears in the tent resulted in a two-day suspension of performances at the end of March in order to make repairs. Large audiences of Europeans, Chinese, and Javanese nonetheless jostled one another at performances night after night.

The company subsequently traveled to the nearby town of Madiun, where an expected ten-day run was extended to more than three weeks (2 May–ca. 25 May 1899). "Sasmito," the principle Madiun correspondent for *Bintang Soerabaia,* had in general a low opinion of komedi and like commercial entertainment, believing that "they are without a single purpose and in fact occasionally lead to dangerous arguments between husbands and wives."[28] He describes Madiun audiences as "selective" and "completely unwilling to see shows that are less than beautiful."[29] Sasmito could be severe in his reviews, describing for example the Bogorsche Club, a komedi stambul troupe from Bogor, as "a zero, good only at making dirty jokes."[30] The correspondent initially expressed reservation and suspicion that Peranakan India could turn a profit in Madiun. Advance word might have had it that the troupe was very comical and gave high-quality performances, but Sasmito warned that "if it is not beautiful, it should not perform in this city, as it will . . . [lead] only to financial loss."[31] His opinion shifted when he learned that Peranakan India was directed by Mahieu, as when "his company performed here last in 1896, performances were as sweet as sugar candy."[32] Sasmito went so far as to encourage unemployed Chinese men to work as canvasmen for the company, saying that there is no shame in hard labor. When the troupe departed at the end of May, Sasmito pressed for other troupes of this caliber to come quickly, as "when the weather is good, normally Natives here like to watch quality shows at night."[33]

The Komedie Opera Peranakan India invested in a new tent for the Madiun performances, reportedly costing six hundred guilders, including the bamboo struts and palmwood frame. Performances attracted large audiences, with European and Chinese devotees who came night after night throughout the run. Audiences particularly appreciated the polished humor, and nothing that had been seen previously in Madiun could compare to the group's costumes and backdrops.

Concessions were offered to draw Javanese viewers to the theater. The plays performed by Peranakan India were more Indic than those enacted by prior stambul groups. One of these plays, referred to by a correspondent as "the play in which the King of Jamantoran is tortured by his older stepbrother and killed by a robber chief," was performed in Madiun in early May.[34]

1. A young prince from the kingdom of Jamantoran named Sahid Muksim has a stepbrother named Ali Sanggar who has evil inclinations toward Sahid Muksim, as the latter is the son of the senior queen (*pademi*) [and thus the first in the line of succession.]

When the old king of Jamantoran dies, Sahid Muksim becomes king of Jamantoran. Ali Sanggar becomes angry that he is not made king. He is older but the son of a secondary wife. Despite all this, Sahid Muksim appoints him his principle vizier.

2. One day, Ali Sanggar makes a verbal agreement with a robber chief to kill Sahid Muksim, in order that Ali Sanggar can become king. Ali Sanggar agrees that the robber chief, named Palsanam, will become his principle vizier as recompense.

3. One night, as Sahid Muksim is sleeping in his pleasure garden, he dreams that he meets a girl named Siti Rudina, the daughter of the king of Tosanbrangka. He awakes and is full of longing for the princess and gives his viziers instructions to propose marriage to the princess.

4. The king of Tosanbrangka accepts Sahid Muksim's proposal with a happy heart, and writes a letter to Sahid Muksim declaring his willingness to give him his daughter in marriage. He sends his daughter to him that very day.

5. As Rudina travels through the jungle, she is captured by a robber chief. Ali Sanggar arrives and brings the robber chief to the royal palace.

6. At midnight, Ali Sanggar and the robber chief kill Sahid Muksim and throw the corpse into a river. Siti Rudina is asked if she will marry Ali Sanggar, but she refuses, and she is put into a cask which is nailed shut and set adrift in the sea.

7. Sahid Muksim's body flows downriver and washes up on the shore. It is found by two traveling performers who make their living from playing the violin and drum. They lift Sahid Muksim from the river and see that he is not in fact dead but only unconscious. The three agree to work together to make a living.

8. The king of Sea of Fire, named Jamajuja, sits on his throne and observes a cask tossed by the waves. He orders it to be retrieved and brought to the palace.

9. Once it has arrived at the palace, he orders it to be opened and he catches sight of Siti Rudina. He falls in love with Siti Rudina at first glance and wishes her to be his principle queen, but Siti

Rudina asks for him to wait, as she is exhausted from being nailed shut inside the cask.

10. One day, as Siti Rudina sits in the garden, Sahid Muksim arrives. He is wearing women's clothes and is accompanied by the violinist and drummer. They request that King Jamajuja hire them to perform. The king commands a performance. Sahid Muksim's singing alludes to Siti Rudina and everything that has happened. Sahid Muksim and the drummer and violinist then depart. King Jamajuja searches all over for Siti Rudina, but she has gone after Sahid Muksim. They recognize each other and exchange intimacies and then run away together. Jamajuja chases after Siti Rudina when he realizes she has run off.

11. Siti Rudina and Sahid Muksim arrive at the abode of a raksasa [ogre]. The raksasa sees Siti Rudina and falls in love and wishes to marry her. Siti Rudina agrees, but on the condition that the raksasa kill King Jamajuja. The raksasa agrees to this. Not long after, King Jamajuja arrives and fights the raksasa. Both die. But before his soul departs, the raksasa informs Siti Rudina that he has an arrow and whoever is struck by this arrow can be transformed into anything. With this, he gives the arrow to Siti Rudina.

12. Siti Rudina shoots the arrow at herself and transforms herself to resemble King Jamajuja. She then goes to Sea of Fire and orders all the soldiers to take up arms and attack the kingdom of Jamantoran. The viziers and soldiers depart because they believe it is their own king who has given the order.

13. In the palace of Jamantoran, Ali Sanggar is enjoying himself with his two wives, Siti Ulma and Siti Aisa, whom he has just married. Sahid Muksim arrives with the violinist and drummer and they are hired to perform by Ali Sanggar. They approach the king and Ali Sanggar is killed. The viziers are about to capture them, when Siti Rudina arrives and the viziers are filled with fear. In the end, Siti Rudina is struck with the arrow and resumes her normal form. She tells the viziers everything that has happened. The viziers only then recognize Sahid Muksim, who is reanointed king. The violinist is married to Siti Ulma and the

> drummer is married to Siti Aisa and both men are appointed viziers.[35]

The production of the King of Jamantoran's tribulations merited an exclamatory Wah! (wow!). Spectators lapped it up, without a thought about the cost of tickets.[36] Stories of this sort play on motifs that are familiar to Javanese more from Indic tales enacted as wayang and topeng than from the *Arabian Nights*. Magic arrows, men posing as women and women as men, hand-to-hand combat with raksasa, deposed kings posing as beggars, bodies cast adrift at sea. All these are devices found in tales that have existed in Java for at least a thousand years. With a bit of tweaking, the same plot could be transposed to the mythical universes of the Mahabharata or Panji.

Komedie Opera Peranakan India's repertoire is redolent of a move to indigenize the stambul form and reach out to rural Javanese audiences. Mahieu experimented with performing a wayang kulit play, *Sembodro larung* (Sembodro cast adrift), the story of the death and resurrection of Arjuna's beloved wife Sumbadra, one of the most frequently performed episodes from the Javanese version of the Mahabharata.[37] This play was performed "just as in *wayang purwo* [classical shadow puppet theater], the only difference being that the words are in high Malay. Everything else is the same."[38] The production was acclaimed and attracted a sellout crowd when it was performed in Solo in March or April 1899, and when it was performed in Madiun in May there was great anticipation. "We shall see if it is good or not. Perhaps it will be even better than wayang. People are astonished that it will really be done. . . . Pay heed! When Tuan [Mahieu] performs this play it should be announced by ringing the *bende* [signal gong] so that Natives will clearly be alerted."[39] The intermediate state of Peranakan India, between Javanese tradition and modern komedi, is signaled by the title of an article announcing Peranakan India's arrival in Solo: *Wayang Orang of* [or] *Commidie Stambool.*[40] Peranakan India had acquired some distinctly Javanese characteristics and could be considered either or both genres.

Yet despite this sort of artistic innovation (or regression, depending on one's point of view) and the monetary investments made in equipment, Komedie Opera Peranakan India stopped functioning soon after its Madiun appearance. There are reports of an unnamed komedi stambul troupe playing the small towns of Ngawi, Padangan, and Blora in May through July 1899 that might have been Mahieu's company. This troupe is described as "something resembling komedi stambul," a phrase that suggests that it was combining features of stambul with one or more other cultural forms.[41] Among the beautiful actresses in the company is a certain "Nona Nelie," who might have been Mahieu's ex-wife, Nellie Vos, assuming that relations with Mahieu remained cordial enough for her to act alongside Mahieu after their divorce. The company seems to have been appreciated. It received a command performance at the bupati of Ngawi's mansion, and a pantun about the actress playing (or named) Siti Aisah whose "face shines like the full moon" was said to be so often quoted in Blora as to give the local correspondent a headache.[42] It is not known if the company was profitable, however.

Like so many other stambul outfits operating at this time, Peranakan India was a company that emerged, gained the public's attention, made some money, faltered, and then was sold.

Komedie Opera Peranakan India had increased in size and run up much debt by August 1899. The company of fifteen actors and fifteen actresses was purchased from Vaillant by a seventeen-year-old aspiring actress named Helena "Lena" Mavinne Coppiëns, originally from the east Javanese town of Pasuruan. Lena Coppiëns's age suggests that she applied to family members for the necessary funds to make the purchase. The stambul company later provided employment for two actors named Th. Coppiëns and W. Coppiëns, both of whom joined the troupe in the middle of 1900. More than likely these were Lena's brothers or cousins. The stambul company might have been conceived from the outset as a kind of family investment.

Lena Coppiëns was half the age of Mahieu when she took over the company, but their relation seems to have been intimate from the start. The couple married on 3 September 1900, and Mevrouw Mahieu gave birth to twins exactly three months later.[43] Lena Coppiëns (who tended to use her maiden name for professional purposes) was initially not the most polished of actresses in the troupe; she was considered neither very beautiful nor good at acting in front of the public. She was prone to giggling fits and tended to laugh out loud at theatrical clowning, to the distraction of the audience. Although her skills improved with experience, from the very first she was taking on leading roles—one suspects because of her position of ownership.

The new proprietorship resulted in an immediate change of direction for the troupe. The wayanglike stories of the sort that dominated Komedie Opera Peranakan India's repertoire were out, and a renewed attention to contemporary social issues was in. The company went through a number of name changes in its first half year under Coppiëns's ownership. It was announced that she was renaming the troupe Sinaraja (Great Light) after her purchase, but by October 1899 the name had become Sinar Stamboel (Light of Stambul), while around January 1900 it was changed to Komedie Sinar India (Light of the Indies).[44] This last name was the one that stuck. For a company that saw its purpose in enlightening audiences about social issues through theater, it was an apt designation. Many persisted in referring to any company headed by Mahieu as the Komedie Stamboel. Addressing Mahieu in print, Otto Knaap notes that while there are now many other similar troupes with various names, "'your' troupe of *cabotins* remains known as the Komedie Stamboel."[45] The rechristening might have been Mahieu's idea. At any rate, the Sinar India name articulated a distinction he was keen to maintain.[46]

The first two years of Sinar India's existence was indeed a period for Mahieu to experience more than "a trace of pride." It was a high point in Mahieu's career, and the linkage to an emergent politics of solidarity allowed him the opportunity to regain his former glory and celebrity. As one admirer put it: "while many groups under the name of Stamboel depart from and arrive on the face of the earth, it is only Sinar India that remains active, due to the astute efforts of its director, Mahieu."[47]

SINARAJA PREMIERED in Yogyakarta in August 1899 and played mostly for Javanese spectators. Attendance was poor, despite Coppiëns's investments in decor, in part due to competition with the Warren Circus and an acrobatics troupe known as the Flying Jordans. A gratis promotional show brought out the crowds, but overall audience turnout was not as good as when the Komedie Stamboel had last played Yogyakarta. Merchants hoping to collect on outstanding debts owed by the former owner of the company were disappointed.

Mahieu's company toured the coastal towns and cities of central and western Java between October 1899 and April 1900. This was a different sort of audience that Komedie Opera Peranakan India had played in its last months of operation, more cosmopolitan, less devoted to Javanese tradition.

Sinar Stamboel (as Mahieu's company was then known) played Semarang in October and November 1899, a time of centennial excitement and change. Semarang's first automobile was received at this time by a certain Heer Stoop, who took it on a pleasure trip from Semarang to Rembang. Sinar Stamboel scored a major hit with a benefit performance on 16 November 1899, with proceeds going to the Transvaalfonds, a charity set up to support "the Boer fighters" (*de Transvaalsche strijders*) in the Anglo-Boer war. Once again contemporary events in a theater of war inspired Mahieu to make links between his dramatic activities and the world stage of imperialism.

The war between Britain and the Boer settlers of Transvaal and Orange Free State had been long in coming. A British buildup of troops along the border led Boer leader President Paul Kruger to issue an ultimatum for their removal. That ultimatum was ignored and the Transvaal forces attacked on 11 October 1899. This was generally recognized as a preemptive move to prevent British annexation. The Boer settlers scored some initial victories in the first months of the conflict, before British reinforcements arrived by steamship. Subsequently, the Boers engaged the British in guerilla warfare, which resulted in the conflict's protraction to three years and massive loss of lives and property.

Newspapers reported events from the Transvaal front daily, and the war was much discussed in clubs and street corners around the Indies. The Boer settlers' war against the mighty British army engaged the sympathies of people of Dutch descent around the world.[48] Officially, the Dutch position on the Anglo-Boer War was neutral. The Dutch colonial empire was propped up by British navy gunships. The protracted Dutch struggle to wrest control of Aceh from its Muslim rulers was only possible due to the tacit consent of the British. Unofficially, most Dutch were pro-Boer. The tension between the pro-Boer Dutch public and the neutral government was so severe that it nearly brought the government down.

The origin of pro-Boer sympathy can be attributed to the Algemeen Nederlandsch Verbond (ANV; General Dutch Alliance), a nationalist organization originally headed by the great Leiden Indologist J. H. C. Kern. The ANV championed the idea of linguistic and cultural unity among speakers of Dutch in the Netherlands, Flanders, South Africa, and the Netherlands Indies, and promoted a utopian vision of a greater Netherlands as a political entity. The organization attracted adherents and members in the Indies who imagined themselves as "culturally belonging" to the greater Netherlands.[49] At stake in the Anglo-Boer war, from the point of view of the Indies' ANV-oriented ideologues, was not merely possession of the Transvaal's gold mines. What mattered was the self-determination and autonomy of a Dutch settler population that people of long residence in the Indies (so-called blijvers) imagined to be much like themselves.

There was some debate in Batavia before the war about how to express public support for the Boer settlers without giving affront to the British citizens residing in the Indies. A Boer folk song programmed for inclusion in a musical offering at Batavia's Harmonie Club was canceled due to fear of offending the club's British members. The cancellation sparked considerable debate, pro and con. When war broke out, public sympathy rallied around the Boer cause. Boer songs were sung and played everywhere and local Transvaalfonds were established in all cities and large towns of the Indies, much in the way that Lombokfonds had been established in 1894.

Sinar Stamboel's Transvaalfonds benefit performance succeeded in drawing a prestige audience. Thirty seats were reserved for members of the Women's Committee (Dames-Comité) of Semarang's local Transvaalfonds. The resident attended along with his wife, Mevrouw Verspyck, as did a general and his wife, officers and soldiers, and many prominent European citizens.[50]

The play performed at Sinar Stamboel's benefit show, *The Roc's Egg,* was a staple of the stambul repertoire, but the tableau vivant that followed was not: it depicted Joseph Chamberlain, Britain's secretary of state for the colonies, and Paul Kruger striking "symbolic" (*zinnebeeldige*) poses.[51]

The "crowning event of the evening" was a Boer anthem Mahieu translated into Malay, sung at the benefit performance's conclusion. It seems this song was a loose adaptation of "Kent gij dat volk" (Do you know that nation), a Boer anthem composed in 1875 by Catharina van Rees.[52] Mahieu's inspiration for this translation was possibly the fact that the Transvaal national anthem had played to a standing audience at the benefit soiree variée at the schouwburg two weeks before his own benefit.

—Ada bangsa gaga brani	There is a brave and strong people
Lama turut prenta	Who have long lived in domination.
Ini bangsa orang tani (landman of boer)	This is a race of farmers (peasants or Boer)
Tinggal di Afrika	Who live in Africa.
Bangsa Ingris suda mau	The British desire
Bekin semuwa ancur	To crush everything,
Tapi Alla tida kasi	But God will not allow this
Sebab dia orang jujur	For they are honest.
Hip hip hura! hip hip hura!	Hip, hip, hooray! Hip, hip, hooray!
Hip hip hura! hip hip hura!	Hip, hip, hooray! Hip, hip, hooray!
—Ini orang bangsa blanda (Hollander)	They are a Dutch people
Waktu dulu perang (80-jarige oorlog)	Who during a past conflict (the Eighty Years' War)
Mundur di negri Afrika	Retreated on the African continent
Bekin perhimpunan (Republiek)	And formed a new entity (republic)
Bangsa Ingris selamanya	The British always
Dia orang busuk ati	Have had a corrupt heart.
Mau ambil negeri nya	They wish to seize their nation

Tapi banyak ingris mati	But many British have died.
Hip hip hura!	Hip, hip, hooray!
—Negri Transvaal maski baru	The Transvaal nation is still young
Tida takut perang	And not afraid of war.
Bangsa ingris dapet malu	The British have lost face
Tida bisa menang	As they are unable to win.
Orang Transvaal menang perang	The Transvaal people will win the war
Sebab muda pada Alla Tuwan	For they are favored by Lord God.
Orang ingris dia kala	The British will lose
Sebab dia turut setan	For they follow the devil.
Hip hip hura!	Hip, hip, hooray![53]

The audience sang along with the song's chorus. Dutch spectators left the performance "with greatly pleased hearts" for having assisted the Boer fighters.[54] Dutch- and Malay-language newspapers subsequently published and reprinted the Malay lyrics.

Sinar Stamboel's war effort was part of a swell of support for the Boer settlers. Artists and cultural organizations around the Indies were busy organizing war benefits, expressing their full-hearted support for the Boer cause. Sri Ratoe Indra Bangsawan, owned by the Batavia entrepreneur Oeij Kiat Djin and directed by Wim Cramer, organized a benefit performance of *Aladdin* on 4 November 1899 in Batavia. The next day, a large-scale picture of the Anglo-Boer War was displayed on the stage of Yogyakarta's European club, De Vereeniging. A flag of the Transvaal Republic was also unfurled and Boer folk songs were sung. There were plans to start up a new theater club called "Thalia" in Makassar the same month to do benefit performances to support the Boer cause. This club was to be composed of twenty European men, who intended to dress in Boer costumes, sing Boer songs, and conclude their shows with a tableau vivant showing "Transvaal freeing itself from British domination."[55] Sinar Stamboel was not even the only stambul group playing Semarang to organize a war benefit. S. E. Scipio, director of the Mataharie Stambool, which was playing the Chinese neighborhood of Gambiran at the same time as Sinar Stamboel was performing in Semarang's alun-alun, attempted to organize a war benefit as well on 20 November 1899. This performance had to be rescheduled until 23 November, as not enough people showed up at the first date. Apparently, Europeans were reluctant to see theater in Semarang's Chinatown, and competition for audiences with Sinar Stamboel was fierce until Mahieu's company left Semarang at the end of the month.

It is evident that Mahieu was at the cusp of a wave, with good links to Europeans elites and in synch with public sentiment. Mahieu's company was starting to transform, becoming something other than (or in addition to) a commercial theater. Theater, at its root, is a cultural contrivance to realize something that is not here and now in the moment of performance. It involves the active participation of both skilled performers and imaginative spectators to precipitate such a making-present. The repeated call of "Hip, hip, hooray!" in Mahieu's translated war song was as much a statement of belief in Boer victory as an effervescent affirmation of belonging that brought Boer settlers, the Semarang audience, and Sinar Stamboel together as parts of an encompassing, imagined community.

From Semarang, Sinar Stamboel traveled east along Java's coast to Pekalongan and Brebes. No reports are forthcoming from Pekalongan, but a newspaper correspondent writing for *Bintang Soerabaia* describes the company as performing in a tent northwest of the central market area of Brebes, in the Chinese quarter. Those performing included "six European women, four Muslim women, four Dutch men, and ten people of other races."[56] Costumes and backdrops appeared new, and performances of plays including *Ali Baba* and *The Lombok War* were said to be "fairly good" (*lumayan*), and not a waste of twenty-five cents (the price for third-class seats). But profits in Brebes were diminished by rain and the pugnacious reputation of performers: female spectators reported being reluctant to go to the theater for fear that a fight might break out.

Mahieu's company played Tegal in February 1900. This is the first time the company is identified as Sinar India, and it is also in Tegal where

Mahieu joined the Indische Bond (Indies League). Twenty-seven other members of Sinar India followed suit, an absolutely unparalleled institutional commitment to the league.[57] The league provided Mahieu with an institutional affiliation, a language of discourse, and an ideology—resources he drew on and contributed to in his theatrical and other cultural activities.[58]

The Indische Bond was established in 1898 at the urging of the Eurasian journalist G. J. Andriesse. Andriesse was passionate that the permanent "European" residents of the Indies (blijvers)—the vast majority of whom were in fact Eurasian—were entitled to a higher degree of political representation in the Indies' governance than the temporary residents (trekkers). The former considered the Indies their permanent home, while the latter were essentially adventurers, who wished to exploit the riches of the Indies and then return to the Netherlands. "He strongly attacked the 'sickening feeling of justice in the hearts of many,' who preached 'Java for the Javanese.' In his opinion 'the Indies were just as much the possession of the Eurasian as of the indigenous people' because if Java was not the fatherland of the Eurasian, where would his fatherland then be?"[59] Or, as Andriesse often railed, "Indië voor de Indiërs."[60] With the support of A. Bijvoet, an early advocate for the eradication of poverty among the Indies' Eurasian population, Andriesse gave a public address in Batavia, and the Indische Bond was subsequently established as a social welfare organization in October 1898.

> The goal of the organization, as laid down in article 2 of the [league's] Statutes, was "the advancement of the interests the members and the rendering of material and moral support to those European residents of the Netherlands Indies who are in need of such support and anxious to receive it." Members of the organization could be drawn from *all Europeans living in the Indies.* This, therefore, was a major departure from the original ideas of Andriesse. Achievements of the "humanitarian" objectives of the Indische Bond were sought in the establishment of cooperative shops, the advancement of small-scale agriculture and the furthering of education.[61]

The organization proved to have substantial appeal, attracting more than four thousand members by 1900, each of whom received the organization's print organ, the *Bondsblad,* with their five-guilder membership fee. Lodges and local chapters were established in towns and cities throughout the Indies. The functioning league departed from the radical ideas of Andriesse, who was ousted from the organization due to his overly confrontational stance. Judging from the debates that raged in the pages of the *Bondsblad,* however, the league certainly had a radical fringe, which did not back away from Andriesse's revolutionary idea for Eurasians to unite in order to unseat the pure-blooded European trekkers from their entrenched position of power.

The Indische Bond was without precedent in the Netherlands Indies, a mass organization that cut across numerous boundaries of class, occupation, locale, and religion. It has been described as "socially thin" and unable to "enlist a popular constituency nor dissociate from its strong identification with the European-born Dutch elite."[62] Much of the debate was internal and utopian, ignoring both the realities of colonial administration and the Indies' majority Asian population in models for the equitable distribution of wealth and power. But it is highly significant for being the first nongovernmental organization where the distribution of wealth and power were discussed openly, and it provided an organizational model for many organizations that followed. The Indische Bond was significantly the first organization that discussed the idea of an Indies nationalism embracing all ethnic groups—European, Chinese, Arab, Indonesian, and others—cutting across bounds of ethnicity and religion. This form of nationalism ultimately failed due in part to centrifugal global forces that enticed various groups defined by religion, region, ethnicity, and ideology to form their own autonomous communal structures and organizations in the first decades of the twentieth century. Had Indies nationalism taken off, the form and sentiment of Indonesia would have been different than it is today.[63]

The goal of the emancipation of the Indo and the concept of Indies nationalism only gradually emerged from the Indische Bond. "In the first two years after its founding it was not yet clear what the Indische Bond was or what it ought to do."[64] What was more significant from the start was instilling a feeling of solidarity among members and the imagining of what some members called *Indo-Europeesche maatschappij* (Indo-European society).[65] This came about through debate, discussion, speech making, writing, and performance.

A key term in this discourse was *Indische,* literally meaning of the Indies or Indies-like, but use figuratively to describe "all cultural phenomena which were composed of mixed European and Indonesian elements."[66] This was a new term on the horizon, although it mapped old patterns of cultural and social amalgamation. The naming of the hybrid condition was a liberating move of great significance. Since the British occupation of Java, indigenized Europeans and their mestizo lifestyles were regularly mocked as culturally degenerate and inauthentic.[67] The rijsttafel (lit., rice table), a colonial meal of rice and assorted side dishes based on Javanese cuisine, was derided as an affront to both European and Indonesian palates, an indiscriminate hodgepodge of clashing textures, colors, and tastes.[68] The identification of the in-between as Indische allowed intellectuals who enjoyed eating rijsttafels, lounging in sarongs, peppering their speech with Malay terms, and so on, to argue that their habitus emerged from particular sociological conditions and possessed distinct cultural logic. The Indische culture, it was argued, was not just arbitrary overlappings and juxtapositions of East and West; it was a perfect adaptation of the culture of Europe to the tropical clime of the Indies. A repertoire of cultural characteristics could be identified as "typically" Indische in guide books and popular writings; a corpus of novels with "origins lying with Indies authors, with the Indies public, or in the Indies life" could be delineated by Hans van de Wall as Indische romans; a hybrid colonial architectural style could be formulated and promoted as Indische.[69]

Mahieu's artistic and social activities gravitated toward league circles in 1900. There were league members in every city and town that Sinar India played, league clubs to visit, league meetings to attend. The league linked Mahieu to a higher class of people than he had previously known in his professional life and allowed him to cultivate respectability. Furthermore, it brought him into contact with intellectuals, including art critics such as Otto Knaap and Van de Wall, with whom he could exchange ideas. The league provided a new configuration for Mahieu's theater—it was Indische theater, theater of and for the Indies.

Mahieu regularly gave benefit performances for the league and sent telegrams to the *Bondsblad,* such as this one, sent after a 3 April 1900 performance of *The Pariah, or Misplaced Trust* (also known as *Ma Husin, or Misplaced Trust*) in Cirebon: "Tuesday performance of *The Pariah, or Misplaced Trust* to benefit Indische Bond, request mention in paper. —*Mahieu.*"[70] Mahieu not only received the requested plugs for his benefit show in Cirebon but others the company gave in western Java. His philanthropy also garnered exclamatory accolades—"Long live Mahieu and company!"—in the *Bondsblad* and other Dutch-language newspapers with regular columns on Indische Bond activities.[71] A cynic might view all this as good publicity: thirty-five hundred copies of the *Bondsblad* were being printed twice weekly as of April 1900, one of the highest circulation figures for any publication in the Indies. But there is something genuinely passionate in Mahieu's embracement of the Indische Bond's vision.

That passion was audible to contemporary observers in Mahieu's discourses. In addition to Sinar India's benefit performances, Mahieu also regularly presented speeches on social issues to Indische Bond members and others, and he fully participated in league discussions. Mahieu's public speaking is described by Otto Knaap, a fellow league member, in his semifictional profile of "Antoine Tardieu." Knaap writes from the perspective of an interlocutor who knew Mahieu well.

> It goes without saying that Tardieu [read: Mahieu] is a social democrat. That alone would be reason enough for the Indies capitalists to count him among the indecent. . . .
>
> Although born and raised in an environment where broken Dutch was spoken, he has been able, thanks to his cultivated feel for language, to compel himself to speak pure Dutch. That is why he gladly raises his voice at meetings and gatherings to disclose his genuine and fancied grievances in a storm of words. His orations are delivered with theatrical gestures. The sound of his own voice seems to stir him. His voice and gestures of his arm continually

> crescendo and an utterance always concludes fortissimo. . . . He is very impulsive and many adroit mischief makers have thus taken advantage of him.[72]

As a stambul actor-manager, Mahieu created plays and realized an artistic vision onstage. He was used to speaking to a rapt audience and being listened to and admired for his skills in elocution and wit. In the league circle, Mahieu was one voice among many clamoring for societal change. It was a heady scene, full of hope, full of possibility.

Mahieu continued to program some the staple plays of the stambul and bangsawan repertoire with Sinar India. In the company's brief run in Cirebon (31 March–4 April 1900), plays offered included the well-worn *Ali Baba and the Forty Thieves* as well as Indische roman *Secrets of Batavia by Day and Night.*

Mahieu took advantage of the presence of the very talented Frans Paulus, the company's musical director and violinist in 1900, to hire out Sinar India's orchestra for private and public functions on nights when the theater was dark. Mahieu intermixed music with "comic speeches" (*komieke voordrachten*). Two such performances took place in early 1900 in Cirebon. Mahieu and his orchestra performed at a gala thé dansant on 24 February 1900 at the house of The Han Tong, lieutenant of Cirebon's Chinese community that went on until five in the morning. Fireworks, a brass band, and champagne also enlivened this event, held to celebrate a family member's wedding. (Chinese opera and a ronggeng social dance troupe from Pekalongan performed on a prior night.) A less elaborate presentation was a 6 April 1900 soirée musicale with comic speeches held at the Phoenix, Cirebon's European club, with tickets priced at one and a half guilders for men, one guilder for women, and seventy-five cents for children. For this occasion, Mahieu used the cover name Andalusia Music Society, omitting reference to Sinar India. Mahieu is listed in advertisements as the Andalusia's "music director."

In April 1900, Sinar India traveled from Cirebon to the nearby town of Indramayu. Another benefit for the Indische Bond was held in this small coastal town, and Mahieu delivered a "speech" (*lezing*) there, presumably to league members. The benefit merited praise in the *Bondsblad* for setting a "positive example."[73] The company spent the next three months touring the highlands of west Java, playing Sukabumi, Bandung, Cimahi, and possibly other towns, giving benefit performances for the League at each stand.

A new assistant resident who had a more liberal attitude toward popular theater than his predecessor was installed in Batavia in 1900. The ban on performing stambul in Batavia, Bogor, and surroundings was still officially in force in 1900, but Mahieu was "so much loved by the people" of this area, with regular letters addressed to Malay newspapers petitioning for his troupe to come, that he was able to circumvent the prohibition and perform in Bogor and Meester Cornelis.[74] Mahieu attempted as well to get a permit to perform in Batavia proper in 1900, but his petition was rejected. Some complained that this was discriminatory, as a bangsawan group known alternatively as the Komedie Sri Latjmi Maja Poean (in Malay) or the Jawi Pranakan Theatrical Company of Penang (in English) had no such problems getting a permit for Batavia's Mangga Besar square, despite considerably less popular appeal. However, even Sinar India's most fervent admirers advised that it would be prudent for the police to be on their guard in the event the company performed in the Batavia area, "so that people will not fear another disturbance of the likes of the Loth incident a few years back."[75]

Mahieu's grand return to the area of the capital did not go as smoothly as might have been anticipated. Mahieu instructed roustabouts to construct a stage and a shed (*sawung*) in Kampung Anyar, near Bogor's railway station, at the beginning of July 1900, while the actors were still performing nightly in Sukabumi.[76] Sinar India opened in Bogor on 16 July 1900, but less than four days later the company was shut down by Bogor's assistant resident for "causing much disruption to families," that is to say for extramarital affairs between performers and locals. Mahieu had reportedly invested approximately two hundred guilders in erecting the stage and shed, but was forced to sell the theatrical edifice to an unnamed hajji for seventy guilders. (The hajji planned to dismantle the makeshift theater for resale or use elsewhere.) An early report stated that not only had Sinar India's permit been revoked, the assistant resident had "promptly expelled" the performers from the residency.[77] An article then appeared in the *Bondsblad* that Sinar India had permanently disbanded.[78]

Reports of Sindar India's departure and demise were premature. Apparently Mahieu was able to work out a compromise with the local government. Performances resumed again in Bogor by the beginning of August, after Mahieu had dismissed a number of actors for dissolute behavior. Spectators again flocked to the theater, but while all admitted that Mahieu was a superb actor and comic, spectators were not pleased with the well-worn physical properties. "All the backdrops are very dirty and don't shine at all! Why doesn't the company's owner replace all the backdrops with new ones? Ones that shine more."[79] Another paper said, "Before it came to Bogor, a number of newspaper correspondents expressed their anticipation of the company's arrival, but after it had arrived, not one of them regularly attended, and in the end Sinar India did not make much profit because the people of Bogor did not appreciate it much."[80]

Sinar India stayed on in Bogor through the middle of September 1900, despite the low audience figures, as Mahieu negotiated performance permits to play Meester Cornelis and Batavia. On one of his trips to the capital, Mahieu also stopped by the *Bondsblad* office and spoke with the editor to set the record straight that Sinar India was still solvent. Apparently the false news of the company's dissolution had been reported by two disgruntled former Sinar India employees who wished to harm their former employer. Mahieu claimed not to have read the article. Mahieu and Lena Coppiëns, who was six months pregnant, registered their marriage on 3 September; Mevrouw Mahieu née Coppiëns subsequently traveled to east Java, presumably to be close to her family during the pregnancy's last trimester, and delivered twins Carel and Emile Mahieu in Mojokerto on 3 December 1900.[81]

Sinar India gave a benefit performances on 6 September 1900 for the Indische Bond in Bogor, as was its custom, performing *The Pariah, or Misplaced Trust*, followed by a tableau vivant entitled "The Indische Bond in 1910." Mahieu's tableau of the future, almost certainly filled with hope for a bright tomorrow, was said to have met with popular approval, encouraging him to do more work in this line.

SINAR INDIA's long run in Meester Cornelis (24 September–6 December 1900) was in many respects the pinnacle of Mahieu's career, a vindication for the abuse that he and his theater had suffered for much of the last six years and a validation of his work's cultural significance.

Sinar India made numerous physical improvements before the opening, crafting new costumes and scenic properties and taking on new performers, filling out the cast to twelve actresses and thirty actors. "Almost all the actresses are young European women selected for their attractiveness and beautiful figures, and what is more they are famed for their performance skills and are very capable of acting before an audience."[82] As if this was not enough, Mahieu advertised at the end of November that "for the pleasure of the Komedie S.I.'s audience I have added many young women and men who are good actors" to the company.[83] This was a strong company of actors, memorialized decades later by "Opa Samson" as including "well-known figures such as Dirk van Sprew and Bram Wagner (clowns), Hunter, Pietje Portier (*bongkok udang*), Marie Oord."[84]

Opa Samson reached back to teenage memories to paint a vivid image of the physical environment of Mahieu's theater in Batavia circa 1900.

> Outside the tent, there were the lights of food and drink sellers. You could get a cold drink from the *tukang aer batu* [iced drink vendor] and hot drinks from the coffee vendor or the *tukang bandrek* [hot ginger drink vendor]. You could also get a hot meal, rice with vegetables and side dishes. This was for the many people who came to the stambul straight from work in order not to be too late to buy a ticket. . . .
>
> You see people streaming in through broad doors . . . You see a man over there wearing a panama hat, a captain of industry! The one wearing a tie is from the press. The woman fanning herself in the first row has a carriage waiting outside. The Chinese *tuan toko's* [store owners] from Pasar Baru and from the lower town are well

> represented and come with their wives. Their wives have sparkling diamonds on ears and fingers. . . . The entire hall seated about six hundred people.
>
> Two juxtaposed flying angels holding trumpets were painted at the top of the proscenium arch. Between the angels was a harp festooned with requisite decorations. The columnar sides of the proscenium arch were painted. There were curtains and musical instruments here and there. On the front curtain was an image of a woman in white with a diadem on her head, reclining on a thick multicolored carpet and playing a stringed instrument. She was depicted as looking on a grove of trees. A deer could be seen among the trees.
>
> The side scenes represented the places where plays were set. For stories from *The Thousand and One Nights* there were mosques with minarets and there was a fountain at the center. . . . There were also side scenes depicting views of rice fields with mountains in the background and a fountain in the foreground. . . . You must not imagine that these were only roughly executed images. . . . If you were to inquire into who did all the painting, an unassuming Indo young man would be told to step forward. . . . At night he plays supporting parts, and in the day he works with palette and pencil in hand.[85]

As can be seen from Opa Samson's description, the company's repertoire was extremely diverse, encompassing plays from Parsi theater and bangsawan, the staples of the stambul repertoire, European operatic adaptations (*Faust* and *Aïda*), and Indische romans. There was a play based on a Siamese chronicle, *The Battle of Achmad Mohamad: The Origin of the Genie King,* also known as *The Monk King, or A War Tale Concerning the King of Siam.* A play entitled *The Transvaal War* was performed on 25 November 1900. This was promoted as a story that spectators "had never before seen, though they might have heard the story, as it is heavily reported in the newspapers. Whoever comes tonight can see for themselves the very strange clothes and behavior of Boer men and women."[86] Two weeks later, a motion picture tent show in the

Tanah Abang district of Batavia played a short film about the Anglo-Boer War. Probably this film, like most early war "documentaries," was about as authentic as Mahieu's theatrical spectacle of war.[87]

Audiences reacted viscerally as individuals and as a social body, as described in one of the most touching tributes to Mahieu's company by a newspaper correspondent who wrote under the humble Javanese nom de plume Wong Betawi (a person from Batavia).

> People work in the city of Batavia for the sake of their physical sustenance—that is, to pay for food, clothes, and accoutrements. Is it not surprising, then, that the Sinar Hindia company, and its accomplished director, have been accepted with open arms and hearts?
>
> Every night that Sinar Hindia performs at Meester Cornelis, the people of Batavia and surroundings indicate that they understand how great the benefits are that accrue in receiving food for the soul. I have always looked after myself and insured that the food supplied to my body and soul are in balance, but I feel that Mahieu's performances are a sort of new sustenance serving to reinvigorate the nerves and elevate thoughts from the commonplace.
>
> Starting from the performance of *Nyai Dasima,* a story that causes tears to flow from the eyes of girls and women, Sinar Hindia has continually healed the ailing souls of the people who live here. . . . Over the last nights, I have seen spectators from all parts come to the theater, where this community [*kaum*] is treated by the performing ensemble onstage, which is so lively and attractive in all aspects, including the smallest details, so that in the melancholic sections all the spectators look for a handkerchief to dry their eyes, and when it is animated [onstage] everyone feels that they live in fellowship.[88]

So much of the history of komedi stambul up until this moment had been conflict ridden. Friendship between company and audience was sometimes evoked, particularly around benefit performances. As with the British music hall at the time, this sort of komedi friendship was effectively "a fragile membrane of good intentions" that "promised stability and certitude in [a] slippery and capricious microcosm of a larger world."[89] Fellowship might have been intensely desirable, but it was generally illusory. Stambul did not, as a rule, tap into and reinforce communal structures and values of affiliation like the communally produced performances of traditional Java or the artistic productions of enthusiastic Dutch dilettantes. The theater at Meester Cornelis was something other than typical stambul. Sinar India was generating communitas, breaking down social barriers and healing selves.

The development of communitas and solidarity was, in a sense, Mahieu's proclaimed aim. Mahieu attended an 18 November 1900 meeting of the Meester Cornelis chapter of the Indische Bond at the lodge house De Ster in het Oosten (Star in the East). Meester Cornelis's league chapter was the largest and most active in the Indies, and its meetings were regularly reported on in the Batavia press. Mahieu argued at this meeting that from now on one should use the more inclusive term Indiërs (people of the Indies) rather than the divisive term Indos, which had come to connote the poorest and least educated sector of Eurasians. Mahieu went on to say that "the Indiërs living in the kampung," the Eurasians who lived in a way essentially indistinguishable from the Muslim population, "for various reasons never attend meetings. They nevertheless contribute whatever little bit they can muster [to the league]. The more fortunate of their league brothers must stay in touch with them if they are to be firmly committed to their party."[90] Mahieu also suggested that the league appoint district commissioners who could tour to small towns such as Tegal and Pekalongan to lead discussions with local members, thus "contributing to the flourishing of the league."[91] He was clearly thinking of his own itinerant experience and the social networking his touring had created.

An Indische Bond benefit performance was organized at Meester Cornelis on 14 October 1900, which raised one hundred thirty guilders. At the 18 November league meeting, Mahieu also unveiled plans to hold three benefit performances for the local league chapter at an engagement planned for Batavia's schouwburg. The announcement merited applause from the Indische Bond members attending the meeting. Mahieu's application to perform at this most elite bastion of European culture was not in the end accepted, however, despite his direct plea for support from Agerbeek, president of Meester Cornelis's Indische Bond chapter.

The Meester Cornelis benefit performance for the league featured a play and tableau vivant that seem to have been expressly created for the occasion.[92] This play, entitled *Bin Lail, or The Son of Blackest Night,* was characterized in one description as "an allegorical fantasy piece" concerning relations between Europeans born in Europe and Eurasian Indiërs.[93]

> A certain king of Tanah Datar [Malay for lowlands] has two sons. The elder is named Yanudin Kassa [Dutch for cash] and is loved and privileged by his father above his bastard brother Bin Lail [Arabic for son of the night]. Bin Lail is unappreciated, slighted, and neglected, and in the end he grows tired of living in his father's palace and resolves to seek his fortune elsewhere.
>
> After adventures of all kinds, he arrives in the kingdom of Hindia [Malay for the Indies] where he renders the king a great service. As a reward the king grants the hand of his daughter and appoints him as his deputy and recognizes him as the heir to the throne.
>
> In the meantime, Yanudin Kassa has succeeded his father on the throne and rules over Tanah Datar. He is drawn into a war with various neighboring princes and is driven off his throne and out of his land. He wanders the world until at last he arrives at his brother's land. His brother receives him kindly and treats him with great generosity. He applies his power and influence and helps his brother regain his throne.[94]

After the play there was a "grippingly beautiful" tableau vivant with the Dutch title "Ende desespereert nimmer" (Never give up), representing the League of the Indies and the *Nederlandsche maagd,* or Dutch maid. The latter was a well-known icon of the Dutch nation, a woman with long tresses and a Grecian helmet, that featured on posters and banknotes and was as familiar to people of the Indies as Uncle Sam is today to Americans. In the tableau, it is the representative of the Indies

League that stretches out its hand to Jong Indië, an icon of the Indies' future, in a protecting gesture.[95]

The benefit performance was much discussed, and tickets were scarce. The play's allegorical meaning was said to be so "transparent as to nearly make commentary meaningless."[96] The play tells us that the ensconced Netherlands will only be able to maintain its power with the assistance of the adventurous dark-skinned Indiërs. The tableau further suggests that it is these Indiërs, and especially the Indische Bond, that offers protection and assistance for all the people of the Indies. The colonials, based in the Netherlands, stand by and do nothing.

The promotion of *Bin Lail* in the *Bondsblad* was cast in a new sort of language that had rarely been applied to stambul in the past. "Nobody with the slightest feeling for Eastern poetry and art should miss this timely performance," *Bondsblad* wrote in its preview.[97] And when it was over, a review read: "The performance was irreproachable, permeated completely with a typical Eastern character."[98] The *Bataviaasch Nieuwsblad* used much the same language in its review of *Jula-Juli*. "A habitué of the Théatre Française or the professional Opera in Paris might be able to make some not ungrounded criticisms of the acting and singing, but we are not in Europe, and I can strongly recommend that anyone who wishes to see something extraordinary, something that is typically Indische, go acquaint themselves with the Sinar India theater company."[99] Sinar India had been rhetorically uplifted to a cultural emblem of a new ideal, the fusion of "Eastern" and "Western" culture into a uniquely Indische blend.

The company was not immune to the usual criticisms. Wong Betawi recognized that "visiting Sinar India causes young men to have dark thoughts because the actresses' faces are too beautiful, causing souls to wander outside the boundaries that Nature has ordained for them."[100] There was also a story of a mother who abandoned her three-year-old child in a dos-à-dos outside the theater so that she could flirt and carry on with an actor backstage. The coach's driver waited outside the theater for hours and was in the end forced to seek the assistance of the sheriff to reunite the child with the mother. "Men or women will forget everything without fail when goaded by the devil," concluded the article.[101]

These criticisms were minor and only obliquely implicated Sinar India. The blame for neglecting a child or allowing one's thoughts to "wander outside the boundaries" was placed on the spectators.

The 18 November league meeting at the Star of the East concluded with perhaps the single greatest honor Mahieu received in his life: "Mr. Agerbeek, president of the Meester Cornelis chapter, asked . . . if this was not the place to offer a token of appreciation to Mr. Mahieu, who has manifested support and upheld the concerns of the league whenever possible, on various occasions and in many respects. Loud applause from everyone present demonstrated the concurrence of the assembly."[102] Two intimate portrayals of Mahieu by Otto Knaap and Hans van de Wall (writing as Victor Ido) come out of Mahieu's involvement with the Indische Bond during 1900. Both accounts are fictionalized, at least in part, and are motivated by particular ideological reasons. I have already drawn on both for what they reveal about Mahieu's character and biography, not without recognizing historiographic problems. (Other commentators have referred to them less critically.) My purpose in examining them at this juncture is to show something about how Mahieu was perceived by Batavia's intellectual elite in 1900 and how they understood his theatrical efforts as relevant to their ideological programs.

Otto Knaap (1866–1917) was the foremost art critic of the Indies at the turn of the century, as well as a dedicated classical violinist.[103] Although an Indo born in the city of Cirebon, he was educated in literature at Leiden and was extremely knowledgeable about modern European art. Knaap wrote knowingly in *Java Bode* of the latest cultural trends and polemics in Paris, London, and Berlin. He was forthright as an art critic and condemned the dilettantism that dominated the Indies' European art scene at the turn of the century. Legal troubles in 1900 led to him being banned from working as a journalist and contributed to his decision to move to Europe in 1901. In Europe, Knaap continued his career as an art critic, living in Paris and writing for the major Dutch newspapers. Knaap's portrait of Mahieu, entitled "De Indische Antoine: Antoine Tardieu," originally appeared in the *Algemeen Handelsblad,* published in Amsterdam.[104]

From his portrait, it is evident that Knaap saw much of Mahieu in meetings and performances as well as less formal occasions in 1900. Knaap's concern in writing about Mahieu was not biographical. He was interested instead in saying something about the moral purpose of art and conveying to a foreign readership some insights into the conditions of theater making in colonial Indonesia. The use of a pseudonym for Mahieu frees Knaap of the necessity of historical accuracy and allows him to appropriate Mahieu as a symbol of the Eurasian struggle for recognition. Mahieu's parents, for example, can be described simply as paupers, without reference to the various low-level colonial service jobs occupied by Johan Mahieu. There is no need to mention that Mahieu was not the company's first director, nor is Yap Gwan Thay's extensive involvement in the Komedie Stamboel's founding discussed. ("Tardieu" was instead said to have secured a loan from a fictional "Arab money lender" in order to establish the theater.) Theater is the most social of art forms, but in Knaap's portrait "Tardieu" emerges as a heroic personality. Mahieu, in this telling, strove to create a "harmonic whole" out of Eastern tradition and classical Western theater. He was "innovator, actor, director, impresario and much more" in theater, ready to sacrifice all in the "temple of art." Mahieu's theater is viewed as emerging directly from his social democratic political inclinations. The whole enterprise becomes an allegory for class struggle.

Hans van de Wall configures Mahieu in his 1912 novel *De paupers* (The paupers) in a similar, albeit more complex, manner. Van de Wall's biography is similar to Knaap's, and they were indeed collegial until a spat in Batavia's press in 1897. Van de Wall was born in the Indies in 1869 but attended gymnasium in Delft, and received a strong education in classical music. He returned to the Indies in 1891 and worked as an art critic for the *Bataviaasch Nieuwsblad* and a church organist, and wrote novels, essays, and plays under the alias Victor Ido. (It is likely that Van de Wall was the author of the *Bataviaasch Nieuwsblad* review cited above, representing Sinar India as a "typically Indische" theater.) *De paupers* is arguably Ido's masterpiece, an intimate and sympathetic glimpse into the lives, aspirations, and limitations of poor Eurasians. In the novel's last five chapters, Mahieu appears under the guise of "Karel

Reumer," director of the "Komedie Hindia." His character provides an ideological orientation and a role model for the poor Indos who are the novel's central characters, allowing them to find purpose and direction in their lives.[105]

Reumer is introduced to the novel's protagonist in chapter 14 over a meal of bami noodles in a Chinese food stall. The Komedie Hindia is said to be one week into a two-month engagement in "the big field in the upper part of the city," a more or less accurate representation of the circumstances of performance in Meester Cornelis from September to December 1900. With little preamble, Reumer launches into a heated address concerning the importance of the league, or brotherhood, uniting Indos throughout the Indies. Reumer speaks of systematic discrimination over hundreds of years against Eurasians, in favor of Europeans, Chinese, and Natives, and of his own efforts as an impresario to create a theater to provide employment for Eurasians: "I am myself an Indo and feel much for the poor siblings of my race."[106]

The complicity of Ido (and Knaap) in the elevation of Mahieu to the status of autonomous creator marked stambul as something more than just a commercial entertainment. The theater was transfigured into a feature of a larger narrative of the self-recognition and communal imagining of the Eurasians of the Netherlands Indies. It is not incidental that the play the Komedie Hindia enacts in *De paupers* is *Romeo and Juliet.* The point of depicting the Komedie Hindia performing Shakespeare is not to provide a historical commentary on the actual repertoire of stambul at this time.[107] There is no historical evidence that Sinar India performed *Romeo and Juliet* in 1900, although versions of *Hamlet* and other Shakespeare plays were performed by stambul and bangsawan companies beginning as early as 1899. Rather, the representation of *Romeo and Juliet* as a stambul play performed by Komedie Hindia is a strategic move, presented with much flourish. There is pride evident in Reumer's voice when he explains, "I have thus adapted a piece of Shakespeare into high Malay. We have had much success with it."[108]

Appropriating Shakespeare provides a singular possibility for exploring emotional depths and alien sensibilities. This is borne out in the discussion after *Romeo and Juliet* in *De paupers,* which centers on romantic love. Nini, sitting in the audience and romantically interested in "Reumer" (who is playing Romeo), had been overwhelmed by the staged passions to the point of jealousy of the Juliet playing opposite Reumer. Reumer admits that the story is based on fact but is skeptical that such a love unto death could exist in real life. Nini is convinced of such a love's possibility, for she herself experiences such a passion for Reumer.

The use of a Shakespeare play also allows Ido to address issues of hybridity. Before the *Romeo and Juliet* performance, when Reumer dialogues with the Eurasian protagonists, the contrast between the place of Eurasians in the Netherlands Indies and British India is explicated by Reumer: "They say you are either a full-blooded Englishman or you are not. There is no middle way. If you are not an Englishman, you are colored. They don't consider you as being at all like themselves. And at least you know how you are apprehended. But here, for us, our legal position is equivalent to that of the Europeans. In theory, we are equal to the Europeans. But in practice, they consider you inferior and exclude you from many positions and privileges. This is perfidy. It is grounded in a lie."[109] Reumer continues to say that it was "solidarity" with the "poor members of my race" that caused him to drop out of high school and establish a theater company—thus providing work for unemployed Eurasians.

Shakespeare, it is hardly necessary to say, is iconic of Englishness. Englishness, in the particular Indo reading articulated by Van de Wall/Ido/Reumer/Mahieu, means perfect definition in racial bounds: all Shakespeare is "European"; there can be no "colored" Shakespeare. Enacting Shakespeare as an Indiër is thus not simply a "color-blind" casting decision; it is an active, symbolic assertion of European privilege by the Eurasian underclass and an assault on Dutch colonial perfidy. As in many colonial countries, adapting the Bard into an emergent poetic literary register was part and parcel of a project to realize group identity in the modern world system.

Rob Nieuwenhuys, in a capsule summary of Mahieu's life, writes that Mahieu "withdrew from public life in 1900."[110] This is not accurate in the strictest sense, as Mahieu remained active as an actor-manager, but it is certainly the case that Mahieu did not enjoy much celebrity after 1900, and his name goes unmentioned in the pages of the *Bondsblad* until his death in 1903.

It seems that Sinar India remained in western Java following the last show in Meester Cornelis on 6 December 1900. Mahieu and his "musical corps" presented a "soirée musicale with comical speeches" at the Nederland, the clubhouse of the Indische Bond chapter of Cirebon on 1 February 1901. Admission was fifty cents for league members and one guilder for nonmembers, and a social dance followed the performance. Sinar India subsequently gave shows over eight nights (14–21 February 1901) in the Panjunan area of Cirebon, performing a mixture of *Arabian Nights* plays, Indische romans, European romances, and Indian tales. Ticket prices were the lowest that Mahieu had ever charged: one guilder for first-class seats, fifty cents for second class, and twenty-five cents for third; children under ten years paid half price. Sinar India advertised in Cirebon's Dutch-language newspaper, but there are no articles about performances. The plummeting ticket prices and the location of the theater in the Arab quarter of Panjunan—rather than the more prestigious Kebumen Square, where the company had performed in the past—suggest a major decline in the company's fortune.

Sinar India returned to Batavia around 1 June 1901 and performed for approximately two months in the Glodok field (Tanah Lapang Glodok) near the Chinese quarter. The plays performed were basically the same mixture that the company had presented in Meester Cornelis in 1900. Spectators came from as far away as Meester Cornelis and Tangerang, but performances evoked relatively little interest or commentary in the Dutch or Malay press. One report notes that the serialization of stories over two or three nights dampened audience enthusiasm and that the company should complete a story in a single night. (The length of the Indische romans in particular had contributed to the practice of serialization.) Another commentator noted the need for installing lights outside, on the north side of the theater, where there were puddles and muddy ground.

Among the plays more actively promoted in Batavia were the Indische roman *Revenge, or Oeij Kim Nio and Lie Koen Njan* (27 July 1901) and the engagement's farewell performance of *The Transvaal War* (30 July 1901), at which "Tuan and Nyonya Mahieu gave many thanks to all their friends in Batavia who had come as spectators and assisted in the advancement of the company."[111] The show that attracted the most public interest was Mahieu's adaptation of *Aïda,* entitled *Aïda, or Adiama,* which was said to be produced "at great cost" and featured both Mahieu and Lena Mahieu née Coppiëns in leading roles.[112] The plot basically follows the story of Verdi's 1871 opera, with small variations in motivation and a different ending.

> The king of Egypt meets with his head priest about the king of Ethiopia, who has refused to pay a requisite tribute. The head priest advises the king of Egypt to appoint his minister Radamias [Radames] as the commander of the armed forces of Egypt and order him to wage war against the king of Ethiopia.
>
> Radamias receives the sword of state and goes to the temple of Orkan to ask for the gods' blessings so that he can be victorious in battle. He vows to be loyal to his king. Before he departs for Ethiopia, he says goodbye to the daughter of the king of Ethiopia, Adiama [Aïda]. Adiama is a slave to the king of Egypt, and Radamias loves her.
>
> Radamias wins the battle and captures Adiama's father. Radamias is received with honor upon his return to Egypt. Sadness prevails when Adiama meets the king of Ethiopia, who is then thrown into jail.
>
> The king of Egypt speaks with Amaniras [Amneris], his daughter, and tells her that he will marry her to Radamias. The princess agrees to her father's request, for she loves the young man. Radamias, who loves Adiama, is not capable of refusing his king's request, but he asks for the marriage to the princess to be postponed. The king of Egypt agrees to his request.
>
> Adiama has arranged for a rendezvous with Radamias in front of the temple to Mewifis [Memphis] and is waiting for him to arrive. But Adiama's father, who has escaped from prison, shows up unexpectedly and orders Adiama to tell him the military secrets of

> Egypt. At first Adiama refuses to obey him, but when her father threatens to curse her she promises that she will comply to her father's wishes.
>
> When Radamias arrives at the temple, Adiama embraces him and requests that he tell her the military secrets. Radamias is torn, as if he reveals the secrets he will appear disloyal to his king, and if he refuses Adiama's request it will appear as if he does not love her. A short time later, the king of Ethiopia shows up and makes things even harder for Radamias.
>
> At this moment, the chief priest emerges from the temple and captures Radamias. The king of Ethiopia runs away with his daughter, Adiama, but she subsequently separates herself from her father to go look after Radamias, who has been sentenced to death by starvation. Amaniras, the daughter of the king of Egypt, offers to aid Radamias, but he refuses the princess, and in the end Amaniras goes mad [and dies].
>
> The final scene takes place in the temple of Orkan. Beneath it is the subterranean prison cell in which Radamias has been sentenced to death. All the priests recite prayers in the temple. Amaniras's corpse is placed on a slab of stone that covers the entrance to Radamias's subterranean cell. Adiama excavates a tunnel to Radamias's cell, and the two young people die together as they embrace each other.[113]

The play was promoted as "emotionally stirring" and this indeed proved to be the case: the last embrace of Radamias and Adiama in the prison cell—the scene in Verdi's opera in which the lovers sing their farewell to the earth ("O terra addio")—was said to be particularly touching.[114] The actors depicting Radamias and Adiama were said to be beyond reproach, but some of the other actors came up for criticism in a *Bintang Betawi* review. The actors playing the king of Egypt and the head priest were criticized for forgetting lines, and the reviewer notes that it is "actually not appropriate for the king of Ethiopia to act the clown, nor should he use dirty language when he meets with his daughter Adiama."[115] Performing the well-known staples of European opera and theater evidently placed the company under particular performative obligations. Reviewers had formerly allowed Mahieu much dramatic license in his adaptations of European sources. More fidelity was demanded in Batavia in 1901. Educated spectators, including theater reviewers, knew the plots in advance and expected a degree of respect for source texts.

One witness to Sinar India's Batavia performances, journalist and playwright Jan Fabricius (1871–1964), acutely expressed this sense of obligation to sources. Fabricius provides a sepia-tinted account of Sinar India's 1901 engagement in Mangga Besar in his nostalgic collection *Tempo doeloe: Uit de goeie ouwe tijd* (Times past: From the good old days).[116] The collection was published in Holland in 1949, during the same months as the Netherlands was evacuating its occupying troops from Indonesia and was arranging for the transference of sovereignty. Fabricius wrote in order to hold onto the "goodness" and colonial order of his youth; he activated memory to structure an unruly present. Fabricius titled his stambul essay "Verguld goud" (Gilded); his central concern was to show the superficiality of the adoption of European culture in Indonesia.

The scanty surviving documentation of the 1901 Batavia performances means that it is hard to judge the degree of accuracy of Fabricius's description. Only one of the plays he cites as having been performed—*Ali Baba and the Forty Thieves*—is known with certainty to be part of Sinar India's repertoire. There is no evidence of Sinar India performances of other plays he notes. I have found no record of Mahieu adapting Alexandre Dumas père's play *Napoléon Bonaparte* (1831) nor his novel *Les trois mousquetaires* (1844). Fabricius notes plays by Victorien Sardou including *Fédora* (1882), *Don Quichotte* (1864), *La Tosca* (1887), and *Madame Sans-Gêne* (1893) (the last written with Emile Moreau) and dramas by Henrik Ibsen, but none of these are noted in adverts or reviews either. It would be hard to imagine any theater company introducing such challenging plays in such short order. Once again, it appears that a Dutch author writing on Mahieu and his theater in a literary vein was less concerned with historical veracity than with ideological concerns—in the case of Fabricius, depicting stambul theater makers as raiders of the European literary canon.

Fabricius's sense memories of the experience of being present at the stambul theater in 1901 bear an emotional truth, however, that makes them worth recounting. Fabricius characterized himself as a young European man among others who came to the theater "especially toward the end of the month," in search of cheap entertainment. He depicts himself taking his place in the back stands, "priced at twenty-five cents." He owned up to not understanding the "stately Malay" used onstage by the main characters, "but the jokes of the comics, normally spoken in house- or garden-variety Malay, were well worth" the price of admission.

> The walls of the large building were made of plaited bamboo, while the roof was made of thatched palm leaves. There was no flooring and the numerous seats of all sorts were situated on the grass. In the middle of the "hall," a single coconut tree was growing. The local authorities had refused permission to chop it down, for one reason or other. The theater was thus literally built around the tree. There was an opening in the roof to accommodate the top of the coconut tree. During the western monsoon, when torrential rain fell on some days, the opening naturally let the rain in, but the seats in the immediate vicinity of the coconut tree were occupied. For accommodating souls who agreed to put up with the inconvenience, ticket prices for seats around the tree were set at two cents.
>
> In a corner on one side of the stage, was the orchestra: three violins and a pianist. . . . In the other corner of the stage was the buffet, made up of four or five buttressed planks, at which one could buy Chinese Cap Kuda [Horse Brand] beer or fried plantains.[117]

Much of the remainder of Fabricius's rambling account is devoted to a summary of Mahieu's adaptation of *The Merchant of Venice,* which Fabricius says was translated, to the best of his memory, as *Saudagar dari pada Venezia.* In fact, Sinar India did perform a play at Mangga Besar on 28 July 1901 with a Malay title that more-or-less translates as *The Merchant of Venice: Sudagar-Bandar* (lit., the merchant of the port city).[118]

"*The Merchant of Venice*—in the komedi stambul, oh gods! . . . Who knows, the event could turn out to be a highpoint in Shakespearian history," Fabricius reflects with heavy sarcasm.[119] His Dutch readers know beforehand that the performance by necessity will turn out otherwise. Apparently, seeing a European culture god served up as popular Eurasian melodrama could only be understood as travesty. The "offenses" against Shakespeare in Mahieu's updated adaptation, including the use of a telephone, are commonplace, even banal, by contemporary theatrical standards. It is hard to see what Fabricius finds so amusing in what he sardonically describes as Mahieu's "improvements" to the bard.[120] The use of an instrumental version of "Silent Night, Holy Night" to accompany the scene of the choice of the three caskets might be trite, but it hardly seems comical.

Fabricius wrote his account from memory after an interval of nearly half a century. It might be inadmissible as a historical document of a performance, but it can be taken as an index of a dominant mode of perception of Mahieu's theater at that time. Sinar India was taken as an appropriate object of ridicule. Not only did it not merit the serious attention of the art critic, it was interpreted as kitsch or camp. There was no discussion during 1901 of Mahieu's unique contributions to Indische culture. The effervescent moment of the celebration of Sinar India as an Indische theater was over.

Sinar India concluded its Batavia engagement at the end of July 1901 and immediately departed by steamship to Pontianak, a city of seventeen thousand people on Borneo's west coast.[121] Pontianak had established itself in the eighteenth century as the west coast's major center of trade and industry. Borneo's gold-mining industry attracted Chinese coolies, which led to the formation of Chinese kongsi that organized workers and controlled smuggling and other industries and trades. These kongsi were seen as overly powerful by the Dutch government, and a series of so-called kongsi wars were waged between 1850 and 1885, eventually resulting in the loss of political power for all Pontianak's kongsi. Pontianak remained (and remains to date) a very Chinese city. In 1901 there were fully 5,500 Chinese (mostly Teochew), as well as 300 Arabs, 186 Europeans, and about 11,000 Javanese, Malays, and Buginese residing in Pontianak.[122] While kongsi no longer wielded actual political power, Chinese social, religious, and welfare organizations of various sorts remained defining elements in Pontianak's civic life. Children were educated in classical Chinese texts at Chinese schools. The numerous *toapekong* (general temples) as well as three clan temples played major roles in defining a sense of community.

Chinese life in Pontianak and the rest of the west coast of Borneo had more in common with mainland China than the Chinese mestizo cultures of Malaysia, Singapore, and Java. Even as late as 1920, more than 99 percent of the west coast's Chinese spoke a Chinese language as their primary language rather than Malay; Hakka effectively functioned as an interethnic lingua franca.[123] Chinese opera troupes, imported from China via Singapore, attracted large audiences night after night in tent shows held in Pontianak, Singkawang (known as the Hong Kong of Indonesia), and other towns on Borneo's west coast with substantial Chinese populations. Muslims, Europeans, and other non-Chinese attended the Chinese opera. Non-Chinese spectators might not have understood dialogue or been able to follow plots, but often Chinese opera was the only public entertainment in town.[124] A sort of Sino-Malay theater originated in Pontianak in the 1870s or 1880s that was subsequently imported to Singapore and Sumatra, but the details are imprecise.[125]

Bangsawan and stambul were popular in eastern and southern Borneo, where a dialect of Malay (now known as Banjarese) was spoken by many as a first language. The stambul troupe known as Komidie Opera Vergeet Mij Niet is recorded as having toured southern Borneo as early as 1897.[126] Bangsawan troupes had long included the coastal and riverine cities and towns of this part of Borneo on their touring itineraries. Itinerant troupes originating in southern and eastern Borneo were capable of long-distance travel and could compete with visiting Malaysian and Javanese companies. One itinerant troupe known as Komedi Pulo Borneo (Island of Borneo Theater) toured Java in 1902. Another troupe from Banjarmasin (southern Borneo) under the direction of a *panghulu* (village chief or Muslim leader) and land council member named Haji Abdulhalim, toured Samarinda and presumably other parts of eastern Borneo for more than three months in the same year. Troupes from these regions of Borneo were as multiethnic as their Malaysian, Javanese, and Sumatran counterparts. A popular troupe from Banjarmasin that toured to Martapura in 1902 was directed by Entjik Tjaat, a Malaysian of Indian descent from Penang, and featured Banjarese actors.

The situation was very different for western Borneo. Bangsawan troupes had occasionally come to Pontianak, but there is no indication that a stambul troupe had played that city before Sinar India. Stambul's popularity was an unknown, and traveling to Pontianak thus entailed great risk for Sinar India.

Possibly Sinar India was "contracted" (*dipacht*) to come to Pontianak by one or more Chinese organizations, with a formal agreement that guaranteed a fixed income in exchange for a predetermined number of shows. If so, this same local organization would also be responsible for arranging the necessary permits with the local authorities, doing advance publicity, and the like. Such arrangements were customary for theater troupes performing in Indonesia's outer islands. Being contracted was in theory a surefire way for a theatrical company to make a profit, but in practice it had many pitfalls. Companies were paid from income generated from ticket sales, which often fell short of projections. The books could also easily be cooked by predatory middlemen, making it appear that there was a deficit. Sponsors were legally required to fulfill their obligations to the theatrical companies they hosted, but not all possessed such scruples, and it was difficult to prosecute recalcitrant sponsors, who often wielded considerable political influence at local levels. Steamship fares in the Indies were high, and permits were required for interisland travel. (Traveling without such permits resulted in fines or imprisonment.) A company could easily be stranded (*terlantar*) in distant shores, without sufficient money to return to its point of origin. A company owner or director might manage to scrape together enough funds to travel to the next stand, but if unable to pay company members, it was likely that most if not all of his performers would leave the company.[127]

A mishap of unknown nature but disastrous proportions struck Mahieu and his troupe some months after their arrival in Pontianak in

August 1902. An account by Saligi, a Pontianak correspondent for *Bintang Soerabaia,* indicates that Sinar India went bankrupt not long after its arrival in Pontianak.[128] Mahieu and all his performers were then recruited to perform with a locally owned bangsawan company named Komedi Bangsawan Kioe Kong Hap, and they continued to play the area of Pontianak until February 1902. It was at this point that Mahieu and former Sinar India company members were scouted by an English agent of Indra Zanibar during his visit to Pontianak. Indra Zanibar, a major bangsawan company owned by S. Kasim, had played Pontianak prior to November 1899. It is likely that Kasim's agent was in Borneo to arrange for a return visit. The meeting with Mahieu was fortuitous.

An offer to join Indra Zanibar was too good for Mahieu and his fellow performers to refuse, for it meant free passage to Singapore and a chance to return on tour to Java. "Only [violinist and orchestra director Frans] Paulus and his wife stayed on with Komedi Bangsawan Kioe Kong Hap."[129] All the rest of the former Sinar India company members seized the chance to join Indra Zanibar and left by steamship to Singapore in February 1902. Returning to Java meant severing social ties with Pontianak locals, and it is likely that to effect Mahieu's engagement Kasim's English agent was first required to settle outstanding debts owed Kioe Kong Hap and Pontianak merchants. Saligi reports the following about an actress referred to as Nona Nellie or Si Nellie (perhaps Mahieu's ex-wife, Nellie Vos) which suggests that the departure was made with great haste.

> Nona Nellie had married a scribe of corporal rank who wept like a small child weaned of his mother's breast, poor thing!!! He was left with only a short letter that read as follows:
>
> > Dear Corporal!
> >
> > Do not cry or be heartsick that I have departed without forewarning you. I left without first asking your leave because I was afraid you would prevent me from going. I am going to Semarang to see my papa because I dreamt that I saw him dressed in white [a Javanese symbol of death], and I do not know if he is sick or worse! I will certainly

return to you after I have seen my papa, and I will write to you on 1 March, love and kisses:

—Nellie

The Corporal cried not because his wife ran away but because he treasured a small gold watch and a gold ring a relative had given him—both of which Si Nellie took with her.[130]

Saligi closes his report from Pontianak to express his doubt that "Si Nellie" would ever return to her husband and his incredulity regarding Nellie's dream. The steamship that the former Sinar India actors had boarded was, after all, taking Mahieu, Nellie, and their colleagues not to Semarang, but to join Indra Zanibar in Singapore.

Indra Zanibar, also known as Wayang Kasim, after its owner Bai Kasim or S. Kasim (also spelled Kassim), was the most financially successful and arguably the most innovative Malay-language theatrical company between 1898 and 1910. Bai Kasim was a Malay Indian (*peranakan India*) from Bombay.[131] He was a musician and composer, as well as a troupe owner, and was renowned for his intimacy with troupe members. Kasim lived profligately, and though theater made him rich, it is said he did not leave enough money upon his death to purchase a burial shroud.

Wayang Kasim originated in Singapore, though it was sometimes represented as a Penang company. (Possibly Kasim lived in Penang prior to moving to Singapore.) Indra Zanibar was highly mobile and traveled widely throughout Malaysia, Indonesia, and Thailand. It did well enough in Thailand, in fact, to mount a two-month engagement in Bangkok in 1902, though likely only a smattering of spectators understood the Malay dialogue.[132] Wayang Kasim's two initial tours to Java in 1899 and 1900–1901 established it as one of the most important theatrical troupes to have played the island. It was particularly celebrated for its music and comedy. An appearance of Wayang Kasim, especially in smaller cities and towns, was a major event; the director-playwright Andjar Asmara recalls that many years after the company appeared in Padang (around 1905), he still "regularly heard the name Wayang Kasim referred to by people."[133] The troupe performed in public theaters in urban areas, and even before its first tour of Java it had also performed at the palaces of the sultan of Pontianak and the king of Siam, while in 1900 it played before the sultan of Johor. Reportedly, the sultan of Pontianak was responsible for granting the royal title (*gelaran*) the company used in its later years of existence, the Zanibar Royal Theatrical Company of Singapore.[134]

Kasim did not regularly travel with the company but entrusted the organizational management to agents and the artistic supervision to stage directors. Kasim's agent from 1899 to 1901 was E. Zorab (various spellings), a Parsi born in Bombay who also performed magic shows under the stage name Professor Zorab on Thursday nights, traditionally a dark night for bangsawan theater, out of respect for Islamic custom.[135] As an illusionist, it is more than likely that Zorab had a hand in devising special effects for the troupe, such as the "dance with fire on the head" in an *Arabian Nights* play.[136] Zorab was replaced for a short time around late 1901 or early 1902 by an agent named Sarkies, who was in turn replaced in July 1902 by an English agent, known alternately as Thomas Edward and Edward Thomas.[137] Thomas remained with the troupe for many years, and when Indra Zanibar performed in Bangkok in 1910, "HM the King of Siam . . . presented Mr. E. Thomas, the manager, with a silver and gold cup bearing the king's monogram."[138]

Wayang Kasim's artistic directors are not routinely credited in notices or advertisements, perhaps to foreground Kasim's own active involvement in the company. One of the early directors who worked for Indra Zanibar was B. B. Wanteh, who is listed as directeur in 1899 advertisements. Wanteh had worked for troupe owner Abubakar Siddij as the director of the Komedi Indra Bangsawan Empress Victoria Jawi Pranakan Theatrical Company of Penang in 1896 and later established himself as the owner of his own troupe, the Penang-based Komedie Tjindra Bangsawan. Wanteh was evidently a literary man; when Tjindra Bangsawan played Batavia in 1903, the company advertised itself as performing "Malay chronicle literature" (*buku hikayat*) serialized over two to three nights.[139]

Indra Zanibar's selection of play was diverse from the start, and as it toured it broadened to include tales that were popular with local audiences. During its first tour of Java in 1899, plays performed included not only Parsi theater and bangsawan standards such as *Hawai Majelis* and *Indra Sabha,* but also Malay chronicles, an adaptation of Shakespeare's *Hamlet,* and the perennially popular Indische roman, *Nyai Dasima.* In later years, Indra Zanibar went on to include Javanese legends and Chinese romances.

Indra Zanibar emphasized magical and spectacular scenic effects. A 1902 performance of *Jula-Juli* "depicted an open carriage with three strikingly beautiful fairies in it, traveling over the ocean and pulled by several geese," and "in the intermission, a woman flew through the air and did somersaults, just like the acrobatics in the Harmston Circus."[140] A 1911 production of the play *Wonders of the Deep* showed "the view of the bottom of the sea with mermaids swimming about."[141] Wayang Kasim appears to be the first Malay troupe to include "extra turns" inserted between acts and scenes of plays, starting with the aerial acrobatic display of 1902. In 1903 the company added a "set of dances by eight of the company" as an attraction.[142] Throughout its history, Wayang Kasim remained innovative in music and dance, incorporating Spanish dance, cakewalks, Hungarian dance, Cossack dance, sailor dances, and the like.[143] Some of these were performed by specialist performers, recruited to the company especially to do their turns. Among its many novel performers were "Lolita, the graceful and charming Spanish dancer" and "the youngest clown in the world" who was "only five years old."[144] Wayang Kasim also employed European clowns such as the White Russian Adolf Klimanoff, formerly of Ott's Circus.[145] All these special effects, acts, extra turns, and comic bits took up much time. The curtain at a 1909 performance of *The Merchant of Venice* "timed to drop at 12 P.M., did not do so till past 1 A.M.," and even so "the whole plot was not gone through."[146]

Oral history has it that when Mahieu and the other Indo performers joined Indra Zanibar they exerted a negative moral influence on the company's Malaysian members. In the initial stage of his company's existence, Kasim had "closely monitored the social behavior and morals of his company members, especially in the *rumah kongsi*.[147] Escorts insured the good character of company members. But after this period, it was said that company members did not behave properly and were not monitored. Many of them behaved immorally. This happened as the company mixed with Indos who were accustomed to gambling and drinking."[148] The veracity of such a historical claim is hard to judge. One might argue that the shift in behavior was inevitable due to Indra Zanibar's itinerant nature and was independent of any influence exerted by the former Sinar India members who joined en masse in 1902. What is clear is that Mahieu and the other Sinar India performers contributed to major artistic changes. From this point on, stambul and bangsawan were inextricably connected.

Mahieu, Lena Mahieu née Coppiëns, and the other former Sinar India members evidently spent some months touring British Malaya with Indra Zanibar and then traveled with the company to the Netherlands Indies. Mahieu had been at the lowest point of his professional career in Borneo, working for a little-known company far from the cultural vitality of Java. His return to the stages of Batavia and other cities offered new possibilities. Still, audience tastes were eternally capricious, the prospects for theater people always unknown.

> A girl named Isa went a number of nights ago to see the bangsawan company in Mangga Besar. When she returned home, there was no end of her praise for the excellence of the company, the likes of which she had never seen for her entire life.
>
> "I swear, Mother," said Isa to her parent, "that if I had enough money I would want to go every night. I would even agree to work as a servant for the company owner, as long as I could get a complimentary ticket every night."
>
> As she was talking in this way, Si Isa undressed. Only then did the girl see that her brooch, worth sixty guilders, was missing. She did not know where it had fallen. More than likely it was pilfered by one of the "land crocodiles" who loiter outside the theater tent, waiting for their prey.

Si Isa cried bitterly as she recalled the brooch, saying, "I vow never to go to see that company again, or any like it, no matter how much I enjoy these shows."[149]

Indra Zanibar arrived in Batavia on 3 May 1902. It was one of the biggest and most impressive Malay theater troupes ever to hit the capital. There were twenty-three actresses, thirty-two actors, and ten musicians in Indra Zanibar. About half the cast was said to be carefully selected Europeans. It is likely that the company's elaborate scenery, incandescent lights (*lampu gas glui-licht*), flying machinery, traps, and various equipment required a crew of at least a dozen people to rig and operate.[150] Newspaper reports indicated that no other company could compare to Indra Zanibar's spectacular scenic decor or the polish of its musical orchestra. An advertisement for a performance of *Mahiransyah* promised that "fairies will emerge from the earth and flowers and descend from the heavens."[151] *Hawai Majelis* featured flying nymphs that ascended and descended, and a moon that split open for a reveal scene.

The company mounted a more aggressive advertising campaign in Batavia than was customary in order to fill its circuslike tent at Mangga Besar for the duration of its long run in Batavia (7 May–27 July 1902). Indra Zanibar was accustomed to renting dogcarts in order to hand out promotional leaflets and announce the titles of plays to be performed. It also used the Malay newspapers extensively to print preperformance publicity as both paid advertisements and advance notices. A promotional statement released to newspapers for a play entitled *Siti Yohana: A Woman with a Faithful and Honest Heart, Who Obeys Her Husband,* said that it was "truly very necessary to bring your family to see this play, because it will be a beautiful show, and will provide excellent advice and good guidance for all women."[152] A promotion for the final show of the Batavia engagement (a comical play entitled *Ajaib and Telasam*) had it that: "Whosoever wishes to laugh until they cry must come tonight. Laughter is indeed a necessity for all humans, because laughter brings pleasure to the heart, excises all troubling thoughts, and refreshes the human body. Thus whoever does not *like* or is *unable* to laugh is better off dead, because a person like that does not have friends, and whoever does not have friends is better off not living long in this world."[153] In other words, if you don't come see Indra Zanibar, you're better off dead. This was a new sort of advertising for popular entertainment in the Indies. This sort of moralizing was a promotional strategy more characteristic of snake oil salesmen than theater companies. Not all took kindly to this sort of hard sell. One reader wrote to *Bintang Betawi* to complain about Indra Zanibar's unfulfilled promises to hold a benefit show for Semarang's poor, citing the Malay proverb "There is thunder but no rain ever comes."[154]

Indra Zanibar's comedians and a number of the established company members merit mention in reviews, but the headliners were Auguste and Lena Mahieu, described familiarly as "old acquaintances" of the Batavia public.[155] Both were considered major assets, "the flowers of the company."[156] "Nyonya M." (Lena Mahieu-Coppiëns) was said to have had a "more healthy-looking figure, be more beautiful, and be a more capable actress than formerly, she no longer giggles so much onstage, though sometimes she has to contain her desire to laugh when she sees the actions of [the clowns] Si Malang and Si Badjingan, who are humorous beyond compare."[157]

Auguste Mahieu's talents were also mined to the fullest. Many of the plays Mahieu had developed for the Komedie Stamboel, Sinar India, and the other companies under his direction were incorporated into the Wayang Kasim repertoire. An advertisement for *Ali and the Magic Violin,* Mahieu's signature comic fantasy piece, notes explicitly that the role of the eponymous hero "will be performed by Tuan Mahieu."[158] Mahieu even took on two roles in a *Jula-Juli* performance, playing the male lead, King Darsa Alam, in the first half of the show and a comic (*banyol*) role afterward, allowing a lesser actor to take over the Darsa Alam role. The reviewer for *Bintang Betawi* found such role doubling unaesthetic. "It is not customary for someone to be replaced in a role, and if the company was indeed short of actors the person responsible for casting should have found a way to insure that all the parts were covered. . . . Did they think that the public would not take note of this?"[159] But undoubtedly there were also those in the audience who derived pleasure from Mahieu's extra exposure in this well-known play.

Fig. 5.2. Advertisement for Indra Zanibar performing *Ali and the Magic Violin* in Batavia. "This play will be realized by Tuan Mahieu." *Bintang Betawi,* 13 June 1902.

All Indra Zanibar's performances received extensive publicity. Even such a tried-and-true staple as *Ali Baba and the Forty Thieves* benefited from a press release promising that "even if you have seen it a hundred times, you will not be bored, as everything is excellent and funny, and what is more the instrumental accompaniment, songs, and singing are guaranteed to please the hearts of those who come."[160] A number of productions were promoted particularly heavily, however. One of these was an Indische roman entitled *Rosina* (various spellings), based upon the *Bintang Betawi* serial by the Minahasa journalist F. D. J. Pangemanann.[161] The *Rosina* story had already been dramatized by Mahieu, and Sinar India had performed it as a two-night serial in Meester Cornelis in 1900 (4–5 November 1900) as well as Batavia (30 June–1 July 1901). The play was nonetheless promoted as "never before enacted by another company" and was touted as "better and more funny than the story of *Nyai Dasima,*" the gold standard for all Indische romans.[162]

Pangemanann's novelette is set about two hundred years in the past, in the surroundings of Batavia. The eponymous heroine is a beautiful Balinese slave of the Eurasian Nyonya Van der Ploeg. After Rosina is beaten by her mistress for a minor offense, Rosina's slave-husband, Apol, takes bloody revenge, killing Nyonya Van der Ploeg and her two young sons. Subsequently, Rosina runs off with a robber chief named Joyo, lured by a false promise that he will take her back to Bali. Joyo has his way with Rosina and keeps her as a prisoner in his forest lair, but after a while he grows bored with her and kidnaps the beautiful Annie Kramer, daughter of a Batavia doctor, with the intention of making her his next mistress. Annie is rescued with her honor intact by the police with the help of Apol, and Rosina is reunited with her husband. The robber's nest is broken up and Joyo sentenced to death. Annie marries her sweetheart, the handsome and brave Van der Laan, at a gala reception at which Van der Laan announces that Apol has been pardoned by the governor-general of all past crimes.

Like many Indische romans, Pangemanann's novelette was said to be based on actual historical events, and it was promoted in press releases as "a story that actually happened in western Java, an account of the present time."[163] The sensationalist plot's triple homicide and kidnapping clearly made the novelette interesting dramatically, but a perhaps less expected selling point of the play was that it represented the police investigation of Annie Kramer's kidnapping. When *Rosina* was performed outside Batavia, the piece was promoted as an accurate depiction of the ways and customs of Batavia's authorities and police.[164] Clearly, official tolerance for popular theater had progressed considerably since the worries in 1893 about Mahieu's "subversive" depiction of the police. Another salient feature was the fact that the play ended with "Dr. Kramer hosting a big wedding party for the marriage of his daughter to Mr. Van der Laan, at which many gentlemen and ladies are shown dancing."[165] In the segmented and hierarchical society of colonial Indonesia, it was still considered a rare privilege to be able to gaze on the exclusive rituals of European marriage and sociation.

The claims of realism made for *Rosina* as "an imitation of the ways, customs, and costumes of the past" opened the production to a critique by *Bintang Betawi* for misrepresentation. Rosina's costume, including a silk *kebaya* blouse, was deemed far too rich for a slave; "as far as we know female slaves wore white wraparounds as tops." The ball scene that concluded the play was said to be "lively and amusing," but "the bridegroom appeared not to be very capable of dancing in the European fashion."[166] And even more grievously, Mr. and Mrs. Van der Ploeg were inexplicably dressed as an Islamic king and queen.

Also much promoted by Indra Zanibar in Batavia and in subsequent stands on its tour of Java were a raft of plays featuring Chinese characters or set in China, foremost among them *Sampek and Engtay,* the tale of the butterfly-lovers. This folk romance set during the Eastern Jin dynasty (317–420 CE) is a *Yentl*-like love story about a young woman named Engtay who disguises herself as a young man in order to obtain an education.[167] She befriends a male classmate named Sampek and gradually falls in love with him. Sampek is innocent to Engtay's true sex, and only reciprocates when he finds out by accident she is a woman. By then it is too late. Engtay's parents have already arranged for her to marry another man. After their deaths, Sampek and Engtay transform into a pair of butterflies. This tale was translated into Malay as early as 1873, and following Indra Zanibar's production it became a popular theater staple, performed in a wide variety of regional and national styles to the present.[168]

Initial publicity stated that Indra Zanibar's version was "adapted from a Chinese book," but later the play was explicitly identified as being "based or adapted from a poetic narrative written by the late Sian Sing, Babah The Tin Lam," that is *Boekoe sairan dari tjeritanja Samphek Eng Tay tersalin dari boekoekoe Tjina* (A poetic telling of the story of Sampek and Engtay based on a Chinese book).[169] Advance publicity promoted this "excellent, humorous, and very lively" production as a dramatic realization of a "story that actually happened in ancient China," using "authentic Chinese costumes appropriate to the play."[170] A special invitation was issued for Chinese spectators.

The initial performance of *Sampek and Engtay* in Batavia on 3 June 1902 received strong notices. Both Nyonya Mahieu (as Engtay) and a cross-dressed Nona Meli (as Sampek) were praised for shedding real tears in their heart-rending scenes, to the pleasure of the audience. Only Sampek's father came in for criticism, for not displaying sadness upon the death of his son, but instead "playing the scene for laughs" (*menunjuk kejinakatannya*).[171] The play was repeated in Batavia "by popular demand" on 6 July 1902.[172]

Indra Zanibar's *Sampek and Engtay* production maintained a more or less respectful attitude to Chinese culture, and while the play was presented with the popular theater's characteristically lively humor, the jokes do not appear to have been at the expense of the Chinese as a national or racial entity. The same cannot be said about Mahieu's comic caricature of a *cina sengke* (unnaturalized Chinese immigrant) in a 13 June 1902 performance of *Ardan Zanggi.* The play's title suggests that the Chinese were not the only ethnic group caricatured in this play. *Zanggi* is the Malay form of *Zangi,* the standard term for East African black slaves through much of Asia and the Middle East, and a pejorative term for black Africans more generally. No details of plot are forthcoming, but most likely the play's eponymous hero, Ardan Zanggi, was a "delineated Ethiopian" played by an actor in blackface.[173]

Most of the actors in the company reportedly found *Ardan Zanggi* a difficult play to perform and had trouble acting their parts. Mahieu's depiction of a cina sengke, however, was said to be so funny that "one laughed whether one wanted to or not."[174] This impersonation is not detailed, but more than likely it pilloried "typically Chinese mannerisms, such as speaking at the top of the voice, walking with a swagger, lolling inelegantly in chairs, slurping, sucking the teeth and burping while eating, mispronouncing the 'r' sound, and so on."[175] "One reviewer commented, "I observed a number of Chinese nyonya who sat with sour faces and were unable to contain their desire to laugh whenever Mahieu took on the manner of a cina sengke, but there were a number of Chinese who did not much like having the ways of their 'own race' [*bangsanya*] imitated."[176]

The comic delineation of Chinese people has a double significance in terms of the history of stambul. We have seen how the Komedie Stamboel originated as a Chinese cultural enterprise that appealed to the subversive spectacle of categorical Europeans forced to dress up in absurd

"Arabian" costumes to sing and dance before Chinese patrons. Mahieu's impersonation of a Chinese is in effect a mirroring response to this initial degradation and marks in racialist terms a distancing from Chinese patronage. It indicates as well a decline in the economic significance of the Chinese as stambul patrons, and presages a period in which they will turn to their own culture and history to construct the Malay popular theater known as *cu te hi,* or *opera derma.*[177]

Indra Zanibar, despite its technical sophistication, was in many ways a gauche theater that dished out equal amounts of disrespect to many (if not all) societal elements. One of the highlights of the 1902 repertoire was a comic play entitled *Merchant Bahiram, Baktoom, and Baktim,* which featured a caricature of Betawi kroncong musicians that "naturally had great success" in Semarang and a clownish striptease that greatly displeased the "many polite ladies and girls" in attendance when this same play was performed in Batavia.[178] Its offensiveness was no doubt due to Indra Zanibar's highly itinerant nature. This Singaporean company had no real core audience to address and appease, and it could afford to play to lowest-common-denominator sensibilities. One might even make a stronger claim that it enabled the fashioning of a mass audience that encompassed the Malay world—the region that now includes Indonesia, Malaysia, and other parts of peninsular and insular Southeast Asia.

INDRA ZANIBAR swept out of Batavia at the end of July and traveled to Semarang, where it opened with a special performance of *Merchant Bahiram* in the schouwburg on 3 August 1902 and began to give shows in its tent pitched at the alun-alun on 6 August 1902. Mahieu is listed as the company's orchestra director (*orkest-directeur*) in advertisements appearing from 2 August onward. Advertisements rarely noted orchestra directors, but highlighting Mahieu's name had evident publicity value.

The company's schouwburg premiere received a good notice from *De Locomotief,* though reportedly some of the actors were "hard to understand."[179] The paper did report later that the tent was a fire hazard and complained that the collection of a twenty-five-cent "tax" on food stall owners who had set up their stands in the vicinity of the theater was unlawful.[180]

Indra Zanibar performed in Semarang until the end of September 1902 and then traveled to Surabaya, where it performed in the Chinese quarter of Sidodadi from early October through December 1902. The Mahieus' names are not noted in publicity or reviews, and from this it is reasonably clear that Auguste and Lena had left Indra Zanibar after the end of the Semarang engagement.

Most likely the Mahieus used their earnings from Indra Zanibar to bankroll a new troupe that they took on the road in central Java some time after September 1902. They retained the old company name of Sinar India. It is not known how many Indra Zanibar company members left Indra Zanibar to join the reformed company. Mahieu conceivably recruited Semarang actors and musicians for his troupe. He knew Semarang's theater scene well and had recruited actors there before. A newspaper report suggests that he "raided" a local stambul company for some of his actors. "A Chinese man who owns a komedi stambul troupe in Semarang has recently suffered a major loss. His mistress ran off with two young Indos from his stambul troupe, taking his possessions with them. The police went in search of the mistress and located her, but the possessions were all sold off and the money used for pleasurable activities by the two young Indos."[181] Possibly the Chinese owner's mistress (who was likely to have been an actress herself) and the two actors broke with their Semarang employer in order to join Sinar India. This, admittedly, is speculation. There seem to be no reports referring to the newly reformed Sinar India until after Mahieu's reformed company arrived in the central Javanese town of Bumiayu in January 1903.

Auguste Mahieu's decision to leave the security of steady employment with Indra Zanibar was dicey. There was intense competition in the commercial entertainment field in 1902. A large town such as Malang typically had as many as three komedi companies playing simultaneously. New centers of amusement opened up as Java's transportation networks consolidated. "The railroad shifted the hinterland-coastal commercial traffic network from old arteries to . . . new one[s]. This caused a remarkable expansion of new interior road networks linking up with the railroad. New markets grew as centers of commercial activity and communications to cater to the increasing rural commercial activities. The railroad acted as a stimulus and magnet for rural traders and villages and linked the rural economy more closely to larger marketing units, such as Semarang and other big towns. All this acted to open rural villages further to imported commodities and world economic influences."[182] Facilitated by the expansion of rail lines, stambul troupes were now routinely visiting even small, out-of-the-way towns such as Tuban, Jember, Jombang, Klakah, Klaten, Brebes, and Tangerang. Such towns had rarely if ever seen such commercial entertainment in the nineteenth century. Semipermanent theaters, typically rickety sheds, were constructed by local entrepreneurs in cities and towns as dedicated performance spaces for rental by touring troupes.[183] The news that a stambul troupe owned and directed by Wim Cramer was coming to Krawang evoked the following reflection from a newspaper correspondent. "In the past, nobody ever heard of a bangsawan troupe or other commercial entertainment coming to Krawang (except for Chinese opera, which was performed annually at the Shejit festival at the temple). But for the last three or four years now, an almost continual stream of various shows has come to perform in Krawang, such as komedi stambul, motion pictures, wayang wong, and so on. One troupe performing here replaces the next."[184]

One analysis of this increase in troupes had it that owners and producers saw komedi as a safe investment in a time when "making a profit in trade was very hard." The profit to be made from commercial entertainment made it attractive to investors who had previously shied away from going into the entertainment business because of its ignoble reputation. "Work that was once viewed with contempt must now be seen as equivalent to other sorts, as it makes an equivalent profit."[185] The growing number of komedi troupes around the turn of the century is also a reflection of the rapid urbanization of Java and the growth of a public with disposable income.

In addition to other live shows, stambul now had to contend with the motion picture as an alternative form of entertainment. The first narrative films were not made until 1903, but Indonesian audiences were already expressing great enthusiasm for this technological wonder. A newspaper correspondent who attended one of the first public cinematic presentations by the American Biograph in Batavia had it that "the pictures displayed were no different than human actions, except that those pictured could not talk."[186]

Any sort of stambul troupe that Auguste and Lena Mahieu could muster up in late 1902 could not compete with the large commercial outfits dominating Indonesian cities. Their only option was to tour small towns off the beaten track. There is a biological indicator that they were optimistic of success. The couple conceived a child around the beginning of November 1902, suggesting they believed that it was only a matter of time before Sinar India's star rose once again.[187]

On 14 January 1903, Auguste Mahieu arrived in Bumiayu with the reformed Sinar India. Bumiayu was a small Javanese market town in a primarily agrarian region where rice and coffee were cultivated. It was distinguished for being the station of a controller of the colonial government, and for little more.[188] It was the sort of town that Mahieu would have passed over in his gravy days; the arrival of this well-known figure amazed at least one Bumiayu resident.

Mahieu was in a state of ill health when Sinar India came to Bumiayu. Life on the road was physically taxing, and various sorts of ailments were constant hazards. Illness had long haunted Mahieu and other members of his troupe. Actor Johan Frederik Alexander Fortijn had been the first stambul actor to die of illness, immediately before the Komedie Stamboel's departure for its tour of Java in November 1891. The Komedie Stamboel's cashier Tan Swi Tjwan had died of a fever in August 1892. A fourteen-year-old Ambonese boy connected with the Komedie Stamboel "who suffered from asthma" died when the company played Cirebon in August 1894.[189] When Sinar India played Batavia in June and July 1901, the company was "not only plagued by rain, but plagued by illness, for the company members keep getting sick, one after the other."[190] Illness was also said to be rampant among Indra Zanibar when the troupe played Batavia a year later, so much so that a deficit of healthy members actually was detrimental to performances. A rumor circulated in July 1902 that one of the Indra Zanibar actors had died of cholera, resulting in a police investigation. The rumor turned out to be false, apparently started by a disgruntled spectator who had been refused a complimentary ticket. Nobody had died of cholera (dreaded for its epidemic quality), but it was true that an actor had died of fever, likely brought on by malaria.[191]

Illness was exacerbated by the living situation typical of stambul performers. During the months of the rainy season, stambul actors sometimes retired to the kampung, living in a way not distinguishable from the indigenous populace. A 1902 short story concerning a stambul actress describes such a rainy season domicile, "located deep in the countryside":

> The house was small and had only one room, where Nona Ida and her husband, the director of the komedi stambul company, slept. There were woven mats spread out on the ground for sleeping, and above them a sheet and pillows. Theatrical costumes of all sorts were drying on clotheslines suspended between poles. On the floor tiles were a few dirty bowls that had been filled with coffee and the remains of bananas consumed by company members. There was a row of chairs from the theater against the wall.[192]

When touring—with the exception of some company owners and their agents, a very small number of star actors, and actresses who were mistresses, or kept women—company members lived collectively in a large house or small number of smaller houses fitted out as dormitories. These houses were known as rumah kongsi or *rumah stambul,* rented accommodations with minimal furnishing "where company members lived together for as long as they were situated at a particular stand."[193] Actor Tan Tjeng Bok recalled, "when the leader said, 'You are to stay here,' we would stay there regardless of circumstances. Sometimes we'd get a house that perhaps had not been inhabited for ten years. There was one that people said was a house where someone had hanged himself. There was another house that people said was once a hospital. But we had to live there regardless."[194] Andjar Asmara, Tan Tjeng Bok's colleague in Dardanella, has high praise for the way that Piëdro, the director-owner of Dardanella, arranged the living space in a rumah kongsi. In contrast,

> space in the rumah kongsi was fought over in the bangsawan companies of old. Everyone wanted to occupy the best space, especially the prima donnas or leading men, who considered themselves privileged, as the company depended on them. Much jealousy was evoked over fights for space, and when someone felt slighted they might rent a separate room or house for themselves. . . . In the old days, many company members lived onstage. When I was a small boy in Padang, I saw that the members of Juliana Opera lived in the area of the stage. They put up screens only a few meters from where they performed, and that is where they slept, as well as put on their makeup and costumes before shows.[195]

As the Janitz trial revealed to the world (see chapter 4), most stambul actors in Mahieu's day had footloose private lives, moving among and between a number of beds, changing sexual partners, and haphazardly showing up at performances. Mahieu had a reputation for discipline, but he lived among performers drawn to stambul for wine, women, and song, and his lifestyle could not have differed significantly from the average actor after Sinar India folded. That lifestyle posed severe threats to the health of performers and made them particularly vulnerable to contagious illnesses.

Mahieu died on or around 24 January 1903. The cause of death was variously given as malaria or *demem* (fever). Both terms might refer to one and the same illness. Some form of demem was rife in the area of Bumiayu in January 1903. In the nearby village of Tanjung, which had a population of three hundred at the end of 1902, fifty people died of demem between 1 and 13 January 1903.[196]

Mahieu's death was first reported in *De Locomotief* on 31 January 1903: "The well-known Mr. Mahieu, founder of Java's first stambul troupe, died the day before yesterday in Bumiayu, in the regency of Brebes, where he was giving performances, following an illness of short duration."[197] His death was not national news, and only a few additional obituaries trickled in. *Bintang Betawi* reported Mahieu's death as below.

> The *Semarang Courant* relates that Tuan A. Mahieu has died of demem in the district of Bumiayu in [Kabupaten] Brebes. If there is anyone who has known suffering in this world, that person is Tuan Mahieu. He received an adequate education at a Sekola Raja [secondary school] as a youth, but he did not wish to continue his studies because he preferred to wander from city to city to earn money and find permanent employment. The very first komedi stambul was opened by Tuan Mahieu, filling him with restlessness. Whoever has seen this gentleman perform is certain to praise his acting, regardless of whether he played the role of king or the role of servant. And whoever was in difficult circumstances and saw Mahieu perform was certain to laugh. Mahieu's parents, if I am not mistaken, are still alive and live in Malang.[198]

Selompret Melajoe reported more simply, "What Semarang resident does not know Tuan Mahieu of the Komedie Stamboel? It has been reported that this man has recently died a sudden death in Bumiayu."[199] A more disparaging account of Mahieu's life was contained in a *Bintang Soerabaia* obituary: "Word has it that A. Mahieu, the komedi stambul director, has died in the Kedu area. This man received a good education and was not ignorant, for he was once a student at the Sekolah Raja here. But he did not put his intelligence to good use, and instead made a living on a path not praised by the general public."[200]

The longest report of Mahieu's death was published some months after, in the pages of the *Bondsblad.* It had been some years since Mahieu was active in the Indische Bond, and the delay in publishing an obituary suggests that Mahieu was no longer in the public eye.

> On 14 January 1903, we were surprised by the arrival in our lovely town of Bumiayu, located in the residency of Pekalongan in the Brebes section, of a stambul troupe named Sinar India, with den Heer H. [*sic*] Mahieu, well known to all, as director. He was the founder of the first stambul troupe and was always one of its key

supporters. The last years had not been kind to den Heer Mahieu; he had to contend with many difficulties. Lack of proper care—as well as the sleeping sickness—had exceedingly weakened his exhausted body. He was struck by a recurrent attack of malaria here, was ill for three days, and died. What a pitiful death! Steeped in poverty and lodged in a foul Javanese house with his troupe, he breathed his last breath on a bale-bale [elevated platform serving as a bed] on the night of 24 January.[201] Entirely forsaken, far from his family and many friends, he found his solitary grave in Bumiayu, a grave as yet unmarked by a stone.

No . . . I should not say entirely forsaken, for he had his friends here as well, who now wish to appeal to your humane and sympathetic magnanimity. Recall how much good the deceased did during his life. He helped many in need and would give away all he possessed to help a poor person in desperate need. Come friends, let us all pitch in and contribute a small token in memory of den Heer Mahieu. His grave should be marked by at least a simple stone. I have no doubt that many of his friends are willing to contribute a small sum to the construction of a tomb.

—M. J. B., Bumiayu, 24 June 1903[202]

M. J. B.'s "In Memoriam" was followed by an editorial comment by J. H. W. de Brussel Assé seconding the appeal for a proper marker at Mahieu's grave. De Brussel Assé had no doubt that Mahieu's many friends would be able to raise a sufficient sum, volunteering space in the *Bondsblad* to note donations received. He also quoted from Otto Knaap's portrait of Mahieu and stated that the paper would reprint the entire article in the following issues.[203]

Individual donations, thirty-two in all, trickled in between 18 July and 29 August 1903. Most were contributions of one guilder, yielding a sum of 60.50 guilders. Two communal fund-raising efforts were also conducted in Semarang and Bogor among members of local league chapters. The letter circulated in Bogor described Mahieu as "the creator of the Malay theater and a fervent advocate of the concerns of Indiërs," as well as "a zealous propagandist for the Indische Bond."[204] Any money not spent on the tombstone, it was promised, would be donated to needy

Eurasian widows and orphans. These communal efforts in Semarang and Bogor brought in 50 and 42 guilders, respectively. The mailbox-style listing of contributions continued to run in the *Bondsblad* for a few months after the donation from the Bogor chapter was reported (19 December 1903), but no further contributions were forthcoming. The sum collected topped out at a modest 152.50 guilders—hardly sufficient for a genuine monument.

MAHIEU'S DEATH was not marked by great ceremony, but retrospectively it did signal an end of an era for Indonesia's popular theater. Many of the innovations from 1891 to 1902 are attributable to Mahieu; his public personality and steadfast dedication to the stage greatly contributed to stambul's popularization. In the decades that followed his passing, the popular theater scene was dominated by bangsawan groups from British Malaya, such as Indra Zanibar and their Indonesian imitators. These groups followed a variety format, in which acts of plays were interspersed with popular song and dance routines and the like.[205] Indonesian theater people active during Mahieu's career, including Yap Gwan Thay, Marie Hoogeveen née Oord, Wim Cramer, and the Hunter brothers, continued to create stambul, but their work showed little originality. Gramophone recordings were released of stambul songs and plays beginning in the twentieth century's first decade, but the Dutch and Malay presses did not actively cover stambul, and Chinese and European spectators no longer gave stambul much heed.

Two companies that emerged in the mid-1920s, Orion and Dardanella, propelled Indonesian popular theater to the center of public attention once again. Orion and Dardanella both produced plays that emphasized psychological realism, with songs consigned to extra acts inserted between dramatic scenes. International cinema heavily influenced repertoire, dramaturgy, and style. Both companies insisted on being called *tooneel* (Dutch for theater) to mark their affinity with mainstream European theater and distinguish themselves from stambul and bangsawan. Multiethnic audiences again flocked to the theater and press coverage exploded. Miss Riboet, Orion's prima donna, became Indonesia's first major recording star. Dardanella transformed into a

Fig. 5.3. Members of the stambul troupe Eendracht Maakt Macht, some of whom formerly acted under Mahieu. Standing are Wim Hunter and Rudolf Hoogeveen. Seated are Hunter-Portier and Marie Hoogeveen-Oord. Reprinted from Nieuwenhuys, *Komen en blijven,* 159.

dance troupe and toured Europe and the United States. Devi Dja, the star of Dardanella, eventually settled in southern California, where she made a career teaching dance at Ruth St. Denis's dance school and working in Hollywood as a dancer, choreographer, and MGM contract actor. The history of this later phase of Indonesia's popular theater, however, is properly the subject of another book.

Chapter 6

MAHIEU'S LEGACY

Many forms of itinerant entertainment prevalent in the islands of Indonesia during the nineteenth and early twentieth centuries were ephemeral; they had little enduring significance. These entertainments did not disappear entirely, but neither did they survive. There are still traces of the acrobatic and circus troupes that toured Indonesia in the past in marginal forms of spectacle such as *genjring akrobat, sirkus alas roban,* and *kobrasiswa*. Such *atraksi* (attractions) are localized in rural areas and are little known in urban Indonesia, though small numbers of troupes continue to operate in perfunctory fashions.[1] The residue of acts of Indian, Chinese, and European magicians who entertained Indonesian audiences in the past likewise might be located in the performances of magic presented by roadside snake oil merchants hawking their wares to the credulous. A small number of circuses and itinerant *lumba-lumba* (dolphin) shows tour Indonesia today, and numerous buskers perform small-scale dog-and-monkey shows—generally referred to as *topeng monyet* or *komedi monyet*—on street corners and at markets throughout the archipelago. These animal shows are largely aimed at children and have minimal appeal for most adults. Komedi stambul is distinguished from its commercial rivals by its long-term importance in Indonesian cultural life. Komedi stambul might have ceased functioning as a theatrical genre with the beginning of the Japanese occupation in 1942, but it remains an important landmark in the emergence of modern theater and Indonesian culture generally.[2]

Much work has been done by government officials and scholars alike to conceptualize and encourage Indonesia's cultural and linguistic unity in diversity. This book suggests that komedi stambul was one of the critical conduits for establishing Malay language and associated urban culture in the consciousness of ordinary people throughout the islands of Indonesia. Knowledge of Malay was largely restricted to the spheres of officialdom, army barracks, and urban Chinese and Eurasians in Java and other Indonesian islands until the end of the nineteenth century. (Knowledge of Malay in Sumatra was perhaps more widespread.) The popularity of stambul and related Malay-language theaters were critical factors in Malay's move "out into the marketplace and the media," and help to explain why Malay was so avidly "picked up by *inlanders* [Natives]" lacking formal education in fin de siècle Indonesia.[3] In Mahieu's day, Indonesian actors performed in Malay to audiences who did not speak the same dialect of Malay as they did, and they acted onstage together with actors from all over the archipelago and as far away as Singapore and Penang. Grammarians had been struggling to define a transregional form of Malay for decades; in stambul theater a panlocal Malay became a living reality spoken aloud in theatrical dialogues before and with mass audiences.

The overwrought acting style so characteristic of many so-called regional theater (*teater daerah*) forms, as well as Indonesian television and film, is a reflection of stambul acting.[4] The ideal is not to internalize character but to project movements to the audience. The legacy of stambul acting lives everywhere in the stagy gestures and affected intonation automatically deployed by so many Indonesians when speaking bahasa Indonesia. Although bahasa Indonesia is officially the national language of Indonesia, it remains for most Indonesians an "un-native" language.[5] It requires a modulation of the self, and the way the self is situated in terms of others, in order to shift oneself from the habitus associated with a mother tongue and inhabit the linguistic worldview of bahasa Indonesia. It requires speakers to dissimulate, to act. Stambul and its theatrical derivatives have provided models for how to do this.

Komedi stambul was also a critical conduit for literature and criticism, as Pramoedya Ananta Toer has pointed out.[6] The audiences attracted to popular stage adaptations of newspaper serials and books were far larger than the number of readers of the published texts. Pramoedya also rightly states that the informed critics who reviewed these productions for newspapers preceded the first literary critics by at least a decade. The language and norms of Indonesian criticism developed around stambul and were only later applied to nondramatic art forms. The diverse generic forms represented onstage during the theater's first decade of existence molded an emergent Indonesian structure of feeling.

Komedi stambul's emergence preceded the arrival of the motion picture in Southeast Asia by only a few years and prepared Indonesian audiences for it. In the 1890s variety troupes and circuses commonly provided demonstrations of cinematic precursors such as the Ripograph, Cinematograph, or Kinetoscope between acts and items. The introduction of the cinema or *gambar hidup* (lit., living picture) to the Indies in 1899 allowed "people of all sorts to gain awareness of the state of the world with all the things it contains and the variety of creatures that inhabit it."[7] Komedi stambul had traded on much the same attraction. The theater served to frame expectations of what cinema should do and mean—but in the theater the actors spoke.

Ben Anderson has persuasively argued that komedi stambul exerted critical influences on twentieth-century Indonesian political culture. The theater provided a model for "elocution and gestural repertoire" for early twentieth-century politicians.[8] "The borrowing seems quite natural if we reflect that it was for the first time in stambul and bangsawan that 'natives' stood up onstage and addressed large numbers of people they did not know with words more or less fully prepared or memorized."[9] Anderson goes on to suggest that the expectations of audiences at political rallies and meetings were shaped by the theater. Audiences attending political functions expected to be able to participate in political spectacles that mirrored their degree of participation at the theater.

Anderson also elaborates on the importance of scripts for developing "a conception of *representation.*"[10] Audiences of traditional theater expected actors and puppeteers to improvise dialogue within the constraints of time-honored norms of characterization. Stambul actors worked from prepared scenarios that demanded them to take on particular rather than general sorts of characters.

> Scripts came to the fore with what we can call *representative* interpretation. If a stambul troupe put on a Malay version of *The Merchant of Venice,* the actors needed scripts because no one in the cast or audience had any solid idea of who Shylock was, how he should gesture, or what he should say. For one thing, no character in traditional drama had been a Jew or a moneylender. In the event, Shylock could only be played "sociologically," as a representative of intersecting, more or less contemporary, group categories—say, moneylenders, foreign minorities . . . , protective fathers of rebellious daughters, etc. The actor had no way to improvise the role, and thus came to depend on a memorized script and the ability to interpret it according to vague standards of social verisimilitude. Shylock "worked" to the extent that his player managed to convince the audience that he was just like, i.e. re-presented (or mechanically reproduced) groups or social types out there in the contemporary real world. In this way the new dramatic forms paralleled the echo effect of the newspaper, conjuring up in the consumer's mind *general categories of similar persons.*[11]

Political leaders used the conventions of stambul acting to convince their constituents that they were legitimate representatives of certain types—socialist, leader, revolutionary. As Anderson states, "anyone, in principle, could 'act' [such roles] if they chose so to do."[12] There was no need for justifying leadership on hereditary grounds, nor did leaders have to conform to traditional imaginings of what rightful leaders should look like and behave. They simply had to be able to present convincing interpretations of social categories.

Komedi stambul encouraged experimentation with roles more generally, and encouraged mobility. Audiences at theater performances observed how actors took on new roles nightly through the assumption of particular styles of gesture, verbal mannerisms, costume, and makeup.

Those sitting in the audience also put on shows by dressing for the occasion and behaving in public in ways that differed from ordinary life, testing the limits of social liberties.

Komedi stambul has been portrayed as an emblematic mestizo cultural form in which differences among Chinese, Indonesian, and European were erased and social boundaries were crossed.[13] We have observed that stambul was a multivalent cultural field that actively involved participants from all of colonial Indonesia's major ethnic groups, including Muslims, Chinese, Europeans, Eurasians, Arabs, and others. Rather than being a melting pot for ethnicity and race, however, onstage and offstage relations in the theater served to dramatize social and ethnic difference. Contrast and conflict came into the limelight in this most public of spaces. The dramatization of ethnicity (which was not specific to one dramatic text, but informed all aspects of production and reception) had general importance to all subsequent imaginings of identity and community. Particular patterns of social relation were instituted in the theater. In particular, komedi stambul established the Eurasian appearance as the preferred object of spectatorial pleasure for Indonesian audiences of melodrama; as such, stambul has rightly been called "a precursor of the contemporary Indonesian 'Sinetron' or soap operas."[14] The pattern of Chinese "exploitation" of non-Chinese performers also largely began with stambul. Chinese bankrolling of Indonesian artists and culture workers continues to be characteristic of nearly all forms of Indonesian entertainment involving large sums of money, including the recording industry, television, and film.

Perhaps most important, komedi stambul was an engine that fired the imagination to conceive of the world as a picture, one of the hallmarks of modernity, in the analysis of Martin Heidegger.[15] Heidegger identifies five essential phenomena as characteristic of the modern age—science, machine technology, the objectification of art as an expression of human life, the valuation of culture as the highest good of man, and the loss of the gods. In the modern era, the world can be represented as a picture, a structured image knowable in its entirety from a human (i.e., not divine) perspective. Stambul played a decisive role in securing, organizing, and articulating a modern worldview in nineteenth-century Java and other islands of Indonesia. It marked a break with the traditional ethos and worldview most prominently displayed in wayang kulit.[16] Java's traditional shadow puppet theater enacts a stratified world of gods, nobles, demons, and commoners, in which characters are inherited types rather than novel creations. Performances are contingent on ritual functions and dedicated to ancestors and tutelary spirits; the puppeteer is both entertainer and ritual officiant. Stories might be new creations based on the characters and situations of oral tradition, but resolutions are fixed: there is always a return to the status quo. The Javanese language employed is often purposefully archaic and obscure, demanding linguistic expertise from both performers and audience. Stambul staged a modern model for representation, both in theater and in real life. As commercial entertainment performed in readily accessible Malay language in public theaters, depicting characters mechanically reproduced or re-presented from social life, it was not contingent on expert spectators, local religious practices, or place spirits. The theater was a platform for mimesis and translation, in which "a huge variety of stories were imitated or enacted."[17] Plays were typically narrative transformations of literary and journalistic sources, but the companies were free to take substantial liberties with dramatic sources as these were not fixed by the legacy of a performing tradition. It was, in other words, a site for play. It was a place for the exploration of possibilities, including ones overtly forbidden by the colonial regime.

The longevity of the stambul style is related to its conditions of emergence. W. T. Lhamon Jr. makes this point in his cultural history of the legacy of blackface minstrelsy in the United States. Lhamon contrasts the continuing presence of blackface gestural vocabulary and imagery in American popular culture with the limited impact made by imported forms of entertainment, such as Arab acrobats, that existed at the same time. Minstrelsy's endurance was related to the way it "was built up in the Atlantic markets and other working places where men and women rubbed against each other under the stresses that produce cultural form. . . . It grew out of the way the blackface figure always resisted, or did not easily fit into, other people's forms—and so gradually forced a form that gave it room of its own."[18] Likewise, stambul's lasting interest comes from the way it emerged a year into the Gay Nineties and the vicissitudes of its development over that decade. The theater's dynamic responses and adaptations to societal obsessions and change, the ways it rubbed together men and women of different backgrounds and social orientations—Chinese entrepreneurs, Eurasian and Malay performers, multiethnic audiences, moralistic newspapermen, sardonic European cultural observers, engaged Eurasian activists—produced a hybrid cultural form that borrowed on the conventions and technologies of other forms but demanded room of its own.

Komedi stambul and its history have been the objects of occasional scrutiny by historians, artists, and activists over the last century. Mahieu assumed an iconic significance among the Indo population of the Netherlands starting in the 1950s. There have been various performative interpretations of or responses to the legacy of stambul enacted in postcolonial Dutch and Indonesian theaters. A paucity of sources about Mahieu and the earliest period of stambul history has allowed for a diversity of interpretations, presented from contrasting positions.

One motif recurring in early twentieth-century writings is that the Mahieu years of stambul represented a high point in theatrical history and that groups that followed in the footsteps of Mahieu, Yap Gwan Thay, Kasim and the other theatrical innovators of the late nineteenth century were degraded or fossilized imitations. This narrative of innovation and decline was used strategically in order to justify new waves of innovation in Indonesian theater practice. One finds an early example of it in the introduction of Lauw Giok Lan to his Malay-language translation of *Karina-Adinda* by Victor Ido, a play originally written in Dutch for performance by Ido's own theater group. Lauw justified his translational effort as a way to improve on degenerate standards of theatrical performance. The translator understood printed playtexts as functioning to bring structure and order to rehearsal and performance. He hoped that by publishing a playtext he could restore the order that once existed in Malay-language theater but no longer did.

> The performance of European theater has steadily become more modern, though there is heavy competition from film. In contrast,

> the performance of theater by Eurasians, Chinese, and Natives of the Indies . . . has become degraded. Let the reader try to recall how orderly the komedi stambul performances of Yap Gwan Thay were more than twenty years ago. Compare these with the komedi stambul and bangsawan groups of today. Certainly, you will be able to perceive a major difference. It can be upsetting to see the most recent troupes. They are no longer orderly. They are incapable of attracting any spectator with the least education.[19]

This same charge was reiterated under similar circumstances by Kwee Tek Hoaij in the introduction to *Allah jang palsoe* (The false gods), a play Kwee adapted from a short story by E. Phillips Oppenheim: "komedi stambul has been produced for decades without undergoing any progressive change. In fact, it has regressed much in comparison to the erstwhile Komedie Stamboel owned by Yap Gwan Thay and headed by A. Mahieu."[20]

These impressions by two Chinese playwrights were amplified by Andjar Asmara (writing under his real name, Abisin Abbas) in one of his many essays concerning theatrical history. Andjar Asmara was also concerned to justify his own theatrical practice, and to distance his form of tooneel from the stambul companies of the past.

> Mahieu began performing stories from *The Thousand and One Nights,* like *Ali Baba, Aladdin and His Magic Lamp,* etc. The performance of these stories was grounded in the techniques of Western opera and the Parsi theater. Stories were presented through song. For decades, song of this type was still used onstage. Even today there still exist small stambul companies (though the number has declined due to competition with modern technologies), which still insist on using such songs. The Mahieu period existed for a long time without change. Performers only imitated and continued Mahieu's working methods, without making any substantial changes. One might be able to notice alterations in acting and staging, but the basic performance technique was that which Mahieu created at the outset. . . . Mahieu was an educated man who greatly loved music and art. It appears his creation was grounded in a kind

of idealism, but his aspirations were not carried through by those who imitated him. All that was imitated was the [outer form of] stambul, and that was done in such a way that it remains a stain on the good name of Indonesian tooneel.[21]

There was in fact much continuity between the sort of tooneel promoted by Andjar Asmara in his theatrical practice and journalistic writing and the stambul theater that preceded it. Many of the star actors of Dardanella, the theater troupe that Andjar Asmara was most closely associated with, began their careers in the stambul theater. These performers brought their honed performance skills to bear on the psychological spoken-word dramas preferred by Dardanella and like groups, as well as to the "extra turns" of song, dance, and comedy that were inserted between acts. Andjar Asmara credits Mahieu with initiating a "new movement" in Indonesian theater, but mandated a categorical break with the stambul of yore.[22] The immoral behavior of stambul artists (Andjar Asmara mentions theater owners serving as pimps for their actresses) had tarnished the image of stambul to such a degree that an entirely new name for theater was deemed necessary.

An important essay by Tzu You on Malay-language theater displays a similar logic. Tzu You was quite critical of the "old-fashioned" sentimentality, loose dramaturgy, and overuse of song in early komedi stambul. Yet he also recognized the importance of Mahieu, Yap Gwan Thay, and Kasim as "trailblazers" (*pembuka jalan*) who "developed a theater-loving public."[23]

A VERY different critical take is articulated in late colonial European writings about stambul. This understanding is related to an emergent appreciation of the artistry of "authentic" or "pure" artistic expressions of Java, Bali, and other islands of Indonesia. Few European researchers before the twentieth century examined Indonesian performance, and when they did, they treated it as epiphenomenal. Dutch scholars of wayang kulit, for example, regarded shadow puppet theater as a form of literature and analyzed texts for literary value, mostly from a philological point of view. Some of the most important nineteenth-century

Dutch scholars of the performing arts, such as museum anthropologist L. Serrurier, author of an important 1896 book on wayang kulit, had never been to Indonesia nor seen actual performances. This began to change in the first decades of the twentieth century, with the emergence of devoted scholars of music, theater, and dance such as Jacob Kats, J. S. Brandts Buys, Jaap Kunst, Theodore B. van Lelyveld, Theodore Pigeaud, and Colin McPhee. All these scholars understood the Indonesian arts to be aesthetically different from the arts of Europe. They especially valued what was unique to the classical and courts arts of the archipelago. This sense of distinction was reinforced in the public presentations of performers from the Indonesian archipelago at international exhibitions and world fairs in Europe and the United States. These packaged cultural performances were also publicly valued in terms of cultural difference. Experiential distance and stress on singularity yielded an emphasis on exotic presentation. Members of the traditional indigenous elite were sympathetic to this project of cultural differentiation to the extent that it supported their own interest in maintaining cultural legitimacy.[24] Many among the elite embraced European methodologies for studying performance, or lent active support to European scholars studying Indonesian art forms.

The flip side to this attention, one is tempted to say fetishization, of the authentically indigenous performing arts was the devaluation of everything hybrid or mixed. Performing arts that appropriated European forms and ideas were generally condemned as ridiculous in both popular and scholarly writing. Johannes Fabian, discussing anxious European reactions to popular African culture, including hybridized "forms and places of entertainment," has suggested that the denunciation of "the ridiculous" is a "defensive-aggressive reaction" to a perceived assault on colonial distinctions among European colonizer, authentic (rural, traditional, Other) Native, and alienated (urban, modern, educated) Native.[25] Scholarly attention to and validation of traditional cultural genres and concomitant ridicule of hybrid popular genres serves to shore up constantly endangered boundaries between the ideal and the typical. The treatment of komedi stambul in late colonial writing by Europeans is in line with Fabian's African observations.

Komedi stambul in Mahieu's time was viewed by most Europeans as a marginal art form associated with both non-Europeans and Eurasians. Certain revisions in Kalff's 1893 account of his visit to the Komedie Stamboel mark an epistemological shift. Kalff opened the 1918–19 revision of his essay with a statement that it was a curiosity in seeing how non-Westerners treated Western theatrical arts that drew Europeans to come see Komedie Stamboel performances, and he interpreted the noise that elite Chinese spectators made in the theater as a way for them "to demonstrate that this is their own komedi."[26] Such clearly marked racial distinctions—between European self and non-European Other, Chinese ownership and non-Chinese spectatorship—were absent in the original version of the essay. By consigning the Komedie Stamboel to the category of the non-Western, Kalff erased possibilities of European complicity in a hybridized cultural field. The representation of stambul as the work of others facilitated Kalff's representation of stambul as "abominable vandalism" by others of "his" own music and theater.[27] Komedi stambul and related Malay popular theaters were seen by Kalff and other early twentieth-century Dutch and other European colonial observers as unbearably grotesque and ludicrous, an infantile travesty of high art. "A German who attended a stambul performance of Hamlet in Menado in 1922 was not favorably impressed by the sight of the Prince of Denmark and his mother singing a duet to the strains of the 'Blue Danube' played on violin, piano and flute. A similar reaction was recorded by the Englishman H. S. Banner to Gounod's Faust, in which a clown scored a great success with his rendition of 'Daisy, Daisy, Give Me Your Answer Do.'"[28] Some observers still managed to take a kind of camp pleasure in stambul. As J. Th. Koks noted in 1931, "a European no longer goes to see stambul for the play that is performed but in order to take pleasure in how it is botched up."[29] One can hear a trace of the subversive pleasure taken in the trashing of European cultural icons.

> The Comedy Stambool, the latest novelty in the theatrical field, tries, by means of Malay-speaking actors, to introduce, after a fashion, the masterpieces of the European drama, not without success,

> notably so in the coast towns. Instead of Prabu Suyodono, King of Astino, baffled in his pursuit of the beautiful Princess Pregiwo by her brother Angko Wijoyo, the Comedy Stambool exhibits for instance Hamlet, robed in something between a dressing-gown and the uniform of Napoleon's grenadiers, discussing the merits of a dusky Ophelia, who violently agitates her Japanese fan, with the rollicking ghost of his father in turban and top-boots, and given to the most daring puns. Though there is much of the tragic element in the Comedy Stambool, jealousy, frenzy, madness and murder galore, out of regard for a mirth-loving public the clownish low comedians are entrusted with any part and permitted to make it attractive after their own sweet will, to crack their jokes, and sometimes very good ones too, independently of the characters in which they appear.[30]

An enjoyment of travesty accounts for much of the reason why casual European observers repeatedly privileged stambul treatments of Shakespeare and Goethe over other plays performed.[31]

In contrast to travel writers and journalists, Dutch scholars afforded themselves no such pleasure in their observations of stambul. Their writings have a much more sober and moralizing tone underpinned by a palpable anxiety. In the general introduction to his magnum opus, *Music in Java,* Jaap Kunst described how Western influences had caused a "regression" in Javanese arts, which were under dire threat of degeneration.[32] The threat to the extinction of gamelan and other traditional Indonesian performance forms was not due to competition with Western popular music, such as jazz, for in Kunst's understanding "European-American civilization is so utterly foreign to Indonesian cultures that it cannot be assimilated by them." (More recent musical developments have of course proven Kunst incorrect.) Rather it was stambul and kroncong that were to blame: "The monotonous and characterless wail going under the name of 'Stambul' or 'kronchong' music . . . causes Indonesians to become more and more estranged from their own art. . . . In a faster tempo it is either dying away or degenerating." Kunst's anxiety was outwardly directed toward the music of Java, but one senses that Kunst had more at stake than just the fate of the object of his scholarly research. Indeed, Kunst characterized his own scholarship on classical gamelan as a rear guard action against cultural degeneration and saw the death of classical arts as unavoidable. He wrote of "the anxious and increasing anxiety . . . of musical authorities, both native and European, about the future of Indonesian music" due to the increasing popularity of "the lowest forms" of music in Indonesian society. Surely Kunst counted himself among the anxious. A fair modicum of European anxiety regarding the deleterious effects of popular culture on classical Javanese art hinged on an uncomfortable feeling of complicity in the "bastardization" of European art music, a term applied by Kunst's ethnomusicological rivals, Brandts Buys and Brandts Buys-van Zijp, to stambul music. "We are not even sure whether poor Mozart might be one of the grandfathers of the monster," the two wrote about a hybrid stambul-gamelan performance.[33]

Looking at stambul, these educated Europeans could only see discomfiting reflections of themselves and their own cultural baggage. They saw stambul as something derivative of their own culture and could not see past that. One hears echoes of this same attitude in references made in postwar American writings. Faubion Bowers, in a standard introduction to Asian theater published in 1956, describes how the troupe of Mahieu (who is referred to not by name but as "an Indo-European") "performed extravaganzas like the *Arabian Nights,* with a Western orchestra, many songs, and the declamation exaggerated into a sort of caricature of the grand, heroic Shakespearean style."[34] Why Bowers types stambul as a caricature of Shakespearean acting is puzzling, as it is unlikely that he saw any stambul himself. One wonders about the informants who prompted this negative comparison, and about Bowers's quickness to affirm such prejudice in the absence of empirical evidence. Clifford Geertz likewise describes stambul as "something on the order of our earlier musical comedies or Victor Herbert–type operettas in which a kind of artificial and sentimental declamatory plot was interspersed with *kroncong* singing and popular dancing, the plots being taken from popular folk stories and such sources as the 'Thousand and One Nights.'"[35] It is hard to see how a comparison to Victor

Herbert might assist a reader in understanding the cultural object of description, other than to evoke a prior bias against "light" entertainment prevalent among members of the Euro-American cultural elite circa 1960. Both Bowers and Geertz appear to have inherited a colonial prejudice against hybridized entertainment forms, wittingly or unwittingly. Neither were colonizers, but in relation to stambul they both appear as colonialist.

The one colonial scholar who felt that stambul should be considered as more than a mere travesty of European art was the Dutch philologist Theodore Pigeaud. Pigeaud believed stambul should be approached as a reflex of urbanization, and while he lamented its popularity as an index of alienation from traditional culture, he recognized its sociological logic and its place in the life of Eurasians and those "parts of Java which have undergone a high degree of foreign influence for a long while."[36] He did not back away from revealing, in a noncritical way, how stambul historically influenced the development of rural performance traditions in his major study of Javanese folk performance, *Javaanse volksvertoningen*.[37] While he shows no enthusiasm for the popular theater, neither does he demonstrate a noticeable degree of prejudice against it.

Komedi stambul resisted all these colonial attempts to frame and tame it. As colonial historian Rudolf Mrázek has suggested, the "loud, flagrant, irreverent, dazzling," stambul was part of the "subtlest kind of rebellion." It made "a fool of anybody who might suggest a bridge or translation." "Diving into everything Western," komedi stambul contributed to breaking "the wholeness of the colonized."[38]

Eurasian writings from the same period represented stambul in another way altogether. We have seen that many of the early stambul troupes were made up primarily of Eurasians, and that Mahieu in particular was keen to use stambul to benefit Eurasians as individuals and a collective. The link between stambul and Eurasian life and culture was played up in late colonial writings by and about Eurasians. This was seemingly at odds with the many changes happening in the popular theater field at this time. In a 1931 account of Indo life, J. Th. Koks states that stambul might have originated from Indo actors and mestizo society, "but for a long time it has not been a genuinely mestizo culture. Native actors account for the large majority of performers in a stambul troupe; the language of performance is also the dialect of Batavia."[39] This demographic shift was related to a gradual socioeconomic upward drift of the Eurasian population. Eurasians maintained a limited linguistic identity through speaking creolized languages. In Batavia, Indos spoke *petjo* to one another. Petjo has been described as a dialect of Dutch with Malay syntax and morphology and heavy borrowing of Malay nouns.[40] In Semarang, Indos spoke a form of Javanese-inflected Dutch that has been dubbed Javaindo.[41] Eurasians continued to wear sarongs when lounging at home, eat rice as a staple food, and indulge in many Indonesian pastimes for their personal amusement, but higher levels of education in the last decades of colonial rule created access to high-status jobs, and few Eurasians felt an economic compulsion to join stambul troupes. This resulted in a loss of a feeling of involvement and investment in stambul and related popular theaters. Rather than attending and participating in the contemporary theater, Eurasians in late colonial Indonesia began to reminisce about the origins of stambul, paying particular attention to Auguste Mahieu, who was commonly figured as stambul's creator (*schepper*).

The most important piece of Indo writing on stambul during the late colonial period was Alvares Theodorus Manusama's short book *Komedie Stamboel of De Oost-Indische Opera* (or The East Indies Opera) published in 1922.[42] Manusama worked as a librarian in Batavia. He was also involved in the Ambonsche Studiefonds, a social-cultural organization, and wrote in Dutch on subjects connected to Ambonese traditional culture and Christianity. Other publications included a novelization of the Nyai Dasima story, published in both Malay and Dutch, and a short book on kroncong music. Manusama's stambul book is noteworthy in the way it centralizes Mahieu as the creator and originator of stambul.[43]

From the first sentence of the first chapter, the book focuses its attention on Mahieu, who is represented as a heroic individual. Manusama prognosticates that "the name of Mahieu shall remain inseparably connected" to stambul.[44] Manusama's book functions as agent in this historiographic cause. Manusama's principal informants, judging from his book's collection of programs, likely included Rudolf Christiaan Hoogeveen or Hoogeveen's wife, Marie Hoogeveen née Oord, owners of the stambul company Eendracht Maakt Macht (Strength is unity). They are represented (along with Wim Cramer and W. F. Hunter) as "students" of Mahieu's "school" who formed their own troupe almost as an homage to their "teacher." (Later secondary sources compound this misrepresentation by suggesting that all competing stambul troupes were formed only after Mahieu's death.) Mahieu's theater is described as a "charming" combination of Western and Eastern theatrical elements. Manusama depicts Mahieu's end in the remote town of Bumiayu as the voluntary act of retirement of a world-weary visionary.[45] All those involved in Mahieu's enterprise, it is suggested, shared intimately in the creator's passion for creating a new form of entertainment with appeal to the heterogeneous population of the Indies. There is an evident sense of joy taken in the way that this theater, in its heyday, brought together all the different ethnic groups of the Indies in the same auditorium. This pleasure in togetherness was no doubt in part nostalgic, for when Manusama's book was published, Java and the rest of the Indies were beset with industrial strikes, rallies, and party politics that emphasized differences in race, ethnicity, class, and religion.

There are two major stories to be told about the legacy of stambul after the end of Dutch rule over the Indonesian archipelago and the international recognition of the Republic of Indonesia's independence in 1950. One concerns how stambul was discursively and performatively revived and reimagined by Indo repatriates to the Netherlands as a vehicle for Eurasian cultural definition, autonomy, and recognition. In postcolonial Holland, stambul was framed as a cultural accomplishment of the Eurasian community in nostalgic performances as well as writings and photographs published by Eurasians who migrated to the Netherlands following Indonesia's independence. Auguste Mahieu was canonized by Eurasians as an ethnic hero. The other story concerns how stambul was reinterpreted by Indonesian theater artists and commentators as a vehicle for the construction of a national theater in the service of national integration. Stambul has also occasionally engaged the attention of "outside" scholars who are partisans of neither Dutch nor Indonesian cultural scenes but have contributed to both. The existence of traveling theories and texts means the different "stories" are not as separate as they might appear at the outset.

A COMBINATION of Indonesia's unstable economy, confrontational politics, and questionable security and educational conditions resulted in the mass migration of at least one hundred thousand Eurasians from independent Indonesia to the Netherlands between 1945 and 1958.[46] These migrants, as well as a minority of the "pure blooded" (*totok*) repatriates, suffered acute trauma in their relocation. Indische Nederlanders, or "Netherlanders from the Indies," initially experienced the mother country as a cold and unfriendly place.[47] The repatriates had generally enjoyed affluence in colonial Indonesia. Most had employed domestic servants such as nannies and cooks before the Japanese occupation of Indonesia (1942–45) and were accustomed to lives of relative luxury. Internment in camps during the occupation, monetary inflation during the postwar years, unemployment, and postcolonial nationalization of Dutch-owned industries had diminished or eliminated their economic advantages. Most repatriates arrived in Holland with little or no savings and encountered immediate difficulties in finding suitable sources of employment. Differences in culture, language, and skin color between Indische Nederlanders and the majority Dutch population were continual reminders for many Dutch of the humiliating loss of the colonies and the decline of Holland's imperial stature. Governmental efforts to integrate Indische Nederlanders into preexisting structures of Dutch society initially met with only limited success.

Aspects of the cause as well as the remediation of the "problems" of assimilation were associated with performance. Social issues surrounding the integration of Indische Nederlanders with Dutch society were brought to the attention of the general public most forcibly in a youth riot between young Indische Nederlander men and young Dutch men in The Hague in the summer of 1958. The cause of the riot was understood by a Children's Police officer as arising from "jealousy for girls: the dark Indo-European boys are attractive to a 'certain kind' of Dutch girl; these boys are good looking, they are well dressed in their modern narrow trousers, they are good dancers and their behavior is polite, pleasant, and graceful. They are much more popular with these girls than their clumsy and plump Dutch brothers. Sexual jealousy is aroused!"[48] Young Indische Nederlanders also introduced a version of rock and roll in the Netherlands, giving birth to a genre of popular music eventually known as Indorock. This new form of music was viewed with much suspicion in conservative Holland but was embraced in Germany and made a central contribution to the development of Eurorock.[49]

The performative competencies of Indische Nederlanders in music, social dance, and "graceful" behavior functioned as a source of group pride as well as contestation. Performing was a way for Indische Nederlanders to communicate their cultural distinction to Dutch society at large. It was also an opportunity for reflexivity in the interest of group solidarity. This combination of communicative and reflexive action is particularly evident in a series of charity performances that took place in the mid-1950s. These shows were perceived by at least one of their creators as revivals of the Eurasian legacy of stambul.

Political scientist Justus Van der Kroef sees the beginning of the postcolonial reimagination of stambul as a Eurasian cultural legacy. He argues in favor of the full assimilation of the Indo population remaining in Indonesia after decolonization into mainstream Indonesian society. To counter the claim that the Indo could not be fully Indonesian due to divided loyalties, Van der Kroef asserts that in postcolonial Indonesia,

> the Indo can play an indispensable role in the synthesis of East and West. In the past his function in this connection has often been unique. One is reminded, for example, of the stambul, the popular Indonesian opera, invented by a Eurasian, who translated the score[s] of European operas into Malay, transposed the music often in a most original way and used Indonesian characters. Stambul was immensely popular among all population groups in the nineteenth

and early twentieth century, a unique form of cultural synthesis of Eurasian origin.[50]

This same argument about the possible future role of Eurasians as cultural mediators, mustering the same evidence of the mediating significance of stambul, could be applied to those Eurasians who settled in Holland as well.

A key figure in the restoration of stambul was Eurasian writer and cultural activist Jan Boon, better known as Tjalie Robinson.[51] Robinson organized cultural activities (most important, the annual Pasar Malam in The Hague), published a magazine on Indische Nederlander life and culture under the title *Tong Tong,* and wrote anecdotally about Eurasian life in colonial Indonesia and postcolonial Holland. Robinson has been described as "spokesman for and guru of the exiled Indo society."[52] Boon also wrote "serious literature" under the nom de plume Vincent Mahieu, an homage to Auguste Mahieu. Despite the paucity of hard data about Auguste Mahieu's life and art (or perhaps because of it), Boon idolized him as a great Eurasian writer.[53]

Featured prominently in Robinson's cultural programming in the 1950s were cabarets and cultural evenings. These events were, in Boon's imagination, a postcolonial form of komedi stambul or bangsawan. All the shows were charity benefits, produced on minimal budgets, with performers and production personnel donating time and services. "It was the funniest thing," Robinson's widow, Lilian Ducelle, recollected in an interview. "We were immigrants, we were poor. [Yet] we were raising money for other people. (*Laughs.*)"[54] The evenings took a variety format, with music, dance, dramatic sketches, and speeches. Many of the actors and dancers in the dramatic sketches and dance numbers were inexperienced, though the music making was consistently at a professional level. The events were focal points for gathering Indische Nederlanders, who had been repatriated to areas around the Netherlands, in a single time-space in order to make and apprehend a work of culture. Once can view the cultural evenings as precursors to the Pasar Malam (Night Fair), but they were more than that as well.[55]

One of the first of the evenings directed by Robinson was the Grote Indische Feestavond (Big Indies Celebration Evening). This event was produced by the missionary association Bond van Oud-Steurtjes at the auditorium of the zoo in The Hague on 7 July 1956.[56] It was a ninety-first birthday celebration of Johannes van der Steur (better known as Pa van der Steur), and a fundraiser for Van der Steur's missionary work in Indonesia and New Guinea. Approximately seventeen hundred attended, coming "from the farthest corners" of Holland. There was "mystical Buddhist temple dance and a modern Apache dance" by De Exotische Dansgroep from The Hague, under the direction of Dé Reindorp. Steel guitarist Rudy Wairata performed with his two bands: the Hawaiian band the Mena Moeria Minstrels and the Ambonese band the Amboina Serenaders.[57] A color film about colonial Indonesia was screened. There were comic sketches written by Tjalie Robinson and friends performed under the rubric of the music, theater, and dance group Las Palmas. The evening began at eight and concluded at eleven thirty with a "modernized" version of the kroncong standard "Terang bulan" (Clear moon). A ball with music provided by the Mena Moeria Minstrels and the Esquire Quintet followed, ending at three in the morning.

It is not coincidental that July 1956 also marked the appearance of the first issue of *Onze Brug* (Our bridge), a magazine dedicated to Indische Nederlander issues under Robinson's editorship. Robinson had launched a magazine called *Gerilja* (Guerilla) in 1955, but that periodical had quickly ceased publication. *Gerilja* was dedicated to "self-preservation amidst civilization for the outcast of the masses," had an explicit policy of "no culture," and excluded "old men" and "clergymen."[58] In contrast, *Onze Brug,* like the Grote Indische Feestavond, reached out to the nostalgic old colonialists and clergymen who were at the core of the Bond van Oud-Steurtjes and like organizations. Much of *Onze Brug* was concerned with the people and politics of western New Guinea, a part of the former Netherlands Indies that remained a Dutch colony until 1962. But *Onze Brug* was not only a bridge to the New Guinea colonists, it was from the start also concerned centrally with the Indische Nederlanders as a community. The failure of *Gerilja* and the success of the Indische Feestavond and *Onze Brug* demonstrated that inclusive, culturalist initiatives were more viable than confrontational, political projects in generating solidarity among members of the internally heterogeneous Indische Nederlander population.

Robinson followed up the Grote Indische Feestavond with an Indische Avond (Indies Evening) in December 1956.[59] This time the event was produced by Robinson's own organization, the Onze Brug foundation, and was a benefit for Hungarian refugees in the Netherlands. Once again, the location was the zoo auditorium in The Hague; more than sixteen hundred people were in the audience. Dé Reindorp's dance group presented a revue of world dance, showing "American Patrol, a Harem dance, a Kraton dance and *Potong Padi* [rice harvesting], Hawaiian Nights, a fantasy-rich Apache dance, an improvised Chinese dance, a Viennese waltz, a Surinamese dance, and an electrifying South American dance." There was a fashion show of batik clothes designed by Robert Mahieu, embraced as "our only Indische fashion designer in Holland."[60] The Bee-Bee Sisters, the Manhattan Quintet, and Rudy Wairata and his Mena Moeria Minstrels performed music. Again, social dance followed the show. A. G. de Grave-Terwogt, chairperson of the Onze Brug foundation, gave an address where she reported that the Indische Avond was firstly a gesture of solidarity with the Hungarian refugees from a population that has itself survived considerable upheaval, including the "Japanese terror" and the Indonesian struggle for independence. The second purpose of the evening was to raise awareness of the periodical *Onze Brug* and the way that it is a bridge not only between repatriates in the Netherlands Indies and New Guinea colonists, but among Indische Nederlanders as a community.

The Tweede Indische Avond (Second Indies Evening), organized by the Onze Brug foundation in collaboration with the Centrum Nederlanders uit Indonesië, took place at The Hague's zoo on 18 May 1957. This event was more ambitious in its representative claims and aimed to establish a high level of artistic accomplishment. There were "classical Eastern dances" by the Ramayana dance group under the direction of Lakshmini Devi. These dances included a Hindu offering (*puja*) to the goddess Lakshmi, a Minahasa "love dance," classical Janger dance from Bali, and a *tari piring* (plate dance) from Padang. The Novelty Quintet, under the direction of guitarist Hans de Water, performed Hawaiian music. Tjalie Robinson contributed comic dialogues. The famous Indische Nederlander songwriter Ben Snijders performed his own compositions, accompanied by his wife Jos Snijders on piano. One of these compositions—a piece that "should be heard, not read"—was the petjo song "Indisch ABC." The piece begins as a litany of longing for foods, pastimes, types of people, and comfort not available in the Netherlands and ends as a plea for solidarity.[61] Snijders's petjo song invokes particular sense memories—the smell of jasmine in an Indische garden, the pungent aroma of fish paste and *jengkol* beans, the tightly packed *opelet* buses, the festive atmosphere of the Pasar Malam—in order to establish commonality among audience members. These shared memories are contrastive. The European is typed as a complainer. The European thinks that the spicy *rujak* fruit salad so much enjoyed by Indonesians and Indische Nederlanders, particularly women, is little more than "crap" (*smurrie*); he prefers the banana, a tropical fruit that has a low status in Indonesia as it is not seasonal.[62] Standard spoken Dutch (*Hollands spreken*) is described as difficult (*moeilijk*) at the same time as Snijders revels in typical petjo turns of phrase and vocabulary.

The evening overall was consciously an attempt to demonstrate performative competence, build a sense of group awareness through shared laughter and memories, and establish a culture. These goals were explicitly noted in framing remarks delivered at the evening by A. G. de Grave-Terwogt and reports on the evening by Tjalie Robinson and others in the pages of *Tong Tong*.[63]

The Indische Cabaretavond (Indies Cabaret Evening), performed on three consecutive evenings (28 February–2 March 1958) at The Hague's zoo and repeated in April 1958 at the Royal Institute for the Tropics (KIT) in Amsterdam, took the themes and structures of the previous cultural performances to a new level. This was a remarkable occasion, in the ways that it involved the most significant Indische Nederlander artists and intellectuals, reached out to the Dutch public, and actively linked the present to the past history of the Indies, particularly the popular theater of stambul and bangsawan.

The Indische Cabaretavond was a benefit for the Red Cross, the Central Committee of Religious and Private Initiatives for the Social Care for Repatriates, and a charity for repatriates known as the Noodgironummer 777 (after the charity's bank account number); in all five thousand guilders was raised. The evening was produced by Tong-Tong, the organization that replaced Onze Brug. Tong-Tong took its name from the slit gong, a traditional Javanese instrument used to sound alarms and assemble communities in times of crisis and need. The name change signaled a new understanding of the relation of the Indische Nederlander population to the general populace.

> *Tong-Tong* [is] a name that cautions preparedness and watchfulness. The word "our" is gone. We do not want and cannot afford to form a separate group in Dutch society. We must instead strive to inform a broad audience far outside of our characteristic circle. We need to attract the entire Dutch public into our sphere of interest and . . . tell other people who we are and what we can do. Only then can the *Indisch* group in the Netherlands (a quarter million souls!) become a positive, useful and constructive element of the Dutch people.[64]

This understanding of the importance of public outreach and contributing to civil society was displayed in the Indische Cabaretavond.

The Indische Cabaretavond included kroncong music directed by Mary Brückel-Beiten, comic speeches by Tjalie Robinson, Indische songs by Ben and Jos Snijders, Indische compositions by violinist Fred Belloni, calypso music and Elvis Presley impressions from Los Muchachos del Tropical, a fashion show of Robert Mahieu's designs, and a series of dramatic sketches with a cast including Johan Fabricius, Rob Nieuwenhuys, and Tjalie Robinson. Cabinet minister Marga Klompé opened the event with a short speech. Klompé had an established reputation as an advocate for Indische Nederlanders: her famous 1957 radio address was instrumental in galvanizing the Dutch public to offer assistance to repatriates.[65] Klompé expressed her hope in her opening remarks that the Netherlands' cold climate was compensated for by the warmth of reception that the Indische Nederlanders had been shown. The appearance of Queen Juliana at the KIT show was more than a photo opportunity. Juliana's candid expression of enjoyment of the evening, and her admiration for the musical talents of Indische Nederlanders, was a validation of the sense of cultural merit of an immigrant group.

The dramatic sketches were collaboratively written by Robinson, Lilian Ducelle, Fabricius, Nieuwenhuys, and others. They were meditations on memory, possibility, and contradiction, mixing parody and farce together with serious social commentary. Tragedy and comedy were sleeping together in the same bed. Humor was posited as a coping mechanism for the sense of loss experienced by this diasporic group as well as social glue that amalgamated individuals around a shared cultural sense of the absurd.[66]

Het oordeel (The judgment), an "allegorical sketch" coauthored by Robinson and Fabricius, showed how "the ordeal of the world is experienced by exiled populations." The sketch displayed schematically the diverse meanings of displacement and resettlement for different elements of society—a planter (played by Johan Fabricius), the wife of a civil servant (played by Mary Brückel-Beiten), an old woman named Tjang (Ang van Ameyden-van Duym), Tjang's youngest grandchild (Lucian Boon), an adventurer (Tjalie Robinson), and a judge (Rob Nieuwenhuys). The repatriated Indische Nederlanders are shown wearing signs with letters around their neck—the signs used to sort them into different groups upon their arrival in Holland. No information was provided about the meaning of these arcane signs; some speculated that "A" meant that they were to be settled in Amsterdam. "They treated us like cattle, just like cattle," Lilian Ducelle recollected.[67] In the sketch, old woman Tjang complains about how she is unable to cope with the climate or the Dutch people and wishes to return to Indonesia. Tjang's young grandson chides her on her inflexibility—and embraces repatriation as an opportunity to go to university.

This weighty drama was juxtaposed with lighter sketches harking back nostalgically to the colonial past and dealing with the cultural contradictions of diaspora. The sketch *Mijn avontuur* (My adventure) showed a young streetwise man (Ben Snijders) on the lookout for girls. He ends up unexpectedly falling for an older, more traditional woman

Fig. 6.1. Repatriates arriving in the Netherlands in *Het oordeel* (The judgment). Photograph courtesy of Lilian Ducelle.

(played by Thea Roïs). *Viva la vida* (Live life to the fullest) was billed as a "Spanish sketch," and used Latin music and Mexican decor and costumes, including sombreros. Much play was made on the similarities and differences between the tropical Indies and tropical Latin America. The "Toreador's Song" from *Carmen* and references to bullfighting led into a song-and-dance number called *Kijk uit voor de stier* (Look out for the bull). The fierce "bull" is revealed to be a very docile *kerbau,* the domesticated Javanese water buffalo—enacted in the manner of a panto

Fig. 6.2. Botol Kecap and Aspirin in the comic sketch *Het raadsel* (The puzzle). Photograph courtesy of Lilian Ducelle.

cow. *Het raadsel* (The puzzle) was a comic dialogue between two clowns named Aspirin and Botol Kecap (Soy Sauce Bottle). Each clown tries to get the better of the other in order to obtain full possession of a bicycle. The sketch was consciously modeled after the comic interludes of stambul; Mahieu is mentioned by name in the program as the founding figure of this "sort of half Eurasian, half Indonesian 'Three Penny Opera.'"

The connection between this performance initiative and the past of stambul was elaborated in a speech delivered by Robinson in Amsterdam before Queen Juliana.

> In his opening remarks, Tjalie Robinson . . . brought the ghost of the past onto the planks. He recalled the first truly Indische theater, the *opera stambul,* "invented" by August Mahieu in Surabaya in 1904, a theatrical art rejected by Europeans but enthusiastically received by Asians. Other operas sprouted like mushrooms in Java and Sumatra. Before long they conquered the whole of the Indies, crossing over to Melaka and later, with such stars as Miss Riboet and Miss Dja, even crossing the Pacific. *The first operas were nearly entirely "manned" by Eurasian actors. When the Indo captured his place in European society, he distanced himself from Indische way of*

life including the stambul, which increasingly became influenced by Malay elements. During the war (when all Indische Nederlanders were imprisoned), the final "sentence" was executed against it. All Indo actors disappeared from stambul and the new name bangsawan *was coined.*

The arts of theater, cabaret, and revue are unknown in [traditional] Asian art (wayang is an entirely different formation!). It was an Indische man who was responsible for importing this uniquely Western cultural element to the East. Nobody realizes what an enormous contribution an Indo has made in the Asian acceptance of Western culture. Millions and millions of Asians have attended opera stambul and bangsawan and have thereby learned about real-life social problems in dialogue and drama that can be investigated and dealt with. . . .

But the stambul is dead. Dead and forgotten. What the artists of Tong-Tong have done was to bring out a ghost of the past on the planks for an evening. Is it possible that among the quarter million repatriates in the Netherlands there is enough original talent to create a new philosophy of life (for the theater is a different formation than a philosophy of life), one in which the European can derive as much enjoyment as Asians did from opera stambul?[68]

Robinson's representation of theatrical history might be partisan and inaccurate. It was, for example, the term *sandiwara,* which replaced *bangsawan, stambul,* and *tooneel* during the Japanese occupation of Indonesia. Dja and Riboet were properly stars in the revue theater known as tooneel (or tonil), not stambul; Mahieu did not "invent" komedi stambul in 1904.[69] Robinson's intent was earnest and heartfelt, however. Robinson believed that it was stambul that stimulated an interest among the mass of Indonesians, Malaysians, and other Asians to take on board European cultural forms and ideations.[70] Through stambul, Eurasians are represented as having historically played a valuable role as cultural brokers between Europe and Asia. The trotting out of the ghost of stambul onto the planks was more than a demonstration of past accomplishment. It was a cultural strategy for asserting that Indische Nederlanders are gifted with a unique ability to play a positive role in generating new mediating cultural formations, including a philosophy of life (*levensbeschouwing*) that can benefit Europeans in understanding the complexities of the postwar world.

Robinson latched onto stambul to provide recognition and valuation for Eurasian cultural accomplishment in the eyes of Eurasians and the larger Dutch public that he and his compatriots wished to engage with but not assimilate to. The postcolonial restored performances were in a sense incomplete. They needed discursive framing and prior knowledge of performance and a particular understanding of cultural history. Robinson's idealism was high, as were his expectations in regard to his audience. Seen in this light, it is not surprising that Robinson considered the Indische Cabaretavond only a partial success. He admitted that the performance standard of the actors in the dramatic sketches was amateuristic and that many of the actors had trod the boards for the first time. In a 1967 piece Robinson describes the Indische Cabaretavond, typed as "the last stambul performance in the Netherlands," as a *rommeltje,* a diminutive form of the word for rubbish or jumble that might be translated as a "little throwaway." In the same text, Robinson accused the Dutch press of not attending in sufficient numbers and being unable to comprehend the purpose of the evening—which was to recover or restore (*terugvinden*) "all—literally all!—elements of the Indo's komedi."[71] There is genuine anger in a 13 April 1958 letter that Robinson wrote to Louis de Bourbon in the immediate wake of the Cabaretavond.

> My Indisch cabaret-evening. Why does one think that it is just a portion of Indisch fun? . . . One obviously doesn't know that the Indonesian bangsawan that dominates today over all of East Asia, is of Dutch origin. That a halfblood, August Mahieu, was the founder of the so-called Opera Stambul, from which many operas originated, which in the long run (in terms of the repertoire) became more and more Asian? That among the originally performed dramas *Genoveva of Brabant* was proudly staged next to *Hamlet. The Two Orphans* next to *Macbeth,* that Fairy tales from *Thousand and One Nights* were performed and ancient Hindu tales were

> prepared for the stage. That millions and millions of Asians, because of this European bangsawan, became interested in Western culture? Ah, Holland does not recognize her own sons! We just say: such a colored person, is he Indonesian or Ambonese or Surinamese! [English in original:] Very, very, very stupid![72]

This perceived lack of public recognition for the accomplishment of performance contributed to Robinson and Tong-Tong pouring their energy into Pasar Malam starting in 1959. The Pasar Malam is not a cultural performance with clear divisions between spectators and performers but a participatory celebration incorporating goods, food, games, services, performance, vendors, performers, spectator-consumers, and organizers into a common field of play. This configuration ultimately has proven to be the more enduring vehicle for the articulation of Indische Nederlander identity, although in recent years the various Pasar Malam, and particularly the Pasar Malam Besar in The Hague, have become less attuned to Indische Nederlander sentiments and have transformed into commercial fairs with more diverse Asian accents.

There have been other noteworthy cultural evenings organized by Tong-Tong and affiliated organizations. Some of these were within the Pasar Malam frame, but not all. Robinson and Ducelle produced a number of Indische cultural evenings when they were living in California in the early 1960s. A few of these were collaborations with the former Dardanella dancer-actress Devi Dja, who migrated to the United States during World War II.[73] Upon returning to the Netherlands, Ducelle wrote and directed a 1970 musical farce entitled *Blauwbaard's achtste* (Bluebeard's eighth), which was directly inspired by komedi stambul. The music was by Harry van den Brink, and the leading roles were played by kroncong singer Guus Becker and well-known entertainer "Tante" Pim Eisinger.[74] Ducelle also wrote and directed a dramatized journey through the musical history of the Indische Nederlander community entitled *Moesson's Musical Memories*. This 1986 potpourri production featured a cast of hundreds. Ducelle recalls it as one of her greatest cultural accomplishments.[75]

Fig. 6.3. The author and his daughter going to the Pasar Malam Besar in The Hague, 2000. Photograph by Aviva Kartiningsih Cohen.

Tjalie Robinson's interest in restoring komedi stambul onstage might have declined after 1958, but his magazine *Tong Tong* published a raft of articles exploring the history of this theater between 1958 and 1971.[76] Interest in komedi stambul was conditioned on a heartfelt belief that it was a manifestation of "our history," "our culture," "our art"—phrases that come up repeatedly in the pages of *Tong Tong*. W. F. W. Schardijn, in a letter addressed to Robinson accompanying an article on a stambul version of the play *Jula-Juli bintang tiga,* stated explicitly that he hoped Mahieu's art would provide an example for young Indische Nederlanders.[77]

The Pasar Malam Besar features to date an Auguste Mahieu "street." This is a tribute as much to the actor-manager as to Robinson's enduring interest in him.

Robinson was a major authority and important voice on colonial culture in postwar Holland, and his insights into and understanding of stambul filtered into academic works by Dutch and foreign scholars. Stambul appears mysteriously, as if entering through a trapdoor, in a variety of writings concerned with colonial history starting in the 1960s. Stambul also features as an example of "Indische culture" in the work of American historian Pauline Dublin Milone. Milone, who conducted research in both Indonesia and the Netherlands between 1961 and 1963, extends the theoretical insights of Dutch sociologist W. F. Wertheim into the mestizo society and culture of the Indies. Milone's central research focus was on premodern Batavia (until circa 1875), but she manages to sneak in a discussion of stambul as a late "development of Indische culture" and a cultural "expression of the poor to middle-income population."[78]

Stambul also slips into a thesis by Australian historian Heather Sutherland. Sutherland's primary concern in her thesis is with social and cultural life of Batavia during the last decade of colonial rule, with a particular focus on the intellectual elites associated with the literary journal *Poedjangga Baroe.*[79] Sutherland nonetheless includes an extensive discussion of stambul, which she describes as one of the primary forms of "institutionalized and therefore accessible entertainments" of late colonial Batavia, "popular entertainment for the modern Indonesian common man, who lived in a complex and changing world, of which the Europeans and their technology were part."[80] Sutherland also explicitly cites a 1966 conversation with Robinson as a stambul source.

The inclusion of a discussion of stambul "as a sort of extra" in Rob Nieuwenhuys's influential book on Dutch writings about Indonesia, *Oost-Indische spiegel* (Mirror of the Indies), might also be due to Robinson's influence.[81] Stambul also figures in Nieuwenhuys's three-volume photo essay *Tempo doeloe,* enjoying pride of place over other performance genres. It is not incidental that four pages of text and pictures on stambul are followed immediately by a comparable number of pages dealing with Tjalie Robinson.[82]

The descriptors attached to stambul show a recuperative upward drift. American historian Paul W. van der Veur describes stambul as an "artistic achievement" of the lower class of the Eurasian community.[83] Librarian, translator, and short story writer Fredrik "Frits" van den Bosch dubs stambul a "cosmopolitan spectacle."[84]

Stambul has continued to have interest for second generation Indische Nederlanders. The research project that has resulted in this book began in the Netherlands while I was a research fellow at the International

Institute for Asian Studies in Leiden, with support, interest, and competition from members of this generation. Before I began my research, Melanie Tangkau, an arts promoter and archaeologist, had already conducted research on stambul and kroncong using Dutch-language sources and interviews with elderly first generation Indische Nederlanders, with the financial assistance of Tong-Tong. Rob Dumas was completing his dissertation on Abdul Muluk theater in South Sumatra at Leiden University at the time I initiated my research on stambul, but he had already written on stambul and was anticipating writing more. To mark the hundredth anniversary of the death of Auguste Mahieu, Dumas presented a talk on Mahieu for a general audience at the Pasar Malam Besar in The Hague.[85]

It was also at the Pasar Malam Besar where I first saw displayed a *Toneel van Java* T-shirt produced by the Sarapan company of central Java. The sepia-tinted T-shirt has an illustration of a disorderly stambul company lounging about onstage, with a Dutch caption that translates, "Modern forms of theater developed slowly from old traditions in large part in the cities of western Java. One of these forms is the sandiwara illustrated above, a quickly paced burlesque that gave performers opportunities for all sorts of gags." During a trip from Yogyakarta to Solo in 1999, I made a quick visit in 1999 to Sarapan's workshop in Kalasan. Upon questioning the manager, I found out that the image on this shirt and others in Sarapan's line of colonial nostalgia items were reproduced from illustrations in yellowing Dutch books housed in Yogyakarta research libraries. The books had been borrowed by Sarapan employees studying at Yogyakarta universities. A manager at the workshop stated that the line was aimed primarily at nostalgic tourists from the Netherlands visiting Indonesia.

THE LEGACY of stambul conforms to a different cultural logic in postcolonial Indonesia. The Japanese occupation of Indonesia brought a halt to the small-scale stambul troupes that continued to eke out a marginal existence in the face of competition from modern media, large-scale tooneel groups such as Miss Riboet's Orion, and variety companies during the late colonial period.[86] Ludruk, ketoprak, and other regional

Fig. 6.4. T-shirt on sale at the Pasar Malam Besar in The Hague, 1999. Photograph by the author.

transformations and derivatives of stambul, performed in regional languages and dialects, flourished in western Indonesia through the first two decades of independence, with the active support of political parties and their cultural wings. There was also sandiwara theater in the national language of Indonesian, aesthetically dominated by what Clifford Geertz terms "a socially conscious romantic realism."[87]

An important effort to understand stambul within the context of national culture was made by novelist, playwright, and cultural critic Armijn Pane in an important 1953 essay on fictional film in Indonesia.[88] Pane had long been a champion of hybrid Indonesian culture, including kroncong and stambul.[89] Citing American anthropologist Melvin Herskovits on acculturation and culture contact, Pane interprets film as a possible cultural tool for the establishment of national unity. In Pane's view, film potentiated the integration of Indonesia's various regional cultures and borrowed Western culture and technology. Stambul figures in this essay as both a precursor to Indonesia's film industry as well as a precedent for an art form involving active participation of a spectrum of the archipelago's ethnic groups and a reliance on Western artistic form and technology.[90]

> At the end of the last century . . . a type of theater was born at the initiative of a person of European descent, assisted by an Indonesian and a Chinese capitalist. In short, this theater can be classified as an acculturation of techniques and structures of European theater and opera as they existed around 1900, combined with the techniques and structures of the extant Malay theater, already influenced by India and Persia. This person of European descent arranged the cross between the two streams in such a way that it would be appropriate for the general Indonesian public of the time. At first, the stories were drawn from the *Thousand and One Nights* collection, slightly adjusted for an Indonesian taste and understanding, a type of taste and understanding that sprang from the mixture of many peoples. At this time, the society was already mixed. One might productively compare it with conditions in America in the past, before the reification of a sort of "way of life"

> [English in the original] supported by various American ethnic groups. In accord with this acculturative outlook, the actors were likewise mixed: there were Indonesians, there were people of mixed Dutch descent.[91]

Armijn Pane, it is important to emphasize, saw stambul as being strictly relevant to its time and place; he did not support its revival. Rather, he discussed stambul in order to demonstrate that the seeds for national integration and unity across ethnic groups did not lie in the support of individual ethnic cultures (a prevalent view in Indonesia then and today) but in the promotion of dominant forms of hybrid and interstitial cultures of the archipelago.

Stambul was put to a rather different use by Tengku Syed Abdulkadar and Zen Rosdy in *Sejarah seni-drama* (The history of dramatic art).[92] Theirs was the first attempt to write a textbook for Indonesian readers dealing with both the history of European and American drama (from the Greeks and commedia dell'arte to Sartre, Tennessee Williams, and the Actor's Studio) and Indonesian drama (from bangsawan and stambul to Usmar Ismail, Utuy Sontani, and the Akademi Teater Nasional Indonesia). The motivation for writing this bicultural history is nationalistic: the book concludes with a long argument for the founding of a national theater. Bangsawan and stambul are understood by Tengku and Zen to have an identical function in Indonesia as that played in Europe by commedia. Actors are described as taking on stock roles in plays and improvising dialogue around well-known moralistic stories. Like commedia, which went through various transformations in the hands of Shakespeare and subsequent European theater practitioners as a transnational root culture, stambul and bangsawan are shown to be alive in Indonesia's present, in new versions of *Nyai Dasima* by Suryosumanto and S. M. Ardan, new theatrical tellings of old folktales by Utuy Sontani, and the itinerant commercialism of the Padang Panjang–based sandiwara company Ratu Asia. The book's purpose is to make the forms and features of stambul and other theaters of the pasts of Europe, the United States, and Indonesia available for appropriation by contemporary Indonesian theater practitioners.

According to its authors, *Sejarah seni-drama* is "not a theoretical book, but a practical and direct guide to theatrical production" intended to "give new impulses to the development of the art of drama."[93] In contrast, Boen Sri Oemarjati's *Bentuk lakon dalam sastra Indonesia* (Dramaturgy in Indonesian literature), is a more conventional literary history of spoken drama in Indonesia.[94] The author recognizes stambul as occupying a critical position in the historiography of Indonesian theater, as the oldest "modern" theater.[95] Stambul is represented by Boen as being at a lesser level of development than scripted drama in the West or in postcolonial Indonesia, due to its use of improvisation and lack of fixed scripts. Boen interprets stambul's high degree of audience involvement and absence of permanent theatrical buildings as marking a low level of theatrical evolution: "The function and status of the public or spectatorship was not as ordered as the function and status of the public in Western theater. The major principle was to serve the public will, and because performances still often happened at the sides of roads or on fields, the public had a direct hand in things and could easily influence or even change the doings onstage."[96] This emphasis on order and control and the corresponding wariness of the public's involvement misrepresents the tradition of popular participation in Western theater by reifying an East-versus-West divide. More to the point, Boen articulates a paranoia of popular participation in a theatrical field of action. This sort of paranoia was characteristic of President Soeharto's New Order military regime (1966–98) as a whole. There is no suggestion that stambul merits revisiting in any way outside the pages of Boen's book. The eclectic and the unpredictable are not to be restored or celebrated but to be excised in the interest of "the appearance of order."[97] Stambul was necessarily recognized as part of Indonesian theater history, but it was dealt with as what theater historian and arts bureaucrat A. Kasim Achmad terms "transitional theater" (*teater masa transisi*), an outdated art "on the way to modern theater" and its scripted performances and orderly audiences.[98]

Suspicion of theatrical disorder abated in Indonesian academic writings that followed Boen's book. In a pair of essays penned in 1973, both Subagio Sastrowardojo and Goenawan Mohamad, two of New Order

Indonesia's most noteworthy cultural critics and poets, cast aspersions on the ideological divide separating the world of "high culture" from the hybrid popular culture emblematized by stambul.[99] Goenawan and Subagio viewed the wave of avant-garde theatrical experimentalism initiated with W. S. Rendra's *minikata* (nearly wordless) drama *Bip-Bop* (1968) as a continuation of an organic theatrical hybridity that dates back to the 1891 founding of the Komedie Stamboel. This is a sort of hybridity that is not experienced as strange or alien but as authentically Indonesian "because of its intimate ties with the growth of public taste."[100] Stambul's low status was elevated to an extent through the attention of these public intellectuals. Their point was not to appropriate popular culture as fodder for more refined art aimed at the educated elite. Rather the theatrical arts of the lower classes and the marginalized were viewed as having interest and appeal in and of themselves. Goenawan and his peers could sit in the open-air theater of Taman Ismail Marzuki, Jakarta's main arts center, and savor performances of lenong and related popular theater genres without feeling a need for intellectualizing or overinterpreting their pleasure. Stambul subsequently achieved recognition and value as what playwright and cultural bureaucrat Saini K. M. has referred to as "trans-ethnic" theater.[101]

Stambul has also been restored in performance through the efforts of Indonesian playwrights and directors. The most important of these has been by director, playwright, novelist, journalist, and editor Nano Riantiarno, who has brought back stambul's tradition of raucous musical comedy to the national stage with over one hundred productions staged since 1977 by his company Teater Koma (Comma Theater).[102] Teater Koma has a loyal following that expects to see plays involving a mixture of social and political satire combined with entertaining song and dance. The cultural roots of this theater are a complex mélange. In addition to a self-conscious linkage to the popular theater of the late colonial period, there is an obvious influence of the regional theater that Riantiarno imbibed as a child in Cirebon. Riantiarno has also conducted informal studies of other Indonesian regional theaters, extensively mining central Javanese wayang wong in a series of productions.[103] He has studied Chinese opera as well and has used Chinese operatic conventions and devices in his adaptation of *Sampek Engtay* and other works. The absurdist theater Riantiarno studied at the Akademi Teater Nasional Indonesia and performed as an actor in Teguh Karya's Teater Populer in Jakarta in the late 1960s and early 1970s has had a lasting impact on him. The Broadway musical and the epic theater of Bertolt Brecht are evident in about equal portions. Politics are never far from the surface, and Riantiarno's theatrical work gained a degree of notoriety toward the end of the Soeharto regime due to the banning of a number of productions on political grounds.[104] Audiences might not be aware of all the cultural borrowings and influences, but the plays presume awareness of current events and knowledge of Jakarta slang and are aimed at a liberal, young to middle-aged audience of at least moderate means.

The designation preferred by Riantiarno for his plays and productions is opera, which intentionally harks back to colonial-era popular theater groups.

> Their opera was not the opera that developed and matured in Italy or Germany. Their opera actually should be called cabaret or operetta. Their trusted recipe could capture the attention of spectators by a mixture of dance, singing, music, humor, and acting. Sometimes this was supplemented with displays of martial arts or fencing skills. Or magic.
>
> And in their time, these professional groups could be said to have had great success in attracting spectators. Actors and actresses could make a reasonable living from their profession, regardless of the debates that often transpired regarding the quality of their performing art. These [debates] could often be violent during this period. Teater Koma has chosen the style once used by professional theater groups in Indonesia in the period around 1925, and has wedded that style to that of the Broadway musical.[105]

Riantiarno has not only modeled his theatrical style of production after colonial-era popular theater, he has also recreated the social milieu of the popular stage in one of Teater Koma's most successful productions, *Opera Primadona* (The prima donna opera), which was originally

Fig. 6.5. Program cover for Teater Koma's 1988 production of *Sampek Engtay,* written and directed by N. Riantiarno.

produced as a stage play in 1988, adapted into a television miniseries in 1990, and revived as a stage play in 2000. This play depicts the passage of decades in the intersecting lives of theater people on- and offstage, based to a considerable extent on the biography of actress Devi Dja.[106] The play is not only about popular theater; the production's use of tried-and-true theatrical formulae reminded at least one critic explicitly of colonial-era stambul.[107]

Riantiarno has long dwelled on the possibility of reestablishing a professional touring theater along the lines of the large-scale tooneel companies of the late colonial period that communicated to mass audiences. The full realization of such a company, which would provide both full-time employment for actors as well as a medium for artistic expression, has continually eluded him, despite his success in a range of other cultural enterprises. The problem is in part historical, for, as Riantiarno has pointed out, the period of the transregional professional theater ended around the time of Indonesia's independence. "We have lost its tracks, for nobody has ever written about this period in detail. What was the process of production used, its management, creative process, and related matters?"[108] Riantiarno's own theater, Teater Koma, is perhaps the best approximation of a performative restoration of the theater of Mahieu and those who followed that trailblazer. It has been one of the goals of this book to re-mark the lost tracks of Mahieu and his generation of theater makers to provide a road map for future cultural production.

Appendix

PLAYS AND TABLEAUX PERFORMED BY THE KOMEDIE STAMBOEL

The following are my English translations of the titles of known plays and tableaux vivants listed chronologically according to the first known date of performance by the Komedie Stamboel and subsequent stambul groups headed by Auguste Mahieu.

Plays

1891

The Fisherman and the Genie
Giafar
Abu Hasan, the Chief of Thieves
Bedreddin Hassan, a Very Honest Man
Nureddin
Ali Baba and the Forty Thieves
Aladdin and the Magic Lamp
Asam and the Spirit Queen
The Prince of Zanzibar
Bukabik
The Barbary Brothers
Amgiad and Assad, the Two Wronged Princes
The Woodsman and the 'Ifrit
The Hunchback

Raelaman bin Rachmat, or The Rinaldo Rinaldi of Arabia
Abuhassan, the Sleeper Awakened
The Contending Kings Murat Khan and Harun al-Rachmat
Brahmin, the Woodsman Prince
Sultan Yahya and His Three Children Made Kings
Young King Rildoan and Baraldoan
The Enchanted Prince Alur al-Haad and Achmat Saman
The Introduction to the Thousand and One Nights, or The Cleverness of a Woman
Fathul Achmat, or The Faust of Arabia
Osup, the Sluggard
He Is Not Jealous
The Lost Son, Yosup bin Diab
The Crippled King, Ali al-Yufri, Later Helped by the Queen of the Spirits Named Siti Anjani
Siti Senimbar, or Innocence Protected by Divine Grace
Budraim bin Hasap, or Retribution
The Hatred of Brothers
The Revenge of the Sultan of Alvia
The Adventure of King Isa bin Asbedi, the Hindi
The Three Crippled Princesses
The Chastised King of Persia Sach Zaman and Queen Siti Ratema

1892

Brahmin, or Unwavering Love
The Arabian Rose
Husin and Sagsamat, or From Fruit Basket to Throne
The Roc's Egg, or The Demon King
Three Bad Men Turn Good
The Three Penitent Sinners, or The Punishments of Hell
The Murder Mystery, or Deceitful Mother Love
From Bows and Arrows to Emperor
The Father's Curse

Hasdam, the Prince Carried Away by Vice
Prince Albraha of Zanzibar
The Arabian King Brahim bin Asat Bubaham
Marhava, or Three Jealous Sisters
The Spirit Queen and Prince Paribanu
Ali and the Magic Violin
The Jealous Heart
Three Deaf Men
The Two Skulls
The Dream of Kings
Baraldoan, the Prince in Exile
The Beginning and End of the Thousand and One Nights

1893

Laili
Brahim's Dream
Bubakam, or Bluebeard
Siti Safira, or Divine Retribution
Sleeping Beauty
Normadi
Akhid, or Retribution
Damsi, the Sunbeam
White Tiger's Milk, or A Child's Love for a Parent

1894

Siti Sarita
Asiad, the Hanged Prince
The Woman without Jealousy
The Sleepyhead
Snow White
Love and Artifice

Sahir Zaman, or The Revenge of the Four Gods
The Somnambulist
Hasan and Ramania, or A Tailor
Kamaralsaman and Badur
Hawai Majelis, the Sun Princess
Badarel Dunia, or The World Star
Genoveva of Brabant
The Hunchback and the Loquacious Barber
Muratkhan, or The Horned King
Brachman Patnaba
He Is Not Jealous and He Is Too Jealous
The Fall of Sin Island, or Treason Punished [banned]
Jupiter

1895

The Expedition to Chili Pepper Island
The Death of Jantik

1896

Punishments of the Afterlife
The Lombok War
The Cakranegara Battle

1897

Sahari Jenahar, or The Sun's Daughter
Abuhassan the Sculptor, or The Galathea of the East
Dewa Laksana Dewa, or The King of Monsters
The Merchant of the Port City
Samsu Alam

1898

Indrajaya, or A Princess' Savior, Who Was the Prey of a Dangerous Sea Serpent
Skylight, or The Destruction of the Kingdom of Women
The Sajratenur Flower
Puran Wahat, or A Beggar Marries a Fairy King
Doimi Adelam
A Dragon's Tears, or The Ghost of Princess Cahya Muntiara
Singa-Braya, or Fear of the Wild
The Grave's Secret
The Magic Bag
Cahya Warna, the Priest's Daughter
The Garden of Bakasari, or Queen of the Dark
Secrets of Semarang by Day and Night
Laili and Majenun, or The Power of Love

1899

Ali Baba Jr., or Merchant Sheikh Albaru
Dudarsani, the Fire Sea King's Child
The Third Star Jula-Juli
Sardui Hassan and Siti Sulmu
Lord Rawa, the Monkey King
Hamid, or The War of Four Princesses
Gehor Alam Syach
The Conquest of the Kingdom of Women

1900

Hassan Husin, or Fratricide
Ma Husin, the Pariah, or Misplaced Trust
Secrets of Batavia by Day and Night

Cloring and Clowong
Nyai Dasima
Glittering Flower
Wahat Alam
Basir Mohamad Afadi
The Punishment for Sin
Bin Lail, or The Son of Blackest Night
The Maradilem Bird
Dancing Water, Singing Tree, Speaking Bird
Rosina
The Sun's Daughter, or Jenar Jenahar
Si Conat, the Bandit Chief of Tangerang
The Magic JarPrincess Bradadani
Zulmi Asela
Bahrul Azham
The Transvaal War
Mohamat Asari, or A Priest's Praise
The Daughter of Prangan Cahya, or A Debt of Shame Repaid with Shame
The Battle of Achmad Mohamad: The Origin of the Genie King
Laela Candra, or The Four Slaves Crowned as Kings
Starlight
True Soul Flower

1901

Gangga Indra, the Ape King
Laela Mendara, Enchanter of Princes
Siti Rohaya: A Tale from Batavia
Laila Surmana
Adiama
Water of Victory
Mohamad Assehari, or The Priest's Son Becomes King
Brachman-Alda: Cahaya Rani's Daughter
The Magic Lute

Baddarel-Feerdaus, or Asmaru and Saida, the Sultan and Queen of Ghemina
The Bakawali Jug
Revenge, or Oeij Kim Nio and Lie Koen Njan
Ardan Jangge
The Horned Princess
Garden of Bakawali, or The Native Girl Angga-Rani

Tableaux Vivants

1891

"The Sultan Harun al-Rachid, Beset by His Head"
"Devils"
"The Prophet Solomon Punishing Two Recalcitrant Genies"
"Fathul Achmat in the Afterlife"
"Mohamad Achir, or The Don Juan of Arabia"
"The Departure of the Steamship *Prince Hendrik*"
"A Struggle between Angels and Devils in a Stormy Sea"
"The Poor Benefactor and the Rich Miser at the Entrance to the Afterlife"
"The Three Ages of Man, Namely: Youth, Maturity, and Old Age"
"Adam and Eve Driven from Paradise"
"Angels Fight with the Devil over a Soul"

1892

"Symbol of Pain"
"Death of a Valiant Robber Chief"
"Jupiter and His Retinue"
"Arabian Shipwreck"
"A Mother's Hope and a Mother's Care"
"Group of Angels"

"Battle between Angels and Devils"
"Neptune in His Kingdom"
"An Indian Attack"
"The End of *From Bows and Arrows to Emperor*"
"The Guardian Angel of Innocence"

1893

"The 1873 Paris Fire"
"The Eruption of Krakatau"
"The Assassination of Prince Willem of Orange by Balthazar Gerards"
"The Symbolic Birth of Sleeping Beauty"

1894

"The Discovery of America"
"The Fisherman's Dream"
"Faith"
"The Death of Captain Revière at Hanoi"
"Battle in America"
"Amor, the God of Love"
"Sleeping Beauty in Paradise"
"Death of General Dupierre in Tonkin"
"The Maid of Orleans"
"Sleeping Beauty"
"Boebaham in the Hands of His Victims"
"Abel Murdered by Cain"
"A Hunter's Dream"
"Talking Angels"
"Faith, Hope, and Love"
"Jacob's Dream"
"Protector of the Innocents"

"Slaughter of the Innocents at Bethlehem"
"Ali Baba's Flight"
"The Wreck of the *Chancellor*"

1895

"The Justice of Solomon"
"Garnot's Death"

1896

"King Kilap on His Throne"
"A Person's Ease, Prohibition, and Fortune"
"The Death of General Van Ham"
"A Virgin"

1897

"The Grand Pensionary Johan van Oldenbarneveldt Executed on the Scaffold"
"The Giant Goliath Slain by David"
"Hearing, Seeing, and Being Silent"
"An Allusion to Sleeping Beauty"

1898

"The Throne of a Fairy Queen"
"A Shepherd's Dream"
"The Heaven of Marhaji and the Hell of Fathul Achmat"
"The Triumphal March of a Fairy Queen"
"Albrecht Beijling Buried Alive"

"A Tiger Hunt"
"The Nymph Queen"

1899

"A Symbolic Representation of General Chamberlain and Paul Kruger"

1900

"The Indische Bond in 1910"

"Never Give Up"
"A Ship Burning at Sea"

Notes

Notes on Sources and Acknowledgments

1. Scott Merrillees, *Batavia in Nineteenth Century Photographs* (Richmond, Surrey: Curzon, 2000), 232.

Introduction

1. The Netherlands Indies (also referred to as the Netherlands East Indies or the Indies) was a Dutch Southeast Asian colony that became the Republic of Indonesia with independence in 1945. Malay was spoken as a first language in nineteenth-century Indonesia by Chinese, Eurasians, and the majority of the population of Batavia (present-day Jakarta). It was also used as a lingua franca by urbanites in other parts of the Indonesian archipelago. Malay was subsequently adopted and adapted as the national language of Indonesia, *bahasa Indonesia*. For a succinct overview of the history of Indonesian, see Stuart Robson, *From Malay to Indonesian: The Genesis of a National Language* (Clayton, Victoria: Monash Asia Institute, Monash University, 2002).

2. Hildred Geertz, "Indonesian Cultures and Communities," in *Indonesia,* ed. Ruth T. McVey (New Haven: Southeast Asian Studies, Yale University, 1967), 41.

3. Homi K. Bhabha, *The Location of Culture* (New York: Routledge, 1994), 35.

4. W. F. Wertheim, *Indonesian Society in Transition: A Study of Social Change,* 2d ed. (The Hague: W. van Hoeve, 1956), 174.

5. "Foreign Asian" was a legal category in the Netherlands Indies whose boundaries varied over the course of the colonial period but generally included Chinese, Arabs, and Indians. Eurasians (sometimes referred to as Indo-Europeans, or Indos) were legally equated with Europeans, and

subject to the same laws and regulations, as long as they were admitted as legal progeny of a father of European status. Period sources refer to indigenous people of the Indies mostly as Native (*inlander* or *bumiputra;* lit., "son of the earth") or Muslim (*orang islam* or *orang slam*). I use both in this book.

6. W. Basil Worsfold, *A Visit to Java with an Account of the Founding of Singapore* (London: Richard Bantley and Son, 1893), 207.

7. J. F. Scheltema, *Java* (London: Adam and Charles Black, 1912).

8. R. J. Wilkinson, *A Malay-English Dictionary (Romanised)*, 2 vols. (London: Macmillan, 1959), 2:810.

9. Pauline Milone, "Queen of the East: The Metamorphosis of a Colonial Capital" (Ph.D. diss., University of California at Berkeley, 1966), 567.

10. Alfred R. Wallace, *The Wonderful Century* (New York: Dodd, Mead, 1898), as cited at "Alfred Russel Wallace and the Wonderful Century," http://www.udayton.edu/~hume/Wallace/wallace.htm. (All internet sources cited in this book were last accessed in January 2005.)

11. Georg Simmel, "The Metropolis and Mental Life," in *The Sociology of Georg Simmel,* ed. and trans. Kurt H. Wolff (New York: Free Press of Glencoe, 1964), 409–24.

12. Milone, "Queen of the East," 9.

13. W. F. Wertheim, "Colonial and Post-Colonial Cities as Arenas of Conflict," *Bijdragen tot de Taal-, Land- en Volkenkunde* 143, no. 4 (1987): 539–43.

14. Ann Kumar, "A Swedish View of Batavia in 1783–4: Hornstedt's Letters," *Archipel* 37 (1989): 253–54.

15. Milone, "Queen of the East," 459–512, 561–68.

16. Michael R. Booth and Pamela Heckenberg, "Touring the Empire," *Essays in Theatre* 6, no. 1 (1987): 49–60.

17. *Tontonan,* a Malay word meaning spectacle or show (lit., that which is observed), is derived from the same root as *nontonner,* from the Batavia Malay word *nonton* (to observe).

18. *Angéline* was written by Armand d'Artois and M. E. G. M. Théaulon de Lambert. N. P. van den Berg, *Het tooneel te Batavia in vroegeren tijd* (Batavia: W. Bruining, 1880), 76.

19. The word *komedi* was also sometimes used interchangeably with *schouwburg* to refer to a European-style theater with a proscenium stage.

20. *Selompret Melajoe,* 14 October 1893.

21. For a cogent discussion of sorcery and modern magic, see James W. Cook, *The Arts of Deception: Playing with Fraud in the Age of Barnum* (Cambridge, MA: Harvard University Press, 2001), 163–213. Meditations on the aesthetics of aneh in central Javanese culture can be found in James T. Siegel, *Solo in the New Order: Language and Hierarchy in an Indonesian City* (Princeton: Princeton University Press, 1987). My discussion of attractions

and the aesthetics of astonishment draws tacitly on Tom Gunning's seminal analyses of early cinema.

22. D. Iken and E. Harahap, *Kitab arti logat Melajoe* (Weltevreden: Visser, 1918).

23. F. de Haan, *Oud Batavia,* 2 vols. (Bandung: Nix, 1935), 1:602.

24. G. H. von Faber, *Oud Soerabaia: De geschiedenis van Indie's eerste koopstad van de oudste tijden tot de instelling van den Gemeenteraad (1906)* (Surabaya: Kolff, 1931), 372.

25. *De Preanger Bode,* 30 August 1897.

26. See, e.g., *Bintang Soerabaia,* 27 December 1893, on the dislike of komedi among Sidoarjo's priyayi. Class bias is one of the reasons that komedi has mostly been ignored by scholars, who have tended to concentrate mostly on the "refined" culture of the elite to date.

27. Henk M. J. Maier, "From Heteroglossia to Polyglossia: The Creation of Malay and Dutch in the Indies," *Indonesia* 56 (1993), 148–49.

28. *Bintang-Barat,* 4 October 1890.

29. Claudine Salmon, "Commerces ambulants et insertion sociale à Surabaya vers la fin du XIXe siècle," *Archipel* 37 (1989): 297–326.

30. Anderson, "Language, Fantasy, Revolution," 37.

31. Liok An Djien, "Dua jago silat di Java," in *Kesastraan Melayu Tionghoa dan kebangsaan Indonesia,* ed. Marcus A. S. and Pax Benedanto, 25 vols. (1935; repr., Jakarta: Kepustakaan Populer Gramedia, 2002), 5:242.

32. Kees van Dijk, "Sarongs, Jubbahs, and Trousers: Appearance as a Means of Distinction and Discrimination," in *Outward Appearances: Dressing State and Society in Indonesia,* ed. Henk Schulte Nordholt (Leiden: KITLV Press, 1997), 39–83.

33. Cf. Anderson, "Language, Fantasy, Revolution."

34. Much of this violence took place across lines of race. Compare the comments of Janet Davis, who describes the "recreational fighting" of American men at circuses as "displaced abjection" and an expression of "familial or class-based divisions within a community." Davis, *The Circus Age: Culture and Society under the American Big Top* (Chapel Hill: University of North Carolina Press, 2002), 190.

35. *Bintang-Barat,* 25 June 1895.

36. During the 1890s one guilder (which contained 100 cents) was worth approximately US $0.40, or about $8 adjusted for inflation.

37. *Bintang-Barat,* 31 October 1890.

38. *Pembrita Betawi,* 23 September 1895.

39. *Bintang-Barat,* 24 August 1895.

40. Geoff Harmston, "Harmston Circus," http://www.dharmston.freeserve.co.uk/page3.html.

41. Milone, "Queen of the East," 160–61.

42. Cook, *Arts of Deception,* 83; *Times* (London), 21 November 1822.

43. *Times* (London), 6 July 1827.

44. Davis, *Circus Age,* 128–31.

45. *Pembrita-Bahroe,* 22 June 1895.

46. Jules Verne, *Around the World in Eighty Days* (1872), 187. Published online at http://etext.lib.virginia.edu/etcbin/browse-mixed-new?id=VerDays&tag=public&images=images/modeng&data=/texts/english/modeng/parsed.

47. Benedict R. O'G. Anderson, *Language and Power: Exploring Political Cultures in Indonesia* (Ithaca: Cornell University Press, 1990), 276.

48. Raymond Williams, *Marxism and Literature* (Oxford: Oxford University Press, 1977), 120.

49. Michael Geyer and Charles Bright, "World-History in a Global Age," *American Historical Review* 100, no. 4 (1995): 1048.

50. James Clifford, *Routes: Travel and Translation in the Late Twentieth Century* (Cambridge, MA: Harvard University Press, 1997), 2.

51. The term *pre-Indonesian literature* was coined by Pramoedya. See Pramoedya Ananta Toer, ed., *Tempo doeloe: Antologi sastra pra-Indonesia* (Jakarta: Hasta Mitra, 1982).

52. For important insights into Indische nationalism and the subsequent fragmentation into ethnic and religious politics its failure engendered, see Jacques van Doorn, *A Divided Society: Segmentation and Mediation in Late-Colonial Indonesia* (Rotterdam: CASP, Erasmus University, 1983).

53. The term "the Mahieu period" (*pariode Mahieu*) is derived from Abisin Abbas, "Tooneel Indonesia, ditengah perhatian oemoem," in *Kunst, tooneel en journalistiek* (Fort de Kock: Malakka, 1935), 16–17. Abisin Abbas, more generally known as Andjar Asmara, was a writer and director and Indonesia's foremost theater critic during the late colonial period.

54. Unless otherwise indicated, all translations are by the author. Practical limitations prevent inclusion of the Malay and Dutch originals.

55. *Bintang Soerabaia,* 12 December 1893.

56. Vanessa R. Schwartz, *Spectacular Realities: Early Mass Culture in Fin-de-Siècle Paris* (Berkeley: University of California Press, 1998), 36.

57. *Pembrita-Bahroe,* 21 October 1895. The newspaper correspondent, who signs his name Ali Babah, is here reporting on Garut performances by Opera Konstantinopel, a stambul company from Cirebon founded in 1894 and directed by S. S. b. S. Basalama.

58. Davis, *Circus Age,* xiii.

59. Pramoedya Ananta Toer, *This Earth of Mankind,* trans. Max Lane (London: Penguin Books, 1990), 17–18.

60. Timothy Mitchell, "The Stage of Modernity," in *Questions of Modernity,* ed. Timothy Mitchell (Minneapolis: University of Minnesota Press, 2000), 18.

Chapter 1

1. Batavia, in contrast, had a population of 110,669 in 1893. See William Hayward Frederick, "Indonesian Urban Society in Transition: Surabaya, 1926–1946" (Ph.D. diss., University of Hawaii, 1978), 25. The European population of Surabaya, which encompassed "Eurasians, Christian indigenes and a variety of others besides Dutch citizens," grew quickly in the last two decades of the twentieth century, from 4,293 in 1880 to about 7,000 in 1895 to 9,000 in 1900. For these and other population figures, see Frederick, as well as "Soerabaja," in *Encyclopaedie van Nederlandsch-Indië,* ed. P. A. van der Lith, A. J. Spaan, F. Fokkens, and Joh. F. Snelleman, 4 vols. (The Hague: Martinus Nijhoff; Leiden: E. J. Brill, 1905), 4:29–31.

2. Frederick, "Indonesian Urban Society," 16. *Indisch* is used by Frederick to refer to the mestizo lifestyle enjoyed by long-term European residents, Eurasians, and a small number of affluent Muslims. For a discussion of stambul as Indische theater, see chapter 5.

3. H. W. Dick, *Surabaya, City of Work: A Socioeconomic History, 1900–2000* (Athens: Ohio University Center for International Studies/Ohio University Press, 2002).

4. Frederick, "Indonesian Urban Society," 18.

5. On the dimensions of kampung life in Surabaya, see particularly William H. Frederick, "Hidden Change in Late Colonial Urban Society in Indonesia," *Journal of Southeast Asian Studies* 14, no. 2 (1983). 354–71.

6. See, e.g., *Soerabaija-Courant,* 15 June 1891.

7. Leslie H. Palmier, *Social Status and Power in Java* (London: Athlone Press, 1960), 108–9.

8. For a history of Surabaya's Chinese community, see Claudine Salmon, "La communuanté chinoise de Surabaya: Essai d'histoire, des origines à la crise de 1930," *Archipel* 53 (1997): 121–206.

9. Milone, "Queen of the East," 375.

10. Worsfold, *Visit to Java,* 70. Worsfold is actually describing Chinese houses in Batavia's Chinatown.

11. Von Faber, *Oud Soerabaia,* 79–80; "Soerabaja," in Van der Lith et al., *Encyclopaedie van Nederlandsch-Indië* 4:29–51.

12. For a nostalgic photo essay of colonial clubs, see Hein Buitenweg, *Soos en samenleving in tempo doeloe* (The Hague: Servire, 1966).

13. Cf. Ann Laura Stoler, *Carnal Knowledge and Imperial Power: Race and the Intimate in Colonial Rule* (Berkeley: University of California Press, 2002).

14. "Soerabaja," in *Uitkomsten der pauperisme-enquête,* 2 vols. (Batavia: Landsdrukkerij, 1902), 2:1–14.

15. Frederick, "Indonesian Urban Society," 15.

16. J. Helsloot, "St. Nicholas as a Public Festival in Java, 1870–1920: Articulating Dutch Popular Culture as Ethnic Culture," *Bijdragen tot de Taal-, Land- en Volkenkunde* 154, no. 4 (1998): 628.

17. See *Tjerimai,* 30 August 1905.

18. Cf. J. S. Furnivall, *Netherlands Indies: A Study of Plural Economy* (New York: Macmillan, 1944).

19. Von Faber, *Oud Soerabaia,* 333–36.

20. Peter Downes, *The Pollards: A Family and Its Child and Adult Opera Companies in New Zealand and Australia* (Aotearoa, New Zealand: Steele Roberts, 2002). On a demonstration of the kinetoscope by the Pollards in Singapore, see *Pinang Gazette and Straits Chronicle,* 24 April 1897.

21. Milone, "Queen of the East," 479.

22. Eliza Ruhamah Scidmore, *Java: The Garden of the East* (Singapore: Oxford University Press, 1986), 102. Scidmore's travelogue was originally serialized in the *Century* in 1897.

23. *Selompret Melajoe,* 16 April 1898.

24. On ludruk, see James L. Peacock, *Rites of Modernization: Symbolic and Social Aspects of Indonesian Proletarian Drama* (Chicago: University of Chicago Press, 1987).

25. For more on commercial wayang wong and its banning in western Java, see Matthew Isaac Cohen, "On the Origin of the Komedie Stamboel: Popular Culture, Colonial Society, and the Parsi Theatre Movement," *Bijdragen tot de Taal-, Land- en Volkenkunde* 157, no. 2 (2001): 313–57.

26. Scidmore, *Java,* 262.

27. At the Rebutan celebration, "lavish offerings of food were made on a platform to the ghosts of the dead, after which the assembled poor were permitted to climb up and seize the food, resulting in a disorderly rush (hence the name Rebutan or Free-for-all)," Susan Abeyasekere, *Jakarta: A History* (Singapore: Oxford University Press, 1989), 62.

28. Von Faber, *Oud Soerabaia,* 51.

29. *Bintang Soerabaia,* 21 November 1888.

30. *Bintang-Barat,* 31 October 1894.

31. For more on Yap Gwan Thay, see my forthcoming essay "A Chinese *Pujangga* from Surabaya? Yap Gwan Thay in an Age of Translation," in an anthology edited by Henri Chambert-Loir on translation in Indonesia and

the Malay world. Yap's name is spelled in many ways in press reports. I use standard Indonesian orthographic convention.

32. *Bintang Soerabaia,* 19 May 1899.

33. Lauw Giok Lan, "Oetjapannja Penjalin," in Victor Ido, *Karina-Adinda: Lelakon Komedie Hindia Timoer dalem Tiga Bagian,* trans. Lauw Giok Lan (Batavia: Tjing Koen Bie, 1913), ii.

34. Abisin Abbas, "Tooneel Indonesia," 15.

35. For a detailed exploration of the relation of Komedie Stamboel to the Parsi theater, see Cohen, "Komedie Stamboel."

36. Others emphasize the role that Malay-language Chinese opera played in establishing the commercial theater. See e.g., Abisin Abbas, "Tooneel Indonesia."

37. H. A. Salim, cited in Armijn Pane, "Dardanella," *Poedjangga Baroe* 1, no. 10 (1934): 381.

38. The Royal Theatre of Hyderabad, which played Batavia in May and June 1883, was described as "still a novelty," but this does not necessarily mean it was the first troupe of its sort. See *Java Bode,* 2 May 1883. Further investigation is needed of popular theater in the 1870s and 1880s.

39. A good introduction to Parsi theater is Somnath Gupt, "The Parsi Theatre: Its Origins and Development," trans. and ed. Kathryn Hansen, *Sangeet Natak* 36, no. 1 (2001): 3–31; no. 2 (2001): 3–29; nos. 3–4 (2001): 23–38.

40. *Bintang-Barat,* 3 October 1890. Wayang Parsi was the name used in Malaysia to refer to Parsi theater and Malay imitations. See Cantius Leo Camoens, "The Wayang Parsi, Tiruan Wayang Parsi, Komidi Melayu and the Bangsawan, 1887–1895," *Malaysia in History* 25 (1982): 1–20. It is not clear when wayang Parsi was first practiced in Indonesia, but likely it was after the 1883 performances of the Royal Theatre of Hyderabad. Wayang Parsi was not, in any case, being practiced in Java by 1890.

41. *Soerabaiasch-Handelsblad,* 16 January 1891.

42. A report that appeared later this same month notes that "one of the princes of the Komedie Stamboel is presently being judged by the Board of Justice for crimes against tram employees on 1 January of this year. A few of his fellow performers are being called as witnesses. The director will be present at the sessions." See *Soerabaija-Courant,* 24 January 1891. This suggests that the actors and Hartens were on good enough terms to see each other socially and ride the tram together.

43. Rob Nieuwenhuys cites in this regard a statistic computed in 1900 by the Netherlands Indies Teachers Society that 41.5 percent of "European" elementary school children spoke no Dutch, 29.3 percent a little, and only 29.2 percent spoke Dutch fluently. His conclusion: "Malay was *the* language of expression for most Eurasians, not Dutch." Nieuwenhuys, *Oost-Indische*

spiegel: Wat Nederlandse schrijvers en dichters over Indonesië hebben geschreven, vanaf de eerste jaren der Compagnie tot op heden (Amsterdam: Querido, 1972), 304; emphasis in original.

44. Abisin Abbas, "Tooneel Indonesia," 17.

45. *Soerabaiasch-Handelsblad,* 28 February 1891.

46. *Soerabaija-Courant,* 22 January 1891.

47. Ibid.

48. *Soerabaiasch-Handelsblad,* 22 January 1891.

49. Theodore G. Th. Pigeaud, *Literature of Java,* 4 vols. (The Hague: Martinus Nijhoff, 1967–80), 1:213.

50. Ibid., 257.

51. Mattani Mojdara Rutnin, *Dance, Drama, and Theatre in Thailand: The Process of Development and Modernization* (Bangkok: Silkworm, 1996).

52. Cohen, "Komedie Stamboel," 337.

53. "Whoever has read these chronicles will certainly not wish to stop reading, because one will want to know the end of this very fine story. The chronicle is well composed, and whoever read it can understand its meaning, because it is written accessibly." *Selompret Melajoe,* 9 October 1894.

54. Armijn Pane, "Keboedajaan sandiwara Indonesia," *Pandji Poestaka* 20, no. 37 (1942): 1330.

55. This play was known in Dutch as *Machmoed, of de visscher en de geest* and in Malay as *Tukang ikan sama jin.* Komedie Stamboel play titles were typically given in both languages, and the "same" play often had multiple designations. Malay and Dutch titles for all plays performed by the Komedie Stamboel in its first ten months of existence can be found in Cohen, "Komedie Stamboel."

56. *Soerabaiasch-Handelsblad,* 21 January 1891.

57. *Soerabaiasch-Handelsblad,* 19 January 1891; *Pembrita bahroe,* 20 January 1891.

58. *Soerabaiasch-Handelsblad,* 9 November 1891.

59. *Soerabaija-Courant,* 19 January 1891.

60. *Pembrita-Bahroe,* 20 January 1891.

61. *Soerabaija-Courant,* 19 January 1891.

62. *Pembrita-Bahroe,* 20 January 1891.

63. *Soerabaiasch-Handelsblad,* 9 November 1891.

64. The now-standard Indonesian word for rehearsal, *latihan,* is also quite rare in classical Malay texts; the root *latih* appears only once in the Malay Concordance Project's fifty-seven texts, in relation to military training.

65. *Soerabaija-Courant,* 19 January 1891.

66. The Malay word *stambul* also referred to that typical article of Turkish dress: the fez.

67. *Soerabaiasch-Handelsblad,* 9 November 1891.

68. The actor Tan Tjeng Bok used the term *ladon-diladon* in a 1971 interview. See Tan Tjeng Bok, interview by Haji Misbach Yusa Biran, tape recording, 27 March 1971, Sinematek Indonesia, Jakarta.

69. *Soerabaiasch-Handelsblad,* 21 January 1891.

70. The imminent "loss" of the Italian Quintet in November 1891, when an offer was made to play in Batavia with a guaranteed income of eight hundred guilders a month, was the cause of some anxiety to Surabaya's polite society: "Who will play at our bals champêtres?" See *Soerabaija-Courant,* 24 November 1891.

71. *Soerabaija-Courant,* 28 January 1891; *Soerabaiasch-Handelsblad,* 15 April 1891.

72. *Soerabaiasch-Handelsblad,* 22 January 1891; *Soerabaija-Courant,* 22 January 1891.

73. *Soerabaiasch-Handelsblad,* 21 January 1891.

74. *Soerabaiasch-Handelsblad,* 22 January 1891.

75. *Soerabaija-Courant,* 23 January 1891.

76. *Soerabaija-Courant,* 26 January 1891.

77. *Soerabaija-Courant,* 26 January 1891.

78. *Soerabaiasch-Handelsblad,* 27 January 1891.

79. *Soerabaija-Courant,* 23 January 1891.

80. *Hindia-Olanda,* 1 June 1894.

81. A. Th. Manusama identifies Yap Gwan Thay as the source of the loan and says that it was only with "great difficulty" that backing was obtained. Manusama, *Komedie Stamboel of de Oost-Indische Opera* (Weltevreden: Favoriet, 1922), 4. Knaap states that the loan was from a rich Arab and was obtained due to Auguste Mahieu's great eloquence. The loan, which Knaap states amounted to a few thousand guilders, was to be repaid with interest and was also conditional on a share of the profits. See Otto Knaap, "De Indische Antoine: Antoine Tardieu," *Bondsblad,* 18 July 1903, 25 July 1903.

82. Sophie Volpp, "The Literary Circulation of Actors in Seventeenth-Century China," *Journal of Asian Studies* 61, no. 3 (2002): 949.

83. Abeyasekere, *Jakarta,* 80.

84. "Tambahsia: Suwatu cerita yang betul sudah Kejadian di Betawi antara tahun 1851–1856," in Marcus and Benedanto, *Kesastraan Melayu Tionghoa* (1915; repr. 2002), 5:29.

85. *Bintang Betawi,* 13 August 1902.

86. *Bintang Soerabaia,* 13, 15 July 1891.

87. *Bintang-Barat,* 30 September 1890.

88. *Soerabaiasch-Handelsblad,* 31 January 1891; *Soerabaija-Courant,* 22 January 1891.

89. *Soerabaiasch-Handelsblad,* 16 March 1891.

90. Tan Sooi Beng makes a similar case for the development of bangsawan theater in Malaysia, arguing that the popular theater served as an open-access leisure alternative to the exclusive British clubs. Tan Sooi Beng, *Bangsawan: A Social and Stylistic History of Popular Malay Opera* (Singapore: Oxford University Press, 1993), 31.

91. *Soerabaija-Courant,* 3 February 1891.

92. *Soerabaiasch-Handelsblad,* 7 February 1891.

93. Nieuwenhuys, *Oost-Indische spiegel,* 303.

94. Others sometimes associated with the origin of the Komedie Stamboel are Djfar Turki (Jafar the Turk) and Kassim. The former was in fact the owner of a major stambul troupe active in the first two decades of the twentieth century. Tan Tjeng Bok, one of the most famous Indonesian actors of the late colonial period, worked in this company as a youth and recalls that Jafar was originally from the Malaysia and was of Turkish descent. The company was multiethnic, with Indo, Arab, Afrikaan, and Palembang actors, and had an amazing forty-nine painted curtains at its disposal. Tan Tjeng Bok, interview by Haji Misbach. Another source asserts that Jafar was originally from Medan. See Amir Pasaribu, *Musik dan selingkar wilajahnja* (Jakarta: Perpustakaan Perguruan, Kementerian P.P. dan K., 1955), 59. Kassim was a bangsawan troupe owner who attained prominence in the late 1890s: his significance in the development of stambul is discussed at length in chapter 5. There is no substantial evidence that either Jafar or Kassim had anything to do with the Komedie Stamboel's founding.

95. *Soerabaiasch-Handelsblad,* 28 February 1891.

96. Tan Sooi Beng, *Bangsawan,* 157.

97. Kusbini as cited and translated in Ernst Heins, "Kroncong and Tanjidor: Two Cases of Urban Folk Music in Jakarta," *Asian Music* 7, no. 1 (1975): 26.

98. R. M. Dumas, "Meerdere generaties van het geslacht Mahieu op Java," *Indische Navorscher* 15, no. 1 (2002): 1–6. I thank Dr. Dumas for his careful reading of my manuscript, and for providing additional information not (yet) contained in his publications.

99. Simon Winchester, *Krakatoa: The Day the World Exploded, 27 August 1883* (London: Viking, 2003), 46.

100. J. Fabricius, *Tempo doeloe: Uit de goeie ouwe tijd* (The Hague: H. P. Leopold, 1949), 76; Hein Buitenweg, "Komedie Stamboel," *Tong Tong* 12, no. 8 (1963): 9.

101. Elise gave birth to three more children while residing in Bangkalan. The first, Alex Oscar Theodorus Mahieu, was born on 31 March 1870.

Perhaps encouraged by his brother Auguste, Oscar Mahieu was an actor in Komedie Stamboel in the 1890s but took a job in 1902 in a sugar mill in Mojokerto. Oscar Mahieu died in Semarang in World War II and likely served as an informant for Andjar Asmara, who notes in a brief historical overview of Indonesian theater that he "received much valuable information" from a *sdr.* (an abbreviation for *saudara,* meaning either "relative" or "brother") of Auguste Mahieu living in Semarang. See Abisin Abbas, "Tooneel Indonesia."

102. For an overview of the history of Padang, see Freek Colombijn, *Patches of Padang: The History of an Indonesian Town in the Twentieth Century and the Use of Urban Space* (Leiden: CNWS, 1994).

103. Ch. E. P. van Kerckhoff, "Het Maleisch tooneel ter westkust van Sumatra," *Tijdschrift voor Indische Taal-, Land- en Volkenkunde uitgegeven door het Bataviaasch Genootschap van Kunsten en Wetenschappen* 31 (1888): 302–14. The complex relations of bangsawan theater with stambul will be explored at length below.

104. On Surabaya's HBS, see von Faber, *Oud Soerabaia,* 269–72.

105. Knaap, "Indische Antoine."

106. The year 1880 was the first year that girls were admitted to Surabaya's HBS: five of them entered the first year class. In the period 1875–1900, 1,052 students attended the school—with only two Javanese and four Chinese pupils amongst them.

107. Knaap, "Indische Antoine."

108. For a fascinating account of Kruseman's years in the Indies, see Olf Praamstra, *Een feministe in de tropen: De Indische jaren van Mina Kruseman* (Leiden: KITLV Press, 2003).

109. Dumas, "Meerdere generaties," 1.

110. Megenlijk subsequently left Surabaya to teach at Batavia's HBS. See G. H. von Faber, *Dingen die niet kloppen: Fictie en historie uit het oude Indië* (Surabaya: Nieuw Soerabaiasch Handelsblad, 1955), 110.

111. Newspaper reports refer to occasional dramatic events involving Surabaya HBS students.

112. *Bondsblad,* 5 October 1900; Manusama, *Komedie Stamboel,* 4.

113. *Bintang Betawi* 3 February 1903. Elsewhere the young Mahieu is characterized as "bohemian." Opa Samson, "Het lied van de Indo," *Tong Tong* 2, no. 21 (30 June 1958): 5.

114. Two sources published some decades after Mahieu's death corroborate that Mahieu held a government job. Opa Samson states that "Mahieu had completed five years of HBS. With his diploma, he obtained a good position from a government Department." See Samson, "Het Lied van de Indo," 5. See also Opa Samson, "De Stamboel," *Tong Tong* 3, no. 8 (30 October

1958): 4. Andjar Asmara states likewise that Mahieu "came out of HBS with skills in music and high aspirations in the field of theatre. Because of these aspirations, he quit his job in a government office in Surabaya and threw himself into the world of theatre." See Andjar Asmara, "Tonil Anak Negeri," *Pandji Poestaka* 13, no. 93 (22 November 1935): 1815.

115. *Bintang Soerabaia* 18 August 1891; *Pembrita-Bahroe,* 24 December 1891.

116. Abisin Abbas, "Tooneel Indonesia," 17.

117. T. R. [Tjalie Robinson], "Marie Oord had een eigen Indo 'Penny Opera," *Tong Tong* 12, nos. 11–12 (1967): 4.

118. For a fictionalized encounter with Mahieu (referred to as Reumer), see Victor Ido, *De paupers* (The Hague: Thomas and Eras, 1978). I discuss this novel in chapter 5.

119. Knaap, "Indische Antoine."

120. See *Soerabaiasch-Handelsblad,* 26 February 1891; *Soerabaija-Courant,* 26 February 1891. The latter story is also translated into Malay in *Pembrita-Bahroe,* 27 February 1891. In the translation, the director's name is noted as I. W. W. Seket, which may be a misprint.

121. *Soerabaiasch-Handelsblad,* 28 February 1891.

122. *Soerabaija-Courant,* 28 February 1891.

123. *Bintang Soerabaia,* 7 April 1894, 23 July 1894.

124. Christian August Vulpius's adventure novel *Rinaldo Rinaldini, der Räuberhauptmann* (Rinaldo Rinaldini, chief of the thieves), was translated into many languages and was a popular theatrical source throughout the nineteenth-century world.

125. *Pembrita-Bahroe,* 2 March 1891.

126. *Soerabaiasch-Handelsblad,* 26 February 1891.

127. *Pembrita-Bahroe,* 5 March 1891.

128. *Soerabaija-Courant,* 25 March 1891.

129. *Soerabaija-Courant,* 19 March 1891.

130. *Soerabaiasch-Handelsblad,* 19 Mar 1891.

131. This unnamed Parsi theatrical troupe did not actually appear.

132. *Soerabaiasch-Handelsblad,* 30 May 1891.

133. *Pembrita-Bahroe,* 14 August 1891.

134. *Java Bode,* 15 February 1893.

135. *Soerabaiasch-Handelsblad,* 1 September 1891.

136. Among the *Arabian Nights* plays mounted during the first weeks under Van der Laan were *The Fisherman and the Genie, Giafar,* and *Ali Baba.*

137. Cf. *Mataram,* 18 August 1892.

138. *Pembrita-Bahroe,* 21 September 1891.

139. Gounod's opera, with its libretto in French by Jules Barbier and Michel Carré (based on Goethe), was most likely Mahieu's direct source. This opera was often performed by itinerant companies, and its music and story were well known to lovers of elite culture.

140. *Pembrita Betawi,* repr. in *Bintang Soerabaia,* 13 August 1894. This article states explicitly that "the story is adapted from European opera."

141. *Soerabaiasch-Handelsblad,* 23 September 1891. "John Chinaman" was a racialist way to refer to the average Chinese man in nineteenth- and early twentieth-century discourse; the term is English in the original.

142. The Malay translation for *tableau vivant* is problematic. The earliest reference in Malay to a tableau vivant performed by the Komedie Stamboel speaks of *kasih tunjuk pigura* (lit., taking a look at a frame). See *Pembrita-Bahroe* 18 August 1891. Later on the term *gambaran hidup* (living picture) is sometimes employed, but more commonly the foreign term *tableau vivant* (often misspelled) would be used.

143. *Soerabaija-Courant,* 14 August 1891.

144. It is unclear which of the three *Prins Hendrik* steamships owned by the Stoomvaart Maatschappij Nederland was represented. For brief details of the three ships, built in 1871, 1874, and 1890, see Stoomvaart Maatschappij Nederland/Netherlands Steamship Co., http://www.theshipslist.com/ships/lines/nederland.htm.

145. Anita Callaway, *Visual Ephemera: Theatrical Art in Nineteenth-Century Australia* (Sydney: University of New South Wales Press, 2000), 73; Jack W. McCullough, *Living Pictures on the New York Stage* (Ann Arbor: UMI Research Press, 1986), chapter 8.

146. Hart entertained privileged visitors to Naples in a "secret art gallery" by impersonating antique Greco-Roman statues. One of these visitors to the ambassador's residence was Johann Wolfgang von Goethe, who was greatly impressed by the display of "attitudes" he witnessed in 1787. Goethe popularized the tableaux vivant in his novel *Die Wahlverwandtschaften* and a collaboration with Johann Heinrich Meyer at the Weimer court enacting paintings by Guérin and David and a new composition by Goethe featuring river gods, nymphs, fauns, Apollo, and the Muses. See Kirsten Gram Holmström, *Monodrama, Attitudes, Tableaux Vivants: Studies on Some Trends of Theatrical Fashion, 1770–1815* (Stockholm: Almquist and Wiksell, 1967).

147. Mary Chapman, "'Living Pictures': Women and *Tableaux Vivants* in Nineteenth Century American Fiction and Culture," *Wide Angle* 18, no. 3 (1996): 26.

148. Whitman, cited in Chapman, "Living Pictures," 25.

149. McCullough, *Living Pictures.*

150. Chapman, "Living Pictures," 30.

151. Davis, *Circus Age* (see introduction, note 34), 83–85.

152. McCullough, *Living Pictures.*

153. Callaway, *Visual Ephemera,* 60, 84.

154. C. G. van den Steen, head of Surabaya's foremost amateur theater club, the Vereeniging Apollo, made tableaux vivants her specialty. In 1883, some 8,000 guilders were spent to fit Surabaya's schouwburg with electrical lighting, largely to light Van den Steen's tableaux with focused lights. See von Faber, *Oud Soerabaia,* 344.

155. Cf. Schwartz, *Spectacular Realities* (see introduction, note 56). Also see Matthew Isaac Cohen, "Traditional and Popular Painting in Modern Java," *Archipel* 69 (2005): 5–38.

156. On the relation of forgery to the Komedie Stamboel, see my forthcoming essay "A Chinese Pujangga from Surabaya?"

157. *Bintang Soerabaia,* 1 September 1893.

158. *Pembrita Betawi,* 27 September 1895.

159. *Bataviaasch Nieuwsblad,* 20 April 1894.

160. Winchester, *Krakatoa.*

161. *Tjerimai,* 18 November 1893.

162. Samson, "Stamboel," 5.

163. *Soerabaija-Courant,* 9 February 1892; my emphasis.

164. I base myself particularly on *Tjerimai,* 15 November 1893; S. Kalff, "Een avond in de 'Komedie Stamboul,'" *Indië* 2 (1918–19): 757–78; Manusama, *Komedie Stamboel.* Kalff's essay was originally published in *Java Bode,* 15 February 1893.

165. On this practice for New York tableaux vivants, see McCullough, *Living Pictures,* 25.

166. S. Kalff, "Avond in de 'Komedie Stamboul.'" Spectators of Javanese wayang kulit also tend to disperse before the formulaic ending scenes.

167. *Pembrita-Bahroe,* 21 September 1891.

168. See C. Fasseur, "Cornerstone and Stumbling Block," in *The Late Colonial State in Indonesia: Political and Economic Foundations of the Netherlands Indies, 1880–1942,* ed. Robert Cribb (Leiden: KITLV Press, 1994), 31–56.

169. An early ad promises to "create various sorts of peoples as they existed in the past as tableaux vivants." See *Pembrita-Bahroe,* 19 August 1891.

170. Hydrochloric acid mixed with a copper salt is used in theater to produce blue-green flame for special effects.

171. *Soerabaija-Courant,* 24 October 1891.

172. *Bintang Soerabaia,* 2 November 1891.

173. *Soerabaiasch-Handelsblad,* 21 October 1891.

174. Both resident and bupati were in fact Dutch-appointed offices. The bupati, charged with overseeing Native affairs at the level of the regency,

was responsible to the resident. But the bupati's noble descent and connections to the royal houses of central Java and Madura, made him an object of veneration to the populace. Many residents also affected Indonesian noble trappings and status markers.

175. See J. F. van Bemmelen and G. B. Hooyer, *Guide to the Dutch East Indies Composed by Invitation of the Koninklyke Paketvaart Maatschappij (Royal Steam Packet Company),* trans. B. J. Berrington (Batavia: Kolff; London: Luzac, 1897), 73. See also "Pasoeroean," in Van der Lith et al., *Encyclopaedie van Nederlandsch-Indië,* 3:236.

176. Louis Couperus, *The Hidden Force,* trans. A. T. de Mattos (London: Quartet, 1992), 45.

177. *Soerabaija-Courant,* 22 August 1891. The Malay translation of this phrase, *cobalah dateng liat adanya,* was less commonly employed.

178. *Bintang Soerabaia,* 22 August 1891.

179. *Soerabaiasch-Handelsblad,* 25 August 1891; *Pembrita-Bahroe,* 28 August 1891.

180. *Pembrita-Bahroe,* 28 August 1891.

181. It is possible that the number of seats was exaggerated; later reports refer to an audience capacity of around six hundred.

182. Booth and Heckenberg, "Touring the Empire," 56.

183. *Soerabaiasch-Handelsblad,* 24 October 1891.

184. Mahieu had previously functioned as a temporary substitute for Van der Laan in October when Van der Laan was serving a jail sentence for absenteeism from his civil guard job in early October.

185. *Soerabaiasch-Handelsblad,* 9 November 1891.

Chapter 2

1. Lit., "There are as many opinions as leaders." *Soerabaiasch-Handelsblad,* 25 November 1891.

2. Onghokham, "The Residency of Madiun: Priyayi and Peasant in the Nineteenth Century" (Ph.D. diss., Yale University, 1975).

3. Madiun performances were avidly reported by the numerous Madiun correspondents who wrote for newspapers in Semarang, Batavia, Surabaya, and elsewhere. The large troupes preferentially played the alun-alun; smaller companies erected tents in empty lots and performed in fenced-off enclosures (*gerbungan*) adjacent to the central market.

4. Scidmore, *Java,* 253–62.

5. Ibid., 252.

6. *Djawi Kondo,* repr. in *Bintang Soerabaia,* 8 December 1891.

7. *Selompret Melajoe,* 19 December 1891; *Bintang Soerabaia,* 12 December 1891.

8. This north-coastal rail line was extended to Juwana later in the 1890s.

9. On colonial Semarang, see B. Brommer, E. Budihardjo, A. B. Montens, S. Setiadi, A. Sidharta, A. Siswanto, Soewarno, and Th. Stevens, *Semarang: Beeld van een stad* (Purmerend: Asia Maior, 1995). For a rich online collection of colonial Semarang images, including a number of late nineteenth-century images, see Semarang Photo Archives, http://www.semarang.nl.

10. The economic and social history of Semarang's Chinese community is chronicled in Liem Thian Joe, *Riwajat Semarang* (Semarang: Ho Kim Yoe, 1933).

11. An important portrait of the cabang atas and the opium trade more generally is to be found in James R. Rush, *Opium to Java: Revenue Farming and Chinese Enterprise in Colonial Indonesia, 1860–1910* (Ithaca: Cornell University Press, 1990). Rush derives the designation *cabang atas* from Liem Thian Joe.

12. For a fascinating portrait of Oei Tiong Ham and his times, see Onghokham, "Chinese Capitalism in Dutch Java," in *The Thugs, The Curtain Thief, and the Sugar Lord: Power, Politics, and Culture in Colonial Java* (Jakarta: Metafor, 2003), 181–223.

13. Cf. Rush, *Opium to Java,* 249.

14. There is no record of the schouwburg shows actually occurring, and it is possible that the Semarang Chinese sponsors did not fulfill this part of the arrangement.

15. *Bintang Betawi,* repr. in *Bintang Soerabaia,* 31 December 1891.

16. *Soerabaija-Courant,* 22 January 1892.

17. See *Soerabaiasch-Handelsblad,* 26 January 1893. Providing advance moneys remains a standard way for Javanese troupe owners to insure that actors and musicians remain with a company. Only after this debt is fully paid off are performers free to leave.

18. *Bintang Soerabaia,* 9 March 1892.

19. "Sair Balon," in *Pembrita-Bahroe,* 11 January 1892.

20. *Soerabaija-Courant,* 13 January 1892.

21. *Bintang Soerabaia,* 27 January 1892. It is common in Java for sacred objects to be presented with offerings at monthly or yearly intervals, as well as before their use.

22. This appears to be a printing error; the text should read "Wednesday and Sunday," not "Wednesday and Thursday."

23. *Soerabaija-Courant,* 24 February 1892.

24. *Bintang Soerabaia,* 23 February 1892.

25. *Bintang Soerabaia,* 3 February 1892. The suggestion to use live music might have been inspired by circus parades.

26. *Pembrita-Bahroe,* 30 December 1891.

27. Ibid.; *Soerabaija-Courant,* 10 March 1892; *Bintang Soerabaia,* 21, 29 January 1892; *Soerabaija-Courant,* 29 January 1892.

28. *De Vorstenlanden,* 24 December 1870, cited in Anthony Day, "Ranggawarsita's Prophecy of Mystery," in *Moral Order and the Question of Change: Essays on Southeast Asian Thought,* ed. David K. Wyatt and Alexander Woodside (New Haven: Yale University Southeast Asia Studies, 1982), 217.

29. Calabressini is noteworthy as one of the first showmen to demonstrate the phonograph on public stages in the Netherlands Indies.

30. See, e.g., *De Locomotief,* 22 October 1895.

31. *Bintang Soerabaia,* 13 July 1891.

32. Calabressini's magic lantern and associated plates were subsequently purchased for six hundred guilders by Yap Gwan Thay, who used them for early-evening magic lantern shows for children in 1892 and 1893.

33. *Soerabaija-Courant,* 31 July 1893. This article actually discusses a Kapasan performance of the Komedie Spanjool, another stambul troupe owned by Yap Gwan Thay, which was at the time managed by actress-manager Brouwer. But the technology, genre, theater, and audience are identical to those of the Komedie Stamboel.

34. *Pembrita-Bahroe,* 12 March 1892.

35. *Pembrita-Bahroe,* 27 January 1892. *Sambeyan* appears to be an alternate spelling for *sanxian,* a long-necked lute with three strings particularly popular in northern China. It can project loudly, has a wide range, and is extensively used for accompanying folk song, opera, and other musical genres.

36. *Bintang Soerabaia,* 16 January 1892; *Bintang Soerabaia,* 1 February 1892.

37. *Bintang Soerabaia,* 9 March 1892; *Soerabaiasch-Handelsblad,* 5 February 1892; *Bintang Soerabaia,* 1 March 1892; *Soerabaija-Courant,* 15 March 1892.

38. *Pembrita-Bahroe,* 16 February 1892.

39. The quote is from *Soerabaija-Courant,* 9 January 1892, and the other comment from *Soerabaija-Courant,* 19 January 1892. The former is from an ad for *Brahmin, or Unwavering Love,* the latter for *The Roc's Egg.* Other names that appear in reviews and notices at this time are the comic actors Lassiak and his wife E. Rensing, and also an actress named Hofman.

40. *Selompret Melajoe* as cited in *Pembrita-Bahroe,* 4 April 1892.

41. *Bintang Soerabaia,* 20 May 1892.

42. *Bintang Soerabaia,* 25 May 1892.

43. See, for example, the advertisement in *Mataram,* 4 August 1892. Neither Dinsbach nor Lassing appear in notices after the company left on tour in June 1892, and nothing more is heard of them.

44. Yap's various enterprises were cross-linked, as was commonly the case for the cabang atas (highest branch) of Indonesian Chinese. See Rush, *Opium to Java,* 98–107.

45. *Bintang Soerabaia,* 23 June 1892.

46. *Bintang-Barat,* 25 July 1892.

47. *Selompret Melajoe,* 30 July 1892.

48. Scidmore, *Java,* 266–77.

49. *Mataram,* 4 August 1892.

50. "Pertjakepan Petroeq dan Soroito," in *Selompret Melajoe,* 13 August 1892. Petroeq (spelled Petruk in contemporary Indonesia) and Soroito (also spelled Saraita) are both clown servants in wayang kulit. Dialogues between the clown-servants of the wayang kulit theater are often featured in colonial newspapers. The clowns commonly reported on local events, and spoke directly for the author and his circle. Wilson's Circus, under the direction of Anna Wilson, toured Indonesia in 1883 to great acclaim.

51. Claudine Salmon, "The Batavian Eastern Railway Co. and the Making of a New 'Daerah' as Reflected in a Commemorative Syair Written by Tan Teng Kie (1890)," *Indonesia* 45 (1988): 49–62.

52. *Bintang Soerabaia,* 17 August 1892; Tan Tjiook San, ed., "Sair Komedi Stamboel" in *Almanak bahasa Melajoe boeat taoen 1893* (Yogyakarta: H. Buning, 1892), 256–73.

53. Tan Tjiook San, "Sair Komedi Stamboel," 256–73.

54. Ibid., 261–62.

55. Ibid., 256.

56. Ibid., 258.

57. *Mataram,* 11 August 1892.

58. Seating royalty onstage during dramatic performances was a common practice of the time in European theater. Joseph R. Roach has argued that "stage spectators acted the roles of an ideal or surrogate audience. The public wanted to enjoy their enjoyment, seeking in their responses a reaffirmation or perhaps a correction of their own." Roach, *Cities of the Dead: Circum-Atlantic Performance* (New York: Columbia University Press, 1996), 164.

59. *Mataram,* 11 August 1892.

60. *Bintang Soerabaia,* 24 August 1892.

61. *Mataram,* 23 August 1892.

62. Tan Tjiook San, "Sair Komedi Stamboel," 271.

63. *Mataram,* 23 August 1892.

64. Tan Tjiook San, "Sair Komedi Stamboel," 279–80.

65. Women from military families made particularly good actresses; one stambul actress working for the Komedie Rusticana (Liem Kiem

Swie, owner) in 1902 was said to be an able actress, as "she formerly often associated with the families of officers, so that she came to understand the norms for performing komedi." See *Bintang Soerabaia,* 31 October 1902.

66. It is likely that the Ambon militia's play was based on the Komedie Stamboel's *Abuhassan, the Sleeper Awakened,* an *Arabian Nights* play.

67. *Selompret Melajoe,* 24 November 1892.

68. For example, *De Locomotief* suggested that the management provide better chairs for the loge and first-class seats, as those initially available were "a real torture" to sit on after a few hours. The management acted on this suggestion the same day the article appeared, replacing the chairs by that evening's performance. See *De Locomotief,* 5 September 1892; *Selompret Melajoe,* 6 September 1892.

69. See *De Locomotief,* 11, 29 August 1892. After Indonesia's independence the main street of Blakang Kebon became known as Jalan Imam Bonjol.

70. Cf. *De Locomotief,* 13 September 1892.

71. *Bintang Soerabaia,* 1 September 1892.

72. *De Locomotief,* 10 September 1892.

73. *Selompret Melajoe,* 27 August 1892; *De Locomotief,* 13 September 1892. Yap's investment figures were widely cited after being reported in *De Locomotief.* If accurate, it is likely that the figure of one hundred thousand guilders included the cost of constructing the Kapasan theater. A more sober estimate of Yap's investment in the Komedie Stamboel figured it at forty thousand guilders—including the Kapasan theater and its accoutrements, tents, costumes and props, and advance monies to the actors.

74. See advertisement in *De Locomotief,* 29 August 1892.

75. *De Locomotief,* 25 August 1892.

76. *De Locomotief,* 26 August 1892.

77. *Selompret Melajoe,* 30 August 1892.

78. *Selompret Melajoe,* 13 September 1892.

79. *Selompret Melajoe,* 3 September 1892.

80. *Selompret Melajoe,* 6 September 1892.

81. *Selompret Melajoe,* 15 September 1892.

82. *Selompret Melajoe,* 22 September 1892.

83. *Selompret Melajoe,* repr. in *Bintang Soerabaia,* 16 September 1892.

84. *Selompret Melajoe,* 6 October 1892.

85. *Selompret Melajoe,* cited in *Bintang Soerabaia,* 15 October 1892.

86. This version is from *Selompret Melajoe,* 13 October 1892. Simons's name is spelled Simens in some accounts.

87. On Lien Gemser, see chapter 4.

88. Scidmore, *Java,* 25.

89. Milone, "Queen of the East," 262.

90. *Soerabaiasch-Handelsblad,* 17 January 1891.

91. Ibid.

92. *Bintang-Barat,* 29 January 1891.

93. *Bintang-Barat,* 29 September 1892.

94. *Bataviaasch Nieuwsblad,* 17 October 1892. The play in question is *Siti Senimbar.*

95. *Bintang-Barat,* 4 October 1892.

96. Ahmat B. Adam, *The Vernacular Press and the Emergence of Modern Indonesian Consciousness (1855–1913)* (Ithaca: Southeast Asia Program, Cornell University, 1995), 32.

97. The *Courant Deminggoe dari pada Bintang Barat,* a Sunday supplement to *Bintang-Barat* that began publication in 1894, was Indonesia's first Malay-language literary magazine, with feature articles of general interests, poems, short stories, and serialized novels.

98. Suggestions included lowering the ticket prices, providing complimentary tickets for police officers, moving the buffet farther from the auditorium to avoid noise spillover, and using brighter stage lights.

99. *Bintang-Barat,* 6 October 1892.

100. *Hindia-Olanda,* 13 October 1892. Kieffer and Wiggers left *Bintang-Barat* in 1893. The newspaper came under new ownership in 1894, and in years to come little attention was paid to Malay-language theater.

101. Mangga Besar (sometimes spelled Manga Besar) was known in Dutch as Prinsenlaan.

102. Augusta de Wit, *Java: Facts and Fancies* (Oxford: Oxford University Press, 1985), 48–51.

103. *Bintang-Barat,* 28 September 1892. Abdul Muluk was a popular Malay theater that was introduced to western Java from Kalimantan or Sumatra in the 1870s, banned by police for the licentious behavior of female fans in 1882, but performed in the open again by the mid-1890s. According to one source, Abdul Muluk theater (also known as Dermuluk) was performed in Batavia until the 1930s. See Nirwanto Ki S. Hendrowinoto, H. S. Djuratap, Susianna D. Soeratman, H. Anwar Tandjung, *Seni budaya Betawi menggiring zaman* (Jakarta: Dinas Kebudayaan DKI Jakarta, 1998), 118–19. On Abdul Muluk theater in Sumatra, see Robert Martin Dumas, *Teater Abdulmuluk in Zuid-Sumatra op de drempel van een nieuw tijdperk* (Leiden: CNWS, 2000).

104. *Bintang-Barat,* 7 October 1892.

105. *Java Bode,* 1 October 1892.

106. *Bintang-Barat,* 4 October 1892.

107. Ibid.

108. *Bataviaasch Nieuwsblad,* 6 October 1892.

109. *Bataviaasch Nieuwsblad,* 1 October 1892.

110. *Bintang-Barat,* 6 October 1892.

111. *Hindia-Olanda,* 5 October 1892.

112. *Bintang-Barat,* 7 October 1892.

113. *Pembrita Betawi,* repr. in *Bintang Soerabaia,* 17 October 1892.

114. *Bintang-Barat,* 14 October 1892.

115. *Bintang-Barat,* 4 October 1892; *Bintang-Barat,* 15 October 1892.

116. It is possible that the Komedie Stamboel gave a one-off performance in the schouwburg on 14 or 15 October 1892 as a charity benefit for Batavia's poorhouses, before opening in Gambir. But details are vague on this. See *Bintang-Barat,* 12 October 1892.

117. De Wit, *Java,* 30.

118. De Haan, *Oud Batavia,* 602–3 (see introduction, note 23).

119. *Bintang Soerabaia,* 17 October 1892.

120. *Bintang-Barat,* 6 October 1892.

121. *Bintang-Barat,* 24 October 1892.

122. De Wit, *Java,* 183.

123. Scidmore, *Java,* 49.

124. De Wit, *Java,* 183.

125. Van Bemmelen and Hooyer, *Dutch East Indies,* 29.

126. *Bintang-Barat,* 17 November 1892.

127. *Tjerimai,* 15 November 1893.

128. Ibid. The two plays announced by Moll are *Fathul Achmat, or The Faust of Arabia* and *Ali and the Magic Violin.*

129. *Bintang Betawi,* 24 June 1902; emphasis in original.

130. *Bintang-Barat,* 1 December 1892.

131. *Bintang-Barat,* 7 December 1892.

132. Ibid.

133. On this point, see also G. H. von Faber, "Van Krontjonglied tot 'Lagu Modern,'" *Cultureel Nieuws* 9 (1951): 28.

134. *Mataram,* Thurs 11 August 1892.

135. *Selompret Melajoe,* 27 October 1892.

136. *Bintang-Barat,* 18 November 1892.

Chapter 3

1. *Soerabaiasch-Handelsblad,* 9 March 1893.

2. *Soerabaiasch-Handelsblad,* 8 February 1893.

3. *Bintang-Barat,* 11 February 1893.

4. *De Locomotief,* 1 November 1894. For a summary of *Laeli,* see *Pembrita Betawi,* repr. in *Bintang Soerabaia,* 20 July 1894.

5. Justus van Maurik, *Indrukken van een 'totok': Indische typen en schetsen* (Amsterdam: Van Holkema and Warendorf, 1897), 126. Maurik purports to describe "a Malay opera, a so-called Comédie Stamboul," but in fact is discussing a bangsawan troupe from peninsular Malaysia.

Both "Daisy Bell" (also known as "A Bicycle Built for Two") and "Ting-a-Ling-Ting-Tay" are British music hall songs written by Harry Dacre in 1892. "Champagne Charlie" is another perennially popular British music hall song, with words by George Leybourne and music by Alfred Lee, composed in 1867. "Die Wacht am Rhein" (The watch on the Rhine), composed in 1840 by Max Schneckenburger, was adopted as Germany's national anthem in 1922. "Wilhelmus van Nassouwe" is a sixteenth-century Dutch nationalist song, commonly played at state occasions in the Netherlands and its colonies.

The characterization of Van Maurik's book as "chummy and banal" is from Rob Nieuwenhuys, *Mirror of the Indies: A History of Dutch Colonial Literature,* trans. Frans van Rosevelt (Singapore: Periplus, 1999), 141.

6. Katherine K. Preston, *Opera on the Road: Traveling Opera Troupes in the United States, 1825–1860* (Urbana: University of Illinois Press, 1993), 13.

7. Cf. Preston, *Opera on the Road,* 16. For a musically sensitive account of a stambul adaptation of Richard Wagner's *Lohengrin,* see Een Habitué, "Lohengrin in de Komedie-Stamboel," *Tong Tong* 6, no. 12 (30 December 1961): 7. Harry Dacre's popular song "Daisy Bell" (1892) is interpolated into this *Lohengrin* due to technical problems in getting the swan onstage.

8. *Soerabaiasch-Handelsblad,* 29 March 1893; *Soerabaiasch-Handelsblad,* 30 March 1893.

9. *Java Bode,* 1 October 1892.

10. Kalff revised his essay a quarter of a century later for publication in *Indië,* a photo journal published in the Dutch city of Haarlem, under the title "Een avond in de 'Komedie Stamboul.'" The description of the play remains substantially the same, though the framing and general tone is not—it is rewritten in a mood of nostalgia, gently describing a cultural scene of the past. The loose translation that follows below incorporates elements of the revised essay as well as the original publication. I discuss revisions Kalff made to his 1893 essay in chapter 5, below.

11. Ibid., 757.

12. Ibid., 758.

13. On the celebration of St. Nicholas Day in Java, see Helsloot, "St. Nicholas as Public Festival" (see ch. 1, n. 16).

14. Abubakar later became the manager of the famous Wayang Yap Chow Thong troupe. See Tan Sooi Beng, *Bangsawan,* 28.

15. Bangsawan companies toured extensively in Sumatra and Borneo in the 1880s, but do not appear as regular visitors to Java. See Matthew Isaac Cohen, "Border Crossings: Bangsawan in the Netherlands Indies in the Nineteenth and Early Twentieth Centuries," *Indonesia and the Malay World* 30, no. 87 (2002): 101–15.

16. A. H. Edrus, *Drama dan perkembangan bahasa Melayu,* vol. 3 of *Persuratan Melayu* (Singapore: Qalam, 1960).

17. Wilkinson, *Malay-English Dictionary,* 1:81; Edrus, *Drama;* Camoens, "Wayang Parsi," 2, 5, 8, 14–17.

18. *Bintang Soerabaia,* 13 March 1893.

19. *Soerabaiasch-Handelsblad,* 4, 6 March 1893.

20. *Bintang Soerabaia,* 25 May 1893.

21. Abubakar's company was only the first of a number of Malaysian companies to play the Kapasan theater in 1893. Less successful was the Komedie Hajji Mohamat Lanang, which played at Kapasan in April 1893. This company was deemed inferior to Abubakar's as "the actresses are as [dark-skinned as] Papuans and not a single one of them is attractive." See *Bintang Soerabaia,* 11 April 1893. It is possible that Mohamat Lanang's unprepossessing company folded in Surabaya and that Sri Soerabaia subsequently absorbed actors and musicians from it. (Mergers and takeovers of this sort were common in years to come.)

22. *Djawi-Kando,* 24 October 1893; *Bintang Soerabaia,* 1 August 1893.

23. Marmoyo is a character in the Menak story cycle who stole the clothes of a bathing woman at Sendang. This same device of stealing the clothes of women while they bathe is also famously associated with the tale of Jaka Tarub.

24. *Djawi-Kando,* 24 October 1893.

25. Van der Laan himself remained active in Malay theater for years to come, directing the short-lived multiethnic Djangan Loepa Kita (Don't forget us) company owned by The Swi Liang (sometimes also referred to as Tan Swi Liang) in 1896; acting in the Sri Stamboul company in 1896; and directing Komedie Opera Zoetelief in 1899.

26. A. van Schaik, *Malang: Beeld van een stad* (Purmerend: Asia Maior, 1996), 22.

27. Van Bemmelen and Hooyer, *Dutch East Indies,* 84; "Malang," in Van der Lith et al., *Encyclopaedie van Nederlandsch-Indië,* 2:452.

28. The characterization of Malang's alun-alun as splendid is from Van Bemmelen and Hooyer, *Dutch East Indies,* 84.

29. Presumably Jagalan was the area of Malang where the company rented a house as a dormitory.

30. This book was likely of the same sort available in Malang. It is described as a *syair hal laku-lakunya komedie stamboel* (poem about the actions of the Komedie Stamboel) and might in fact have been a poetic description of the plays performed. See *Djawi-Kando,* 2 May 1893.

31. *Djawi-Kando,* 19 May 1893.

32. *Selompret Melajoe,* 11 May 1893.

33. This sort of eclectic instrumental ensembles was common in central Java in the past. See Sumarsam, *Gamelan: Cultural Interaction and Musical Development in Central Java* (Chicago: University of Chicago Press, 1995), 36, 83, passim.

34. On Chinese-sponsored tayuban, see Clara Brakel-Papenhuyzen, "Javanese talèdhèk and Chinese tayuban," *Bijdragen tot de Taal-, Land- en Volkenkunde* 151, no. 4 (1995): 545–69.

35. *Bintang Soerabaia,* March 1893.

36. *Selompret Melajoe,* 27 June 1893.

37. *Bintang Soerabaia,* 18 July 1893.

38. *Bintang Soerabaia,* 19 February 1894.

39. *Bintang-Barat,* 16 April 1894.

40. *Bintang Soerabaia,* 21 November 1894.

41. On Tan Hoe Lo, with particular reference to his personal account of an 1889 visit to Europe, see Claudine Salmon, "Le voyage du Marchand Tan Hoe Lo à Paris (1889)," *Archipel* 54 (1997): 177–88.

42. *Bintang-Barat,* 17 April 1896.

43. *Bintang-Barat,* 28 May 1898.

44. *Pembrita Betawi,* 10 January 1895. "Stambul Bunga Mawar" was likely a song from the Komedie Stamboel's production of *Sleeping Beauty,* while "Stambul Aladdin" similarly likewise derived from its *Aladdin.*

45. *Selompret Melajoe,* 20 May 1893.

46. *Mataram,* 29 May 1893.

47. *Bintang Soerabaia,* 22 June 1893.

48. One of the reasons for Harmston's failure to draw crowds was that it did not allow Chinese spectators to sit in the fifty-cent bleacher seats, reserving these exclusively for Muslims. Chinese spectators reasoned that it would be better to spend one guilder and get a seat at the Komedie Stamboel than spend one guilder and sit in the bleachers at the circus.

49. *Bintang Soerabaia,* 22 June 1893.

50. *Bintang Soerabaia,* 3 July 1893.

51. Stuart Robson and Singgih Wibisono, *Javanese-English Dictionary* (Singapore: Periplus, 2002), 120.

52. This is of course the same as *Ali Baba and the Forty Thieves.*

53. For a lively description of semiprofessional stambul shows in the 1930s, see E. V. Solomon, "The Krontjong: Java's Ukelele," *Lloyd Mail* 3, no. 6 (1933): 237.

54. *Bintang-Barat,* 14 March 1893.

55. H. Krafft, *Boekoe Komidi Terpake bagi Komidi Stamboel* (Batavia: Regina Orientis, 1893), i–ii.

56. *Bintang-Barat,* 13 July 1893.

57. *Bintang-Barat,* 8 July 1893.

58. *Bintang-Barat,* 24 July 1893.

59. *Djawi-Kando,* 18 July 1893.

60. *Bintang Soerabaia,* 18 July 1893.

61. *Bintang-Barat,* 25 July 1893.

62. *Bintang-Barat,* 17 July 1893.

63. *Advertentieblad voor Tegal en Omstreken,* 19 September 1894.

64. *Bintang-Barat,* 17 July 1893.

65. Widow Twankey is the name of Aladdin's mother in British panto. The role is normally played in panto as a "dame," a male in extravagant drag, but in the Komedie Stamboel, Aladdin's mother was played by a woman.

66. *Mataram,* 11 August 1892; *Bintang-Barat,* 10 October 1892; *Bintang-Barat,* 25 February 1892.

67. *Bataviaasch Nieuwsblad,* 6 July 1893.

68. *Bintang-Barat,* 14 July 1893. This article graphically illustrates the hybrid nature of the Komedie Stamboel's mythology. It refers to Adam and Eve as *nabi* (prophets), consistent with Islamic terminology, but depicts them as being in a state of undress prior to the Fall (the Judeo-Christian version of the myth), while in Islamic tellings of the Adam and Even tale, they are fully clothed before the Expulsion and are degraded with a loss of clothing with the Fall. The "Adam and Eve" production seems never to have materialized, though the tableau vivant "Adam and Eve Driven from Paradise" was frequently performed.

69. *Bataviaasch Nieuwsblad,* 6 July 1893.

70. *Bintang-Barat,* 17, 31 July 1893.

71. *Bintang Soerabaia,* 1 August 1893.

72. *Bintang Soerabaia,* 3 August 1893.

73. *Bintang-Barat,* 20 July 1893.

74. *Bintang-Barat,* 21 July 1893.

75. *Soerabaija-Courant,* 29 July 1893; *Bintang Soerabaia,* 1 August 1893.

76. There is a substantial literature on kroncong. Some of the more important sources include A. Th. Manusama, *Krontjong als muziekinstrument,*

als melodie en als gezang (Batavia: G. Kolff, 1919); Rosalie Grooss, *De krontjong guitaar* (The Hague: Tong Tong, 1972); Kusbini, *Sedjarah kehidupan-perkembangan dan asal-usul seni musik kerontjong Indonesia dengan demonstrasi dalam kata-nada-rupa* (Yogyakarta: Sanggar Olah Seni Indonesia, 1972); Judith Becker, "Kroncong, Indonesian Popular Music," *Asian Music* 7, no. 1 (1975): 14–19; Heins, "Kroncong and Tanjidor" (see ch. 1, n. 97); Bronia Kornhauser, "In Defense of Kroncong," in *Studies in Indonesian Music,* ed. Margaret J. Kartomi (Centre of Southeast Asian Studies, Monash University, 1978), 104–83; and Margaret J. Kartomi, "Portuguese Influence on Indonesian Music," in *Festschrift Christoph-Hellmut Mahling,* ed. Axel Beer, Kristina Pfarr, and Wolfgang Ruf (Tutzing: Schneider, 1997), 657–66.

77. Pranga (also written *prounga*), marisku (also written *moresco*), and dangsu cikote are all subgenres of kroncong music. On the first two subgenres, see esp., Manusama, *Krontjong als muziekinstrument.*

78. *Bintang-Barat,* 14 February 1893.

79. Kornhauser, "In Defense of Kroncong," 155.

80. On the significance of stambul troupes in the popularization of kroncong, see esp. von Faber, "Van Krontjonglied tot 'Lagu Modern,'" (see ch. 2, n. 127); Kornhauser, "In Defense of Kroncong," 131–32.

81. Samson, "Stamboel," 4. "Dirk" here is Dirk van Sprew and "Bram" is Bram Wagner, both members of Mahieu's company in 1900.

82. Kusbini, *Sedjarah kehidupan.*

83. It is not evident why only Batavia instituted such permit fees. E. de Waal suggests that since it was mostly Chinese sponsors who were taxed, the smaller Chinese populations of Semarang, Batavia, and other cities did not make instituting a tax worthwhile. De Waal, *Aanteekeningen over koloniale onderwerpen,* 3 vols. (The Hague: Martinus Nijhoff, 1863), 1:435. Another argument made was that while multiracial Batavia would always have a variety of entertainments, with or without permit fees, the institution of fees outside Batavia would reduce the number of performances to such a degree that the "Natives" would turn to even more contemptible forms of entertainment, particularly gambling. On this point, see *Bintang Betawi,* 23 July 1901.

84. Abdul Muluk had been banned in Batavia in 1882, and Wayang Wong in 1890, on moral grounds. Both were said to have exerted deleterious influences on families. Marriages were ruined due to the infatuation of women with Abdul Muluk's male actors, while both men and women fell for the attractive wayang wong actor-dancers. Officially, these two performance bans were still in place in 1893.

85. Michael Theophile Hubert Perelaer, *Baboe Dalima, or The Opium Fiend,* trans. E. J. Venning (London: Vizetelly, 1888 [1886]), 87–88 (ch. 7).

86. See Waal, *Koloniale onderwerpen,* 1:433. Batavia's authorities went so far as to forbid wayang performances to be held in the vicinity of gambling tents in 1901 to protect vulnerable Muslims from the vice of gambling. *Bintang Betawi* argued that it should be gambling that is prohibited, not theater, and that in fact Muslims were more likely to attend topeng, wayang kulit, and bangsawan than Chinese opera. See *Bintang Betawi,* 28 October 1901.

87. Statute Book 1849, no. 52, art. 20, sect. T. The quote from this article is from Waal, *Koloniale onderwerpen,* 1:435.

88. This regulation is found in Statute Book 1862, no. 126, which is a clarification of Statute Book 1849, no 52, sect. L. See Waal, *Koloniale onderwerpen,* 1:432–33.

89. On this point, and on the nature of revenue farms in general, see Rush, *Opium to Java.*

90. *Pembrita Betawi,* 2 October 1895; *Djawi-Kando,* 22 December 1898.

91. Liem Thian Joe, *Riwajat Semarang* (see ch. 2, n. 10). The opium farm was by far the most valued revenue farm of nineteenth-century Java; farm fees regularly ran into the eight digits. See Rush, *Opium to Java,* 44.

92. *Bintang-Barat,* 10 October 1883.

93. *Bintang-Barat,* 27 July 1893. There is a noteworthy tendency for the company to use the designation Opera Stamboel or Komedie Opera Stamboel when in Batavia, but a preference for the familiar Komedie Stamboel when playing elsewhere. I thus continue to refer to the company as the Komedie Stamboel below.

94. *Bataviaasch Nieuwsblad,* 29 July 1893; *Selompret Melajoe,* 10 August 1893.

95. *Bintang Soerabaia,* 23 March 1894.

96. *Pembrita Betawi,* 29 July 1895.

97. *Tjerimai,* 18 November 1893.

98. Karen Sri Kartomi Thomas, "Tradition and Modern Indonesian Theatre" (Ph.D. diss., University of California, Berkeley, 1994), 51.

99. Cf. Manusama, *Komedie Stamboel.*

100. Victor Ido [Hans van de Wall], "De Bataviaasche tentoonstelling in 1893: Een resident in de knel," in *Indië in de goeden ouden tijd,* 2 vols. (Bandung: Nix, 1949), 1:157–65.

101. *Hindia-Olanda,* 8 September 1893.

102. Walter Benjamin, *The Arcades Project* (Cambridge, MA: Harvard University Press, 1999), 18.

103. *Bintang Soerabaia,* 3 September 1893.

104. On the D'Arcs marionette company, see John McCormick, Clodagh McCormick, and John Phillips, *The Victorian Marionette Theatre* (Iowa City: University of Iowa Press, 2004).

105. *Bintang-Barat,* 11 July 1893.

106. *Selompret Melajoe,* 30 September 1893.

107. *Hindia-Olanda,* 21 October 1893.

108. *Bintang-Barat,* 19 October 1893.

109. *Hindia-Olanda,* 21 October 1893.

110. *Bintang-Barat,* 25 October 1893.

111. *Hindia-Olanda,* 24 October 1893.

112. *Bintang-Barat,* 25 August 1893.

113. See, e.g., *Bintang-Barat,* 21 August 1893; *Hindia-Olanda,* 30 August 1893.

114. *Hindia-Olanda,* 16 September 1893. This same promotion, with minor variations, is printed in *Bintang-Barat,* 16 September 1893: the fact that it appeared the same day in two papers demonstrates that it was a promotional piece given to newspapers by Permata Johor and not a piece written independently by a journalist. The piece was also repr. in *Bintang Soerabaia,* 30 September 1893.

115. *Bintang-Barat,* 16 September 1893.

116. See Camoens, "Wayang Parsi," 3. This period of bangsawan theater differs substantially from the hybrid variety period of the twentieth century described at length in Tan Sooi Beng, *Bangsawan.*

117. John Hoffman, "A Foreign Investment: Indies Malay to 1901," *Indonesia* 27 (1979): 65–92; Benedict Anderson, *Imagined Communities: Reflections on the Origin and Spread of Nationalism* (New York: Verso, 1991).

118. Hoffman, "Foreign Investment." For a brief description of some of the most prominent linguistic features that distinguish "low Malay" from standard Indonesian, see Ellen Rafferty, "Languages of the Chinese of Java: An Historical Review," *Journal of Asian Studies* 43, no. 2 (1984): 247–72.

119. *Bintang Soerabaia,* 3 October 1892. An exception should be noted here. Muslim spectators in the principalities of Surakarta and Yogyakarta apparently had some difficulty with the Komedie Stamboel's language. Malay-language skills were weak and Javanese was used preferentially as a lingua franca in the principalities through the early twentieth century.

120. *Mataram,* 11 August 1892; *Advertentieblad voor Tegal en Omstreken,* 25 November 1893.

121. Fabricius, *Tempo doeloe,* 74.

122. *Hindia-Olanda,* 20 July 1893.

123. *Pembrita Betawi,* repr. in *Bintang Soerabaia,* 16 September 1893.

124. *Bintang-Barat,* 20 September 1893.

125. *Bintang-Barat,* 25 September 1893.

126. *Bintang-Barat,* 18 September 1893.

127. *Hindia-Olanda,* 22 September 1893. "Malaccan Malay" (*Melayu Melaka*) should be taken as meaning the sort of formal, written Malay used in Malaya—Melaka in the legendary past was the epicenter of the Malay world and stands iconically for classical Malay tradition. See James Sneddon, *The Indonesian Language: Its History and Role in Modern Society* (Sydney: University of New South Wales Press, 2003).

128. *Hindia-Olanda,* 25 September 1893.

129. *Pembrita Betawi,* repr. in *Bintang Soerabaia,* 2 October 1893. *Pembrita Betawi* was a staunch supporter of Permata Johor, regularly printing story outlines of plays to be performed in October and November 1893. The language of these bangsawan play summaries is indeed stilted and somewhat hard to follow, suggesting that *Bintang-Barat*'s defense of the Komedie Stamboel's accessibility is justified.

130. The wayang wong, wayang kulit, wayang golek, Abdul Muluk theater, and other companies performing at the zoo also tried to avoid paying the pachter wayang—perhaps sensing that the revenue farmer's authority was diminishing—but their resistance seems to have met with less success.

131. At the time, no Malay-language papers were published in Cirebon or Tegal, nor were there attentive Malay-language correspondents writing for Batavia, Semarang, or Surabaya papers.

132. "Cheribon," in Van der Lith et al., *Encyclopaedie van Nederlandsch-Indië,* 1:346–47.

133. Matthew Isaac Cohen, "'Multiculturalism' and Performance in Colonial Cirebon," in *The Indonesian Town Revisited,* ed. Peter J. M. Nas (Berlin: LIT Verlag, 2002), 348–73.

134. *Tjerimai,* 1 November, 11 November 1893.

135. *Pembrita Betawi,* repr. in *Bintang Soerabaia,* 24 April, 25 April 1894. This story summary is for the Komedie Stamboel's performance of the play in Batavia on 16 April 1894.

136. *Soerabaiasch-Handelsblad,* 20 January 1894.

137. *Tjerimai,* 11 November 1893.

138. *Advertentieblad voor Tegal en Omstreken,* 6 December 1893.

139. *Pembrita Betawi,* repr. in *Bintang Soerabaia,* 26 April 1894.

140. "Tegal," in Van der Lith et al., *Encyclopaedie van Nederlandsch-Indië,* 4:288.

141. *Bintang Soerabaia,* 6 December 1893.

142. *Bintang Soerabaia,* 28 July 1893.

143. *Secrets* (*Barang rahsia dari astana Konstantinopel*) was translated from the Dutch and serialized in the pages of *Bintang-Barat* in the early 1880s. It was published in twenty-one volumes by the Batavia publisher Albrecht and Rusche in 1892–99. It has been suggested that the novel was

translated by E. F. Wiggers, the owner and editor of *Bintang-Barat*. See Tio Ie Soei, "Lie Kimhok, 1853–1912," in Marcus and Benedanto, *Kesastraan Melayu Tionghoa* (1958; repr. 2002), 5:489. W. V. Sykorsky's claim that "the name Komedi Stambul is usually explained by its use of themes from *Secrets of the Court of Constantinople*" is spurious. Sykorsky, "Remarks on the Antecedents of Modern Indonesian Literature," *Bijdragen tot de Taal-, Land- en Volkenkunde* 156, no. 4 (1980), 512. As far as I am aware, the Komedie Spanjool was the first stambul company to stage an episode from this source, whose length and complicated plot made it hard to produce.

144. *Genoveva* was also made into an opera by Robert Schumann in 1849. For a *Genoveva* handbill from Indo's Komedie Vereeniging de Eendracht, with a Malay-language story summary, see Manusama, *Komedie Stamboel,* 41.

145. *Bintang Soerabaia,* 5 September 1893.

146. *Bintang Soerabaia,* 12 December 1893.

147. *Bintang Soerabaia,* 14 November 1893; repr. *Bintang-Barat,* 21 November 1893.

148. *Selompret Melajoe,* 21 December 1893, repr. *Bintang-Barat,* 28 December 1893.

149. *Bintang Soerabaia,* 5 December 1893.

150. *Bintang Soerabaia,* 12 December 1893.

151. *Pembrita Betawi,* 20 July 1895.

152. Edrus, *Drama,* 61–62.

153. The use of magic in theater is not limited to Southeast Asia. For an entertaining overview of magic in European and American theater, see Richard Huggett, *Supernatural on Stage: Ghosts and Superstitions of the Theatre* (New York: Taplinger, 1975).

154. Day, "Ranggawarsita's Prophecy" (see ch. 2, n. 29).

155. On Indonesian language as an un-native tongue, see J. Joseph Errington, *Shifting Languages: Interaction and Identity in Javanese Indonesia* (Cambridge: Cambridge University Press, 1998).

Chapter 4

1. *Soerabaiasch-Handelsblad,* 5 January 1894.

2. *Soerabaiasch-Handelsblad,* 18 January 1894.

3. Scidmore, *Java,* 3, 7.

4. See, e.g., *Daily Advertiser,* 10 February 1894. This *Yoshino,* built by the English firm of Sir W. G. Armstrong, Mitchell, and Company for Japan, played a major role in September 1894 at the Battle of Yalu, the largest naval engagement of the Sino-Japanese War.

5. In British usage, a marquee is a large tent.

6. *Straits-Chinese Herald,* or *Surat Khabar Peranakan,* 21 February 1894.

7. Edrus, *Drama,* 54. Edrus does not refer explicitly to the name of the troupe in his account (which is based primarily on oral sources) but suggests that it was the first stambul troupe to visit Singapore, and that it came some time in the 1890s.

8. See *Straits-Chinese Herald,* 20 February, 21 February 1894. The corrected advertisement appeared daily in this paper through 10 March 1894. *Manager* is roughly equivalent to *producer* in contemporary theatrical parlance, while *director* subsumes artistic functions.

9. *Singapore Free Press,* 19 February 1894.

10. *Straits-Chinese Herald,* 21 February 1894.

11. *Straits Times,* 15 February 1894.

12. *Straits Times,* 8 February 1894; *Daily Advertiser,* 17 February 1894.

13. *Straits-Chinese Herald,* 21 February 1894.

14. *Daily Advertiser,* 26 February 1894.

15. The *Giang Ann* (also spelled *Gian An*) was one of three steamships owned by the Tan Kim Tian line that traveled regularly between Singapore and Java. One of Tan Kim Tian's steamships left Singapore for Batavia and Cirebon weekly. The *Giang Ann* had a carrying capacity of 873 tons.

16. Langlang Boewono's narrative, "Wajang Orang Terlantar di Singapoera," was published in two installments in *Hindia-Olanda,* 12 May, 18 May 1894.

17. *Hindia-Olanda,* 11 November 1893.

18. *Pembrita Betawi,* repr. in *Bintang Soerabaia,* 17 April 1894.

19. *Soerabaiasch-Handelsblad,* repr. in *Tjerimai,* 3 March 1894.

20. *Bataviaasch Nieuwsblad,* 9 May 1894.

21. *Bintang Soerabaia,* 18 April 1894.

22. This story summary is based on *Bintang-Barat,* 12 April 1894; *Pembrita Betawi,* repr. in *Bintang Soerabaia,* 18 April 1894; *Pembrita Betawi,* repr. in *Bintang Soerabaia,* 11 August 1894.

23. *Bataviaasch Nieuwsblad,* 11 April 1894; *Hindia-Olanda,* 11 April 1894; *Bintang-Barat,* 11, 12 April 1894.

24. For a summary of *Sahir Zaman,* see *Bintang Soerabaia,* 28 July 1894.

25. *Bintang-Barat,* 3 April 1894.

26. *Bintang-Barat,* 19 April 1894.

27. *Bintang Betawi,* repr. in *Bintang Soerabaia,* 27 April 1894.

28. *Bintang-Barat,* repr. in *Bintang Soerabaia,* 11 May 1894.

29. *Bintang Betawi,* repr. in *Bintang Soerabaia,* 27 April 1894.

30. *Pembrita Betawi,* repr. in *Hindia-Olanda,* 25 April 1894.

31. *Hindia-Olanda,* 18 April 1894; *Bintang-Barat,* 19 April 1894.

32. *Pembrita Betawi,* repr. in *Bintang Soerabaia,* 22 May 1894.

33. *Bintang Betawi,* repr. in *Bintang Soerabaia,* 11 May 1894. For a review of the turtledove turnovers, see *Bintang Betawi,* repr. in *Bintang Soerabaia,* 20 April 1894.

34. *Bintang-Barat,* 13 April 1894. See also *Pembrita Betawi,* repr. in *Bintang Soerabaia,* 17 April 1894.

35. *Bintang-Barat,* 24 May 1894. Kite dueling is a seasonal pastime enjoyed mostly by children and young people today; in times past it was also a betting sport involving adult participation.

36. *Hindia-Olanda,* 1 June 1894.

37. *Bintang-Barat,* repr. in *Bintang Soerabaia,* June 1894.

38. Latumeten might be related or identical to an elderly musical informant identified as "Willy Latumeten, also called Si Kapuk by people or Oom [Uncle] Piet." See Pasaribu, *Musik dan selingkar wilajahnja,* 57 (see ch. 1, n. 94).

39. *Hindia-Olanda,* 15 June 1894.

40. *Hindia-Olanda,* 2 July 1894.

41. See the marriage announcement in *Bataviaasch Nieuwsblad,* 25 June 1894.

42. *Bintang-Barat,* 11 June 1894.

43. For more details on Yap's finances, see Cohen, "Chinese *Pujangga*?"

44. *Bintang Soerabaia,* 14 March 1894.

45. Tjalie Robinson, "De hele wereld, hemel en hel voor f1500.–," *Tong Tong* 12, no. 11–12 (1967): 8.

46. The economic significance of Mahieu to the company was demonstrated by the downturn of attendance when Mahieu briefly left the Komedie Stamboel to direct the Komedie Spanjool in November 1893.

47. *Bataviaasch Nieuwsblad,* 24 May 1894.

48. *Hindia-Olanda,* 26 June 1894; *Bintang Betawi,* repr. in *Bintang Soerabaia,* 3 July 1894.

49. *Bataviaasch Handelsblad,* repr. in *Tjerimai,* 11 July 1894.

50. *Bataviaasch Nieuwsblad,* 30 June, 1 July, 9 July, 10 July 1894.

51. *Hindia-Olanda,* 10 July 1894.

52. *Pembrita Betawi,* repr. in *Bintang Soerabaia,* 20 July 1894.

53. *Pembrita Betawi,* repr. in *Bintang Soerabaia,* 3 August 1894.

54. Ibid.

55. *Bintang-Barat,* 3 August 1894.

56. *Java Bode,* 14 July 1894; see also *Bintang-Barat,* 16 July 1894.

57. *Tjerimai,* 11 August 1894.

58. *Tjerimai,* 22 August 1894.

59. *Tjerimai,* 15 August 1894.

60. *Tjerimai,* 29 August 1894.

61. A special matinee for children that Mahieu organized on 19 September 1894 might have been a response to the carousel, a promotional effort designed to get children (and their parents) to come to the regular nighttime shows.

62. *Bintang Soerabaia,* 22 September 1894.

63. *Advertentieblad voor Tegal en Omstreken,* 12 September 1894.

64. The following account is largely based on Alfons Van der Kraan, *Lombok: Conquest, Colonization, and Underdevelopment, 1870–1940* (Singapore: Heinemann Educational Books, 1980). See also Edwald Vanvugt, *De schatten van Lombok: Honderd jaar Nederlandse oorlogsbuit uit Indonesie* (Amsterdam: Mets, 1994).

65. On the legacy of Lombok, see esp. Vanvugt, *Schatten van Lombok.*

66. *Advertentieblad voor Tegal en omstreken,* 26 September 1894.

67. Ibid.

68. Ibid. My summary of this play here has been edited from Wessels's summary, with comments inserted.

69. Camoens, "Wayang Parsi," 5–6.

70. *Bintang-Barat,* 16 October 1890.

71. *De Locomotief,* 8 October, 12 November 1894; J. M. Portengen, *Tjakranegara marsch* (Semarang: Van Dorp, 1894).

72. *Bintang-Barat,* 3 December 1896.

73. On tableaux vivants depicting the Lombok campaign as an "unholy war," see Knaap, "Indische Antoine." Plays about the Lombok campaign were performed by the Komedie Stamboel and other stambul companies between 1895 and 1900 under the titles *War in Lombok, The Lombok and Bali War,* and the two-parter *The Expedition to Chili Pepper Island* and *The Death of Juntik.*

74. *Soerabaija-Courant,* 28 May 1895.

75. Tan Tjeng Bok, interview by Haji Misbach Yusa Biran, tape recording, 27 March 1971, Sinematek Indonesia, Jakarta.

76. *Pembrita-Bahroe,* 26 September 1891.

77. *Bintang Betawi,* repr. in *Bintang Soerabaia,* 7 June 1894.

78. See, for example, *Tjerimai,* 14 November 1900; *Bintang Soerabaia,* 26 November 1902.

79. *Bintang Soerabaia,* 3 March 1900.

80. For a seminal study of ludruk in the heyday of its popularity in Surabaya in the early 1960s, see Peacock, *Rites of Modernization* (see ch. 1, n. 24).

81. *Pembrita Betawi,* 30 April 1895. The company being compared here to Mahieu's Komedie Stamboel is the Komedie Konstantinopel.

82. *De Locomotief,* 1 November 1894.

83. See *De Locomotief,* 18 October, 8 November, 9 November 1894; Dumas, "Meerdere generaties," 4.

84. *Bromartani,* 22 December 1894.

85. *Mataram,* 14 January 1895.

86. *Soerabaiasch-Handelsblad,* 3 May 1895.

87. Ibid.

88. Malay newspapers published in Surabaya during 1895 have not been available to me; it is possible that copies of such no longer exist.

89. The population figure is from "Pekalongan," in Van der Lith et al., *Encyclopaedie van Nederlandsch-Indië,* 3:247. On Pekalongan's batik industry, see Harmen C. Veldhuisen, *Batik Belanda, 1840–1940: Dutch Influence in Batik from Java: Histories and Stories* (Jakarta: Gaya Favorit, 1993).

90. *Bintang-Barat,* 18 March 1895; *Pembrita Betawi,* 19 March 1895.

91. *Pembrita-Bahroe,* 24, 26 September 1895.

92. The structural causes of this malaise are outlined in Furnivall, *Netherlands Indies,* 214, passim.

93. *Uitkomsten der pauperisme,* 1:13 (see ch. 1, n. 14).

94. *Mataram,* 6 December 1894.

95. *Soerabaija-Courant,* 29 May 1895.

96. For more on Yap's legal problems in 1895 and 1896, see Cohen, "Chinese *Pujangga*?"

97. "Poerworedjo," in Van der Lith et al., *Encyclopaedie van Nederlandsch-Indië,* 3:282–83.

98. Possibly Oei Tan Bie was related or identical to Oeij Tam Lie, the Komedie Stamboel's cashier arrested in 1894 for living outside the Chinese quarter.

99. Tzu You, "Tooneel-Melajoe," *Sin Po* 18, no. 870 (1939): 10.

100. *De Locomotief,* 16 October 1895.

101. *De Locomotief,* 16 November 1895.

102. *Pembrita Betawi,* 27 April 1896.

103. This account is mostly based on the Dutch-language account of the trial of Janitz published in *De Locomotief.* Much of the trial was conducted in Malay and translated by a court-appointed translator. See *De Locomotief,* 17, 18, 19, 21, 22, 23, 24 December 1896.

104. Possibly "Van Sprew" was related to the clown and technician Dirk van Sprew.

105. *De Locomotief,* 17 December 1896. The questioner here is the officer of justice, A. C. J. Helfrich. Cramer is the witness providing the answer.

106. *De Locomotief,* 18 December 1896; emphasis in original. Those questioning Gemser here are the counsel for the defense (*verdediger*) and the president of the court, Mr. L. A. O. Kollmann.

107. *De Locomotief,* 17 December 1896. Cramer is here being questioned by the counsel for the defense.

108. *Mataram* 17 February, 3 September 1896; Knaap, "Indische Antoine." Knaap's article does not refer to Janitz, Cramer, or Gemser by name, and some of the details of the case are slightly fictionalized, but the general import of the case is truly represented.

109. Knaap, "Indische Antoine."

110. *Mataram,* 6 February 1896; see also *Djawi-Kando,* 8 February 1896.

111. *Mataram,* 17 February 1896.

112. *Pembrita Betawi,* 7 May 1896.

113. Sri Sumatra played Padang and Bengkulu, as well as inland towns of the west coast of Sumatra, in 1896 and 1897.

114. Cramer in fact became a recording star, issuing gramophone recordings of kroncong songs and abbreviated stambul plays in the first decades of the twentieth century.

115. Si Nona L., *Pantoen Sindiran* (Batavia: G. Francis, 1896).

116. *Hindia-Olanda,* 30 May 1896.

117. *Pembrita Betawi,* 13 June 1896.

118. *Bintang Betawi,* repr. in *Pembrita-Bahroe,* 26 June 1896.

119. "Perdjalanannja satoe directeur dari komedie stamboel," *Bintang Betawi,* repr. in *Pembrita-Bahroe,* 30 November 1896.

120. Ibid.

121. Robinson, "Marie Oord had een Opera," 5. Cramer was the lead actor for Marie Oord's stambul troupe in the first decade of the twentieth century.

122. *Hindia-Olanda,* 2 June 1896.

123. *Pembrita Betawi,* 5 June 1896.

124. *Hindia-Olanda,* 2 May 1896.

125. *Pembrita Betawi,* 7 July 1896.

126. *Bintang Betawi,* repr. in *Pembrita-Bahroe,* 27 July 1896; *Pembrita-Bahroe,* 28 July 1896.

127. *Pembrita Betawi,* 15 August 1896.

128. *Pembrita Betawi,* 29 June 1896.

129. This is almost a word-for-word translation of a dialogue published in *Pembrita Betawi,* 22 June 1896. I have taken the liberty of putting it into a dramatic form.

130. *Hindia-Olanda,* 25 July 1896.

131. Dumas, "Meerdere generaties," 4.

132. *Hindia-Olanda,* 1 September 1896.

133. *Pembrita Betawi,* 9 September 1896.

134. *Pembrita Betawi,* 26 September 1896.

135. The population estimates are based on figures provided for 1895 in "Muntok," 2:588; "Palembang," in *Encyclopaedie van Nederlandsch-Indië,* 3:181–82. Muntok was more than 25 percent Chinese in 1895, which might account in part for why Sri Stamboel visited this small town.

136. *Bintang-Barat,* 18 November 1896.

137. Robinson, "Marie Oord had een Opera," 4. For playbills and other information related to Marie Oord's company, see also Manusama, *Komedie Stamboel.*

138. *Soerabaija-Courant,* repr. in *Tjerimai,* 21 July 1897; J. F. van Bemmelen and G. B. Hooyer, *Guide through Netherlands India,* rev. Otto Knaap (London: Thos. Cook and Son, 1903), 130.

139. For an overview of the history of Medan, see M. A. Loderichs, D. A. Buiskool, B. B. Hering, C. A. Heshusius, A. Mansoer, and G. O. Prins, *Medan: Beeld van een stad* (Purmerend: Asia Maior, 1997).

140. One well-known crime that happened in Medan in 1899 was the poisoning of the children of Margaretha Zelle—who later took on the name Mata Hari as a dancer. See Sam Waagenaar, *The Murder of Mata Hari* (London: Arthur Barker, 1964), 38. There is no information available regarding Zelle's exposure to stambul in the Indies, but one suspects that the popular theater played a more formidable influence on her exotic dancing style than has previously been suggested.

141. *Tjerimai,* 21 July 1897.

142. *Bintang-Barat,* 24 July 1897.

143. The Indian Circus toured Java from April through November 1894. Advertisements and notices mention trained animals, equestrians, gymnasts, canine and Japanese acrobats, and clowns.

144. *Bintang Soerabaia,* 31 July 1894.

145. In fact, the designation *komedi laijsing* (also spelled *laysing*) became a generic term for variety shows operating in western Indonesia at the turn of the century.

146. This company differs from the Komedie Stamboel Betawi, directed by Theodores van Sornsen de Koste, which was active in Batavia from February to May 1895.

147. *Pembrita Betawi,* 8 November 1895.

148. *Pembrita Betawi,* 6 November 1895.

149. *Pembrita Betawi,* 11 November 1895.

150. The gregarious owner of Permata Stamboel was named Tjali, a common nickname for Indos.

151. *Bintang-Barat,* 28 May 1896; *Pembrita Betawi,* 28 May 1896.

152. *Hindia-Olanda,* 9 October 1896. There is a possibility that Mahieu joined the Permata Stamboel in Sumatra after Sri Stamboel went bankrupt.

153. The narrative that follows is for the most part based on the closing argument of Mr. Van Dijk, the defense attorney for the seven Chinese men accused of murdering Loth. See *Bintang-Barat,* 28, 29 April, 1, 2, 3, 4, 5, 8 May 1899.

154. *Bintang-Barat,* 29 April 1899.

155. Robinson, "Marie Oord had een Opera," 6.

156. Snabilié's testimony on 13 April 1899, as reported in *Bintang-Barat,* 14 April 1899.

157. The seven defendants at the Loth murder trial were Soe Hoen Tjiang, Oeij Ong, Ong Ki Lian, Han Joe Toan, Tjiong Tang Hin, Tjoa Li Joeng, and Lauw Kong In.

158. *Bintang-Barat,* 21 April 1899.

159. *Primbon-Soerabaia,* 9 May 1901.

160. J. H. F. van de Wall, *Victor Ido, Zijn leven en zijn werken,* n.d., Manuscript D H 998, KITLV, 237–42. The sketch was performed in its initial version in Batavia on 12 July 1900. See *Java Bode,* 11, 13 July 1900.

161. Victor Ido, *De paria van Glodok: Episode uit he Indische paupersleven in drie acten* (Bandung: Visser, 1921). The revised play premiered in Batavia on 8 October 1916.

162. NIROM (Nederlandsch-Indische Radio Omroep Maatschappij) was the Dutch colonial state radio that served the Indies. "Goena-goena" (to use Ido's own spelling) was an episode in a nostalgic radio series called *Indië in den goeden ouden tijd* (The Indies in the good old days). These addresses were originally published in 1935. See Ido, *Indië in den goeden ouden tijd.* The version of "Goena-goena" I am using here is from the a single-volume edition of this collection (The Hague: Van Hoeve, 1966), 121–24.

163. Ido, "Goena-goena," 121. The page numbers for subsequent references to this work are given in parentheses in text.

164. On this point, see James T. Siegel, *Fetish, Recognition, Revolution* (Princeton: Princeton University Press, 1997), 76. The most important Indo ghost in Batavia was the spirit of Pieter Ebervelt, who was executed in 1722 for "plotting to overthrow VOC [Dutch East Indies Company] rule in Batavia." Ebervelt's skull was impaled on a public monument. Offerings were regularly presented at this monument to propitiate the fierce spirit of Ebervelt until it was torn down during the Japanese occupation. A re-creation now stands in Tanah Abang, not far from where Loth was killed. See Scott Merrillees, *Batavia in Nineteenth Century Photographs,* 2d ed. (Richmond, Surrey: Curzon, 2001), 74–75.

165. Couperus, *Hidden Force.*

166. Cf. Ellen Boschman, "Goena-goena: Een zoektocht in de literatuur naar betekenis en verbeelding," *Indische Letteren* 15, no. 1 (2000): 37–47.

Chapter 5

1. *Bintang Soerabaia,* 5 May 1899; *Het Centrum,* 4 August 1899; *Djawi-Kando,* 8 August 1899.

2. *Het Centrum,* 10, 13 March 1899.

3. *Het Centrum,* 14 December 1898.

4. Tan Tjin Hian's name is also spelled Tan Tjien Hwa and Tan Tjin Gian in various accounts.

5. *Bintang Soerabaia,* 30 October, 14 November 1899. The characterization of Gresik as *vervallen* (dilapidated or fallen into ruins) is from "Grissee," in Van der Lith et al., *Encyclopaedie van Nederlandsch-Indië,* 1:602.

6. *Bintang Soerabaia,* 3 March 1900.

7. *Laili and Majenun* (also known as *Laila and Majenun*) was a play imported from the bangsawan repertoire. For summaries, see Tan Sooi Beng, *Bangsawan,* 216–17; Manusama, *Komedie Stamboel,* 46–47. Both *Laili and Majenun* and *Hawai Majelis* are evidently based on plays from the Parsi theater, originally written by Nasarvanji Aram and further modified by Husaini Miyan Zarif. See Somnath Gupt, "Parsi Theatre," *Sangeet Natak* 36, no. 1 (2001): 26–27; no. 2 (2001): 4–5.

8. Mahieu and Vos's son Adolphe Joseph Mahieu was born and died in Semarang on 24 August 1896. See Dumas, "Meerdere generaties," 4.

9. The internal quote about Derk van Sprew is from Robinson, "Marie Oord had een Opera," *Tong Tong* 12, nos. 11–12 (1967): 5. Derk (or Dirk) van Sprew was a member of Marie Oord's company in the first decades of the twentieth century.

10. Gerard Termorshuizen, "'Daar heb je waarachtig wéér een Indische roman!' Indische literatuur en literaire kritiek tussen 1885 en 1898," *Indische Letteren* 13, nos. 3–4 (1998): 139–48.

11. Perelaer, *Baboe Dalima.*

12. A number of Malay-language Indische romans have been republished in recent decades. See Pramoedya, *Tempo doeloe;* Marcus and Benedanto, *Kesastraan Melayu Tionghoa,* vol. 1.

13. Andjar Asmara, "Suka-Duka dibelakang lajar sandiwara: Memoires dari Andjar Asmara," part 3, *Varia* 1, no. 22 (17 September 1958): 27. *Rusia* is in fact a Batavia Malay equivalent to *rahasia.*

14. *Rossina* and *Si Conat* were both based on novels by F. D. J. Pangemanann, while *Nyai Dasima* was based on a novelette by the journalist and illustrator G. Francis. All three are reprinted in Pramoedya, *Tempo doeloe.* See below for a summary of *Rossina.* For a good description of *Nyai Dasima* as performed by a Yap Gwan Thay stambul troupe in the first decade of the twentieth century, see Tan Boen Kim, *Tjerita si Riboet, atawa Boenga mengan-*

doeng ratjoen (Batavia: Kho Tjeng Bie, 1917), 3–19. See also Kenji Tsuchiya, "Popular Literature and Colonial Society in Late-Nineteenth-Century Java: *Cerita Nyai Dasima,* the Macabre Story of an Englishman's Concubine," *Southeast Asian Studies* 28, no. 4 (1991): 467–80.

15. *Bintang Betawi,* 20 July 1901.

16. Lynn M. Voskuil, "Feeling Public: Sensation Theater, Commodity Culture, and the Victorian Public Sphere," *Victorian Studies* 44, no. 2 (2002): 263.

17. From a review of a performance in Surabaya's Kapasan theater. *Bintang Soerabaia,* 10 July 1899.

18. The quote is from Balwant Gargi, *Theatre in India* (New York: Theatre Art Books, 1962). On Baliwala, see especially Kathryn Hansen, "Making Women Visible: Gender and Race Cross-Dressing in the Parsi Theatre," *Theatre Journal* 51 (1999): 127–47.

19. Robinson, "Marie Oord had een Opera."

20. Maleman refers to the nights of Ramadhan. Maleman was celebrated with much pomp as a form of royal ritual in late nineteenth-century Yogyakarta.

21. *Het Centrum,* 20, 27 February 1899; *Retnodhoemilah,* 24 February 1899.

22. *Het Centrum,* 27 January 1899.

23. The name India, or "Indië," also refers to the Indies, and it possibly had protonationalist overtones as well. See below for the links between Indische nationalism and Mahieu's theater.

24. *Retnodhoemilah,* 24 March 1899.

25. Although in Malaya the Malay word *si* is "a demonstrative usually expressive of contempt," in Indies Malay *si* is "used before the names of those with whom the speaker and interlocutor is intimate. Wilkinson, *Malay-English Dictionary,* 2:1100; John M. Echols and Hassan Shadily, *An Indonesian-English Dictionary,* 3d ed., rev. John U. Wolff and James T. Collins (Ithaca: Cornell University Press, 1989), 511.

26. Cf. Michael Herzfeld, *Cultural Intimacy: Social Poetics in the Nation-State* (London: Routledge, 1996).

27. *Bintang Soerabaia,* 27 February 1899.

28. *Bintang Soerabaia,* 21 April 1902.

29. *Bintang Soerabaia,* 23 August 1901.

30. *Bintang Soerabaia,* 17 August 1901.

31. *Bintang Soerabaia,* 4 May 1899.

32. *Bintang Soerabaia,* 9 May 1899.

33. *Bintang Soerabaia,* 2 June 1899.

34. *Bintang Soerabaia,* 12 May 1899.

35. *Bintang Soerabaia,* 5 May 1899.

36. *Bintang Soerabaia,* 12 May 1899.

37. An accessible adaptation of this story is Sunardi D. M., *Sumbadra larung* (Jakarta: Balai Pustaka, 1977). Possibly the motif of being thrown into the sea in the play summarized above was borrowed from this same wayang kulit play-episode.

38. *Bintang Soerabaia,* 13 May 1899.

39. Ibid.

40. *Retnodhoemilah,* 7 March 1899.

41. *Retnodhoemilah,* 9 June 1899.

42. *Retnodhoemilah,* 18 July 1899.

43. Ibid.

44. Sinar India is also spelled Sinar Indië and Sinar Hindia.

45. Otto Knaap, "Indische Antoine." The French word *cabotin* means "ham" or "third-rate actor," but also implies "someone who lives and dies for acting." See http://movies.yahoo.com/shop?d=hc&id=1800011568&cf=biog&intl=us.

46. In Victor Ido's 1912 novel *De paupers,* Mahieu, who is semifictionally portrayed as "Karel Reumer," is introduced to the novel's protagonists as director of the "Komedie Hindia":

> "Boong, this is Reumer, the director of the Stamboel. . . ."
>
> "Of the Komedie Hindia," emended Reumer, with just a trace of pride.
>
> "Come now, that amounts to the same thing," teased Perisa, with gaiety.
>
> Ido, *Paupers,* 221–22.

47. *Primbon Soerabaia,* 19 October 1900.

48. On Dutch reactions to the Boer War, see particularly Maarten Kuitenbrouwer, *The Netherlands and the Rise of Modern Imperialism: Colonies and Foreign Policy, 1870–1902,* trans. Hugh Beyer (New York: Berg, 1991).

49. Stoler, *Carnal Knowledge,* 83.

50. *De Locomotief,* 17 November 1899. Gross income was 369.55 guilders from ticket sales, with an additional 83.60 guilders from donations solicited from spectators. When 139.49 guilders were deducted for expenses this yielded a net income for charity of 313.66 guilders—"a splendid result indeed!" The sum raised was directly comparable to the gross income of 468 guilders raised for the Transvaalfonds from a soirée variée held at Semarang's schouwburg on 30 October.

51. *Semarang Courant,* 13 November 1899.

52. Marthinus van Bart to author, e-mail, 16 April 2004.

53. *Semarang Courant,* 17 November 1899.

54. *Bintang Soerabaia,* 15 December 1899.

55. *Bintang-Barat,* 21 November 1899.

56. *Bintang Soerabaia,* 31 January 1900.

57. Mahieu is one of 105 new members registered as joining the league during the second week of February 1900. Members of Sinar India who joined in Tegal in this list are: Brodie, Mrs. J.—actress Sinar India, Drysen, F. H.—actor Sinar India, Haan, Miss M. de—actress Sinar India, Hobyn, J. B.—actor Sinar India, Hunter, J. R.—actor Sinar India, Hunter, W. F.—actor Sinar India, Los, W.—actor Sinar India, Mahieu, A. C. P.—director Sinar India, Mahieu, Mrs. née H. Coppiëns—actress Sinar India, Muggie, W.—actor Sinar India, Paulus, H.—violinist Sinar India, Portier, Miss B.—actress Sinar India, Portier, Miss J.P.—actress Sinar India, Pronk, P.N.—actor Sinar India. See *Bondsblad,* 13 February 1900. Listed as joining the league several months later, at a time when Sinar India was playing Meester Cornelis, are: Buisson de St. Remy, E. J.—actor Sinar India, Coppiëns, Th.—actor Sinar India, Coppiëns, W.—actor Sinar India, Engels, H.—actor Sinar India, Gebhardt, Mej. M.—actress Sinar India, Gussmand, F.—actor Sinar India, Kudding, J. G.—actor Sinar India, Lefebre, W.—actor Sinar India, Ligtvoet, Th.—actor Sinar India, Peterman, F.—actor Sinar India, Petrus, A.—actor Sinar India, Stralendorff, C.—actor Sinar India, Vries, G. A. de—actor Sinar India, Wolf, J. de—actor Sinar India. See *Bondsblad,* 20 November 1900. These two lists provide the fullest record available of company members of any nineteenth-century Indonesian popular theater troupe.

Bataviaasch Nieuwsblad (13 October 1900) notes that Mahieu made sure that all the members of his troupe, "or at least all the male members," joined the league. The mass enrollment of Sinar India suggests one of three possibilities: joining the league was compulsory for Sinar India actors; Mahieu paid for the five-guilder membership of his company members; or Mahieu's ideological conviction in the worth of the league was so compelling and he was such a magnetic personality that Sinar India performers wanted to join on their own individual initiatives.

58. Mahieu's affiliation with the league is not indicative of the entire stambul field. As Ann Laura Stoler observes, the league "was led by Indies-born Europeans who spoke for the Indo poor but whose numbers were rarely represented in their ranks." Stoler, *Carnal Knowledge,* 106. Outside of Sinar India, only a handful of stambul performers joined the league.

59. Paul W. van der Veur, "Introduction to a Socio-Political Study of the Eurasians of Indonesia" (Ph.D. diss., Cornell University, 1955), 82.

60. The Indies is for the people of the Indies. Ulbe Bosma and Gijsbert Oonk, "Bombay Batavia: Parsi and Eurasian Variations on the Middlemen

Theme," in *Mediators between State and Society,* ed. Nico Randeraad (Hilversum: Verloren, 1998), 37.

61. Van der Veur, "Eurasians of Indonesia," 139.

62. Stoler, *Carnal Knowledge,* 107.

63. For an important study on the emergence and failings of Indies nationalism, see Doorn, *Divided Society* (see introduction, note 52).

64. Ulbe Bosma, *Karel Zaalberg: Journalist en strijder voor de Indo* (Leiden: KITLV Press, 1997), 120.

65. The term Indo-Europeesche Maatschappij was used, for example, by J. van Poel in a lecture delivered to Indische Bond members in Cirebon on 22 March 1900. Mahieu was present at that meeting and announced his forthcoming Indische Bond benefit performance.

66. Wertheim, *Indonesian Society in Transition,* 173.

67. Jean Gelman Taylor, *The Social World of Batavia: European and Eurasian in Dutch Asia* (Madison: University of Wisconsin Press, 1983).

68. Onghokham, "De Rijsttafel and the Colonial Dutch," in *The Thugs, the Curtain Thief, and the Sugar Lord: Power, Politics, and Culture in Colonial Java* (Jakarta: Metafor, 2003), 311–22.

69. The internal quote is from Hans van de Wall's essay "Over Indische Romans," published in *Bataviaasch Nieuwsblad,* 20 October 1900. On the concept of Indische, see particularly Frances Gouda, *Dutch Culture Overseas: Colonial Practice in the Netherlands Indies, 1900–1942* (Amsterdam: Amsterdam University Press, 1995).

70. *Bondsblad,* 3 April 1900.

71. Ibid.

72. Knaap, "Indische Antoine."

73. *Bondsblad,* 20 April 1900.

74. *Primbon Soerabaia,* 9 May 1901, repr. in *Bintang Soerabaia,* 10 May 1901.

75. *Primbon Soerabaia,* 19 October 1900.

76. Likely Mahieu constructed a shed in Bogor rather than using a tent as he did not wish a repeat of the unfortunate events of 9 November 1892, when the Komedie Stamboel's tent was destroyed by a storm.

77. *Primbon Soerabaia,* 24 July 1900.

78. *Bondsblad,* 27 July 1900.

79. *Bintang Soerabaia,* 15 August 1900.

80. *Primbon Soerabaia,* 3 November 1900.

81. Dumas, "Meerdere generaties," 4.

82. *Bintang Soerabaia,* 10 November 1900.

83. *Bintang Betawi,* 30 November 1900.

84. Samson, "Lied van de Indo," 5. *Bongkok udang* means literally the "bend of a shrimp." It appears to be a stage name. There were actually two

actors named Hunter in Mahieu's company at this time. Both achieved fame and distinction during the first two decades of the twentieth century. Dirk van Sprew's name was also spelled "Derk van Spreew." Possibly Bram Wagner was the same "crooner" also known as "Bram Atjeh" (Bram of Aceh). See Pasaribu, *Musik dan selingkar wilajahnja,* 56 (see ch. 1, n. 94).

85. Samson, "Stamboel," 4.

86. This notice actually describes a subsequent performance of the play. See *Bintang Betawi,* 30 July 1901.

87. Cf. Kristen Whissel, "Placing the Spectator on the Scene of History: The Battle Re-Enactment at the Turn of the Century, from Buffalo Bill's Wild West to the Early Cinema," *Historical Journal of Film, Radio, and Television* 22, no. 3 (2002): 225–43.

88. *Primbon Soerabaia,* 19 October 1900.

89. Peter Bailey, "Business and Good Fellowship in the London Music Hall," in *Popular Culture and Performance in the Victorian City* (Cambridge: Cambridge University Press, 1998), 100.

90. *Bataviaasch Nieuwsblad,* 19 November 1900.

91. *Bondsblad,* 30 November 1900.

92. It was originally announced that Sinar India would perform *Aïda* on this benefit night; *Bin Lail* seems to have been a late substitution.

93. *Bondsblad,* 16 October 1900.

94. *Bondsblad,* 12 October 1900.

95. *Bondsblad,* 16 October 1900.

96. *Bondsblad,* 12 October 1900.

97. Ibid.

98. *Bondsblad,* 16 October 1900.

99. *Bataviaasch Nieuwsblad,* 26 September 1900. *Jula-Juli* was in fact a bangsawan play imported into stambul. For a plot summary of *Jula-Juli bintang tiga* (Third star Jula-Juli), see Tan Sooi Beng, *Bangsawan,* 209–10. For a reconstruction of a Mahieu performance of *Jula-Juli,* see Manusama, *Komedie Stamboel,* 14–23.

100. *Primbon Soerabaia,* 19 October 1900.

101. *Primbon Soerabaia,* 16 November 1900.

102. *Bondsblad,* 30 November 1900.

103. Biographical information about Otto Knaap can be found in "Het Indische gemopper: Bas Veth en Otto Knaap," *Oost-Indisch Magazijn* 19, no. 188 (1990): 41–42; Reggie Baay, "Perkara's in de Indische kunstkritiek," *Indische Letteren* 11, no. 1 (1996): 17–30. I am grateful to Bregtje Knaap for these citations.

104. F. van den Bosch, "Kosmopolitisch spektakel," *Indische Letteren* 9, no. 1 (1994): 47. It was reprinted in two installations in the *Bondsblad* in

1903, after Mahieu's death, where it was preceded by a brief note from the editor stating that the essay would allow readers to appreciate Mahieu's significance for the Indos' struggle. *Bondsblad,* 18, 25 July 1903. This article was reprinted in *Tong Tong* in 1971, with editorial commentary and photographs. The year of original publication is uncertain—most likely it was 1901 or 1902.

105. Van den Bosch, "Kosmopolitisch Spektakel," 47; Rob Dumas, "Auguste Mahieu, Markant acteur bekend van de Komedie Stamboel," lecture presented at the Pasar Malam Besar, The Hague, 22 June 2003.

106. Ido, *Paupers,* 225.

107. Hans van de Wall was not only a literatteur but also a cultural historian, and I have no doubt that he could have described the Sinar India repertoire more accurately if that was his goal.

108. Ido, *Paupers,* 226–27.

109. Ibid., 225.

110. Rob Nieuwenhuys, *Komen en blijven: Tempo doeloe, een verzonken wereld: Fotografische documenten uit het oude Indië, 1870–1920* (Amsterdam: E. M. Querido, 1998), 164.

111. *Bintang Betawi,* 30 July 1901.

112. *Bintang Betawi,* 13 July 1901.

113. *Bintang Betawi,* 12 July 1901. The names used by Verdi in his opera are in brackets.

114. *Bintang Betawi,* 15 July 1901. Mahieu ends his adaptation of *Aïda* somewhat differently than the Verdi opera. Princess Amneris is alive and sane at the opera's end and prays for the peace of Radames's soul from the temple above his cell. Aïda also does not burrow a tunnel into Radames's cell, as in Mahieu's adaptation, but rather slips into it unnoticed before it is sealed.

115. *Bintang Betawi,* 15 July 1901.

116. Jan Fabricius, "Verguld goud," in *Tempo doeloe,* 74–82. The precise year of the engagement is in fact not provided in Fabricius's account, but many of the details accord with what is known about the 1901 Mangga Besar engagement.

117. Ibid., 74–75.

118. For a summary of a bangsawan version of *Merchant,* entitled *Saudagar Sailok* (Merchant Shylock), see Rahmah Bujang, *Sejarah perkembangan drama bangsawan di tanah Melayu dan Singapura* (Kuala Lumpur: Dewan Bahasa dan Pustaka, 1975), 59–60.

119. Fabricius, "Verguld goud," 76–77.

120. Ibid., 78.

121. For a general overview of Pontianak's history, which I draw upon here and below, see Mary Somers Heidhues, *Golddiggers, Farmers, and Traders*

in the "Chinese Districts" of West Kalimantan, Indonesia (Ithaca: Southeast Asia Program Publications, Southeast Asia Program, Cornell University, 2003).

122. Ibid., 135.

123. Ibid., 193.

124. P. Adriani, *Herinneringen uit en aan de Chineesche districten der Wester-afdeeling van Borneo, 1879–1882* (Amsterdam: H. C. A. Campagne, 1898), 141–45; M. Buys, *Twee maanden op Borneo's westkust: Herinneringen* (Leiden: Van Doesburgh, 1892), 47.

125. Kerckhoff, "Maleisch tooneel," 303 (see ch. 1, n. 103).

126. Vergeet Mij Niet (Forget Me Not), also known as Djangan Loepa Kita, was directed by Charles O. van der Laan in 1896, and T. Lewerisija in 1897.

127. There are numerous accounts of stranded actors and companies. I have already summarized an account of a stranded wayang wong manager in Singapore. See above and *Hindia-Olanda,* 12, 18 May 1894. The most complete of such reports from the period is an 1898 serialized account of a wayang wong troupe that traveled to Singapore and met with financial disaster, resulting in a schism. See *Djawi-Kando,* 3, 5, 8, 10, 12 March 1898. See also *Bintang Soerabaia,* 10 April 1901 regarding a stambul troupe stranded in Makassar and *Bintang Soerabaia,* 19 July 1901 regarding a bangsawan troupe stranded in Banjarmasin.

128. *Bintang Soerabaia,* 5 April 1902. This is the only available account of Mahieu's six months in Borneo.

129. Ibid.

130. Ibid. Most likely the "corporal" was an officer in Pontianak's Chinese community, not a military man.

131. Edrus, *Drama,* passim.

132. Tan Sooi Beng, *Bangsawan,* 18.

133. Andjar Asmara, "Suka-Duka," 28.

134. Edrus, *Drama,* 56.

135. *Bintang Soerabaia,* 15 April 1901. Zorab appears to have been a fascinating character. When Indra Zanibar played Madiun in 1901, it was reported that Zorab was "greatly loved by the Natives here for his many good qualities. It is true that this gentleman is very intelligent. It is a shame he could not settle permanently here. If he lived here, many young people would wish to study how to speak French or Parsi with him, for he knows both languages. He is Parsi himself, but has lived for a long time in Bombay."

136. *Bintang Soerabaia,* 13 December 1899.

137. Tengku Syed Abdulkadir and Zen Rosdy note that the among the most "famous stambul troupes to Indonesia before 1925" was one directed

by a certain "Bai Zoraf," said to be "a man of Indian descent from Singapore." See Tengku Syed Abdulkadir and Zen Rosdy, *Sejarah seni drama* (Singapore: Pustaka Melayu, 1960), 151. It is likely that this was the same person as E. Sorap.

138. *Straits Echo,* 5 October 1910, cited in Tan Sooi Beng, *Bangsawan,* 28.

139. *Bintang Betawi,* 23 January 1903.

140. *Bintang Soerabaia,* 22 October 1902.

141. *Straits Echo,* 19 June 1911, cited in Tan Sooi Beng, *Bangsawan,* 41.

142. Tan Sooi Beng, *Bangsawan,* 44.

143. Ibid., 38.

144. Ibid., 38, 61.

145. Ibid., 40. Klimanoff was the father of Piëdro, the owner-manager of Dardanella and Devi Dja's husband. It was Adolf Klimanoff's accidental death in a balancing act on stacked chairs that resulted in his wife and daughter settling permanently in Java, forming the famous Dardanella troupe in 1926, which propelled Devi Dja to starhood. See Ramadhan K. H., *Gelombang hidupku: Dewi Dja dari Dardanella* (Jakarta: Sinar Harapan, 1982); Lenoa Mayer Merrin, *Standing Ovations: Devi Dja, Woman of Java* (Santa Monica, CA: Lee and Lee, 1989).

146. This newspaper review of Kasim's production of *The Merchant of Venice* performed on 11 December 1909 is cited in Tan Sooi Beng, *Bangsawan,* 110.

147. The rumah kongsi is the communal boarding house rented by itinerant theater groups. See below for more detail.

148. Edrus, *Drama,* 55.

149. *Bintang Betawi,* 26 June 1902.

150. On the use of incandescent lights, see *Bintang Betawi,* 7 May 1902. According to Rahmah Bujang's calculations, even a small bangsawan company required a crew of at least ten. Wayang Kasim at this point was about double the size of what Rahmah Bujang classifies as a "large company." Bujang, *Sejarah perkembangan drama bangsawan,* 91.

151. *Bintang Betawi,* 26 May 1902.

152. *Bintang Soerabaia,* 2 December 1902. This play was performed in Batavia on 20 July 1902. The promotion here is for a later performance in Surabaya on 1 December 1902.

153. *Bintang Betawi,* 26 July 1902; emphasis in original.

154. *Bintang Betawi,* 25 June 1902.

155. *Bintang Betawi,* 9 May 1902.

156. *Bintang Soerabaia,* 13 June 1902.

157. *Bintang Betawi,* 9 May 1902. Si Malang literally translates as Unlucky and Si Badjingan as Scoundrel. Both are typical stage names for clowns.

158. *Bintang Betawi,* 13 June 1902.

159. *Bintang Betawi,* 23 June 1902.

160. *Bintang Betawi,* 24 May 1902.

161. This serial was subsequently reprinted in book form and was collected in an anthology edited by Pramoedya. See F. D. J. Pangemanann, "Tjerita Rossina," in Pramoedya, *Tempo doeloe,* 117–53.

162. *Bintang Soerabaia,* 11 October 1902.

163. *Bintang Soerabaia,* 11 October, 12 November 1902.

164. *Bintang Soerabaia,* 11 October 1902.

165. *Bintang Soerabaia,* 12 November 1902.

166. *Bintang Betawi,* 17 May 1902.

167. On the tale of Sampek and Engtay and its Indonesian transforms, see George Quinn, "Liang Shanbo and Zhu Yingtai: A Chinese Folk Romance in Java and Bali," in *Literary Migrations: Traditional Chinese Fiction in Asia (17th–20th Centuries),* ed. Claudine Salmon (Beijing: International Culture Publishing, 1987), 530–68.

168. For a description of a performance of this play by "Opera Hindia Nederland," see W. B. Peteri, "Stamboel," *De Nieuwe Gids* 37 (1922): 411–19. A particularly interesting production is Teater Koma's *Sampek Engtay,* written and directed by N. Riantiarno. This was first produced in a low-key production at Gedung Kesenian Jakarta (the old schouwburg) in 1988 that attracted Teater Koma devotees. (It was the first performance of live theater I saw in Indonesia.) When it was revised and revived in 1999 at Teater Tanah Airku in Taman Mini Indonesia Indah (Indonesia's national theme park), the production was a celebration of traditional Chinese culture, with dragon dance, acrobatics, and the like. This latter production was restaged in an English translation, directed by Riantiarno, in Singapore in 2000. For the script, see N. Riantiarno, *Sampek Engtay* (Jakarta: Pustaka Jaya, 1999).

169. *Bintang Soerabaia,* 31 October 1902; The Tin Lam, *Boekoe sairnan dari tjeritanja Samphek Eng Tay tersalin dari boekoe Tjina* (Surabaya: Gimberg, 1890).

170. *Bintang Betawi,* 3 June 1902; *Bintang Soerabaia,* 31 October 1902.

171. *Bintang Betawi,* 4 June 1902.

172. *Bintang Betawi,* 5 July 1902.

173. A third play that likely had a Chinese content was *Chow-Chow,* a comic parody in which "seven stories are collapsed into one" (*Bintang Soerabaia,* 2 December 1902). This play was performed as the final show in Indra Zanibar's engagement in both Batavia (27 July 1902) and Surabaya (3 December 1902).

174. *Bintang Betawi,* 15 June 1902.

175. Quinn, "Liang Shanbo and Zhu Yingtai," 547. Quinn notes that such anti-Chinese caricaturing flourishes in areas of Indonesia where the Chinese are economically powerful and resentment runs high among non-Chinese Indonesians.

176. *Bintang Betawi,* 15 June 1902.

177. On cu te hi and opera derma, see Matthew Isaac Cohen, ed., *The Lontar Anthology of Indonesian Drama,* vol. 1 (Jakarta: Lontar, forthcoming).

178. *De Locomotief,* 4 August 1902; *Bintang Betawi,* 7 July 1902. For a summary of a later version of "Bahtoem and Bahtim," see Manusama, *Komedie Stamboel,* 29–30.

179. *De Locomotief,* 4 August 1902.

180. *De Locomotief,* 5, 8 August 1902.

181. *Bintang Soerabaia,* 14 October 1902.

182. Djoko Suryo, "Social and Economic Life in Rural Semarang under Colonial Rule in the Later 19th Century" (Ph.D. diss., Monash University, 1982), 149.

183. See, e.g., *Bintang-Barat,* 1 June 1898 (about Tasikmalaya theaters); *Bintang Soerabaia,* 5 December 1900 (about a newly constructed Arab-owned theater in Surabaya); *Bintang Soerabaia,* 21 December 1901 (about a condemned stambul shed in Semarang).

184. *Bintang Betawi,* 4 August 1902.

185. *Bintang Soerabaia,* 29 August 1902.

186. *Bintang Soerabaia,* 25 April 1899.

187. According to Dumas, Auguste and Lena's third child, August Mahieu, was born on 8 August 1903. Assuming he was carried to full term, he was conceived at the beginning of November 1902. Dumas, "Meerdere generaties," 4.

188. "Boemiajoe," in Van der Lith et al., *Encyclopaedie van Nederlandsch-Indië,* 1:224.

189. *Tjerimai,* 25 August 1894.

190. *Bintang Betawi,* 8 July 1901.

191. *Bintang Betawi,* 21 July 1902. Infant deaths among families who traveled with their children were very common as well. None of Mahieu's children with either Nellie Vos or Lena Coppiëns survived past childhood. Lena Coppiëns-Mahieu herself died in 1913, at the age of forty. See Dumas, "Meerdere generaties," 4, 6.

192. "Dari hal satoe nona Komedie Stamboel" (Concerning a certain Komedie Stamboel actress), in *Bintang Betawi,* 17 May 1902.

193. Andjar Asmara, "Suka-Duka," 27.

194. Tan Tjeng Bok, interview by Haji Misbach Yusa Biran, tape recording, 27 March 1971, Sinematek Indonesia, Jakarta.

195. Andjar Asmara, "Suka-Duka," 27.

196. *Bintang Soerabaia,* 12 February 1903.

197. *De Locomotief,* 31 January 1903.

198. *Bintang Betawi,* 3 February 1903. In fact, Johan Mahieu died in Kertosono on 9 December 1902, while Mahieu's mother died in Probolinggo on 10 June 1915.

199. *Selompret Melajoe,* 3 February 1903.

200. *Bintang Soerabaia,* 7 February 1903.

201. The attentive reader will note the discrepancy between the dates of death given in *De Locomotief* and *Bondsblad.* The authoritative almanac source cited by Dumas agrees with the latter. See Robert Martin Dumas, *"Teater Abdulmuluk" in Zuid-Sumatra op de drempel van een nieuw tijdperk* (Leiden: CNWS, 2000), 57.

202. *Bondsblad,* 11 July 1903.

203. Knaap's article was reprinted in *Bondsblad,* 18, 25 July 1903.

204. *Bondsblad,* 12 September 1903.

205. See Tan Sooi Beng, *Bangsawan.*

Chapter 6

1. Genjring akrobat is associated with the area of Cirebon and Indramayu (West Java); sirkus alas roban is found in Batang (Central Java); and kobrasiswa is practiced in Magelang (Central Java).

2. The characterization of stambul's emergence as a cultural landmark is from A. Teeuw, *Modern Indonesian Literature,* 2 vols. (The Hague: Martinus Nijhoff, 1979), 2:207.

3. Anderson, *Imagined Communities,* 133 (see ch. 3, n. 129).

4. Indonesia's myriad teater daerah genres, including *opera Batak, randai, lenong, tarling, ketoprak, ludruk, kemidi rudat,* and dozens more performed in regional dialects and ethnic languages, are to a significant degree localized versions of stambul. A detailed examination of regional theater is beyond the scope of this book. On the concept of teater daerah, see I Made Bandem and Sal Murgiyanto, *Teater daerah Indonesia* (Yogyakarta: Kanisius, 1996).

5. Errington, *Shifting Languages* (see ch. 3, n. 167).

6. Pramoedya Ananta Toer, "Sepatah Kata Perkenalan," in *Tempo doeloe,* 3–5.

7. *Primbon Soerabaia,* 15 February 1901. The quote is from an article about a tent film show by the Java Biorama in Surabaya, including shorts of world personages such as Queen Wilhelmina, President Kruger, and Major Wilson.

8. Anderson, "Language, Fantasy, Revolution," 36.

9. Ibid., 36.

10. Ibid.; emphasis in original.

11. Ibid., 37; emphasis in original.

12. Ibid.

13. See esp. Charles A. Coppel, "Mestizo Society as an Imagined Community," in *Studying Ethnic Chinese in Indonesia* (Singapore: Singapore Society of Asian Studies, 2002), 124–35.

14. Pauline D. Milone, review of *Java en Madura in de uitvoerende kunsten,* by Victoria M. Clara van Groenendael, *Journal of Asian Studies* 58, no. 1 (1999): 276.

15. Martin Heidegger, "The Age of the World Picture," in *The Question Concerning Technology and Other Essays,* trans. William Lovitt (New York: Harper and Row, 1977), 113–54. See also Mitchell, "Stage of Modernity," 1–34 (see introduction, note 60).

16. A classic formulation of ethos and worldview in wayang kulit is provided in Clifford Geertz, "Ethos, World View, and the Analysis of Sacred Symbols," in *The Interpretation of Cultures* (New York: Basic Book, 1973), 126–41.

17. *Pembrita Betawi,* 7 May 1896.

18. W. T. Lhamon Jr., *Raising Cain* (Cambridge, Harvard University Press, 1998), 59.

19. Lauw Giok Lan, "Oetjapannja Penjalin," i-ii (see ch. 1, n. 33).

20. Kwee Tek Hoaij, *Allah jang palsoe: Satoe lelakon komedi dalem anem bagian* (Batavia: Tjiong Koen Bie, 1919), iii.

21. Abisin Abbas, "Tooneel Indonesia," 16–17.

22. Ibid., 15.

23. Tzu You, "Tooneel-Melajoe," *Sin Po* 17, no. 870 (1939): 10.

24. Cf. Sumarsam, *Gamelan* (see ch. 2, n. 34).

25. Johannes Fabian, *Moments of Freedom: Anthropology and Popular Culture* (Charlottesville, VA: University of Virginia Press, 1998), 23–24.

26. Kalff, "Avond in de 'Komedie Stamboul.'"

27. Ibid., 757. Kalff is in fact citing Van Maurik, *Indrukken van een 'totok,'* 126 (see ch. 3, n. 6).

28. Heather Sutherland, "'Tempo Doeloe' and 'Pudjangga Baru': Aspects of Social and Intellectual Life in Twentieth-Century Batavia, Focusing on the Indonesian Community, 1933 to 1942" (master's thesis, Australian National University, 1967), 101.

29. J. Th. Koks, *De Indo* (Amsterdam: H. J. Paris, 1931), 241.

30. Scheltema, *Java,* 71–72 (see introduction, note 7).

31. For a concise review of European writing about stambul adaptations of Shakespeare, see Kurnianingrat, "An Essay Towards a History of Shake-

speare in Indonesia" (master's thesis, Cornell University, 1958), 19–27. For commentaries on stambul treatments of Faust, see Hubert S. Banner, *Romantic Java as It Was and Is* (Philadelphia: Lippincott, 1927), 86–87; and Adrienne Lantère, "La Comédie Stamboul," *Lloyd Mail* 5, no. 2 (1935): 71.

The same sort of pleasure in trashing European cultural icons is found in a famous essay by anthropologist Laura Bohannan in which the sense and meaning of the plot of *Hamlet* is challenged by Tiv tribesmen in northern Nigeria. Bohannan's essay is often anthologized and assigned in university classes to demonstrate the lack of universality in literature. It is pleasurable to read Tiv ventriloquizing doubts and certainties about canon construction and associated claims to authoritative interpretation. Bohannan, "Miching Mallecho, That Means Magic," in *Magic, Witchcraft, and Curing,* ed. John Middleton (Garden City, NY: Natural History Press, 1977), 43–54.

32. Jaap Kunst, *Music in Java,* 2 vols. (The Hague: Martinus Nijhoff, 1973), 1:4. The first (Dutch-language) edition of *Music in Java* was completed in 1933.

33. J. Brandts Buys and A. Brandts Buys-van Zijp, "Tooneel," *Djawa* 6 (1926): 99.

34. Faubion Bowers, *Theatre in the East: A Survey of Asian Dance and Drama* (New York: Grove, 1960 [1956]), 220–21.

35. Clifford Geertz, *The Religion of Java* (Chicago: University of Chicago Press, [1960]), 306.

36. Th. Pigeaud, "The Present State of Theatre, Dance and Music in Java," in *The Kraton: Selected Essays on Javanese Courts,* ed. Stuart Robson (Leiden: KITLV Press, 2003), 300. Pigeaud's essay was originally published in 1932.

37. Th. Pigeaud, *Javaanse volksvertoningen: Bijdragen tot de beschrijving van land en volk* (Batavia: Volkslectuur, 1938).

38. Rudolf Mrázek, "Indonesian Dandy: The Politics of Clothes in the Late Colonial Period, 1893–1942," in *Outward Appearances: Dressing State and Society in Indonesia,* ed. Henk Schulte Nordholt (Leiden: KITLV Press, 1997), 135.

39. Koks, *De Indo,* 241.

40. Hadewych van Rheeden, "Petjo: The Mixed Language of the Indos in Batavia," in *Mixed Languages: Fifteen Case Studies in Language Intertwining,* ed. Peter Bakker and Maarten Mous (Amsterdam: Institute for Functional Research into Language and Language Use, 1994), 223–37.

41. Miel de Gruiter, "Javindo, a Contact-Language in Pre-War Semarang," in Bakker and Mous, *Mixed Languages,* 151–222.

42. Manusama, *Komedie Stamboel.*

43. This sketch of Manusama is based on Tjalie Robinson, introduction to A. Th. Manusama, *Njai Dasima* (The Hague: Moesson, 1986), 5–11.

44. Manusama, *Komedie Stamboel,* 8.

45. Manusama's account is replete with much fabricated and questionable material. Who could possibly remember a performance that happened twenty-eight years in the past in the sort of detail presented by Manusama?

46. On the politics and culture of repatriation, see esp. Paul van der Veur, "Eurasian Dilemma in Indonesia," *Journal of Asian Studies* 20, no. 1 (1960): 45–60; Andrew Goss, "From *Tong-Tong* to Tempo Doeloe: Eurasian Memory Work and the Bracketing of Dutch Colonial History, 1957–1961," *Indonesia* 70 (2000): 9–36.

47. Indische Nederlanders is current terminology for Dutch citizens of part-Indonesian descent. In the 1950s a variety of labels were in use for this same group, including tropical Netherlanders (*tropen-Nederlanders*) and repatriated Netherlanders (*gerepatrieerde Nederlanders*). Indische Nederlanders are militant that they are Netherlanders (and fully entitled to every aspect of citizenship in the Netherlands) but should not be considered Dutch. The term Indo continues to be used in the United States among Indonesian Americans, including ones of Dutch descent.

48. Topaas de Boer-Lasschuyt, "Eurasian Rapatriants in Holland," *Research Group for European Migration Problems Bulletin* 8, no 2 (1960): 24. I have made some minor grammatical corrections and adjustments to spelling in this quote.

49. L. Mutsaers, "Indorock: An Early Eurorock Style," *Popular Music* 9, no. 3 (1990): 307–20.

50. J. M. Van der Kroef, "The Eurasian Dilemma," in *Indonesia in the Modern World* (Bandung: Masa Baru, 1954), 275–308, 293–94.

51. Much has been written about Jan Boon in Dutch. For valuable English-language discussions, see Winniefred Anthonio, "Tjalie Robinson: 'Reflections in a Brown Eye'" (Ph.D. diss., University of Michigan, 1990); Goss, "*Tong-Tong* to Tempo Doeloe."

52. E. M. Beekman, *Troubled Pleasures: Dutch Colonial Literature from the East Indies* (Oxford: Clarendon Press, 1996), 511.

53. Lilian Ducelle, interview by Matthew Isaac Cohen and Melanie Tangkau, The Hague, 20 November 2003.

54. Ibid.

55. The Pasar Malam is today the most important cultural mode and locus of community building among Indische Nederlanders.

56. Much of the information that follows is based on an album of photographs, press clippings, and programs kindly provided by Lilian Ducelle.

57. On Hawaiian and Ambonese music in relation to Indische Nederlanders, see Mutsaers, "Indorock." Ambon-born steel guitarist Rudy Wairata (1932–81) also spelled his name Rudi.

58. Robinson, cited in Anthonio, "Tjalie Robinson," 107; Anthonio's translation.

59. "Indische Avond," *Onze Brug* 1, no. 7 (1957): 6. No precise date is given for this event in this article, but internal references suggest that it happened in December 1956.

60. Lilian Ducelle, "Robert Mahieu: Meten met 4 maten," *Tong Tong* 6, no. 19 (15 November 1961): 8. Ducelle was at this time also an aspiring fashion designer.

61. Indisch ABC, by Ben Snijders:

A is alles over Indië dat U niet vergeten mag	A is all about the Indies that you must not forget
B dat zijn de baboe die we hier missen iedre dag	B are the *babu* [nannies] whom we miss here every day
C de Chinese klontong met zijn tjoetela bagoes	C are Chinese peddlers and their chocolate sweets
D de doeren toelen lievlingsvrucht van Si Rakoes	D is real durian, the favorite fruit of Si Rakus
E is Es lilin es lilin tjeutjeuk kelapa moeda	E is *es lilin* [popsicles] and coconut popsicles
F is Si Fientje eens de Roos van Manggarai	F is *Si* Fientje, formerly the Rose of Manggarai
REFRAIN:	
'k Zing voor U allen	I sing for you all
dit ABC	This ABC
't Zijn ook Uw belangen	It is also for your sake
Zing dus maar mee	So sing with me
De tekst is eenvoudig	The lyrics are simple
Bijna eentonig het lied	The song is almost monotonous
Maar het is de waarheid, waarheid, waarheid, anders niet.	But it is the truth, truth, truth, and nothing but.
G is goeling die je elke dag bemint	G is *guling* [k.o. pillow] you love every day
H het Hollands spreken dat ik toch zo moeilijk vind	H is speaking *Hollands* [Dutch] that I find so hard
I is ikan asin djambal, gaboes en pedah	I is *ikan asin* [salted fish] from *jambal, gabus,* and *peda.*
J dat is—wah, jahen! Elk schot moesti kena	J is—wow, *jahen* [hunting]! Each shot hits its mark
K de krontjong die een ieder zoo graag hoort	K is kroncong that everyone enjoys so much

L de lucht van trassie, djengkol
enzovoort

L is the *lucht* [smell] of fish paste,
jengkol beans, etc.

Refrain

M is the melatigeur waar de tuin
vol van kan zijn
N–verrek! Die njamoeks! Eeuwge
bron van sjagrijn
O een tienmansvehikel, ge kent
hem wel, de opelet
P de Pasar Malam, rameh, maar
awas toekang tjopet!
Q een querulant die zich
noemt Europeaan
R de roedjak, vindt hij smurrie,
pisang noemt hij banaan

M is the smell of *melati* [jasmine] flowers that can permeate the garden.
N–damn! Those *nyamuk* [mosquitoes]!
The eternal source of chagrin.
O is a ten-man vehicle, you know it
well: the *opelet* [k.o. jitney]
P is the Pasar Malam [Night Fair],
festive, but beware of pickpockets!
Q is the *querulant* [complainer]
named the European
R is *rujak* [spicy fruit salad] that he
thinks is crap, while he calls
pisang the banana.

Refrain

S is sate kambing met
sambal katjang flink pedis
T mijn vriend Si Tolol die niet
al te snugger is
U dat is Uzelf, één voor één mijn
kameraad
V een soort verbondenheid
die tussen ons bestaat
W is whiskey soda, godendrank
in het warme land
X een onbekende, van de roemah
gade een trouwe klant

S is goat satay with very spicy peanut
sauce
T is my friend *Si* Tolol who is not too
bright
U that it is you yourselves, my
comrades each one of you
V is a kind of *verbondenheid*
[solidarity] that exists among us
W is whisky and soda, a divine drink
in a hot land
X is unknown, referring to a regular
customer at the pawn house

Refrain

Y dat is het eiland natuurlijk, waar
ik mijn jeugd heb doorgebracht
Ofschoon ver weg ben ik daar nog
vaak in mijn mooiste dromen
in de nacht
Ik ben nu haast aan het einde
van dit simpel ABC

Y is the island [Java; pronounced Yava
in Dutch], of course, where I spent
my youth
Though I am often away there in my
most wonderful dreams
I am now nearly at the end of this
simple ABC

Draagt Z de Zon van dat Zonne-
land steeds in Uw harten mee
Het alfabet is uit en nu volgt de
moraal
Iets innig dierbaars houdt ons
sterk, U, mij, allemaal.

Always bear Z, the *zon* [sun] of that
sunny land, with you in your heart
The alphabet is finished and now
follows the moral
Fondly beloved things make us
strong—you, me, one and all.

"Indisch ABC: Lied van Ben Snijders," *Onze Brug* 2, no. 7 (October 1957): 4.

62. On differences between Javanese and Dutch opinions of the banana, see Onghokham, "Rijsttafel and the Colonial Dutch," 313 (see ch. 5, n. 69).

63. "Een avond van: Interesssante oosterse dansen, kostelijke humor van de Indische Tijl Uylenspiegel en geestige parodieën op het Indische leven," *Onze Brug* 1, no. 10 (April 1957): 5; F., "Tweede Indische avond," *Onze Brug* 1, no. 11 (May 1957): 3; no. 12 (June 1957): 4.

64. Robinson cited in Goss, "*Tong-Tong* to Tempo Doeloe"; Gross's translation.

65. The long-term benefits of this speech are debatable, however. See Topaas de Boer-Lasschuyt, "Eurasian Repatriants in Holland," 33–34.

66. These comments on Indische Nederlander humor are based on a discussion with Lilian Ducelle in her apartment in The Hague on 26 February 2004.

67. Lilian Ducelle interview.

68. "Onze koningin ontmoet een klank uit het verleden," *Tong Tong* 2, no. 17 (30 April 1958): 2–3; emphasis in original.

69. On the transformation of stambul to tooneel and then sandiwara, see Cohen, *Lontar Anthology.*

70. Robinson believed that stambul historically preceded bangsawan and that the latter genre was derived from the former.

71. Robinson, "Marie Oord had een Opera," 7.

72. Robinson, cited in Anthonio, "Tjalie Robinson," 236; Anthonio's translation.

73. Lilian Ducelle interview.

74. T. R. [Tjalie Robinson], "Blaubaard's achtste," *Tong Tong* 14, no. 22 (1 June 1970): 3–4. On Guus Becker, see the short film by Hans Plas, *Guus Becker: Troubadour van het krontjonglied* (Ridderkerk: Indo Films, 1997).

75. Lilian Ducelle interview. The program for this event is in the library of the KITLV. See *Moesson's Musical Memories: Programma 18 May '86* (The Hague: Moesson, 1986).

76. for references to selected stambul articles in *Tong Tong,* see ch. 1, nn. 100, 103, and 117; ch. 3, n. 7; ch. 4, n. 9; and ch. 6, n. 77.

77. W. F. W. Schardijn, "Djula Djuli bintang tiga," *Tong Tong* 12, nos. 11–12 (1967): 9–13. References to komedi stambul in the pages of *Tong Tong* or its successor *Moesson* became infrequent after Robinson's death in 1974.

78. Pauline Dublin Milone, "*Indische* Culture, and Its Relationship to Urban Life," *Comparative Studies in Society and History* 9, no. 4 (1967): 424–25.

79. Sutherland, "'Tempo Doeloe' and 'Pudjangga Baru.'"

80. Ibid., 90, 104.

81. Nieuwenhuys, *Oost-Indische spiegel,* 302–7.

82. Nieuwenhuys, *Komen en blijven,* 164–72. Nieuwenhuys makes explicit the connection between the two Mahieus by explaining that Robinson's "Indisch pseudonym" of Vincent Mahieu was a reference to Auguste Mahieu. See *Komen en blijven,* 169.

83. Paul W. van der Veur, "Cultural Aspects of the Eurasian Community in Indonesian Colonial Society," *Indonesia* (Cornell University) 6 (1968): 38–53.

84. Van den Bosch, "Kosmopolitisch spektakel." Fredrik van den Bosch (1922–2001) was born in Utrecht but spent much of his youth in the Netherlands Indies before decolonization.

85. Rob Dumas, "Feit en fictie rondom Auguste Mahieu," *Moesson* 48, no. 8 (2004): 18–21.

86. The Japanese ban on European terminology and European dramatic sources effectively ended the life of minor stambul troupes still touring in 1942.

87. Geertz, *Religion of Java,* 306.

88. Armijn Pane, "Produksi film tjerita di Indonesia: Perkembangannja sebagai Alat Masjarakat," *Indonesia* 4, no. 1–2 (1953): 5–112.

89. See particularly Armijn Pane, "Pemandang Pers," *Poedjangga Baroe* 1, no. 10 (1934): 381–85. For recent assessments of Armijn Pane's views of popular culture, see William H. Frederick, "Dreams of Freedom, Moments of Despair: Armijn Pane and the Imagining of Modern Indonesian Culture," in *Imagining Indonesia: Cultural Politics and Political Culture,* ed. Jim Schiller and Barbara Martin-Schiller (Athens: Ohio University Press, 1997), 54–89; Keith Foulcher, "Culture and Colonialism in the Essays of Armijn Pane, 1933–1953," in *Lasting Fascinations: Essays on Indonesia and the Southwest Pacific to Honour Bob Hering,* ed. Harry A. Poeze and Antoinete Liem (Stein: Yayasan Kabar Seberang, 1998), 131–52.

90. For a more extended consideration of the relation between popular theater and early Indonesian cinema, see Taufik Abdullah, Misbach Yusa Biran, and S. M. Ardan, *Film Indonesia Bagian I (1900–1950)* (Jakarta: Percetakan Negara RI, 1993).

91. Armijn Pane, "Produksi film," 8.

92. Tengku Syed Abdulkadar and Zen Rosdy, *Sejarah seni drama* (see ch. 5, n. 139).

93. Ibid.

94. Boen Sri Oemarjati, *Bentuk lakon dalam sastra Indonesia* (Jakarta: Gunung Agung, 1971).

95. This at least is how theater historian Jakob Sumardjo interprets Boen Sri Oemarjati's historiography. See Sumardjo, *Perkembangan teater modern dan sastra drama Indonesia,* (Bandung: Citra Aditya Bakti, 1992).

96. Boen Sri Oemarjati, *Bentuk lakon,* 22.

97. On New Order obsession with the appearance of order, see John Pemberton, *On the Subject of "Java"* (Ithaca: Cornell University Press, 1994).

98. A. Kasim Achmad, "Sebuah pengantar tentang teater tradisionil di Indonesia," *Budaya Jaya* 114 (1977): 648. A. Kasim Achmad is an arts bureaucrat and scholar who is currently a lecturer in theater at Institut Kesenian Jakarta (Jakarta Arts Institute). His views of stambul as a "transitional theater" have been amplified in numerous other publications and unpublished writings. For an independent formulation of "transitional theater," see Ariyasena Jayasekara Gunawardana, "Theater in Modernizing Societies: Some Aspects of Modern Asian Theater Developments" (Ph.D. diss., New York University, 1977).

99. Subagio Sastrowardojo, "Orientasi budaya Chairil Anwar," *Budaja Djaja* 59 (1973): 213–46; Goenawan Mohamad, "Sebuah Pembelaan untuk Teater Indonesia Mutakhir," in *Seks, sastra, kita* (Jakarta: Sinar Harapan, 1980), 91–142.

100. Subagio Sastrowardojo, "Orientasi budaya," 221.

101. Saini K. M., cited in Jorgen Hellman, *Performing the Nation: Cultural Politics in New Order Indonesia* (Copenhagen: Nordic Institute of Asian Studies Press, 2003), 70.

102. For an overview of Riantiarno's work, see Herry Gendut Janarto, *Teater Koma: Portret tragedi dan komedi manusia (Indonesia)* (Jakarta: Grasindo, 1997).

103. See particularly Nano Riantiarno, *Semar gugat* (Yogyakarta: Bentang Budaya, 1995).

104. Michael H. Bodden, "Teater Koma's *Suksesi* and Indonesia's New Order," *Asian Theatre Journal* 14, no. 2 (1997): 259–80.

105. Nano Riantiarno, "Memilih Pelakon (Seputar Ihwal Memilih Pelakon dan proses pembentukan peran)," in *Teater Indonesia: Konsep, sejarah, problema,* ed. Tommy F. Awuy (Jakarta: Dewan Kesenian Jakarta, 1999), 203–4.

106. Nano Riantiarno, *Opera primadona* (Jakarta: Pustaka Kartini, 1988).

107. H. Rosihan Anwar, cited in Tuti Gintini, "Teater Koma's 'Opera Primadonna' Flows Lightly, Amusingly," *Jakarta Post,* 11 August 2000.

108. Nano Riantiarno, "Teater dan masyarakat Teater Koma," in *Interkulturalisme (dalam) teater,* ed. Nur Sahid (Yogyakarta: Yayasan Untuk Indonesia, 2000), 155.

Glossary

alun-alun	A central square in a town or city. In residency towns, the alun-alun was commonly the location of the mansions of the regent and resident. In the court cities of Yogyakarta and Surakarta, there are alun-alun squares to the north and south of the royal courts.
babah	An adult Chinese man; sometimes used as a prefix before a Chinese man's name (e.g., Babah Tjan Tjin Hianak). Also spelled *baba*.
bangsawan	A generic name for the Malay-language popular theater that emerged in Penang in the 1870s under the influence of *Parsi theater*.
bupati	A regent, the highest rank held by Muslims in the colonial civil service. A regent was in charge of Muslim affairs in a regency. Normally regents in Java and Madura were noble elites descended from the noble houses and principalities of those islands; the position was often hereditary, though all appointments were subject to Dutch approval.
dangdut	A form of popular dance music.
gamelan	The classical gong-chime ensemble of Indonesia and Malaysia; refers both to sets of instruments and to a form of music.
Indiër	A person from the Indies; the term preferred by Auguste Mahieu to identify Eurasians and Europeans who considered the Indies as home.

Indische	A Dutch word meaning "of the Indies" but used figuratively to refer to European-Indonesian hybrids. In Dutch, depending on the context, also spelled *Indisch.*
Indische Nederlander	A citizen of the Netherlands of Indies descent; usually refers to Eurasians in postcolonial Holland.
Indische roman	A novel of the Indies, a genre of writing in Dutch and Malay; also refers to plays with Indies settings.
Indo	A Eurasian of mixed Indonesian-European ancestry, the preferred ethnic identity term for Eurasians of mixed Indonesian-European background in the United States and Indonesia today.
kampung	An urban shantytown, inhabited by both Muslims and Eurasians. Also spelled *kampong.*
ketoprak	A form of Javanese-language theater derived from stambul. Also spelled *kethoprak.*
komedi	Commercial entertainment; sometimes also refers to a theater building. Also spelled *komidi.*
Komedie Stamboel	A theater company founded in Surabaya in 1891. The name is capitalized in this book to distinguish the company from the genre it spawned.
komedi Melayu	Malay popular theater, a general designation to describe popular theater in Malay language, including both *komedi stambul* and *bangsawan.*
komedi stambul	A generic name for the Malay-language popular theater that emerged in Surabaya in 1891. The term is lowercased in this book to distinguish the genre from the original company. Also known as *stambul.*
kongsi	A Chinese business association.
kraton	A royal palace or royal court.

kroncong — A genre of popular music originally associated with Batavia that subsequently spread throughout the Indonesian archipelago in association with *stambul.* The kroncong is a ukulele-like stringed instrument prominently featured in this musical form. Also spelled *keroncong.*

lagu stambul — Songs of komedi stambul.

ludruk — A form of Javanese-language folk drama from eastern Java featuring clowning, cross-dressing, and gamelan music. Also spelled *ludrug.*

Muslim — A characteristic designation used for indigenous people in nineteenth-century Indonesia. A person referred to as a Muslim (*orang slam, orang islam*) is not necessarily a doctrinaire practitioner of Islam. The word *Muslim* is used interchangeably with *native* (*pribumi* in Malay, *inlander* in Dutch).

Nights (the) — Abbreviation for *The Thousand and One Nights,* also known as *The Arabian Nights.*

nona — An unmarried woman, usually of European or Eurasian descent. Also spelled *nonah.* See *nyonya.*

nontonner — A Dutch-Malay colonial word used to describe an incidental spectator or onlooker at cultural performances and public events.

nyai — Informal native wife.

nyonya — A married woman, usually of European or Eurasian descent. See *nona.*

pantun — A traditional form of Malay poetry, typically sung in performance. A verse of pantun consists of four end-rhymed lines. Often the first two lines are obscurely poetic, while the third and fourth lines have communicative intent.

Parsi theater — A genre of popular musical theater from India associated with the Parsi population of Mumbai

	that originated in the 1850s and toured Southeast Asia starting in the 1870s.
pasar	A market or bazaar.
pasar malam	A night fair, a hybrid cultural form that emerged in colonial Indonesia and was subsequently adopted and adapted in the Netherlands by *Indische Nederlanders* to celebrate ethnic identity.
peranakan	Of mixed descent, or hybrid cultural orientation. Also spelled *pranakan.*
petjo	A dialect of Dutch with Malay syntax, morphology, and noun borrowing, spoken primarily by Eurasians.
priyayi	The hereditary Javanese and Sundanese elite, usually of noble descent.
ramai	Festive and boisterous. Also spelled *rame.*
sair	See *syair.*
sandiwara	A term for Indonesian, Javanese, or Sundanese spoken drama used since the 1940s.
schouwburg	A European-style theater building with a proscenium stage.
si	A definite article used before a proper name to indicate familiarity, e.g., Si Ahmat Sokrok.
sinyo	A young man, usually of European or Eurasian descent, who wears European clothes and behaves in a European manner.
siti	An Arabic-derived title associated with young women, e.g., *Siti Senimbar.*
stambul	A shortened form of *komedi stambul;* also refers to musical songs of komedi stambul (*lagu stambul*) and the fez.
strijkje	A European chamber ensemble with string and wind instruments.

syair — A poetic narrative generally based on true happenings. Also spelled *sair.*

tooneel — Dutch word for theater, appropriated after 1925 by Indonesian theater artists to refer to popular revue theater. Also spelled *toneel.*

topeng — Masked-dance drama, performed either by solo performers or by groups of actors to *gamelan* accompaniment.

tuan — A prefix or term of address roughly meaning "sir" or "mister" (e.g., Tuan Mahieu); also refers to an adult man, particularly European men. The governor-general of the Indies was known in Malay as tuan besar (lit., big master). Also spelled *tuwan.*

wayang — A general term for traditional and puppet theaters; sometimes used in Malaysia and Indonesia to refer to Chinese opera as well.

wayang cokek — Betawi social dance form accompanied by a hybrid Chinese-Javanese musical ensemble.

wayang kulit — Traditional shadow puppet theater accompanied by *gamelan* music, performed in Javanese and other ethnic languages.

wayang orang — See *wayang wong.*

wayang wong — A form of dance theater in which actors take on the roles of puppets in *wayang kulit* plays and act and dance accompanied by *gamelan* music. Also known as *wayang orang.*

Selected Bibliography

Newspapers

Advertentieblad voor Tegal en Omstreken, 1893–94

Algemeen Dagblad van Nederlandsch Indië (Batavia), 1883

Bataviaasch Nieuwsblad, 1892–1900

Bintang-Barat (Batavia), 1883, 1890–99

Bintang Betawi, 1900–1903

Bintang Soerabaia, 1891–94, 1899–1903

Bondsblad (Batavia), 1900–1904

Bromartani (Surakarta), 1894, 1899

Het Centrum (Yogyakarta), 1898–99

Courant Deminggoe dari pada Bintang Barat (Batavia), 1895–99

Daily Advertiser (Singapore), 1894

Deli Courant (Deli), 1897

Djawi-Kando (Surakarta), 1891–99

Hindia-Olanda (Batavia), 1892–96

Java Bode (Batavia), 1883, 1892–1901

De Locomotief (Semarang), 1891–1903

Makassarsche Courant (Makassar), 1895

Mataram (Yogyakarta), 1892–96

Nieuw Padangsch Handelsblad (Padang), 1897

Pembrita-Bahroe (Surabaya), 1891–93, 1895–96

Pembrita Betawi, 1893–96

Pengadilan (Bandung), 1898

Pinang Gazette and Straits Chronicle, 1897

De Preanger Bode (Bandung), 1896–97

Primbon Soerabaia, 1900–1901

Retnodhoemilah (Yogyakarta), 1895–96, 1899–1900

Selompret Melajoe (Semarang), 1891–94, 1897–98, 1902–3

Semarang Courant, 1899

Sinar Terang (Batavia), 1891

Singapore Free Press, 1894

Soerabaiasch-Handelsblad, 1890–95, 1898

Soerabaija-Courant, 1891–97

Straits-Chinese Herald, or Surat Khabar Peranakan (Singapore), 1894

Straits Times (Singapore), 1894

Sumatra Courant (Padang), 1897

Thieme's Nieuw Advertentieblad (Surabaya), 1892

Times (London), 1822, 1827

Tjerimai (Cirebon), 1893–1905

Books and Articles

Abbas, Abisin [Andjar Asmara]. "Tooneel Indonesia, ditengah perhatian oemoem." In *Kunst, tooneel en journalistiek,* 9–24. Fort de Kock: Persbureau Malacca, 1935.

Abeyasekere, Susan. *Jakarta: A History.* Singapore: Oxford University Press, 1989.

Adam, Ahmat B. *The Vernacular Press and the Emergence of Modern Indonesian Consciousness, 1855–1913.* Ithaca: Southeast Asia Program, Cornell University, 1995.

Anderson, Benedict R. O'G. "Language, Fantasy, Revolution: Java, 1900–1950." In *Making Indonesia,* ed. Daniel S. Lev and Ruth McVey, 26–40. Ithaca: Southeast Asia Program, Cornell University, 1996.

Anthonio, Winniefred. "Tjalie Robinson: 'Reflections in a Brown Eye.'" Ph.D. dissertation, University of Michigan, 1990.

Bemmelen, J. F. van, and G. B. Hooyer. *Guide to the Dutch East Indies Composed by Invitation of the Koninklyke Paketvaart Maatschappij (Royal Steam Packet Company).* Trans. B. J. Berrington. Batavia: Kolff; London: Luzac, 1897.

Booth, Michael R., and Pamela Heckenberg. "Touring the Empire." *Essays in Theatre* 6, no. 1 (1987): 49–60.

Bosch, F. van den. "Kosmopolitisch spektakel." *Indische Letteren* 9, no. 1 (1994): 44–54.

Camoens, Cantius Leo. "The Wayang Parsi, Tiruan Wayang Parsi, Komidi Melayu and the Bangsawan, 1887–1895." *Malaysia in History* 25 (1982): 1–20.

Cohen, Matthew Isaac. "Border Crossings: Bangsawan in the Netherlands Indies in the Nineteenth and Early Twentieth Centuries." *Indonesia and the Malay World* 30, no. 87 (2002): 101–15.

———. "A Chinese *Pujangga* from Surabaya? Yap Gwan Thay in an Age of Translation." In *History of Translation in Indonesia and Malaysia,* ed. Henri Chambert-Loir. Paris: EFEO and Archipel, forthcoming.

———. "On the Origin of the Komedie Stamboel: Popular Culture, Colonial Society, and the Parsi Theatre Movement." *Bijdragen tot de Taal-, Land- en Volkenkunde* 157, no. 2 (2001): 313–57.

Couperus, Louis. *The Hidden Force.* Trans. A. T. de Mattos. 1900. London: Quartet, 1992.

Doorn, Jacques van. *A Divided Society: Segmentation and Mediation in Late-Colonial Indonesia.* Rotterdam: Comparative Asian Studies Program, Erasmus University, 1983.

Dumas, R. M. "Meerdere generaties van het geslacht Mahieu op Java." *De Indische Navorscher* 15, no. 1 (2002): 1–6.

Edrus, A. H. *Drama dan perkembangan bahasa Melayu.* Vol. 3 of *Persuratan Melayu.* Singapore: Qalam, 1960–62.

Faber, G. H. von. *Oud Soerabaia: De geschiedenis van Indie's eerste koopstad van de oudste tijden tot de instelling van den Gemeenteraad (1906).* Surabaya: Kolff, 1931.

Fabricius, J. *Tempo doeloe: Uit de goeie ouwe tijd.* The Hague: H. P. Leopold, 1949.

Frederick, William Hayward. "Indonesian Urban Society in Transition: Surabaya, 1926–1946." Ph.D. dissertation, University of Hawaii, 1978.

Furnivall, J. S. *Netherlands Indies: A Study of Plural Economy.* New York: Macmillan, 1944.

Goss, Andrew. "From *Tong-Tong* to Tempo Doeloe: Eurasian Memory Work and the Bracketing of Dutch Colonial History, 1957–1961." *Indonesia* 70 (2000): 9–36.

Habitué, Een [pseud.]. "Lohengrin in de Komedie-Stamboel." *Tong Tong* 6, no. 12 (30 December 1961): 7.

Hoffman, John. "A Foreign Investment: Indies Malay to 1901." *Indonesia* 27 (1979): 65–92.

Ido, Victor [Hans van de Wall]. *Indië in den goeden ouden tijd.* 2 vols. Bandung: Nix, 1949.

———. *De paria van Glodok: Episode uit het Indische paupersleven in drie acten.* 1917. Reprint, Bandung: Visser, 1921.

———. *De paupers: Roman uit de Indo-europeesche samenleving.* 1912. Reprint, The Hague: Thomas and Eras, 1978.

Kalff, S. "Een avond in de 'Komedie Stamboul.'" *Java Bode,* 15 February 1893. Reprinted in *Indië* 2 (1918–19): 757–78.

Kerckhoff, Ch. E. P. van. "Het Maleisch tooneel ter Westkust van Sumatra." *Tijdschrift voor Indische Taal-, Land- en Volkenkunde uitgegeven door het Bataviaasch Genootschap van Kunsten en Wetenschappen* 31 (1888): 302–14.

Knaap, Otto. "De Indische Antoine: Antoine Tardieu." *Bondsblad,* 18 July, 25 July 1903. Reprinted in *Tong Tong* 16 (1 March 1971): 6–8; 21 (15 May 1971): 8–9.

Krafft, H. *Boekoe Komidi terpake bagi Komidi Stamboel,* Batavia: Regina Orientis, 1893.

L., Nona [pseud.]. *Pantoen sindiran.* Batavia: G. Francis, 1896.

Lith, P. A. van der, A. J. Spaan, F. Fokkens, and Joh. F. Snelleman, eds. *Encyclopaedie van Nederlandsch-Indië.* 4 vols. The Hague: Martinus Nijhoff; Leiden: E. J. Brill, 1896–1905.

Manusama, A. Th. *Komedie Stamboel of de Oost-Indische opera.* Weltevreden: Favoriet, 1922.

Milone, Pauline Dublin. "Queen of the East: The Metamorphosis of a Colonial Capital." Ph.D. dissertation, University of California at Berkeley, 1966.

Nieuwenhuys, Rob. *Komen en blijven: Tempo doeloe, een verzonken wereld: Fotografische documenten uit het oude Indië, 1870–1920.* Amsterdam: E. M. Querido, 1998.

———. *Oost-Indische spiegel: Wat Nederlandse schrijvers en dichters over Indonesië hebben geschreven, vanaf de eerste jaren der Compagnie tot op heden.* Amsterdam: Querido, 1972.

Pane, Armijn. "Dardanella." *Poedjangga Baroe* 1, no. 10 (1934): 381–85.

———. "Produksi film tjerita di Indonesia: Perkembangannja sebagai Alat Masjarakat." *Indonesia* 4, nos. 1–2 (1953): 5–112.

Perelaer, Michael Theophile Hubert. *Baboe Dalima, or The Opium Fiend.* Trans. E. J. Venning. 1886. London: Vizetelly, 1888.

Robinson, Tjalie [Jan Boon]. "De hele wereld, hemel en hel voor f1500.–." *Tong Tong* 12, nos. 11–12 (1967): 8.

———. "Marie Oord." *Tong Tong* 15, no. 8 (1970): 15.

———. "Marie Oord had een eigen Indo 'Penny Opera." *Tong Tong* 12, nos. 11–12 (1967): 4–8.

Rush, James R. *Opium to Java: Revenue Farming and Chinese Enterprise in Colonial Indonesia, 1860–1910.* Ithaca: Cornell University Press, 1990.

Samson, Opa. "Het lied van de Indo." *Tong Tong* 2, no. 21 (1958): 5.

———. "De Stamboel." *Tong Tong* 3, no. 8 (1958): 4–5.

Schardijn, W. F. W. "Djula-Djuli bintang tiga." *Tong Tong* 12, nos. 11–12 (1967): 9–13.

Scidmore, Eliza Ruhamah. *Java: The Garden of the East.* 1897. Singapore: Oxford University Press, 1986.

Stoler, Ann Laura. *Carnal Knowledge and Imperial Power: Race and the Intimate in Colonial Rule.* Berkeley: University of California Press, 2002.

Tan Sooi Beng. *Bangsawan: A Social and Stylistic History of Popular Malay Opera.* Singapore: Oxford University Press, 1993.

Tan Tjiook San, ed. "Sair Komedi Stamboel." In *Almanak bahasa Melajoe boeat tahoen 1893,* 256–73. Yogyakarta: H. Buning, 1892.

Toer, Pramoedya Ananta, ed. *Tempo doeloe: Antologi sastra pra-Indonesia.* Jakarta: Hasta Mitra, 1982.

Veur, Paul W. van der. "Introduction to a Socio-Political Study of the Eurasians of Indonesia." Ph.D. dissertation, Cornell University, 1955.

Wertheim, W. F. *Indonesian Society in Transition: A Study of Social Change.* 2d ed. The Hague: W. van Hoeve, 1956.

Wilkinson, R. J. *A Malay-English Dictionary, Romanised.* 2 vols. 1901–3. London: Macmillan, 1959.

Wit, Augusta de. *Java: Facts and Fancies.* 1898. Oxford: Oxford University Press, 1985.

Worsfold, W. Basil. *A Visit to Java with an Account of the Founding of Singapore.* London: Richard Bantley and Son, 1893.

Index

Page numbers in *italics* refer to figures.